MURDEROUS MINDS ON TRIAL

MURDEROUS MINDS ON TRIAL

Terrible Tales from a Forensic Psychiatrist's Case Book

Stanley Semrau, M.D. and Judy Gale

THE DUNDURN GROUP
TORONTO · OXFORD

Editor: Dennis Mills
Design: Jennifer Scott
Printer: AGMV Marquis

National Library of Canada Cataloguing in Publication Data

Semrau, Stanley
   Murderous minds on trial :
      terrible tales from a forensic psychiatrist's case book

ISBN 1-55022-361-6

1. Murder--Psychological aspects. 2. Murderers--Mental health. 3. Forensic psychiatry--Case studies. I. Gale, Judy II. Title.

HV6535.C3S44 2002   616.85'844   C2002-902373-1

1   2   3   4   5   06   05   04   03   02

THE CANADA COUNCIL | LE CONSEIL DES ARTS
FOR THE ARTS | DU CANADA
SINCE 1957 | DEPUIS 1957

ONTARIO ARTS COUNCIL
CONSEIL DES ARTS DE L'ONTARIO

We acknowledge the support of the **Canada Council for the Arts** and the **Ontario Arts Council** for our publishing program. We also acknowledge the financial support of the **Government of Canada** through the **Book Publishing Industry Development Program** and **The Association for the Export of Canadian Books**, and the **Government of Ontario** through the **Ontario Book Publishers Tax Credit** program.

Printed and bound in Canada.
Printed on recycled paper.
www.dundurn.com

Dundurn Press
8 Market Street
Suite 200
Toronto, Ontario, Canada
M5E 1M6

Dundurn Press
73 Lime Walk
Headington, Oxford,
England
OX3 7AD

Dundurn Press
2250 Military Road
Tonawanda NY
U.S.A. 14150

TABLE OF CONTENTS

Acknowledgements   7
Disclaimer   8
Introduction   9

Section I — The Insanity Defence   15

    Chapter 1.   Mixed Signals   17
    Chapter 2.   The Refugee's Story   29
    Chapter 3.   Defining Moments   40
    Chapter 4.   Dial "Me" for Murder   50
    Chapter 5.   Death Will Save Your Life   67
    Chapter 6.   Not a Simple Case of Road Rage   88
    Chapter 7.   Murder at the B&B   99
    Chapter 8.   Can I Take You for a Ride?   110

Section II — The Intoxication Defence   125

    Chapter 9.   Poor Choice of Movies   127
    Chapter 10. Just Like Dad   148
    Chapter 11. Bad Spirits   158

Section III — Automatism and Provocation Defences   171

    Chapter 12. The Neighbour from Hell   173
    Chapter 13. "Is He CRAZY?!"   185
    Chapter 14. A Tale of Two Little Old Ladies   197
    Chapter 15. A Sort of Frantic Night   212

Section IV — Verdicts and Sentencing   227

    Chapter 16. A Jealous Wife   229
    Chapter 17. Something She Forgot to Mention   236
    Chapter 18. Big Boy   254

Section V — Sentence Administration   269

    Chapter 19. The Ultimate   271
    Chapter 20. Virtual Reality Murder   290
    Chapter 21. Release: Safety, Politics or Medicine?   301

The Psychiatrist's Prescription   315

ACKNOWLEDGEMENTS

The writers would like to express heartfelt thanks to friends, relatives, and colleagues in medicine and law who read and offered valuable comments on the manuscript. We dedicate this book to our families: Dr. Semrau to his, whose kindness and love have always counter-balanced the darkness and horror of his work; Judy Gale to hers, for surrounding her with love and good humour, keeping her grounded while she vicariously experienced these acts of murder.

— Stanley Semrau, M.D.,
and Judy Gale

DISCLAIMER

The stories presented in this book are based on cases from Dr. Semrau's practice. Two subjects, Clifford Olson and Terry Driver, are identified by their real names, as the notoriety of their cases would have made effective concealment impossible. Another subject, Zerom Seyoum, kindly contributed his own story in his own words. All other cases have been disguised to some extent by changes of name, community and other identifying details. This was done to protect victims and relatives, whose pain may be sadly resurrected to make what we believe is an important plea for improvements to our justice system and, in some instances, to shield mentally-disordered offenders doing their best to lead peaceful, low-profile lives in the community. Plot and other details have also been altered for readability and clarity. Therefore, any reader already familiar with a case who correctly discerns its true identity should be aware that the story in *Murderous Minds on Trial* may not accurately represent the real-life case in all respects. Two authors and the forces of fiction have been at work.

— Stanley Semrau, M.D.,
and Judy Gale

INTRODUCTION

Why do people kill? And do many of them really "get away with murder"?

A child is brutally slain. The confessed killer — a scruffy individual who shows no sign of remorse during his trial and who emits small smiles as some of the most grisly evidence is presented — pleads not guilty by reason of temporary insanity, and is acquitted.

The public, media-fed and emotionally charged, is outraged. How can the courts let this happen? Why should one killer "walk" while others are locked up for life? When a life is taken, why should any killer be absolved of blame?

In another case, a pathetic picture is drawn for the jury: a young mother, weeping quietly, smothers her baby, believing with her whole heart that she is actually saving the infant from the devil. It is an act committed by someone distraught beyond reason.

This time the public's anger is directed less at the woman than at her failed support system. Hardly anyone would wish her sent off to maximum security for life. Still, a life has been taken, the law has been broken — even if the defeated figure in the prisoner's box does not fit anyone's image of a killer.

Nor does the well-spoken business executive fit the mold. After months of senseless torture from a neighbour — including, the jury hears, excrement thrown against windows, obscenities directed at his wife, a dead pet on his doorstep, and boom-box "music" pounding through the night — he suddenly shoots his tormentor.

Is this a normal, nice person who "lost it" in a temporary, isolated moment of madness? Or is he afflicted with a mental disease, fighting bigger demons than his neighbour? Or was he "born evil," with his villain side just waiting to emerge?

How can the courts — judges and jurors — decide, and how should they deal with people who are mentally ill, or claiming to be mentally ill? We all want the outcome of a murder trial to be humane, constructive and protective of society, but the pressures are enormous.

In an ideal world, full information and clear, objective rules would efficiently produce a just outcome for every murder trial. But in truth, we stumble through the procedure, amateurs and professionals together, looking at the facts with different eyes and trying to make the justice system work, using a mix of rules, some established centuries ago and fiddled with until they are excessively abstract, confusing and contradictory. Even with the best intentions and ample intelligence on the part of judge and jury, some verdicts and sentences can lead to a murderer being let loose to kill again. And laws based on outdated psychiatric theories can jail an ill person who could have been successfully treated or rehabilitated.

In murder, as any mystery reader knows, no two cases are alike. Each brings to trial its own tangle of evidence, legal parameters, medical factors, social circumstances, timing and personalities.

Often the accused is known to be the killer, but the verdict hinges on this slayer's mental state at the time the killing took place — specifically, on his or her intentions. If the jury or judge decides that the killer was suffering from a mental illness or was under the influence of alcohol or drugs to an extent that rendered him or her incapable of forming a rational intention to kill, the accused was not, under law, fully responsible for his or her actions and cannot be declared guilty of murder.

It is the court that determines whether the accused person is a calculating criminal or the victim of a mental illness, or somewhere in between. And following any verdict but acquittal, it is the court that decides what will happen with the rest of this person's life.

Everyone wants to "do the right thing" by both the accused and society. But the wheels of justice may wobble off in the wrong direction, because many trial participants may be under-informed concerning law, mental illness, intoxication and the relationships between those factors. Juries try to determine if the accused did it, what the killer's mental state was, whether or not the accused and all the witnesses are believable, and even what jargon-wielding lawyers, judges, doctors and other "experts" are saying.

Extracting acceptable, credible evidence is never easy. Murder trials are peopled with liars, cajolers, finks, gangsters, dullards, heroes, saints, average folks and the emotionally ill. On the witness stand they can be sincere, dissembling, frightened, emotionless, crafty, nasty, ignorant, confused, slow-witted, sharp-minded, glib or inarticulate. People who look and talk like slick con artists may be speaking the truth. Innocent or unwell people may be so panicked by the circumstances that their memories get twisted, and self-defensive lies pop out during testimony.

In trials where the plea is not guilty by reason of some kind of mental illness, intoxication or temporary aberration, it is also a daunting task to attempt to reconstruct a person's mind retrospectively, and then to determine whose version of any reconstruction should be accepted.

How can we know what the killer was thinking, when he claims not to know himself? Who can tell best how his mind was working — an eye witness, a psychiatrist, a close family member or a friend? There is no mental equivalent of an aircraft's "black box" to verify human flights of the mind, so attempts to re-create someone's state of mind can sometimes amount to little more than prejudice, speculation or wishful thinking.

One of the biggest obstacles to reaching a just conclusion is posed by the variety of players in the courtroom drama. Jurors, lawyers, judges and medical experts all enact distinct, key roles from disparate perspectives, with wide differences in their knowledge and backgrounds.

Consider the jurors. They must decide the fate of killers in the most basic sense, drawing the line between guilty and not guilty, between "mad" and "bad." Yet juries are randomly assembled groups of people facing horrendously complex issues without expert knowledge. The butcher, the baker, the software maker come to the trial ready, even eager, to do their duty and to be totally fair. Days of mind-numbingly detailed and conflicting testimony follow. They hear psychiatrists and lawyers for both the defence and prosecution speak with equal assurance and erudition. Usually knowing little about either the law or mental illness, beyond what these professionals have just told them, jurors wrestle with the task of determining which side is right.

Mental health practitioners are brought into the courtroom to provide credible evidence concerning the mental state of the accused. Most are seasoned forensic psychiatrists and psychologists, but others — experts in their own fields but inexperienced in testifying — may be unaware of all the legal factors and precedents affecting the case, and unfamiliar with courtroom procedure and strategies. A medical specialist can be ambushed by witness cross-examination tactics shaped to elicit specific responses, and finish feeling mired in contradictions. I speak from experience.

Similarly, few lawyers or judges are trained to recognize behaviour patterns or types of mental illnesses. The defence counsel puts every effort toward acquittal. The Crown counsel advocates for justice. Both counsel insist that the jury focus on whatever evidence is favourable to their case. They can provide DNA tests, witnesses at the scene, smoking guns and confessions that add up to concrete proof of who did it. But an answer to the next question can be harder to argue: exactly how guilty is the killer? Can the lawyer be expected to know whether or not the accused killer was capable of forming intent? What evidence is looked for? What questions are most important to ask an expert psychiatric witness on the stand? And knowing that the verdict can make the difference between a specific jail term or an indefinite time in a psychiatric hospital, how does the lawyer know how to advise an accused client to plead?

Likewise, the judges who hand down sentences can hardly be expected to be familiar with the long-term complexities of mental illnesses. I've heard a sentence based on the belief that a certain condition, schizophrenia in this example, can be cured within some length of time. In fact, the best possible outcome would be to bring the condition under a degree of control — control that can only be achieved and maintained with lifelong, continuous treatment. For such an offender, a short sentence or release into the community without sufficient restrictions can invite dreadful consequences. Judges are sometimes forced to impose sentences they know are out of sync with the reality of individual cases, because the length of sentence and parole eligibility are predetermined by the verdict. Mandatory sentences for first-degree murder are rigid; when the jury delivers a first-degree verdict, the judge must send even the most mentally ill or brain-damaged killer to jail for a minimum of twenty-five years.

Sometimes the players in the drama don't even speak the same language. Considerable trial time can be used to determine the differences between legal, clinical and common definitions of such crucial words as "intent." The psychiatrist might argue that the legal definition doesn't fit with today's medical concept. The lawyer can rebut that the legal definition is nevertheless the one that prevails in court. The public, hearing the same word during a televised report of the trial, may ascribe a third, street meaning to it.

Somehow, trial participants must sort everything out, and make life and death decisions. We dream of the quick-fix of a television-story trial, and an ending that grants the same relief and satisfaction. Real-life cases, however, are messy and complicated.

Outside the courtroom, the general public, politicians and the media are also vital players. They may not influence a particular trial, but their opinions help shape the criminal justice system overall. The public's clamour for justice pushes politicians to make changes in law and the correctional system, and the media that comprise the public's chief source of information. Mass media tend to limit their coverage to the most sensational highlights of the most sensational trials. But they can also force the public to focus on important issues. An entire community can rise up in arms quickly and harmfully, if given shallow impressions, or people can mobilize for improvement, given a deeper understanding of the issues.

Increasing the understanding of all the players in a murder trial is our best hope for bringing the law up to speed, for reducing conflict and tragedy, for increasing the likelihood that the guilty will be convicted and the sick treated. The greater the understanding everyone has about mental illness, criminal law and the court system, the better equipped we are to instigate improvements and to protect the innocent — both accused and potential victims.

Or criminal justice system needs serious reform, particularly where law and psychiatry come face to face in a murder trial. These trials can be seen as high-stakes games played by certain rules. Prosecution and defence do their best to take advantage of the rules to win. Who wouldn't? However, many of these rules, which were originally designed to improve the process, now hinder it. Some are so rigid that the resulting (all-or-nothing) outcome doesn't relate to real, individual people.

Verdicts are too distinctly compartmentalized to reflect the real-world variety of crimes, perpetrators and mental states. There are usually only five available verdicts: Guilty of First-Degree Murder, Second-Degree Murder, Manslaughter, Not Criminally Responsible on account of Mental Disorder (formerly Not Guilty by Reason of Insanity), and Not Guilty. None of these may properly fit the circumstances of a particular case, but whichever comes closest has to be used. You must choose one. Sentencing, too, is fairly inflexible, often not serving the various purposes of retribution, incapacitation (in a legal sense), deterrence and treatment/rehabilitation. Overall, the law frequently fails to keep up with modern knowledge of human behaviour.

The situation is ripe for both calculated abuse and honest misadventure in terms of trial outcomes. The results are that some cases have perverse or unjust outcomes; others result in reasonable verdicts, almost by accident and with great inefficiency; and some perfectly reasonable trials produce decent outcomes in spite of the system.

Changes in the way we treat guilty people (including the desperately ill) who have killed, have evolved too slowly, case by case in the time-honoured way of the law, trailing far behind advances in psychiatric understanding.

Sitting in a courtroom (as a forensic psychiatrist) I have alternately cheered and wrung my hands over the way the system operates. Some elements of the system should be trashed, but the good parts should be incorporated into a new, consistent structure that is more easily understood and allows flexibility of outcomes better related to each specific case. So much courtroom procedure involves elaborate game-playing because of the overly structured approach to verdicts and sentencing. With better flexibility, for example, we could see realistic and sensible bargaining, leading to more guilty pleas and, therefore, more-constructive case dispositions.

The stories in this book are my cases, fictionalised as necessary. They're meant to provide some idea of the problems that must be dealt with when killers go to court, as well as the tools that help and the restrictions that frustrate trial participants.

They are grouped in five sections to represent the difficulties in the three "mental-state defences," in verdicts and sentencing, and in administering the sentences. Some of the verdicts are unsettling. Some of the epilogues are depressing. Sometimes the verdict suggests that the jury or judge concurs with my opinion; at other times, it doesn't. I don't always agree with other mental-health experts, as will be evident. And while I often admire lawyers, I don't always like what they do, particularly when there's a mentally ill person being grilled or when the system forces a defence lawyer into a silly or desperate defence strategy. In my criticisms of the legal system, I have taken advantage of the fact that I am not a member of the legal profession.

The stories are meant to leave you informed, and appalled enough to demand major changes to Canada's Homicide Law.

I

THE INSANITY DEFENCE

No person is criminally responsible for an act committed or an omission made while suffering from a mental disorder that rendered the person incapable of appreciating the nature and quality of the act or omission or of knowing that it was wrong.

— Section 16(1) of the Criminal Code of Canada

CHAPTER ONE

MIXED SIGNALS

Click! The new door bolt locked in place, and for a fleeting instant fear loosened its grip on John Klevchin. But within seconds he was back in wary mode, eyes sliding around the small apartment, checking that all systems were in place, that everything was working.

He now had five dead-bolts on his door, with two electronic password-locks as back-up. Bars and padlocks were attached to the windows, and he'd also thought to fasten them over the heating ducts from the building's central furnace. His alarm system, complete with motion sensors, lights and siren, was state of the art. And a hidden video camera ran twenty-four hours a day, ready to record the actions of any intruder who did manage to penetrate the defences.

John recalled, with some satisfaction, the installer declaring that his set-up was "in a league with Fort Knox." In the sleepy little community of Rock Creek, the construction business was in a slump, so his purchase of all the latest security devices over the last six months had been welcomed by the town's only locksmith.

It wasn't easy for John, who lived on welfare, to afford all this hardware, but he had to protect himself. He wondered if this new door-bolt would finally stop the intrusions, or if he needed to buy more. Perhaps it would stop them until he received his next welfare cheque, the one thing he could rely on.

Some months ago, he had been officially categorized as disabled from chronic paranoid schizophrenia. He had his doubts about the diagnosis. But being declared disabled, whether or not you were, meant extra money, and he needed that supplement to pay for more security equipment. He let the diagnosis stand.

After all, he told himself, anything, *anything* was better than having God-knows-who slip into your apartment, replace your belongings with carefully-crafted fakes, and poison the food in your refrigerator. Someone was doing that to him, and he had to stop it.

He could tell his personal stuff had been exchanged, several times. Things like belts, shoes, even his after-shave, weren't in their usual places when he came home. As soon as he walked in, he could sense right away that something was different.

Same with the refrigerator. He admired the intruders' cleverness, but he could detect the slight change of flavour in the foods. Subtle poisoning. He knew that was why he had been feeling weird lately.

It didn't seem like anyone was going to help him deal with this. John had complained repeatedly to the police about the break-ins. They were interested enough the first few times, but now they simply suggested he drop into the Rock Creek Mental Health Centre, and tell the folks down there. He was feeling increasingly desperate because no one seemed willing to take his complaints seriously.

A while back, he had been getting injections of a long-acting antipsychotic drug, haloperidol, every four weeks at the Mental Health Centre. Evelyn, his psychiatric nurse, had been calm and reassuring, listening to his accounts of apartment tampering and apparently understanding that there were hushed and mumbled voices rustling around in his head — whisperings of the devil, his dead grandfather, and sometimes even the Rock Creek police. She had explained that the voices and anxiety were the result of his schizophrenia. Some genetic glitch had given him an overload of a chemical, dopamine, in his brain. These shots would help re-balance his chemistry.

Well, some of that made sense; he knew his father and uncle had both been schizophrenic. But no one could tell him the business with his belongings and his food was just a figment of his imagination.

Still, he took the injections for several sessions — partly to qualify for his disability supplement, and partly to humour Evelyn, who was the one person in Rock Creek who hadn't tried to torment him. But the shots were painful, and he started getting muscle cramps. After his last injection three months ago, he had stopped going for the medication.

He ventured out of his apartment less and less. For one thing, he reasoned that being at home would deter intruders, although sometimes he was certain they slipped in while he was in the bathroom or asleep in bed. If he couldn't deter them, perhaps he could catch them in the act. His video surveillance never seemed to record their images, so he suspected they had some devious way to defeat the camera. And without the medication, he had become more and more sleepless and agitated at night, his wakefulness fuelled by his desire to stay alert and on watch.

Constant sexual harassment was the other reason that John seldom left his apartment. Everywhere he went in Rock Creek, people showed their tongues to him. Oh, they disguised what they were doing with normal, everyday actions: yawning, laughing, licking their lips. But it was obvious to him that this displaying of tongues was a sexual come-on directed straight at him.

He didn't mind it so much from the women — he was, after all, a heterosexual — but the men and children were clearly trying to lure him into molesting or doing something homosexual, with their sly seduction attempts. He worried that one way or another, they were going to get him — if not by messing with his stuff and poisoning his food, then by getting him pinned as a sex pervert and coming up with some archaic law that would justify his public castration on the stage at Rock Creek Memorial Hall.

The campaign of terror against him had intensified some time after he stopped his injections. Lascivious tongues slid across lips everywhere he looked, and to make things worse, the voices in his head seemed to intrude more and more.

The police voices were the strongest, and lately a new twist had appeared in their messages: they were telling him that he would be allowed to get away with teaching the citizens of Rock Creek a lesson. By getting his revenge against at least one of the people plaguing him, the voices said, he could scare off the rest. The officers seemed to be offering him a way out of his torment.

Although he didn't know what he might be allowed to do — or to whom, or when — John was encouraged and stimulated by this change of direction. Now the police were not only paying attention, they were backing him up.

He drew support from another source when his readings of the Bible started to take on new meaning. Where the words once seemed to dictate love and forgiveness, John now found clear permission for a necessary act of personal revenge. "The Lord knoweth how to deliver the godly out of temptations and to reserve the unjust unto the day of judgement to be punished," and "Vengeance is mine, sayeth the Lord," and, best of all: "I was made strong, waxed valiant in fight, turned to flight the armies of the aliens." Why had he come across these lines, if they were not sent as a message especially for him?

Suddenly he had the police *and* the Lord on his side. The excitement of doing something righteous with these two powerful and virtuous forces behind him was almost too much to bear. He started feeling edgy, then almost panicky, waiting for a clear sign that he was allowed to act. Before, he had considered suicide as the only way he could escape the terrible tension; he had come very close to it several times. Now he had another way to deal with it, and perhaps he needed to go and search for the sign himself.

He decided to venture out on a Sunday morning, sticking to deserted streets to avoid the disgusting tongue show. He left behind the hairpiece he often used to disguise himself from his enemies; "they" had discovered it in his apartment.

"March for Schizophrenia": the words jumped out at him from a poster tacked to a utility pole. A march was to take place later that day, starting in Mary Hill Park. This *must* be it. He puzzled over the words, trying to decipher the particular message that would be directed to him alone. Finally, it clicked: the date. October 4, could also be written as "10–4"; how many times had he heard that on television? — police code for "Go ahead, proceed." And yes! The location, Mary Hill Park, was an obvious reference to Mary, the Mother of Christ. At long last, he had his cue. Both the police and Jesus had given him clear signals to set matters straight today in Mary Hill Park.

He raced back home and into the kitchen. A quick sniff told him that the food in his refrigerator had been tainted while he'd been out. They would give him no rest until he showed them he could be bullied no more.

A long butcher knife lay on the counter. He wished he had a gun, but if you had been labelled with a problem like schizophrenia, gun-control regulations stopped you from owning firearms of any kind. The knife fit nicely into his deep inside jacket pocket.

When he left the apartment, he was so excited that he didn't even bother with his usual, elaborate lock-up procedure. High on the danger of his task, and eager to get revenge and to stop the torture once and for all, he headed straight for Mary Hill Park.

Some discomfort did lurk in the back of John's mind, a glimmer of recognition that he had always been a quiet, gentle person, an outright pacifist if he thought about it. But he reminded himself that he had received an unmistakable signal, and as he walked along, the urgency of responding to some sort of starting pistol returned. The police voices urged him on, and, for the first time ever, he heard the actual voice of Jesus, quoting scripture in a way that made it clear John's intentions were morally correct.

No one was at the park when he arrived. For a moment he panicked, thinking that something might be wrong with the plan, but then realized he was an hour early for the march. If he simply hung around, though, someone might figure him out and, without a doubt, that somebody would start sexually harassing him. He headed into the public Men's Room and sat down in one of the stalls to wait, anxiously keeping an eye on the washroom though the door crack. After about fifteen minutes, he began to wonder if this was the best place to wait, but at that moment he heard footsteps outside.

Peter and Ruth Jenkins, an elderly couple, had retired to Rock Creek five years earlier, drawn to the community by its quiet neighbourhoods and the chance to be close to their daughter and her family. One of their favourite pastimes was a Sunday morning visit to the park with their three grandchildren. The youngsters delighted in feeding the squirrels and playing their own games among the trees, and the grandparents delighted in the youngsters. This morning, given Peter's increasing prostate problems, the family made their first stop at the park's restrooms.

Peter entered the washroom and stood at the urinal. John monitored him carefully from behind the stall door, not at all sure that this was the right time or place. But then Peter licked his lips and John knew that he had to act. The stall door crashed open and John leaped at Peter, driving eight inches of butcher knife into his back, almost completely severing his aorta and left pulmonary artery. Peter staggered out of the washroom and collapsed at the feet of his stunned wife and grandchildren. He managed a hoarse "I love you" in his dying moments.

John felt as if a tornado had erupted inside his mind. In the washroom, he had felt a wild exhilaration: he had finally had his revenge and the torment was over. But as he emerged and saw Peter's lifeless figure and the hysterical family, he became incredibly confused. What was happening? His police voices were telling him he had done the right thing, but he couldn't hear Jesus. The Devil was back, and he was telling John he would burn in hell. He sat down on a park bench, immobilized by confusion, but still expecting that the police would clear him of any wrongdoing.

His confusion deepened when the police inexplicably arrested him, instead of congratulating him. Maybe they needed to make a public display and would quietly release him later. But the police held him in a jail cell overnight, and the on-call Legal Aid lawyer who was called warned him to keep his mouth shut. What was going on? Maybe they were carrying out a complicated charade, pretending he was guilty, pretending they were dealing toughly with him to avoid public criticism. Perhaps ...

His doubts grew to alarming proportions when he was led before a judge who told him he was charged with murder. Maybe he had been trapped. Maybe the voices and the poster's message had been diabolical tricks to lead him into really big trouble. so the people of Rock Creek could escalate their campaign of terror against him.

By the time he had been transferred, by judge's order, to the Forensic Psychiatric Institute, John's eyes had taken on a wild look, and he moved around his room like a rabbit caught in a box.

Later that day, my telephone rang.

"Dr. Semrau?" My stomach churned when I was told that I had been assigned to the John Klevchin case. I had only been practicing as a forensic psychiatrist for six months. Working out of the Forensic Psychiatric Institute, my basic job was to provide assessments of the mental state of persons accused of crimes, and to present and defend my reports at trial.

So far, my cases involved relatively modest misdeeds — the worst had been a bungled robbery attempt. Now here was a murder: not only a major criminal case, but one that had provided the media with a banquet. Within a few days, public furor with the accused man had risen to a lynch-mob levels in Rock Creek and its neighbouring communities. The prospect of standing up in court and expressing anything like a contrary opinion was daunting, even if I lived and worked ninety miles away.

In Rock Creek, the local paper carried stories about the cold-blooded, merciless killer alongside sympathetic portraits of the victim, his devotion to soccer coaching and the Rotary Club, and his grieving family. Regional television news played and replayed images of the death scene and clips of little children in the park. Radio talk-shows were full of demands to bring back the death penalty.

One of the people I talked to, before I met John, was Evelyn Humphries, his psychiatric nurse at the Rock Creek Mental Health Centre. She told me that when John had been brought to court, officially accused of murder and ordered held in custody while a psychiatric assessment was made, an overflow crowd had watched, seething with hostility. "Stop! Wait till you've heard the whole story!" she had wanted to shout at the people around her. But their anger intimidated her, and apprehension that she might inadvertently violate patient confidentiality in the heat of the moment stopped her. Although she hadn't seen John for more than three months, she felt strongly that his voices and paranoid delusions must have propelled him into this unthinkable act.

Two days after his arrest, I entered John's isolation room alone for the first interview. His fear and agitation had escalated to the point that leaving him in the general psychiatric ward population would have been too dangerous. By now he was convinced that the signal he had received from the poster was a hoax and that a terrifying trap was rapidly closing in. Confined to a locked room containing only a barred window and a mattress with an untearable sheet (so he couldn't hang himself), John alternated between banging on the door, screaming, and cowering in a corner wrapped in the sheet.

"Don't go in there alone. You'll be attacked for sure," the nurses had warned. But it seemed unimaginable to me that approaching a severely frightened, paranoid man surrounded by a bodyguard of burly orderlies would help develop any kind of rapport.

I was dressed to the nines, a fact that did not go unnoticed by the puzzled staff, who were used to my normally casual attire. I had read somewhere that conservative clothing and colours exhude authority, and I also remembered the chief psychiatrist's theory that patients never attack people wearing suits and ties, and who sit on the floor in a totally non-menacing manner. So, suited and tied, I entered the room with a quiet greeting and sat down on the cold tile floor. This image of calm authority seemed to reassure John, and even to arouse his curiosity. Nevertheless, several minutes of complete silence ensued.

"How are you doing, John? Are you getting enough to eat? Are you hungry?" I ventured a few casual questions that appeared to break the ice. John responded in monosyllables, eyes downcast but shooting frequent, furtive glances at me.

"Do you know why you're here?" At this, the first specific question about his predicament, John shut down. Sensing a trap, he would say no more.

Four times over the next few days, I attempted to have a conversation with him — as did the ward nurses — with no success. Meanwhile, John was deteriorating rapidly. He became more withdrawn and depressed. He virtually stopped eating; his fear of being poisoned had resurfaced.

Obviously mentally ill and a danger to his own health, John would have to be certified under the Mental Health Act, a move that would permit involuntary psychiatric treatment for him, including medication if he needed it. This was done. His records, forwarded from Rock Creek, described the success of his curtailed series of haloperidol injections, so I immediately prescribed the same medication.

The results were dramatic. Within two days, John was eating again and carrying on at least partly sensible and relevant conversations with the staff. He was soon well enough to be transferred into the common dormitory and living areas. Finally cooperative in interviews, he began to reveal the story of his thoughts and feelings leading up to the killing. His voices gradually subsided. After three weeks, he had enough insight to know that he had been seriously mentally ill and that he probably had not been plagued by intruders or by people campaigning to have him convicted as a sex pervert.

As his insight grew, predictably his depression worsened. Somehow, he saw a newspaper account, which portrayed him as an unfeeling psychopath. John felt totally bewildered. He knew what he had done, and understood what a devastating thing it was, but he still believed he had only been trying to save himself. He descended into deep depression; one afternoon he almost succeeded in hanging himself in a shower stall. He was put on suicide watch and prescribed an antidepressant, fluvoxamine.

By the time of the trial, six months after the murder, John was no longer suicidal and had begun to ease up on himself. He was starting to accept my explanation that his behaviour — normally peaceful and law-abiding — had been the product of a mind disturbed by illness.

On the first day of the trial, I was probably the most apprehensive person going into the courtroom. Pre-trial meetings with the prosecution and defence lawyers had left me feeling uneasy. The defence counsel had been delighted with my opinion that John was deserving of an insanity defence. She was, however, fairly inexperienced — I could imagine her being intimidated by a hard-nosed prosecutor — and perhaps had something to lose by winning a case that flew in the face of local opinion.

The prosecutor admitted that the insanity defence had merit but, given his role, he could hardly accept that lying down. He warned me to expect ruthless grilling on cross-examination, but that I wasn't to take it personally.

The gallery was packed for the trial. The public's mood seemed to have shifted from a "string-'im-up-now" attitude to a willingness to "sit here until justice is done" — "justice" meaning a life sentence with no chance of parole for ten to twenty-five years. (The death penalty was rescinded, in Canada, in 1976, and has not been brought back in the interim.)

The opening hours of the trial went smoothly. The prosecution's case essentially re-iterated in detail the Agreed Statement of Facts, in which the defence admitted that John Klevchin killed Peter Jenkins deliberately and without lawful reason. I watched the faces of the spectators subside almost into smugness in expectation of a quick trial and a guilty verdict followed by the mandatory life sentence. When instead the defence lawyer rose and began to outline her proposed "Not Guilty by Reason of Insanity" argument, the public gallery erupted. After repeated calls for order and the ejection of two spectators, the trial resumed. At this point, about to provide the key testimony before this crowd, I felt distinctly ill. Despite obsessive preparation to compensate for my lack of experience, I felt that I too was going on trial.

24

The defence lawyer questioned me first:

Q:Dr. Semrau, are you familiar with the requirements of the defence of Not Guilty by Reason of Insanity?

A:Yes. To qualify, the accused must have been suffering at the time of the act froma mental disorder such that he was not able to appreciate the nature and quality of his act, or unable to know that it was legally or morally wrong.

Q:In your opinion, was John Klevchin suffering from a mental disorder at the time of his killing of Peter Jenkins?

A:Yes, he was suffering from chronic paranoid schizophrenia, which had escalated to the proportions of an intense psychotic episode, due to non-compliance with medication at the time of the killing. [*Could I sound much stiffer, I wondered?*] He was suffering from paranoid delusions that his belongings were being tampered with and his food poisoned. He believed that ordinary people going about their business were attempting to seduce him into perverted acts by displaying their tongues at him, so that he could be publicly castrated.

Q:Was he able to appreciate the nature and quality of his act in killing the victim?

A:Yes and no. He certainly was able to know that he was using a knife in a manner likely to cause the death of the victim, but he believed himself to be acting essentially in self-defence, as the result of a campaign of terror against him by the citizens of Rock Creek, who he believed were tormenting him in various ways.

Q:Was he able to know that his acts were legally and morally wrong?

A:No, he wasn't. He believed not only that the police were refusing to provide him with ordinary protection from his tormentors but also that they were communicating with him, through voices in his head and through his interpretation of the "March for Schizophrenia" poster, that it was legally proper for him to kill one of his tormentors in order to strike back and bring this campaign of terror to an end. He also believed that Jesus and the Bible were encouraging and sanctioning his behaviour in the killing, and thus he saw his behaviour as being morally correct. All of these delusional beliefs were the direct result of his mental illness.

I allowed the smallest note of self-satisfaction to ring in my mind, and began to think that perhaps there was a chance I could relax in this role after all. I had sounded fairly competent, I thought. But here was the prosecutor moving confidently in for cross-examination, polish and vigour evident — a major league pitcher coming to throw to a rookie.

Q:Doctor, how can you say that the accused didn't appreciate the nature and quality of his act when he simply ... *cold-bloodedly* ... *stabbed* a stranger with a *large knife* ... in *broad daylight*?

A:[*I swallow*]: He both did and didn't appreciate what he was doing. [*Did I say that? I continue gamely.*] As with most people who are insane at the time of an offence, he largely understood the immediate physical reality of his behaviour, including that a knife can kill someone. However, his behaviour was motivated entirely by a bizarre view of reality in which he was the victim of a massive conspiracy to torment and destroy him without his having any recourse to the normal protection of the law. [*Yes!*]

Q:You're not very experienced as a forensic psychiatrist, are you?.

Surprisingly, this insinuation was just what I needed to boost my credibility. I admitted that although I had been a practicing psychiatrist for several years, I was fairly new to the forensic side. For this reason, I explained, I had obtained a second opinion on the case from a well-known and well-respected colleague, who had concurred with my conclusions. I saw a few heads nod, unconsciously. The prosecutor's questioning continued.

Q:The accused is an intelligent man. Couldn't he have pulled the wool over your eyes with his fantastic story about hearing voices, and his paranoid ideas?

A:That's always possible, but after examining his old psychiatric records, witnessing his mental state after the killing, and seeing

26

the total lack of any other conceivable motive for the killing, I am convinced that he has been telling the truth.

Q:Isn't it true that hundreds of thousands of people suffer from schizophrenia, and yet they are almost never violent? How can you say that delusions and hallucinations caused violence in this case, when otherwise they hardly ever do?

A:It's true that the vast majority of mentally ill people are non-violent. But there is still a slightly higher rate of violence in the mentally ill than in the population as a whole, particularly for patients with paranoid ideas who don't receive or benefit from psychiatric treatment.

Who will become violent and who won't is very hard to predict. It often depends on a particular, unique set of symptoms and circumstances coming together in a tragic combination before any violence will result. John Klevchin's record makes it very clear he is basically a non-violent person who acted totally out of character while in an extremely abnormal, psychotic mental state.

The prosecutor put on a good show, but in the end hadn't argued strongly against the insanity defence. The defence counsel had made her points. Even I felt I had communicated my professional opinion, however stiffly. I had been lucky to start with such a case. John's extreme mental state allowed me to form a clear-cut opinion, unlike many of the "grey-area" cases that were to follow. I had also, as it turned out, been able to witness two very good lawyers at work.

The judge retired to prepare her decision. The defence had elected trial by judge alone, reasoning that the process of attempting to pick an unbiased jury from the local area would have been long, expensive and difficult, and that the odds for a fair verdict in this case ran in favour of a judge from out of the district. The constant undercurrent of hostility during the trial made it appear to have been the correct choice.

The verdict, delivered a week later, was Not Guilty by Reason of Insanity. Rock Creek, at least in the media, went into an uproar. John Klevchin had "managed to talk his way out" of his just punishment for a "cold-blooded murder" with the help of a "bleeding-heart" doctor, lawyer and judge. John was committed back to the Forensic Psychiatric Institute for an indefinite period of time, but this did not seem to quell the community's anger, and the feeling that he had "got off." Evelyn

Humphries and a few of the staff at the Mental Health Centre felt that justice had been served, but they were almost alone.

John accepted his status philosophically, with a realism that served him well through many years during which his future seemed likely to be played out in the Forensic Psychiatric Institute. He knew his situation was better than prison, and he doubted that life on his own in the community could ever really be as humane as where he was, surrounded by understanding hospital staff and other patients who were in the same boat. Not exactly heaven, but a safe haven from others, and perhaps from himself. Today he lives quietly in a group home in another town.

In another time, in another jurisdiction, things could have turned out quite differently. Before schizophrenia, an illness now proven to have a biological cause, was discovered, John might have been convicted of devil possession and "treated" by any of the methods then commonly used, including drowning and burning at the stake.

In 1981, a mentally disturbed young man, John Hinkley, Jr., attempted to murder U.S. President Ronald Reagan in a misguided, delusion-motivated attempt to impress Hollywood actor Jodie Foster. In the backlash following Hinckley's acquittal by reason of insanity, many jurisdictions abolished or severely restricted the insanity defence. In one of these courtrooms, John Klevchin might have been found guilty and given a long prison sentence, even a life sentence without parole. He could conceivably have received the death penalty, although almost everywhere there is overt reluctance to execute the mentally ill.

Even in his own Canadian jurisdiction, the trial could have ended differently. Had he chosen or been forced to be tried before a jury, the academic principles of the insanity defence might have been lost on a jury bent on providing simple and rough justice. In cases like this, I am convinced the prosecutor needs to consent to trial by judge alone. The prosecutor in John's trial was sympathetic and did consent, but other mentally disordered persons have been forced to undergo trial by jury with less reasonable results.

For me, the trial had been an eye-opener. Fascinated, I began a serious study of legal strategies, jargon, and style, and began scrutinizing lawyers at work in the courtrooms. Obviously, I needed to know what to expect in order to respond effectively — and to understand what my responses during testimony would mean for the accused individuals I assessed.

CHAPTER TWO

THE REFUGEE'S STORY

My first killer, John Klevchin, had been diagnosed early in his life as a schizophrenic. He had presented the symptoms, had the family history to back the diagnosis, and had responded well to standard prescribed medications. The tragedy that occurred was the result of his stopping those medications, which threw him directly into a lions' den of hallucinations and paranoia.

Zerom Seyoum was not diagnosed, was not even suspected of being mentally ill, until it was far too late. Long before he was accused of murder, he had spent years living in justifiable fear, in surroundings that were nightmarish. He had come to believe that you had to keep looking over your shoulder and be ready to protect yourself at all times, in order to survive. A bright, right-thinking young man, he carried fresh memories of genuine terror that later helped prevent him from being able to draw the distinction between his life-long habit of apprehensive vigilance and his going over the edge.

He had been literally hunted as a political activist in his native country. When he developed feelings of paranoia in Canada, he failed to recognize the unlikelihood of this being a continuation of his past, and his self-protection mechanisms kicked in, aggressively, out of control.

As this is being written, Zerom is mentally stable and settled. He's an "interrupted academic" who has made use of his skilled and highly trained mind to research various aspects of mental illness and treatment, and to put his findings, as well as the narrative of his life so far, into words. His story is more insightful when he tells it himself, so I will relay it in his words as much as possible. His generosity in allowing me to do so provides a rare opportunity to be privy to a mentally disordered offender's point of view, inhibited by neither the constraints of court-room dynamics nor doctor-patient confidentiality.

Zerom Seyoum was born in Eritrea, a small African nation on the Red Sea coast. This country geographically blocks ocean access to its much larger, land-locked neighbour, Ethiopia. In 1961, when Zerom was 7 years old, Ethiopian Emperor Haile Selassie stepped in and annexed his country, forcing all Eritreans to adopt Ethiopian citizenship. In response, as Zerom describes it, "the people of Eritrea took up arms and fought for more than 30 years." Although Eritrea regained its independence in 1993, hundreds of lives continued being lost each year in the on-going border conflict, until a shaky treaty was signed in 2001.

Zerom completed high school in the now-province of Eritrea, and at 18, entered Ethiopia's only university, in Addis Ababa. That same year, his father died, leaving his mother in Eritrea with Zerom's four younger siblings. During Zerom's second year at the university, a military junta deposed Emperor Selassie. Supported by modern weapons and military advisors from the then-USSR, the junta decided to settle the Eritrean independence question, and, according to Zerom, "declared war on the Eritreans." Many of us remember seeing television news stories of starving Eritreans during that seventeen-year conflict, which included drought and famine as well as bloodshed.

"Most Eritrean students," Zerom relates, "left school to join either the Eritrean Liberation Front (ELF) or the Eritrean People's Liberation Front (EPLF)." Zerom joined ELF, but during field training, he was forced to subsist on a mug of corn a day, and he developed a stomach ulcer. No medicine of any kind was available, so he returned to Addis Ababa and the university, where he joined the strong, pro-democracy, anti-junta student union. Hoping to quash student dissidence, the junta closed all the schools and the university, and created a two-year program called Development for Cooperation, for all students in Grade 10 or higher.

During this time, an underground party made up of university graduates, students and workers was formed, the Ethiopian Peoples Revolutionary Party (EPRP), and Zerom became a member of an EPRP study cell of three university students and two high school students. The younger boys were soon caught in action and shot to death.

Zerom stayed in the city working for EPRP because he had false papers stating that he had to remain there for regular medical check-ups for his ulcer. The success of EPRP's campaign actually caused the re-education to fail. The head of the program was executed.

The university had just reopened when Zerom received devastating news: "My mother had been shot in the head, in front of my 6- and 9-year-old sisters and 12-year-old brother. They were forced to watch while she bled to death. They screamed, but no help came because everyone had closed up their homes. There had been a skirmish between ELF and Ethiopian soldiers. The soldiers had executed 120 civilians on their way out of town."

Zerom raced home, but before he could get back both his brothers had run away and joined the EPLF. And the Ethiopians got more and more aggressive. Eritreans were being killed, jailed and persecuted. Zerom was vulnerable; he had joined an underground EPLF cell, and one of his jobs was to identify people who tortured Eritreans.

"Three times, my house was searched by Ethiopians. I was jailed for a month, tortured and persecuted. They knew I had two brothers in the EPLF; they wouldn't let up."

Deathly afraid for his sisters, he put them in a Catholic mission, and rejoined the university. The elder sister later ran off to join the EPLF, and Zerom felt guilty — if he had taken care of his sister, he anguished, she wouldn't have left. But he graduated with distinction and was soon an assistant lecturer.

The military junta escalated its persecution of Eritreans, so Zerom made two decisions: he would flee across the border into Sudan, and he would apply for a Canadian university scholarship. "I knew that Canada was the most humanitarian country in the world," he says. Once here, he could bring over his youngest sister. He came to the University of British Columbia as a graduate student and teaching assistant in chemistry.

Zerom continues his story.

"Shortly after my arrival in Vancouver, I began to think that people were after me, following me everywhere I went. I couldn't understand. I didn't know what wrong I had committed here.

"Then my landlord started getting telephone calls, and I thought they were talking about me. When I overheard him say, 'I wouldn't do it for that much,' I believed 'they' were offering him $1,000 to poison me. Next time, I heard him say, 'That sounds good,' and I believed they had offered him $10,000.

"There were other reasons I suspected my landlord. In my country, men don't cook. So when I came to Canada, I was unable to cook for and feed myself. I started buying spaghetti noodles, boiled them, added salt and ate them. Later somebody told me to add tomato sauce. I was regularly leaving half the sauce, unsealed, in the fridge, so when the landlord suggested, 'Don't cook three times a day, cook once for lunch and dinner,' I thought he wanted to poison my tomato sauce between meals. Another time he gave me cookies, explaining that they were Christmas cookies and not available in stores; I threw them in the garbage, believing they were poisoned.

"The food and drink were giving me burning sensations and often I vomited. I couldn't eat, drink or sleep. I began having headaches that never went away."

Psychiatrist's note: Had he been mentally well at this point, Zerom might have suspected a return of his stomach ulcer and gone to see a doctor. But his mental illness, in effect, put blinders on him, so that he attributed all adverse experiences — even innocuous and irrelevant ones — to the persecutory plot. Zerom simply believed that everything related to him.

"Then people on buses started laughing at me and talking about me, so constantly that sometimes I forgot where I should get off the bus and ended up three or four stops away from home.

"The graduate students also began mocking me. One day in the chemistry library, I believed that a student was laughing at me, so I moved over to sit opposite her and stared directly at her for 10 minutes. She got scared and left the library.

"I continued to think people were following me. Hundreds of them. And they were poisoning me. I decided to buy my food from the student cafeteria. If I didn't eat the same thing every day, I would be safe, because if they put poison in every dish in the cafeteria to catch me, they would poison the entire student body.

"But I always loved my tea. One day the cashier said, 'Three packets of sugar is enough for a cup of tea,' and she wouldn't let me have my usual six or seven.

"I told Trung, a lab technician and my best friend, about it and he said, 'It's because Canadians don't use as much sugar in their tea, they probably think you take it home.' I said, 'But you know I don't!'

"I couldn't help thinking about it, day and night. Now I knew why I was being followed: they thought I was a thief. But why wasn't it the police who were following me? This is ridiculous! Me, a thief — I couldn't believe it.

"Upset, I went long periods without sleep. I just couldn't understand why I was being belittled like this.

"I said I was going to make tea in our laboratory. Trung bought the kettle, and I bought two kilos of sugar. To my surprise, when I made the tea, Trung didn't have any. I asked one of the undergraduate students to have tea with me. She had tea without sugar. Now I believed that Trung had added poisonous chemicals with the same crystal structure as sugar to my bag of sugar. I began to feel a burning sensation and nausea. When Trung left for home, I dumped the two kilos of sugar into the sink and later bought another two-kilo bag, which I smuggled into the lab early next morning before Trung arrived.

"I had never seen anyone drink tea without sugar, so I believed that the undergraduate student hadn't used sugar because she knew that Trung had poisoned it and she was too scared of Trung to tell me. But with the second bag of sugar, I felt worse than before, with the same burning sensations and nausea.

"Next I thought that camera men were following me. I saw a man taking photos in front of the main library and I believed he was taking them of me.

"At the Chemistry Department Christmas party, there was another incident. A beautiful graduate student approached me, asked my name, whether we were in any of the same classes, and so on. I became suspicious and left her to join the other guys. Later this same student came over and asked if I would like to dance. I said, 'NO!' and got angry at her. Right after that, a man started taking photos of the people there and took three pictures of me.

"I had had enough. The next day I went to the graduate advisor and said, 'Many people that I don't know are following me. They take my picture. I don't know what wrong I have done. I don't know these people, but I know four of their agents.' I explained about the cafeteria cashier, about Trung poisoning my sugar, the graduate student at the Christmas party, who identified me, and the man who took my photo.

"The graduate advisor took me upstairs to the lab, and he had a talk with Trung. He then said, 'If one man was following you, we could go to the police, but since you said there were many, this is a cultural difference.' Afterwards, Trung said to me, 'We people who come from communist countries feel that we are being followed.'

"I didn't believe either of them. But aha! Now I knew why I was being followed. They think I am a communist. This is ludicrous. I hate communism with a passion. That's why I fled home for Canada.'

"But still, I believed that they were going to kill me. They had detectives following me and they were putting snipers on top of high buildings to shoot me without leaving any evidence. They thought I was either a thief or a communist, and I was neither.

"I know now that it was all in my mind. But then, I couldn't hold in my anger. I didn't know what to do.

"I couldn't eat, drink or sleep. And all this time, I had terrible headaches day and night. I went to school and attended classes, not because I wanted to, but because I was afraid that the other students would tell on me if I weren't there taking notes.

"Finally, people started talking to me in my head. The voices sounded like my friends Michael and Selezion, in Eritrea. 'What are you waiting for?' they asked. 'People are conspiring against you, following you and poisoning you. They are dishonouring you.' I didn't even know what 'dishonouring' meant. 'This is self-defence. You will be called hero, hero, hero. You will be all over the newspapers back home: "Our man in Canada revenges himself for being dishonored."' Because the voices were those of my best friends, I believed them.

"Then one morning I got up and started to take action against my enemies. I spread the tomato sauce that my landlord used to poison me all over his food, so he would suffer like me. I took a kitchen knife and went to the bus stop ready to terrorize anybody who stared or laughed at me.

"But my enemies had read my mind, and knew what I was going to do, because they put a guard dog on the bus. A woman with dark glasses had a dog wearing a sign which said, 'Working Dog', so I couldn't do anything but just sit.

"When I got off the bus, I waited for the yellow car which usually parked by the Physics Department. The voices of Michael and Selezion had mentioned a yellow car that followed me. Not knowing if it was a man or a woman, I waited with my knife to terrorize the car's owner.

"Suddenly, I heard a siren approaching. My enemies had found out what I was going to do and were coming after me!"

Zerom panicked. He began running for his life. He took the stairs to the chemistry lab two at a time, his mind a riot of fear, and strange sounds, and the enemy closing in on him. The enemy!

Now he recognized Trung. But Trung ran away from him, screaming, his cries adding to the clamour in Zerom's head. What had happened to him?

Zerom had stabbed Trung, fatally. Trung, the enemy and his best friend.

"I stayed in the lab while people rushed here and there. I still didn't understand. There was so much fog and confusion. Soon I was taken to the police station. I talked and talked about being chased, but then they told me I needed a lawyer. I couldn't understand why, but I did as they told me and picked a name out of the telephone directory. He was a civil lawyer, not a criminal lawyer, but the fact that he was a lawyer was good enough for me — so I insisted he take my case.

"Later that day, somebody put me in the Forensic Psychiatric Institute. After two months on medications, I came to know where I was and that I was accused of second degree murder, of Trung. After six months, I was found Not Guilty By Reason of Insanity."

When I first met Zerom Seyoum, shortly after the homicide, he was absolutely terrified. We soon started him on the road back to recovery with anti-psychotic medications, but the full reality of his circumstances took a while to sink in. He was still assuming that he was going to be killed or tortured — as he likely would have been in Africa, and as he had been persecuted in his delusions.

After initial trust had been established between us and he was able to reach a basic understanding of his legal situation, Zerom began to see me as the person who could save him. I could see he believed I held his life in my hands, as someone who could personally obtain his acquittal with an insanity defence. He didn't expect the court or the legal system to give it to him simply because it was just.

After all, he had recently come from a place where he had seen powerful people able to operate above the law, and rough justice as seemingly the only justice. He was incredibly grateful to me.

Complete trust is a two-edged sword, though. It motivates you to do well by your patient, but makes it harder to retain the cool objectivity of an expert witness.

Zerom, looking back, articulates a clear portrait of the working of his mind those first days after the homicide.

"When voices or paranoia or telepathy compel a mental patient to break a law, jail or punishment never enter his thoughts. He explains his frustrations to the police or a psychiatrist for one reason only. He has to find someone to believe him — to believe that someone was after him and that his actions were justified… to believe that what he did was in self-defence, or to save others.

"When he sees the police, he feels relieved because he thinks they will confirm that he was pushed to the edge. He thinks that the police will protect him and that they will help identify his enemies. When he sees a psychiatrist who says that he needs medication, he doesn't believe that he is sick, and he continues looking for that one person who believes he was persecuted. After I explained my frustrations to the police and the psychiatrist, and they didn't believe me, I still expected Paula, the undergraduate student, would come and explain that Trung was adding chemicals to my sugar to poison me.

"After a while, I began to think that the person who might believe me after all was the psychiatrist. He asked me questions that related to what I was feeling. He didn't justify my actions, but he discovered what I had been experiencing.

"But then I started to suspect that he knew about some things before he asked me about them. So I said to myself, 'He must know what they were doing to me,' and I wouldn't open up after that. I was convinced he was part of 'them', and that he had been sent by my enemies to torture me. But I got over that."

Half a year after the homicide, Zerom's case was tried. We were quite a pair going into the trial. The murder had received enormous publicity; it was still early in my forensic career and I was somewhat wrought with performance anxiety. But Zerom testified competently and ingenuously, I managed to explain his situation with out too many challenges, and the obviously valid insanity defence succeeded.

By then, Zerom was in complete remission, and his lawyer and I both expected that he would be released within two years. It was not to be.

His treatment team recommended conditional discharge after nine months, but the Review Board, which included a Supreme Court justice and psychiatrists, lawyers, clinical psychologists and Crown counsel, turned him down. The following year, both his treatment team and a Review Board recommended a conditional discharge. This time, the Provincial Government cabinet over-ruled the Board, saying discharge would be "premature". In the fourth year, some of Zerom's Canadian friends started talking to the media, saying that he was being unreasonably held at FPI while his treatment team and the Review Board wanted him released. Finally, the cabinet allowed him a conditional discharge. He was now allowed to go where he wanted during the day, as long as he continued to live and receive treatment at FPI.

He enrolled at the British Columbia Institute of Technology (BCIT), in the hope that more education would boost his employment opportunities when all this was over. He did well for two semesters — during which time I moved away, and he was put under the care of another doctor — but then something else interfered.

He had been having difficulties with his anti-psychotic medication all along, on and off. The side effects included insomnia and pain. He kept complaining about it, but because this was the only effective drug of its kind available, all we could do was try reducing the dosage a bit at a time, and try other means to counter the side effects. But let him continue the story.

"They insisted that if I went off the medication, I would get sick again. But the pain was just awful. About a year after Dr. Semrau moved away, I convinced my new psychiatrist to take me off the medication. I was a new man. I could walk faster, express myself properly, sleep soundly; even the food tasted better. I was doing fine at BCIT.

"I thought I was cured, once and for all. I truly believed that my problem had been temporary psychosis. I didn't know that the medication I had been on was simply suppressing my mental illness, keeping it in remission.

"After two months off the medication, I began to have headaches, impaired hearing and dizziness. I became suspicious of what the instructor was talking about, and suspicious of the other students. My attention grew focused on the thoughts in my mind, and no longer on school.

"I thought detectives were after me, although I didn't know what for. The detectives wore hats and dark glasses. I told myself that they couldn't disguise themselves from me, I knew they were following me. But I couldn't understand why.

"Soon every civilian was after me, especially young women hired by the detectives. I started hearing voices telling me that my watch was bugged. Whenever I waited for the bus, young women kept asking me what time it was. So I believed that my watch was bugged, and that was how they found out where I was, and when. I broke my watch into small pieces, as small as could be, so they wouldn't be able to detect my presence. It didn't help.

"All these thought seemed connected together and true, so I tried to solve it myself.

"I took steps to avoid the stares of people on the bus. First, I subscribed to *Time* and *Popular Science* magazines, planning to read them on the way to and from BCIT. Reading on the bus to school was all right. But on my way back, because of the school stress and the headaches, it was impossible to concentrate and focus. I was forced to look around me, and that made me tremble and sweat.

"I tried another solution. Instead of taking the usual two buses to school, I changed routes, taking two different buses plus rapid transit. It seemed there were more of 'them' on this new route. I tried a third route, and a fourth. Nothing helped.

"The staff at FPI figured it out, and asked if I was getting sick. I didn't know that I was sick, so I said 'no'. I also believed that they were in touch with the detectives and wanted to interrupt my schooling. I grew suspicious of them.

"But I had run out of self-solutions. I confided to one of the nurses, who told my psychiatrist, and I had to quit school, and was confined to FPI. When I realized that I was locked up again and on medication, I just gave up. They put me back on the same medications, but despite the side effects, I felt better.

"Before long, though, I grew suicidal. Since that time, I have observed other patients who, like me, thought that no one believed them. They cling to their persecution delusions until the medicine kicks in, time heals, or they commit suicide. The best thing for me, I believed, was to die. The problem was, I didn't know how. When I received grounds privileges, the first thing I did was look — unsuccessfully — for a rope with which to hang myself.

"One of the other patients told me that her father had committed suicide by taking sleeping pills. I told my doctor I was unable to sleep, which was true. She ordered a drug for me, and instead of taking it, I saved every pill until I had 500 mgs. Not enough, so I told the doctor that I was having difficulty sleeping in spite of the pills. She prescribed a different, stronger medication. I saved the new pills up until I had 11,500 mgs. I went to bed after taking both sets of pills with a can of pop, and woke up five days later in the hospital. The nurse watching me said, 'You're not in heaven, you're still on earth.' I had failed and was disappointed.

"Then: turning point. My doctor changed my anti-psychotic medications. Two new anti-psychotic drugs with far fewer side effects became available. Because they were more expensive than existing anti-psychotic drugs, no doctor in British Columbia was allowed to prescribe them until he or she had proven that the older treatments had failed or produced intolerable side effects for the patient. I got them.

"I have been doing well ever since on the new medication. I suffer no side effects. I was soon able to look back and see how delusional I had been. I know now that I have to take my medication all my life, for myself and for others' safety. Most of my problems have been solved."

When Zerom says "most" of his problems have been solved, he is referring to the fact that he is in good mental health. A big hurdle remains in front of him. After twelve years, he is still in the Forensic Psychiatric Institute, caught between a rock and a hard place not of his own making. The Canadian legal system that served him well at the time of the homicide turned what should have been a satisfactory ending to his story into a tragic non-ending.

While he was dealing with his illness, his visa to Canada expired. He was later allowed to apply for refugee status. He was "found credible" in two successive hearings and says he was told he would receive a written decision "after some time". In the interim, his lawyer left the legal aid network. His new lawyer helped him apply for landed immigrant status instead and withdrew Zerom's refugee claim. When Zerom then applied for landed immigrant status, he was told that because he had withdrawn his refugee claim he was not eligible for landed immigrant status. He tried to reopen the refugee status case, and was turned down. He appealed and was rejected.

His last option was to apply for landed immigrant status on humanitarian grounds. Two experts testified that the medication Zerom needs to survive is not available in Eritrea; the European drug companies that synthesize the medications backed up that claim with letters. His lawyer told the Humanitarian Commission that deporting him, rather than allowing him to stay as a landed immigrant, would be condemning him to madness or death. He was turned down, and essentially awaits deportation to Eritrea.

The last twist is that, with more than seven years of mental health and stability behind him, Zerom has long been a clear candidate for reintegration into the community where he would surely become a productive citizen. Yet release from the Forensic Psychiatric Institute would automatically transfer him from provincial to federal jurisdiction, and he would be deported. No Review Board could in clear conscience recommend that he be released in order to be sent to a certain relapse and likely, death. So he waits.

CHAPTER THREE
DEFINING MOMENTS

In one way, the cases of John Klevchin and Zerom Seyoum illustrate how effectively our justice system treats those who used to be called "the criminally insane". Both received the fair verdict of Not Guilty By Reason of Insanity, as it was then called. However, the cases went on too long and although he has been conditionally released, John lost a whole decade when he could have been rebuilding his life as a productive, more socially comfortable person. Zerom remains in a state of suspension, caught in a bureaucratic net.

Society has tried for centuries to figure out how to do the right thing by the mentally ill who commit crimes, even how to separate them from "sane" criminals. A few things we've got right, a lot we haven't, but we're still working on it.

Early in the recorded history of western civilization, there were declarations of acceptance that mentally disordered people should not be held responsible. Ancient Hebrew law and the sixth-century Justinian Code (which had sprung from Roman law) exempted children and the insane from culpability. But that kind of justice was slow in coming to most later societies, including Britain before English common law (the source of our own legal system) began to be formalized in the thirteenth century. Penalties or revenge for crimes committed by the mentally ill or developmentally delayed were often extracted from their families, who were held responsible for taking care of their sick and "idiot" kinfolk at home. Other mentally disordered unfortunates who stepped out of line were believed to be possessed by the devil or evil spirits, and were persecuted or even killed to stop the devil's work, regardless of the level of seriousness of their wrongdoing.

Law and medicine, each in its own way, have been working at defining "mentally ill" for hundreds of years. But our different approaches have resulted in great disparities. Medical people look for cause and effect, a truth or scientific fact, and then a treatment. Legal people need and use precise wording to protect rights or to determine guilt or innocence. Medical advances are made through objective research and testing. Advances in law occur through judgments cast, case by case, by higher-authority opinion. Lawyers abide by the legal definition of "mentally disordered" until new case (or statute) law alters the meaning. We medical people can't just go to them and say, "We don't consider that 'disordered' anymore, and here's the proof." We have to wait for a court case where that specific factor arises and hope the judgment will result in that specific change. In any year, there aren't that many court cases and in only a minority is the insanity defence at issue, so aside from rare systemic overhauls, change proceeds at the proverbial snail's pace.

Lawyers operate in a win-or-lose, all-or-nothing context; the objective is to win the case, not to be "right" or "wrong" but to be a fearless advocate for the client (as a defence counsel) or a minister for justice (as Crown counsel). Acting ethically, professionally and according to the system, a lawyer can take legal wording in isolation and use it in a variety of contexts, to his or her side's best advantage, or, based on rules of evidence, omit salient factors concerning an accused person's mental state. A psychiatrist, on the other hand, has to consider the whole patient when diagnosing and dealing with mental illness: emotions, mental functioning, physical factors, background and environment.

However, medical experts, during testimony, are forced to choose between "mad" and "bad," and they may only use certain legally admissible pieces of evidence regarding the accused's mental state, according to lawyers' instructions and the rules of the court. I've been frustrated many times at not being able to explain fully to the jury the nature of an accused person's illness — or the reasons why an accused person was *not* mentally ill. Juries and judges are in court to make legal decisions, according to legal, not medical, definitions, and using legal, not medical, rules about what information is relevant.

Don't get me wrong. Psychiatrists aren't uniformly scientific, and lawyers aren't unscientific word spinners. Psychiatrists notoriously disagree with one another concerning methods of treatment. Electroconvulsive therapy, prefrontal lobotomies, psychoanalysis, behaviourism, and each theory and drug has its own advocates and opponents. Many therapies have been cast out of favour; others have remained in the toolbox, some in greatly improved form and playing various roles.

And while the evolution of law seems a slow, lumbering process, medical developments can also be a long time coming. In recent years, we have made wonderful advancements in treatment through the development of new medications. Zerom Seyoum was one of the extremely unlucky individuals who suffered agonizing side effects from the best medication that was available when he entered hospital. As soon as he was able to take the new drug, he improved dramatically. But drugs take years to develop. They have to be subjected to a series of time-consuming, extremely costly tests and rounds of approvals before they become available for patients. (While big pharmaceutical companies are often criticized, they do have the incentive and the resources to produce these miracles.)

We psychiatrists can't always claim to meet a higher order of proof than lawyers, either. It is difficult, sometimes impossible, for us to prove anything about the working of one particular human mind much further than "more likely than not." As with the legal profession working on the legal definition of "mental disorder," the medical profession continues to hone our own means and tests for evaluating and diagnosing mental disorders. And it is in assessment, rather than treatment, where we are usually involved with the law. Great strides have been made in improving diagnostic categories, testing techniques and medical technology that allow us to differentiate between different mental disorders and their variations, and to determine the organic causes and effects of some mental disorders. For example, we can now state with complete confidence that schizophrenia is primarily a brain disease with clear genetic and biochemical causes and mechanisms, rather than a sign of weak character or devil possession. That knowledge makes juries much more comfortable rendering insanity verdicts.

British and, in turn, Canadian legal people have been trying assiduously to write fairness into their definitions and practices concerning mental illness since at least 1265. That's when the Archdeacon of Barnstable tackled the issue in his Canon Law of Bracton, which is believed to have started the codification of British common law. In it, he included the connection between a physical behaviour (committing a crime) and a mental process (having a purpose in committing the crime). Since children were too innocent, he wrote, and mad people were considered unable to reason, they could shape no criminal intention or purpose and hence could not be culpable.

As England evolved into a society operating more and more under the rule of law, reason rather than revenge increasingly influenced punishment for crimes. And a developing parliament along with powerful monarchs grew willing and able to enforce domestic peace and order. While the justice system was most occupied with handling typical criminals, a mentally ill person would occasionally clash with some prominent figure, and the ensuing hullabaloo would almost inadvertently lead to refinements in the legal definition and treatment of the "criminally insane."

In 1724, a Lord Onslow was shot by one Ned Arnold, who believed that the nobleman actually lived in Arnold's stomach. At his trial, a few dozen witnesses testified that Ned habitually went around talking to himself and to imaginary creatures, and laughing senselessly. But the judge declared that in order for an accused person to lack criminal responsibility, he "must be a man totally deprived of his understanding and memory and doth not know what he is doing, no more than an infant, than a brute [then meaning a farm animal] or a wild beast [meaning a field animal]". On those grounds, Ned Arnold was found guilty, and the "wild beast test" — referring to lack of intellectual capacity, rather than untamed violence — became a standard.

George III was the intended victim in the next famous case. James Hadfield believed that only his own death could stop God from destroying the world. Suicide was a sin, so he came up with the idea to get himself hanged, by killing the king. He failed on both counts and was found not guilty of attempted murder, by reason of insanity. As a result of this case, the Criminal Lunatics Act of 1800 was enacted. The standard legal definition of mental illness was expanded to include having delusions — referred to thereafter as the delusion test. The Act also instructed jurors to return a special verdict (in essence, not criminally responsible by reason of insanity) when an accused was deemed insane when committing the crime, and that following such a verdict, the court should be ordered to keep the accused in strict, indefinite custody "until his Majesty's pleasure shall be known."

A dozen years after the Hadfield case, John Bellingham assassinated the prime minister of England, Spencer Perceval, and was found guilty of murder, despite another raising of the bar. In the judge's admonition to the jury, the important factor was whether, at the time of the crime, Bellingham "had sufficient understanding to distinguish good from evil, right from wrong, and that the murder was a crime not only against the laws of God but also against the laws of his country." The Bellingham case added the right-from-wrong test, as it came to be known.

In 1840, Edward Oxford was charged with attempting to assassinate Queen Victoria and Prince Albert, but Oxford's acquittal was based on the delusion test. The judge's words also went into legal history: "If some controlling disease was ... the acting power within him, which he could not resist, then he will not be responsible." This reference to irresistible impulse has woven in and out of legal discourse ever since; the idea remains controversial to this day.

The M'Naghten case of 1843 set the standard of standards. The M'Naghten rule has evolved and been refined, but it provided the mother of insanity definitions in British law, and therefore in Canadian, American and all other legal systems based on English law.

In England, Daniel M'Naghten assassinated the secretary to Sir Robert Peel, the Tory prime minister, in an apparent case of mistaken identity. M'Naghten had actually intended to kill the prime minister himself, because, as he testified, Peel and his Tories had hounded him into financial and personal ruin, followed him everywhere, accused him unjustly of crimes and wanted to murder him — all because he, a Scot, had voted against them in the last election. The long trial garnered enormous publicity. Nine well-known medical witnesses, including a psychiatrist brought over from the United States, declared M'Naghten insane, saying he had been laboring under paranoid delusions at the time of the homicide. The verdict was Not Guilty by Reason of Insanity, and Daniel M'Naghten spent the rest of his life in Broadmoor insane asylum.

But the furore caused by his case didn't end with the trial. Much of the public and the House of Lords disagreed with the verdict, and Queen Victoria was royally upset. Fearing that the acquittal of M'Naghten on the heels of Edward Oxford three years before provided no deterrent to would-be assassins, she declared that "everybody" felt that "both malefactors were perfectly conscious and aware of what they did." A panel of judges, including the Lord Chief Justice who had presided at the M'Naghten trial, was soon brought together and, under tremendous public and political pressure, worked out the more stringent formula for determining the legal jnsanity of accused persons, and this became known as the M'Naghten standard.

The new paradigm provided four major rules. One, the accused is presumed sane and responsible until proven otherwise. Two, to be declared insane and hence not criminally responsible, the accused must, at the time of the crime, have been "labouring under such a defect of reason, from disease of the mind, as not to know the nature and quality of the act he was doing; or if he did, that he did not know what he was doing was wrong." Three, the accused is criminally responsible even when he believes he is redressing or revenging a nonexistent wrong (or delusion) for the public good *if*, at the time of the crime, he knew he was acting contrary to criminal law. And four, the accused is not held responsible if the crime was a homicide that was a result of the accused's delusion he was acting in self-defence.

The M'Naghten case set another precedent by allowing expert testimony. Although the legal decision would still rest with the jury or judge, medical experts' testimony concerning the mental state of the accused at the time of the crime was henceforth admissible.

Ironies abound: Daniel M'Naghten himself probably wouldn't have been acquitted under "his" new criteria. He suffered from chronic paranoid schizophrenia, but it was claimed that he knew that what he did was against the law. Later writers said that he had indeed been persecuted, some even suggested that he might have been under contract as a 'hit man' to assassinate the prime minister.

Nearly fifty years later, in 1892, Canada's Parliament incorporated the M'Naghten standards into this country's first Criminal Code, with some modifications. Most significantly, Section 16 read: "[In order to invoke an insanity defence] it must be clearly proved that, at the time of the committing of the act, the party accused was labouring under such a defect of reason, from natural imbecility or disease of the mind that rendered that person *incapable* [new reference to capacity] of *appreciating* [changed and expanded from "knowing"] the nature and quality of the act he was doing, or to know that it is wrong."

As recently as 1980, one of our Supreme Court justices rendered an opinion that underlined the importance of the change from "know" to "appreciate," wording which is still entrenched in Canadian law: "The requirement, unique to Canada, is that of ... an ability to perceive the consequences, impact, and results of a physical act ... This is simply a reinstatement, specific to the defence of insanity, of the principle that intention ... is a requisite element in the commission of a crime."

Canada's original Criminal Code also followed the British model in ordering indefinite custody for the mentally disordered criminal. Following acquittal, the "insane" offender was to be held "in strict custody until the pleasure of the lieutenant governor of the province is known." In practice, that meant each provincial cabinet had virtually absolute authority over these people, without the obligation to follow open, due process, to provide reasons for decisions, or to allow any recourse to appeal to the courts.

It wasn't until 1969 that an amendment to our Criminal Code gave provincial government cabinets the right, but didn't require them, to establish advisory Review Boards to consider individual cases and make recommendations to the cabinet for the person's release or continuing custody. Some provinces established these boards, others didn't. The various boards operated differently and varied in the degree of influence they had on their cabinets' decisions. For this and other reasons, by the 1970s it was commonly felt that the way mentally disordered offenders were treated in Canada was ripe for an overhaul.

A federal Law Reform Commission was struck, and in its 1976 report made forty-two recommendations aimed at significantly improving the system. The federal government reacted to the report by commissioning more research, more consultation, and six years later setting up the Mental Disorder Project to prepare another set of recommendations, which were intended to lead to enabling legislation. More papers, more consultation followed — much of it valuable, bringing in police, mental health professionals and patient advocacy groups, as well as lawyers and politicians. A draft bill was produced in 1986, but that prompted years of quibbling among governments about who would pay for implementing the proposed changes. It was a typically Canadian, let's-look-into-it-further, get-everyone-involved, do-the-right-thing, *I'm*-not-gonna-pay-for-it process.

Then the Swain case of 1986-91 worked its way up to the Supreme Court of Canada, and gave the decisive prod to getting some changes made. Arnold Swain had been accused of assault and aggravated assault against his wife and children. He had frightened and endangered them during a single incident in which he performed some bizarre ritualistic activities in order to protect his family from the devil. Re-examining Swain's trial, the Supreme Court found that two parts of the Criminal Code were actually in conflict with the Canadian Charter of Rights and Freedoms: allowing the Crown to raise the defence of insanity over the objections of the defendant, which violated the accused person's right to control the conduct of his or her own defence, and ordering the accused detained in strict custody for an indeterminate period. The Supreme Court advised the federal government to enact new legislation.

Sixteen years after the Law Reform Commission made its recommendations, Bill C-30, the Mental Disorder Amendments, at last picked up a sense of urgency, moved in almost consensual mode through both the House of Commons and the Senate, and was proclaimed law in early 1992.

The new Section 16 maintains the spirit of the old, while wielding significant changes.

Section 16(1) now reads: *No person is criminally responsible for an act committed or an omission made while suffering from a mental disorder that rendered the person incapable of appreciating the nature and quality of the act or omission or of knowing that it was wrong.*

The words "natural imbecility" and "insane" were removed and replaced with the less-stigmatizing "mental disorder." Not Guilty by

Reason of Insanity has become Not Criminally Responsible on account of Mental Disorder.

Section 16's wording remains relatively vague, so consistent interpretation in the courtroom continues to be difficult despite the accumulation of cases that are narrowing the criteria. Because it is not clear what type of mental disorder can potentially qualify for an insanity defence, the big, well-defined and reasonably well-known illnesses such as schizophrenia are generally accepted, while other conditions such as severe mood disorders, personality disorders and impulse control disorders fall into a grey area. So does another important variable, the degree to which any disorder affects the commission of the individual crime.

These problems will only worsen, as medicine develops more-detailed understandings of certain disorders. For instance, it is conceivable that if we were to discover that decreased gray matter in the frontal lobes was the cause of psychopathy, psychopaths could theoretically become eligible for insanity defences. At present, psychopaths do not fall into this category because they can appreciate the nature and quality of their crimes and know that they are morally and legally wrong, even though morality and law may just be irrelevant abstractions for them. However, knowing that there is a biological basis for any illness or that the illness can or cannot be treated can affect jurors' and judges' decisions when considering the sentencing outcome of potential verdicts. "He couldn't help it" provokes sympathy. For many years, perfectly sane psychopaths occasionally received insanity defences in Ontario and were sent to languish in the Penetanguishene Mental Health Centre.

Debate continues over the fact that Section 16(1) only takes into account so-called "cognitive" factors — the accused person's ability to appreciate, intellectually, the nature and quality of the committed act and to know that it was wrong. There is no consideration of "volitional" factors — the accused person's ability to control his or her behaviour. There may be times when a person in, say, a manic state is acting totally out of control, despite having some appreciation of what he or she is doing and some knowledge that it is wrong. However, proving that someone was acting under an irresistible impulse is extremely difficult, and so that defence has gone in and out of favour, particularly in American courts. It is a fundamental issue, though, and it raises one of the barriers to ever bringing the medical and legal definitions of "mentally disordered" into congruency.

It goes even deeper, in fact, to a basic philosophical difference between law and medicine. The law believes in free will as the basis for individual responsibility and retribution. In contrast, psychiatrists believe in complete psychological determinism. That is, we think that all behaviour is determined by a complex interactive brew of one's genes, brain chemistry, past experience and current circumstances — which makes true free choice an illusion. Our drive is to find genetic or developmental bases for more and more mental disorders, and these would therefore potentially become eligible for the insanity defence. In other words, our principles are subversive to the law, and the law is true to its own principles when it resists the use of psychiatric concepts.

The decision-making role of provincial cabinets was eliminated. Every province and territory was required to establish a Review Board, chaired by a judge or retired judge, with the authority formerly attributed to "the lieutenant governor" to decide whether the accused should be discharged or detained (in hospital) if that decision had not been made by the court. The board's duties and powers were carefully defined, and included a requirement to review each case periodically as long as the person is detained. A board's decision could be appealed to the courts.

A recent Supreme Court of Canada decision — the Winko case — shifted the balance in favour of the detainee by declaring that it is up to the hospital and the Review Board to prove that the detainee would be a danger and not safe for release. Previously, the detainee had to prove he or she was "safe" to be released. Until Winko, most of us working with the "new" Review Boards felt that their decisions were quite protective of public safety, an opinion backed up by the statistics: very few people declared Not Criminally Responsible on account of Mental Disorder (NCRMD) ever re-offended seriously. Their track record was far better than prison inmates released on parole, where the National Parole Board and prison authorities are obliged to release them conditionally, or fully, once part or all of their fixed-length sentence is completed. Now the Winko decision is forcing these Review Boards to release some very scary mental patients because the treatment staff cannot prove they are dangerous. Many of us worry that the law has gone too far in "protecting" the rights of the NCRMD offender.

However, the Mental Disorder Amendments and the Winko decision offer a better chance for release, now that Review Boards include judges and mental health professionals, and representatives of the detainee's own care team and family members may attend the open hearings. Decisions have become less political and more due-process and clinically driven.

Most schizophrenics fit the Section 16(1) definition of a mentally disordered accused. Their symptoms and, probably, the fact that mental illness plays such a major part in their crimes is relatively easy to see and understand by non-medical trial participants. For this reason, the majority of homicide defendants successfully declared Not Guilty by Reason of Insanity or, later, Not Criminally Responsible on account of Mental Disorder have been schizophrenics involved in similar extreme paranoid delusional episodes.

Other mental conditions, and complicated combinations of actual or claimed mental disorders are regularly brought forward in murder trials in the hope of mounting successful insanity defences. In the early days, an NGRI verdict could save a killer from execution, and that provided tremendous motivation. However, capital punishment was outlawed in Canada in 1976. Today, a lawyer might attempt an insanity defence in hope of winning an earlier release than that offered by a mandatory life sentence, or of having the accused detained not in jail but in the less physically brutal atmosphere of a psychiatric facility. The desired verdict doesn't always have the desired result, and many trials are long, provocative and difficult. The case of the Telephone Taunter, which I am about to relate, offered up a smorgasbord of mental disorders — but "not quite" an insanity plea.

Chapter Four

Dial "Me" for Murder

The hoop earrings? Yes. Jeans, denim jackets. *These shoes are sooo ugly. Here, wear my sandals. They'll look good.* It should be a fun evening, the two young women thought. Tanya had met a guy a few weeks ago who seemed nice. He was bringing a friend, she was bringing Misty; the four of them were going out partying for a while, nothing heavy. The girls left Misty's house in Abbotsford at 8:00 p.m. *Are you sure about the sandals? Yeah, they are really, like, cool on ya.*

The boys, B.P. and Pal, picked them up near the junior high school as arranged, then they drove to the liquor store and purchased a bottle. Then, Tanya said suddenly, "I want to see Trev. Just for a second." Trevor was Tanya's boyfriend. B.P. followed Tanya's directions to Trevor's house and she and Misty ran inside. They talked to Trevor for ten minutes, then rejoined the guys in the car, telling Trevor that they were all heading out to Surrey "to party." First, Tanya called home and got permission to stay overnight at Misty's. She was just 15 years old, caught between the desire for thrills and independence and being a good kid.

Back in Abbotsford, a man twice Tanya's age set out for his own evening of thrill-seeking — "scanner-chasing" he called it. Terry Driver had a multi-channel radio scanner on the front seat of his car, and he listened constantly to police and fire bands. He had grown up with scanners — his father had been a police officer. Terry even kept the scanner on during the night, on the headboard of the bed he shared with his wife. This evening he locked onto the Abbotsford police, and did what he often did: cruised the streets in his car, looking for suspicious characters, following up leads he heard on the police channel, attending crime scenes, a self-appointed auxiliary cop.

Hey! A report of a stolen bicycle came over the air. Soon after, he noticed a man on a bike acting suspiciously. Terry followed the cyclist into an apartment complex and called 9-1-1 on his cell phone. When the police arrived, he told them what he had seen, giving them a detailed description of the man on the bike, proud of his ability to "see better at night." Then he left to resume cruising. With the scanner on but nothing apparently happening, he drove up and down the streets, checking out parking lots, behind the Safeway, in public parks, places where he knew there had been fights in the past.

Tanya, Misty, and the other teenagers had, by this time, travelled to Surrey, which is several miles from Abbotsford, where they met some other young people, and hung out in a park with them for a while. Somewhere just after midnight, B.J. and Pal brought the two girls home, dropping them off in front of Misty's.

When the boys had gone, Misty turned to Tanya: "There's a party over on Hazel Street. Let's go, we can walk." They set off down the road, talking as they went, feeling good. It was a quiet night. They noticed only one car on the road, a brown sedan carrying a lone occupant. It drove past them slowly, then pulled into the parking lot behind the hospital a few blocks ahead.

There are two versions of what happened next. The first is Misty's, which she told to the police.

Suddenly, a man wielding an aluminum baseball bat jumped out of a hedge in front of them. "You bitches want to party?" he demanded, at the same time grabbing them both and hauling them back through the hedge, into the bushes.

"Get your clothes off!" he ordered. Misty refused. Tanya lowered her pants and the man undid his zipper, preparing to rape her. He laid down the baseball bat momentarily, and Misty seized it and swung, knocking their assailant on the shoulder. He snatched it back and began hitting her.

"You're going to be sorry, bitch," he told her, "You're going to die!" She screamed, tried to defend herself, but the bat came down and broke her arm, and next time, a finger. She screamed that she would cooperate, that she didn't want to die. She screamed again. After the third or fourth of what the neurosurgeon who treated Misty later would call "homerun swings" to her skull, she lost consciousness.

When she came to, she found herself alone. She was still in the bushes, but about 150 yards away from where the assault took place. She managed to stagger down the path that she knew led to the hospital. About five hours after the attack, Misty stumbled through the doors of Emergency and told the staff that she had been beaten by a man with a baseball bat. An orderly immediately ran outside on the possibility that a person or vehicle connected with her was still there, but there was no movement in the parking lot.

The attending physician treated her for a fractured skull, arm and finger, and reported that her body temperature was 32 degrees Celsius, about four degrees below normal, consistent with her having been out-doors on an October night for several hours. Had she not made it to the hospital when she did, her chances of survival would have been questionable. As it was, medical staff quickly ordered her transferred to a larger hospital, where she was immediately operated upon to treat multiple skull fractures and the skull fragments protruding into her brain.

The second version of the night's events belongs to Terry Driver. I relate it, partly as he told police but mostly as he testified at his trial for the murder of Tanya Smith.

He was scanner cruising in his car when he saw a person run out of the hedge bushes across the street. He couldn't see well enough to describe the person except that it was a male. Thinking that the fleeing man had been involved in a break-in or other crime, Terry Driver parked his car and went through the hedge to have a look. On a grassy spot in the bush he saw two female bodies, one fully clothed and curled in a fetal position, the other lying naked, spread-eagled on her back. . He saw clothes strewn around and a baseball bat near the bodies. "Awestruck and panicked," he went back to his car, intending to call 911 on his cell phone for an ambulance. But he decided he didn't want to get involved; he was known to Abbotsford police and he reasoned that he would be considered a prime suspect. He would go to the nearest convenience store and call anonymously from there.

As he drove, a picture of the scene in the bushes buzzed in his mind, and he found himself aroused at the thought of the naked young woman. He hadn't heard anything reported yet on the scanner, so he figured he could go back, have sex with the girl and leave, making his anonymous call later. He pulled a U-turn and returned, parking his car where it couldn't be seen.

He saw that the fully clothed girl, Misty Cockerill, was alive: she was breathing, and her eyes flickered. He turned his attention to Tanya Smith, who was breathing oddly, but he couldn't see any injuries except for her bleeding nose. He dropped his pants and had intercourse with her; she did not respond. He was about to ejaculate, then realized he didn't want his semen found inside her, but it was too late. He was resting a moment, stroking her and sucking on her breasts, when she suddenly convulsed. It scared him, he said later, and he bit her nipple. She made some gagging noises, then appeared to stop breathing. "Oh, shit," he thought, "Now I'm mixed up with a death." He decided to take the body somewhere and wash off the incriminating semen. He didn't want the other girl to die, so he would take her to the hospital.

He put all the clothes and the baseball bat in the trunk of his car, Then he picked up the limp body of the naked girl and put her in the trunk, too. He got the second girl, who was moaning, into the car's passenger seat and drove into the hospital parking lot, where he propped her up against a cement divider sixty or seventy feet from the Emergency entrance.

Now what? Driver thought of his favourite fishing place along the river, where the water ran swiftly but was shallow; the river would clean up the body easily. It was also a popular place, which meant that the body would be found soon. He drove carefully, using his radar detector and listening intently for police news on the scanner. When he reached the end of the road, he dragged the body along the dirt path to the shore and left it in the river, face down. He threw the clothing into some bushes, and put the baseball bat, his fishing equipment and a few other things on the front seat of the car, planning to throw the bat in a ditch somewhere on his way home. Halfway there, he pulled up alongside a drainage ditch and tossed the bat, his fishing gloves, a towel and shirt into the water. He was home and in bed about 2 a.m. Terry set the scanner up on the bed headboard, and slept fitfully, waking frequently to listen for news.

Just before 4 a.m., Tanya's mother answered the phone to hear an unfamiliar man ask, "Where's Tanya? Where's Tanya? Where is she?" before hanging up.

As soon as Terry's wife left for work in the morning, he checked the car. He found blood in several places, cut out the most bloody section of carpet and cleaned the rest with bleach. By about 9 a.m., he had still heard nothing on the scanner, so he took his two young children and set out for the fishing place, hurling the bloody piece of carpet into some brush along the way. When he arrived, he was not disappointed, because the police and an ambulance were there, and he got in on some of the action. He saw the body being covered up; he directed the ambulance driver as he turned around on the narrow gravel road; and he called his fishing buddy from the crime scene itself to tell him what had occurred at "their" spot. He also alerted a radio and a television station. For the next few days, he was glued to the scanner and the radio, listening for news of the case.

The police investigative team put most pieces of the puzzle together quickly. They eliminated as suspects all the young people the girls had contact with the evening of the attack. They found and identified the discarded clothing items, sandals at one place, earrings at another. They had an autopsy performed, which determined that Tanya Smith had died from drowning, although she had been near death from the terrible beating that preceded. They had fibre and bodily fluid samples under analysis. And they took impressions of the teeth marks on her right nipple, making the decision to keep the existence of this injury as "hold-back" information that only the police and the killer would know. Within a few days, they had determined the site of the attack, and an Abbotsford resident had found the baseball bat. But things weren't moving fast enough for Terry Driver.

The police broadcast a public appeal for help in finding the killer, asking anyone who had seen anything around the time and vicinity of the attack or had helped Misty or seen her being dropped off at the hospital, to call the Task Force Tips Line. The following morning, the fourth day after the murders, Terry Driver made the first of his telephone taunts to the police.

He wouldn't give his name, he wouldn't come in and make a statement, but he was the person who drove Misty to the hospital; he just wanted to let the police have that piece of information — and he hung up. He had made the call from a gas station during his lunch break. In the afternoon, he heard on the radio that the police still didn't know where the attack on the girls had occurred.

Terry thought he'd help with another call.

"Beside a walkway."
"I can't ..."
"Beside a walkway that runs north-south on a grassy knoll behind trees."
"Okay, sir. Where are you getting this from?"
"I'm the killer. Her right nipple tasted pretty good." He hung up.

This call was traced to a pay phone, and investigators were dispatched to get fingerprints and search the area. At this point they were looking for someone who matched a description given them by Misty shortly after her surgery. She was still in shock and her memory was impaired; when she recovered some more, she would provide a description that was very different, but they never quite got it right.

Terry Driver drove home past the pay phone, and to his satisfaction he saw police activity there, and at the crime scene. At home, he watched the early evening news on television and heard for the first time that Tanya had died not from a beating, but from drowning. The news, he would later testify, shocked and upset him. He waited until his wife returned, then went for a drive. He made another telephone call.

"You guys did a real thorough job, but did you think I would be stupid enough to leave fingerprints behind?"

"Pardon me?"

"Do you think I would be stupid enough to leave fingerprints behind when I make a phone call?" End of call, this one untraceable, but recorded. Twenty minutes later, he called again.

"Are you having trouble finding the killer?"

"Uh, do you want to provide information to the police?"

"No. I'm the one."

"You're the…"

"I'm giving you a chance to try and find me. I'll be cruising around looking for someone else."

"What's your name?"

"Just to let you know who I am, Tanya's right nipple tasted really good."

"And what's your name?"

Disconnect. Again, traced to a pay phone, but investigators found nothing there.

A week after the murder, Terry Driver took his children to Tanya Smith's funeral. Police video recorded the event, but they were still looking for someone of a different description. On Halloween, Driver took the kids trick-or-treating, then he went scanner-chasing. Outside a sports bar, he saw a pay phone, and made another call.

"Tonight I'm not going to bite her right nipple, I'm going to bite her [unintelligible]. I'm going to eat her fucking cunt."

"And when is this going to happen?"

"Oh, it's happening to…"

Hanging up, he crossed the street to a restaurant, where he watched the police arrive, examine the telephone booth and go into the bar, then he left.

Several days later, the Task Force released an edited audio tape of all the calls Terry had made to them, hoping that someone would hear it on radio or television and recognize the voice.

"Hey, that voice sounds like you," Terry's fishing buddy joked when he heard it broadcast. Misty Cockerill, by now greatly recovered, recognized the voice as that of her attacker. Over the next two months, the police received hundreds of tips, none of which led them very far. The Telephone Taunter lay low, only once risking being recognized with a 911 call, to report a car-engine fire.

In the early morning of February 17, about four months after the murder, Terry Driver put on his fishing gear and headed for the river. The cemetery where Tanya was buried was on his way. He drove in and pried Tanya's gravestone free with a crowbar. His first thought was to set it at the river's edge where she died. But on the way, he realized that it was now daylight, too late for him to walk to the shore carrying the headstone without being seen. Well then, how about leaving it as a memorial at the crime scene? He couldn't find a parking place near that, so he drove around until he came up with another idea.

The telephone rang in the newsroom at Abbotsford's Radio Max Station.

"Check the Max car in the parking lot," was all the voice on the other end said to the operator in the station's control room. The man went outside and found Tanya Smith's headstone sitting on the hood of the company's vehicle. Felt-pen printing defaced the front of the stone and ran across the photo of Tanya: "She was not the first," "She won't be the last," "I'm still looking," "You won't find me," and "One day Misty." There was a circle around her right chest, an arrow and the words "yummy tit."

The police had no doubt that this was the work of their infamous caller. Two days later, he telephoned again. He would testify in court, later, that the media coverage had become sensational and he was caught up in it, feeding off it, and that the media had speculated that the killer had left town and he hadn't, so he wanted to correct that.

"How did you like my present I gave you guys, huh?"
"I'm sorry, sir, I can't hear you."
"How did you like my present I gave you guys?"
"I'm sorry, I can't —"
"It won't be the last."

The call was traced to a pay telephone at Abbotsford's Rotary Stadium, where a witness gave police a description of the last person to use the booth, and his car.

A few days later, a woman called police to say that a package had been thrown through her front window, shattering it. The missive was an envelope, stapled shut and completely covered with clear tape. A pair of pliers had been attached to give it weight. Written on the front of the envelope was, "From the killer, call 911," and on the back, "From the Abby killer, call 911."

When the police arrived, they discovered a distinct fingerprint on the underside of the clear tape — so conspicuous it might almost have been deliberately planted. The print was subsequently sent out on Canadian and American fingerprint search systems, with negative results. This caused a shift in the task force's approach; they had been looking hardest for a suspect with a criminal record. They changed tactics.

The print was the first of many clues. Inside the envelope they found a computer-printed letter and some newspaper clippings. The clippings included a photo of Misty with "lucky to be alive" penned across her forehead, and a photo of Tanya. The long letter itself was both a confession to the attack on Tanya and Misty and an unsolicited confession to three other assaults on Abbotsford women.

> hello, it's me!!
> yes sir re, tanya's right nipple sure did taste good.
> (by the way tanya was wearing sandals that night and I threw them with her other stuff)....

The letter went on and on, with information about Tanya and Misty, and other "conquests." It ended with a taunt:

> bye guys this is the last you here from
> me till next time.
> Good Luck! ! ! !

The letter had begun with information known only to police and Tanya's killer. Word had got out that Tanya had suffered a bite injury, but not its location. Similarly, her "shoes" had been reported missing; no mention had been made of sandals. Police were not sure that the caller from the stadium had been the same as the person who had called before, claiming to be the killer; the letter said it was.

The references to three other assaults were chilling. The first intended victim was a 12-year-old girl who had been sitting waiting outside a friend's house when someone attacked her from behind, groping her breasts. She screamed and was able to get away, but she gave the police a fairly detailed description of her assailant. The second victim was also approached from behind, then struck in the face so hard she passed out. She was found and taken to hospital, and later was able to provide a rough description of the attacker. (When records were checked, it turned out that, later that same day, Terry Driver had come to the hospital, claiming he had fallen out of a vehicle and injured his hand. His injuries were more consistent with having backhanded someone or something so powerfully that he fractured his wrist.) The third victim mentioned in the letter had been found unconscious and bleeding from head injuries across the street from the hospital. Her nearly-fatal skull fractures were determined to have been caused by "a blunt instrument." Her backpack, minus about $200 in cash, had been found on the roof of an adjacent brick building — details that were included in the letter.

The task force now had a fingerprint, descriptions from more victims, several recorded calls from someone who boasted of being "the Abby Killer," and DNA evidence from the murder victim's body. The final tactic was designed to generate the last pieces of information they needed to find the killer. At a press conference, they released a poster providing an updated description of the suspect, complete with a full-body drawing and a description of his forearm tattoo, along with descriptions of the two vehicles that witnesses had observed. They also released a voice tape containing excerpts from three of the self-proclaimed killer's calls to police.

Results came fast. Donald Driver, Terry's brother, saw the information on TV and called police to listen to the voice again. He then called his mother and asked her to call the police, too. Within an hour, an upset Audrey Tighe telephoned police, requested confidentiality, then said that she and her other children had all listened to the suspect's voice and that they believed it was that of her son, Terry Driver. The physical description was inaccurate, she said, but other details released that morning matched. Terry had told his sister that he had gone to Tanya Smith's funeral. Two weeks after the murder, at a family gathering, Terry had argued with his brother, finally saying, "Don't fuck with me. You don't know me anymore, and you don't know what I am capable of doing anymore."

Police met Terry Driver at his home soon afterwards, claiming he was a look-alike for the suspect, and asking him to voluntarily provide fingerprints and blood samples to eliminate himself as a suspect. Terry pointed out that he did not look like the description, but he agreed to have his fingerprints taken and examined in the presence of his lawyer. The fingerprint found on the package tape was a perfect match, and Terry Driver was arrested and charged.

The Crown prosecutor expected that some sort of mental disorder would be invoked to bolster the accused's denial of guilt, and he asked me to review the case . I was not allowed to examine Terry Driver; the defence would only permit their own appointed psychiatrists to do that, based on the defendant's legal right to remain silent. Yet I had to attend the trial and be ready to testify, in case the defence raised any mental-state explanation.

Frequently, the psychiatrist called by the Crown is refused an interview with the accused, and it is one of the most frustrating barriers to being able to do the job properly. Respecting the rights of the accused means you have only history and other experts' (sometimes conflicting) views by which to judge.

In this case, however, Crown counsel, a seasoned criminal lawyer, was so good at cross-examining the defence's expert witnesses that he doubted he'd need to call any expert witnesses of his own.

Feeling that no jury would acquit the infamous "Abbotsford Killer," Terry Driver chose trial by judge alone. Driver's lawyer entered a not-guilty plea, and said that he was not mounting an insanity plea. However, he claimed that his client's strange behaviour and declarations of guilt could be explained away by the fact that he suffered from Tourette's Syndrome and associated problems of attention deficit hyperactivity disorder and obsessive-compulsive disorder. The lawyer would contend that Terry's compulsions "forced" him to engage in certain behaviours in which he knew perfectly well what he was doing, but was powerless to stop himself.

Terry Driver was presented as someone who had experienced childhood troubles, but who was now settled with a responsible job, wife and family. He was portrayed as handling his Tourette's and attention deficit hyperactivity disorder satisfactorily, his compulsions (listening to the scanner, repetitive hand-washing, and lock-checking) and his "very strong sexual impulse" had been channeled into socially acceptable behaviours until the incident with Tanya. During the trial, expert witnesses for the defence would be called to explain how his disorders were responsible for his bizarre activities following his "discovery" of the two unconscious, beaten-up girls.

Terry took the stand. He said that he had been diagnosed with attention deficit hyperactivity disorder and minimal brain dysfunction when he was 2 years old, had lived in group care from 6 to 11, began developing behavioural tics (headshaking, flexing his neck) at about 12 years, finished high school on a career-preparation program in printing and still worked in the printing industry. He had been diagnosed with Tourette's at 24, married the next year and had two children. He didn't recall being "hyper" as a youth, nor experiencing any conflict with his family because of his behaviour. His dad had been a police officer, so there had always been scanners around, and he guessed that was why he had one and used it all the time.

He related the events of the night the homicide took place, starting with his scanner-chasing, then seeing a man run out of the bushes, then his reasoning about where to dispose of the body, the clothes and the baseball bat, then cleaning out his car — and on through the telephone calls, the gravestone and the package delivered through the window. It was all unplanned, he just did all these things on impulse.

The prosecutor, visibly dripping with contempt, moved in for the cross-examination. He thoroughly intimidated Driver, whose testimony became more contradictory and pathetically untrue as it progressed.

Terry stated that he made the first two calls to police, both from anonymous pay phones, "to help them out with some information."

Why, if you weren't guilty, say "I'm the killer"?

"I held myself responsible for her death [from drowning]. She died from my neglect."

Why say "Her right nipple tasted pretty good" on several calls?

"So they would know it was authentic, so that the call wouldn't be taken as a prank."

Why remove the gravestone?

"I didn't have any plan. I saw the cemetery sign and drove in." The idea to leave it at the radio station "just popped into my head." Writing on the headstone, including the threat to Misty, was to "live up to the media hype. I was feeding off it. I liked the attention." Same with calling police and asking them if they liked "his present." He had intended to throw the package through a police station window, but there were too many people around, so he just tossed it at a randomly selected house window.

He thought some of the police force's public comments made it sound as if the killer was a deranged psychopath, so knowing the note would go to the press, Terry "thought [he'd] give the media what they wanted." He wanted to "egg them [the police] on, to get them going."

Why did he mention that he had used the baseball bat on Tanya and Misty, and on someone else? "The words just came out of my head." He didn't know what the words meant, or why he made the calls, except that he fed off the publicity.

Towards the end of the cross-examination, many of his answers were "I don't know" or "I don't remember." I felt he had been clearly exposed as a sexually sadistic psychopath, and wondered what the defence counsel's tactics would be.

Dr. Mort Duran, who would give a psychiatric opinion on Terry Driver, took the stand for the defence. Although Duran was a general surgeon, not a psychiatrist, he was presented as an expert on Tourette's syndrome (TS), attention deficit hyperactivity disorder (ADHD) and obsessive-compulsive disorder (OCD). He explained that the concept of Tourette's syndrome was changing. Where it was once accepted as an isolated set of uncontrollable physical tics (typically, the neck-flexing and head-shaking exhibited by Terry) and verbal outbursts (swearing, exhibited by a minority of TS patients, excluding Terry), it is now considered part of a broader group of disorders. From 66 percent to 75 percent of TS patients will also have ADHD, OCD and various other difficulties, sometimes including phobias, sleep disorders and learning disabilities.

Dr. Duran's opinion was that Driver had the Tourette's-ADHD-OCD syndrome to a degree. The tics, he said, led to feelings of inadequacy and of being out of control, which in turn led to a need to feel in control and boost self-esteem; ADHD sufferers have a high need for stimulation and hence, according to Duran, an addiction to conflict. Both disorders provide a need to "stir things up," which prompted his taunting of authorities. ADHD victims are characterized by "unfocused behaviour, are non-compliant, have low attention spans, and low frustration tolerance, are quick to anger, have an inability to delay gratification and actively seek turmoil," he said.

Traditionally, OCD victims have been believed to act randomly on obsessions (intrusive thoughts that persist and cause anxiety) and compulsions (repetitive, ritualistic acts such as washing hands repeatedly, sometimes in reaction to an obsession). Dr. Duran felt that "the books are not right" on this one. He said that there is a broader compulsive/obsessive behaviour not associated with fears of harm, as it is usually characterized, but with excitement and pleasure, and that the consequent actions are not random, but based on alleviating a feeling of discomfort by finding some kind of stimulation and/or mounting a show of control. Terry Driver's need to kindle some drama, his impulsive actions, his blurting things out, his need to be the centre of attention all fit this mold. So did the scanner-chasing, the inability to resist raping the naked teenager, the telephone calls, the gravestone incident and the throwing of the package. The obscene references to Tanya weren't meant to be disrespectful to Tanya or to hurt her family; he wasn't thinking of them at all. "When the impulse to stir things up takes over, all other stuff is thrown aside," Duran commented.

That said, he noted, people with these particular disorders have varying degrees of self-control, just as they may be mildly to severely affected by any one of the disorders. The ability and desire to inhibit obsessions, compulsions and tics vary from one person to another. A striking example was now sitting before the court.

A successful practicing surgeon and well-respected citizen, Dr. Duran himself suffers from Tourette's syndrome, attention deficit hyperactivity disorder and obsessive-compulsive disorder. While he was on the stand, he often shook his right hand and touched his suit lapel, his glasses and the microphone in a ritualistic sequence. He told us that, without fail, he lined up his papers at a 45-degree angle, that his tie-downs for his personal airplane always had to be adjusted identically, and that he needed to close the door of the aircraft exactly twenty-six times before leaving it. "If I don't, I'm agitated. I keep thinking about it." When frustrated, he is quick to anger, and he takes minor remarks as personal affronts.

Occasionally, he said, he will lose control, but basically, he can inhibit his tics, and refrain from negative behaviour when it is essential to do so. He makes delicate incisions, ties sutures and does everything else required of a surgeon in the operating room; he intersperses pauses for bursts of tics throughout the surgery. He has long held a pilot's license and is a competent aviator. He can get extremely irritated with air traffic control personnel, but would "never" blow his stack at them, nor have his disorders ever interfered with his ability to fly safely and in control. He recognizes his triggering factors and acts to control his reaction when one occurs. Perhaps Terry Driver's mantra of "I don't know why" (he had done most things) meant he was unaware of his triggers.

Next, a forensic psychiatrist, called by the defence, gave his opinion that Terry Driver had Tourette's syndrome and obsessive-compulsive disorder, with residual ADHD. He observed that although Terry had had severe problems in childhood, he had improved greatly since then, much better than one would have expected — even though it was usual for ADHD to decline or disappear in adulthood. He found that Driver had very little insight into his behaviour, except that he admitted he got intoxicated by the media attention and sought it out. Driver often referred to "cat and mouse" when discussing what had gone on.

He believed Terry was acting out aggressively but not particularly as an anti-authority behavior. It was more likely he was ambivalent about authority. He engaged in pseudo-police activities and had twice applied to be a police officer, but had been rejected. He admired his father and wanted to be like him, but was ignored and beaten by him. His relationships and social skills were poor. He had few friends, and his sexual obsession seemed to be geared towards orgasm, rather than any sort of relationship. Outside his marriage, he satisfied himself with strangers — regular, quick sessions with prostitutes — and masturbation in the washroom at work or in the bushes while fishing. It was hard to tell if he had an irresistible sexual urge or if he simply didn't resist it. The psychiatrist believed he could have resisted the impulse.

He finished by pointing out that although Terry acted impulsively — and compulsively — sometimes, much of his behaviour was planned, and he appeared to be able to think about what he was doing as he was doing it. Under cross-examination, the psychiatrist substantially distanced himself from Driver's and Duran's characterizations of Driver's behaviours as relatively unplanned and meaningless. The doctor agreed that the calls, the gravestone and the letter were linked, and that each indicated some planning on Driver's part, as did the things he did to avoid detection, hide evidence and cover his tracks.

Would the psychiatrist characterize Terry's behaviour as psychopathic? Well, it was bizarre, callous, self-serving and conscienceless ....

Driver had also been tested and interviewed by a forensic psychologist, who agreed with most of the psychiatrist's opinions, including the diagnosis of TS, ADHD and OCD, and Terry's "unusual combination" of impulsive and compulsive traits. He provided more evidence that many of the man's actions were not impulsive. Terry boasted of using a "special phone technique" so as not to leave fingerprints, and remarked that he had made a preliminary visit to the cemetery the night before he removed the gravestone. (Police by now had traced two calls to a sex-line made that evening on Driver's cellular telephone, from or near the cemetery.)

The psychologist added "antisocial, egocentric and narcissistic" to the list of personality adjectives. Teasing the police had made Terry feel superior — triumphant even — and smart. He had been ridiculed and made to feel a failure in life, he said, and he wanted to be taken seriously by the world. Although he had said he wasn't a violent person, there were fairly recent occurrences of slammed doors, broken furniture, holes punched in walls, hitting his wife ("She hit me first"), and of losing control spanking his son.

Driver had not indicated any feelings of guilt for the crime of which he was now accused, and the psychologist felt his actions were consistent with his psychological make-up and with other things he had done during his life.

Terry Driver had had an awful childhood that had apparently rolled into an adulthood of crime, despite his lack of any significant police record. When he was 2 years old, his parents had taken him to hospital for assessment because he was "displaying severe behavioural problems," which continued to escalate until, at the age of 5, he was placed in a day program for troubled youngsters. His parents said they were unable to cope with his aggressive, destructive behaviour — which had included setting a fire at home — and his "unresponsiveness to any type of punishment."

When he was 6, the Drivers gave custody of Terry to the Children's Foundation Residential Care Society. He was tested and assessed while he lived at the Foundation, and reports described a fierce, angry boy, constantly in physical fights with smaller boys or girls, "quick to hit, spit or throw anything within reach," loud and aggressive. He repeatedly claimed he would kill his mother, and seemed more hostile to women than men. He managed to ignite a stick and burn holes in a carpet. He was transferred to another residential home and the negative reports continued: more fighting, dumping garbage containers, tampering with parked cars, shoplifting, lying, and killing fish and chickens "because he was angry." He was extremely "high-strung, belligerent, uncooperative, lacking in self-control and without conscience." He was diagnosed at nine as having ADHD; he had not really responded to treatment.

Terry had been going home weekends, but the Drivers said that they could not handle him full-time and were fearful for their other children if he came home. At one point, his father left home and refused to come back if Terry were returned. At almost 11 years of age, after being in care since he was 6, he did move home. The Drivers separated. Nearly two years later, Grant Driver applied to have Terry live with him, and later obtained custody.

He made it into police files at 13 and 14. He admitted firing his father's pistol, which sent a bullet through a neighbour's window, and he was caught throwing eggs and rocks at another neighbour's house. No charges were laid.

By his own admission, he started pulling off break-and-enter jobs at 17. They gave him an adrenaline rush, he said, so he'd do about one a week. At 18, working in a downtown café, he admitted stealing $450 from his employer's wallet. He agreed to pay it back by paycheque deductions. After the first deduction, however, he was so unhappy that he lodged a complaint against his employer with the Labour Relations Board of B.C. He was fired. A week later, while the restaurant owner had stepped out to make a regular bank deposit, someone with a key slipped into the building and emptied the restaurant till of $550. No charges were laid, but Terry was named as a suspect. Days later, Terry and another youth attempted to entice his former employer into the back lane by knocking on the door and waiting for him to come out, but the suspicious employer and a friend took the precaution of circling the building and approaching from behind. They found Driver crouched behind a garbage dumpster holding a metal pole. The owner wrested the pole from Terry, who said he had "come to see about the money," but ran away when threatened with the police. He was arrested and charged, but the Crown advised that the charges be dropped because there was insufficient evidence of intention to proceed with a robbery.

While he worked at the restaurant, he had traded food for sex with young street girls. Now he used shoplifting and break-and-enters to pay for prostitutes. Terry says he was a systematic shoplifter, careful not to get caught by store security people, and also did some opportunistic trolling for small items, stealing fishing rods from trucks and the like. He was arrested once as he was fleeing from an unsuccessful home invasion, but a Stay of Proceedings was entered. His break-and-enter business tapered off somewhat in the 1990s, and he said he stopped it entirely about two months after the homicide. These smaller crimes did keep him supplied with hookers, whom he continued to use up to the time of his arrest. Ironically, his only conviction was for engaging in prostitution, for which he received a conditional discharge with six months' probation. Other tricks he admitted pulling in adulthood included "ten or fifteen" frontal flashings to female passersby, and setting fire to a garbage dumpster about a year before the murder.

The trial was long and well-covered in the media. Like the murder and the telephone taunting, it aroused public outrage on many levels, including the well-founded anger of sufferers from Tourette's, ADHD, and OCD, who felt they had all been painted as having the capability to do what the Abbotsford Killer had done.

The expert witnesses called by the defence had been fascinating. But in the end we had a Tourette's victim who led an exemplary life in full control of a more severe disorder than Terry's; a psychiatrist who felt Driver had virtually recovered from ADHD, was able to resist impulsive behaviour, had planned most of his actions, and exhibited many of the characteristics of a psychopath; and a psychologist who provided more evidence of planning and psychopathy, including a total lack of remorse.

The judge appeared to have little difficulty in rejecting the argument that the accused was innocent of murder and that, after encountering the results of someone else's crime, he had been forced by his disorders to act in strange ways and utter false declarations of guilt. In his statement, the judge provided a nice straight-forward sound-bite, underlining what needed to be said against such a defence, which stretched psychiatric concepts beyond the breaking point.

Many people suffer from the same disorders, he observed, but they don't go around committing crimes.

Driver was convicted of the first-degree murder of Tanya Smith and the attempted murder of Misty Cockerill, and sentenced to life with no right to parole for twenty-five years.

Since then, he has been convicted of aggravated sexual assault of two women mentioned in the letter he threw through the window. Ultimately, he was declared a Dangerous Offender, and, as such, he is serving an indeterminate, probably lifelong, sentence.

Aside from the defence strategy, what sticks in my mind from the trial is the image of an "uncontrollable" 2-year-old — a toddler — with "an extreme behaviour problem." Couldn't there have been some way to save him then — and thereby Tanya Smith, twenty-eight years later?

I never did testify, and it was probably just as well, because I felt my professional objectivity get wobbly during the trial. As a parent, it was awful to watch this character talk almost cockily about doing something so ghastly, yet trying his hardest to avoid taking responsibility for it. A seductive picture came to mind of me portrayed in the media as a hero conquering evil with my testimony — not the best mindset for a dispassionate, objective case analysis.

CHAPTER FIVE

DEATH WILL SAVE YOUR LIFE

An ex-boyfriend called her Dream Girl. She loved to dance, to draw, to read, to write. She wore flamboyant make-up and big hair, and she signed her name with a flourish: Deborah E. K. LePage. She had two flawless children. And she told stories, although not everyone — sometimes including herself — knew they were stories. She had searched all her life for perfect love.

Her mother's love, she said, had been controlling and highly conditional; her father had sexually abused her as a child, and both parents were alcoholics with bad tempers. She feared their anger and learned not to express her own. She broke up with her high-school sweetheart when her mother threatened to have nothing more to do with her if Deborah married him. She later wed a different man, and the first couple of years with Tyrone were fine, but then she got pregnant; he wasn't happy about that, and began spending nights away, drinking. She moved home with her parents until her daughter, Tiffany, was a few months old, then moved back with Tyrone. He tried, but he wasn't much of a father — or a husband. He added abuse to the turmoil caused by his drinking. She left him, went back to him, and left him, finally, when she became pregnant with her second child, Darren, this time moving from the country into the big city.

Her parents gave her the down payment on a townhouse and helped support her. Although qualified as registered laboratory technologist, Deborah had suffered a back injury in a fall while on the job and was now unable to work; she was involved in a drawn-out process to obtain a disability pension. Unemployed, she threw herself into being "the best mother in the world." She and her children met Tony Starkey in a fast-food line-up. He pursued her avidly, and within a few months they were engaged. Tiffany and Darren liked him, and they made plans to buy a house together in the spring and marry in the fall. But before she sold her house, Deborah decided he didn't love her children enough and she broke the engagement. Tony was heartbroken and kept trying to see her. He had gone ahead with the house purchase and one day several months after the break-up, he insisted Deborah come out to see it. He showed her where all their furniture would go, asked how the children were and, teary-eyed, said how he missed and loved them. When she told him she had found someone else, he got angry, slapped her, and she walked out.

Her "someone else" was Mike Cisco, a divorced man with two young children. His kids adored Deborah. They got along well with Tiffany and Darren, now 10 and 5 years old. Mike and Deborah rode horses, danced, went tobogganing. He wanted to be with her all the time, and made plans for the six of them in the future. A black cloud had appeared when Deborah told Mike about her breast cancer. She took several trips to the cancer clinic for treatment.

Then just before Christmas, she called Mike, bursting with happiness. She said she had just won $220,000 in the lottery. She had Mike take her to his accountant for advice on how to handle the money. Mike suggested she sell her car and buy a better one, but Deborah reminded him that her uncle was about to buy a new Lexus and had promised her his older Cadillac as a hand-me-down. One evening, when they were sitting together on the couch, she had answered a call from Uncle Kurt, and turned to Mike with, "Hey, did you hear that? The Caddy will be here by Easter."

Mike didn't want to rush the relationship, and Deborah told him they had all the time in the world. She hinted that she needed him around to help her deal with her cancer, though. "I'm going to re-write my will," she added, "Will you take care of my kids if anything happens to me?" Mike wasn't ready for that, so things cooled for a few weeks.

Then she called and told him that she had had day surgery for her cancer and it had gone well. Mike asked her to go out dancing the next evening — a big group of friends was going club-hopping to celebrate a birthday. Deborah ran out and purchased a new dress for the occasion, happily telling the sales clerk that she had just won some money in the lottery.

They had a wonderful evening. Mike wore the silver tie she had bought him, and Deborah was at her dramatic, flashy best.

"Let's take all four kids to Disneyland," she proposed.

"I can't afford it, Deborah."

"I'll pay for it, no problem."

They went back to her house. Deborah gave Mike two photographs of herself. They weren't recent, but "I may never get the Valentine's Day photos framed," she said. Mike stayed the night, a sexy night like many others they had spent together. She wore a small bandage on one of her breasts; he assumed it was because of the cancer surgery. In the morning, they drank coffee and watched a movie with the two children. He left in the early afternoon.

Later, Deborah took her children to pick up a video, and stopped to have a hundred lottery tickets checked at a convenience store. She had won $60; she spent $50 on instant-win tickets. They went next door to an automotive place and purchased a gasoline container. "Why are we buying a gas can, Mommy?" Tiffany asked. "In case we run out of gas," Deborah told her. They bought the gasoline to fill it and headed home.

At six the next morning, a neighbor, Simon Schwab, and two men returning home from night-shift jobs discovered Deborah's house ablaze. One of the men called 911 while the other two attempted to get into the house. All the entrances were locked, but Simon managed to break the front door down and crawled on his belly into the hall as far as he could in the choking smoke. From there, he could see one bedroom engulfed in flames and the closed door to another. Assuming the closed bedroom was where any survivors would be, he quickly backed out of the house and ran around to the bedroom side.

Through the window he saw Deborah and her two children in the bed, apparently unconscious. He smashed the window, and with the fresh air, Deborah started to stir. Moving as if drunk or delirious, she tried to pull Tiffany into her lap, then got up and carried the child, to Simon's horror, towards the bedroom door. She laid her daughter down to open the door and wandered alone into the smoke-filled hall. Simon jumped in through the broken window and handed first Darren, then Tiffany to the other man. Shouting, they tried to persuade Deborah to escape by the front door. Just five minutes had passed since the 911 call, and now fire fighters and ambulances arrived, and the emergency crews took over, carrying Deborah safely out and eventually extinguishing the fire.

Simon had noticed blood on both children's nightclothes. Darren was already dead. When the examining physician meeting the ambulance turned his small body over, a bullet fell out. It had gone straight through his chest. Tiffany died in hospital that evening, of a gunshot wound to the head.

Police and fire inspectors went through the house. They found that both doors had been locked and dead bolts set before the rescuers broke in. They found an empty, new gas container on the basement stairs. There were signs that paper had been used to ignite the gasoline in some places, including the house mortgage document. Lottery tickets and family photos were scattered about and a .22-calibre gun was under the bed.

In Deborah's purse, two letters seemed to be confessions of murder and the intention to commit suicide.

"I am so sorry it had to end this way," read one letter, in part. "I have only one regret, that there was no way to protect my children from their grandparents. I could never give them to my folks ... I'm tired of living and pain and worry and indifferent people. I don't care anymore ... If I felt there was something I could do to look after my son and daughter, I would do it ... I hope God forgives me. The children were the only people in this world I loved. I can't leave them alone."

In the hospital, Deborah was given a shot to counteract any narcotics that she might have taken, attempting to overdose and, later, some codeine for back pain. "I'm sorry," she wept, "I don't know what I'm going to do."

She gave her version of the previous night's events. She had watched a movie until just after midnight, then went to bed. She woke up when she felt the heat. She had a feeling that someone was in the house. She got up and went into the living room, where she saw a man. No, the dining room. Her purse was there, and tons of jewelry. Tiffany was crying. Darren was crying. There were shots and a flash. She was having trouble breathing. It was a .22 she heard. She knew because it was her own gun. She usually kept it in a bedroom drawer, but it was out because she had been cleaning it yesterday. It had six shells in it. No, she didn't know what the man in her house had looked like. There were cigarettes all over the carpet and the ashtray was full of butts. There was a gas can. They'd had one in the carport for ages.

By noon, the police had examined and traced the gun. It had been reported stolen a year ago by its registered owner, Tony Starkey.

Neither Tony nor Mike Cisco were implicated in the homicides. City police went to the hospital and read Deborah LePage her rights.

"You mean I am a suspect?" she responded incredulously. They asked her if she wanted to call a lawyer.

"I don't think I need one."

The officers had some difficulty making sure she understood that whatever she had told them before would not count, and that "any threats or promises made by the officer who spoke to you earlier must not influence what you say to us," but that whatever she said from now on could be used as evidence.

They went through the story again. She hadn't locked the dead bolt. The gas container "was tucked behind some garbage in the carport, and had been for months." It was normally kept in the car trunk. Later she confirmed that she had bought the container the previous week. She had had the gun for three years, bought and registered it in North Vancouver to protect her family and herself after one neighbor had been assaulted and another had a break-in.

The officers asked about her finances. She lived on workers' compensation, Canada Pension and her parents' help: about $2,100 a month. She had won $184 on last week's lottery. She had thought she had won more

She said she was restricted because of her back and that she had had a lumpectomy several weeks ago. The story she had related to Mike about the operation a few days before got mixed up with a trip to Victoria to see a cousin, and then she said it had occurred a month ago.

It is a chaotic story she tells of the fire and about noise everywhere and guns and glass and cigarette butts. After the shots, she heard the door close and the gun drop. "The next thing I realized, the kids are lying on the grass wounded and the firemen were breaking the glass to get in the window. Blood. Darren was saturated. Tiffany was at the window trying to open it, but got down when the glass broke. There was a man at the window. I didn't know if the man had come back. I picked up Darren and carried him to see if the ambulance was there. The smoke got to me and I fell, and woke up here in the hospital." She is sobbing, "If I could remember, I would tell you," and afterwards, "I wish Tiffany was here to tell you what happened."

Deborah finally agreed she needed legal advice, and a legal aid lawyer came and talked to her briefly. Medical staff pronounced her fit to be discharged, and she was booked into police cells at almost the very moment her daughter died. She was charged with the murders of both children.

The fire occurred in March. The following January, the Crown prosecutor's office asked me to give them my opinion on Deborah's mental state at the time of the homicides, and on whether or not a Not Criminally Responsible on account of Mental Disorder defence might apply in her case.

It was a complicated case, from medical, psychiatric and psychological standpoints, and it became even more complex when Deborah made two determined suicide attempts at the corrections centre where she was being held. In May, after taking extraordinary precautions not to be discovered, she stabbed herself in the wrists and groin, narrowly missing her femoral artery. In July, she managed to overdose on antidepressants, and teetered between life and death. Deeply comatose and suffering from seizures, she stopped breathing and had to be placed on a respirator. These were not cries for attention, as some suicide attempts are, but the actions of someone who truly wanted to die. And either of these episodes would likely have affected her memory and mental state.

That Deborah led a disordered inner life came as a shock to many people who thought they knew her. She'd had an "all's-right-with-my-world" attitude that covered for her. She appeared to have had no problems with her kids or her parents, no problems with money, no problems with her health — except for her back, although it didn't seem to slow her down, and, towards the end, the on-again-off-again breast cancer.

In fact, she did have a long history of mental and physical disorders — and financial disasters — and towards the time of the fire, her thinking had become more and more fragmented, as she felt her world collapsing in on her.

She described herself as a child as being normal and outgoing with schoolmates, but quiet and restrained at home, where there was always an air of tension brought about by alcohol. That her father sexually abused her from age six to eleven was never investigated, but it is a major theme in her life. Her mother hadn't known, because her father swore Deborah to secrecy, and she didn't tell any medical professional about it until the suicide notes found in her purse after the fire. One was addressed to her psychiatrist.

She gained her certification in MRI technology from a community college. But from her mid-teens on, she had a series of minor medical problems including back pain and insomnia. When she was 23, she had Tiffany. At 26, she was injured helping move a patient at work. She had surgery, but the back pain continued and was unbearable without codeine. At 30, pregnant, she left Tyrone, and never saw or heard from him again. She bought her townhouse, and started having anxiety attacks.

A few months after Darren was born, she experienced feelings of numbness in different parts of her body. Neurological testing was inconclusive, and her doctor felt it might be stress-related and referred her to a psychiatrist, but Deborah didn't like her, so she didn't return. Deborah said later that she couldn't believe that she might have a mental problem.

She found herself weeping a lot, and experiencing full-blown panic attacks. A panic attack can occur for no apparent reason, and they are frightening and disabling. The victim is terrified, thinking he or she is going to die, go crazy or totally lose control. A racing pulse and heavy sweating make it feel worse. Panic disorder can happen to healthy people; it is mostly caused by genetic and biochemical factors.

Now Deborah took the advice of her physician and began seeing a psychiatrist, the one to whom she addressed her "Goodbye" letter. His diagnosis was that she was suffering from unipolar mood disorder (that is, clinical depression) and from panic disorder. She expressed, to him, her frustration at her limited ability to control her life, and her feelings of failure. She couldn't work and had to depend on her parents. She worried about her ability to provide for her family.

In the following two years, Deborah continued to have panic attacks — although now partly controlled by medication — while she underwent several minor surgeries and a hysterectomy. Her doctor tried to help her kick what had become a codeine addiction, but to no avail.

She felt she didn't have enough money to live on, yet couldn't confront her parents to ask for more. Then her claim for increased benefits was turned down, holding her disability pension to $183 a month. A year before the fire, she visited a federal office and was put on an Orderly Payment of Debts program, which required her to pay $200 a month.

In August, Tony, caught with two houses because he had purchased "their" house before selling his, told her he couldn't afford to get married and keep paying for the house. Deborah was afraid to sell her own home. That was one of the real reasons they broke up.

Another was because of an incident in which Darren had asked Tony, "Are you going to be my Daddy?" and Tony had replied, "Only if you're a good boy." That, Deborah said, brought back memories that were too much for her. After the relationship had ended, Tony reported, the four-year-old had spotted him in a mall one day, and had run up and hugged him. Deborah had snatched him away so angrily, glaring wordlessly at Tony, that one of his friends had commented, "Wow! She sure doesn't want anything more to do with you."

In the year before the fire, her psychiatrist was treating her for chronic pain syndrome, panic disorder, recurrent major depressive disorder and borderline personality disorder. Deborah's depressive disorder typically meant that she experienced recurrent bouts of severe depression, during which she would take no pleasure in anything, and she would feel suicidal and utterly hopeless about the future. The personality disorder — something which, perhaps because of the words "borderline" and "personality", non-medical people have trouble accepting as a genuine disorder — meant that her self-esteem was virtually non-existent. She rarely believed herself worthy of anyone's love or attention, and she struggled relentlessly to gain affection and attention to reassure herself of her worthiness.

In his report to the court, Deborah's psychiatrist added, "It should be noted that up to 15 percent of individuals with severe major depressive disorder commit suicide. This risk increases further with accompanying conditions like panic disorder and chronic pain syndrome." Both her physician and her psychiatrist had been treating Deborah with maximum safe levels of medications, as well as insight-oriented and supportive psychotherapy.

Two months before the fire, she "had a sense that I wanted to die," and felt more and more detached and "very far away." She took more than the prescribed amounts of her antidepressant and anti-panic medications — "I did what I could to get through each day", she explained — and was caught stealing a prescription pad from her doctor's office and writing her own codeine prescription. She just couldn't get rid of the pain.

Then Deborah's parents told her they could only give her a monthly allowance of $1,200. They became estranged. She couldn't work, so what would she do? A few weeks later, she told Mike Cisco, whom she had then been seeing for several months, about her $220,000 lottery win. She appeared "on top of the world."

Behind the scenes, the bank was bouncing her cheques and the panic attacks were increasing. Her doctor said she was "constantly worried as to how she would support her children." She told Mike her breast cancer was getting worse, and asked him to be the youngsters' legal guardian if anything happened to her. He said "no"; he wasn't confident of his own ability to be a good father. She called Tony and told him she had terminal breast cancer and was going away for surgery. She asked him to lend her $3,000. She asked him to be the guardian of her children if anything happened to her. He declined on both counts. She left angrily. Tony was shocked when he heard Deborah's version of that visit — as he was on learning many things about her after the tragedy.

She had often called her physician at home with panicky requests for medication. Three weeks before the fire, she called and asked for money. The doctor said she couldn't do that, but asked her to come into the office the next day. It was the last visit before her arrest. They talked about agencies Deborah could see for financial relief. They talked about Deborah entering an addiction treatment centre. Deborah said she couldn't leave her children with anyone for that length of time, especially not with her parents. She felt controlled by them, especially being so everlastingly financially dependent upon them.

In the days leading up to the homicides, things got worse and the border between reality and fantasy seemed to slip back and forth for Deborah. She tried to sell her jewelry. Her church gave her some money. She bought three dresses, a tie and a bracelet, and the cheque was returned N.S.F. She called the Orderly Payment Office and learned she had $10,000 to go. She called the bank where she owed $27,000 on her mortgage, and told them that her "ship had come in," that she'd just won the lottery and would be in to pay everything off. She called the produce store where five cheques had bounced in the last week, and told them the same thing. She went to the Emergency ward of the hospital and was treated for a wound on her breast — the one Mike would assume was from her cancer treatment, but that she described in the hospital as having occurred when she leaned over a knife in the dishwasher.

Out partying with Mike, she told two of his friends that she was terribly sick with cancer and was going into the hospital the next day, repeatedly asking them to visit her there. Looking back, Mike realized some other things had been out of sync. He remembered her house that night as being extremely messy, although she was normally a diligent housekeeper. And the next day, when he left, instead of bouncing onto the couch and waving vigorously from the front window as she always did, Deborah barely raised her hand in goodbye as he went out the door.

Afterwards, Deborah described herself in those last months before the homicides as having been "overwhelmed with life. I had everything to live for, yet I wanted to die. I loathed myself because I couldn't get control of my life." Did she harbour any negative feelings towards her children at the time?

"No. If I had neglected them, I would have felt worse. When I wanted to die, my children were not safe unless [they were] with me or God."

Her last letter, in handwriting less florid and controlled than the letter to her psychiatrist, was written to her parents, although she chose not to address it or sign it.

"I have no reason to keep this secret any longer. I kept my promise to Dad all this time. He tried to pay for his mistakes — the house was the big pay-off. I've punished both of you, you Mom for not knowing what was going on & him for hurting me when I was a little girl — while you were in hospital I consoled Dad by being molested.

"I don't care about anything anymore.

"You will never get your paws on my 2 beautiful children. No Gramma to threaten & love them only when they do as *you say* & he will never hurt *them* the way he hurt me.

"I always wanted to do things right ...

"You will never hurt or hold us hostage again.

"I finally have what I wanted so desperately — control of my life. I choose not to have one."

I didn't have all that background information when I prepared to provide my opinion to the prosecutor in the case, but I had enough to make me realize that there was an escalating pattern of mental deterioration as Deborah approached the catastrophic event. She couldn't deal with reality, so she resorted to fantasy, which she truly came to believe in. But of course these fantasies wouldn't work. There was no winning lottery ticket or cheque in the bank. There was no Cadillac on the way. There was no cancer, and no marriage or support or promises to take care of her children, commitments that she hoped sympathy about the illness would inspire. Her desperation must have mounted frighteningly as reality and the fantasies came into greater and greater conflict. And always, there was the physical pain.

It is like a dam with a few leaks. You make more and more attempts to patch it, but eventually the whole thing breaks. Seeing everything unravelling, combined with the utterly futile outlook of a person suffering from major depression, panic attacks and chronic pain led Deborah to that breaking point. Her distorted thinking made her believe that with this last act — suicide and homicide — she had taken control, plugged the dam, saved her daughters from a fate worse than death. She saw no other options. Uncharacteristically, she didn't even think of seeking medication from her doctors. Had she seen either of them in the days before the fire, she would surely have been hospitalized — and that *would* have stopped the dam from breaking.

My preliminary opinion had been that a verdict of NCRMD was quite unlikely. But the more I learned, the less comfortable I became. I needed to talk to someone else, and that's how, as the saying goes, a funny thing happened on my way to court.

I asked the prosecutor to ask the defence counsel to give me permission to speak to the psychiatrist he had retained, and whose long and comprehensive report I had read. Dr. Q. had originally been ordered by the court to assess Deborah at FPI. He discussed his findings with both defence and prosecution, and eventually was asked to testify for the defence.

As with most jobs, it often helps to talk things over with a colleague. The defence lawyer agreed, so I had what turned out to be a two-hour telephone conversation with Dr. Q., my friend and often courtroom opponent. As part of his assessment, Dr. Q. had spent nearly a hundred hours interviewing Deborah. Then after our discussion and reviewing additional material, I told the prosecutor that there was a reasonable basis for a NCRMD verdict, and listed my reasons.

The next day, his office called to tell me that he would not require my services any longer in this case. My views would be made known to the defence, and I should feel free to testify if they asked.

So I was called as an expert witness by the defence, and on the stand, the prosecutor attempted to paint me as a waffling turncoat.

"You sought the defence counsel's permission to speak to Dr. Q.?"

"I believe it was done through yourself. Yes, I did ask that."

"That's sort of the professional etiquette in the field of psychiatry, is it?"

"Not so much in psychiatry. For an expert retained for the defence, the defence counsel needs to okay that conversation. It's more a matter of legal protocol, I think."

"And you understood that Dr. Q. was the defence psychiatrist?"

"Yes. He's referred to as the defence psychiatrist in that he was retained by the defence. But I think it's important to understand that we don't see ourselves as, and don't try to function as, a psychiatrist for the Crown or for the defence. What we try to do is say the same thing and give the same answer whoever asks us the question. We think of ourselves more as psychiatrists for the judge or the jury, and our opinion is whatever it is."

"I didn't mean to put a label on you. I appreciate that you come to court and tell the truth as best you can, with the abilities you possess."

The prosecutor then questioned me as to when I had made up my mind about Deborah having a legitimate Section 16 defence. Was it after talking to Dr. Q.? I tried to explain that I hadn't completed forming my opinion until I had all the available information to give me a clear sense of Deborah's mental state at the time of the homicide, which after all, was what I was there to assess. I hadn't felt Dr. Q. was trying to push any opinion on me.

"But before you had called Dr. Q.," the prosecutor persisted, "you couldn't really see an insanity defence?"

"My opinion of the mental-status issues has not particularly changed. But the key thing that came to my mind — after the conversation and more thinking and more reading — was about her particular motivation of saving her children. She saw the children being raised by their grand-parents as a fate worse than death, and in my view, that fit with the sec-ond part of the Section 16 defence, which is not 'knowing that [the crime] was wrong.' And that last step in thinking is what occurred to me then."

Had I changed or confirmed my opinion after interviewing the accused? It was confirmed. I had only been able to interview Deborah the week of the trial, because my change in "sides" only then made it safe for the defence to allow me to do so.

It had been an unsatisfying meeting, because of her amnesia (which I felt had been exacerbated by brain damage, fallout from her most recent near-suicide), and teary emotional state. She had completely fall-en to pieces before we could really discuss anything. I tried to make the point that a person's words and behaviour after a homicide are more reflective of the impact of the crime having happened than of the per-son's mental state before or while committing the crime.

"You did not interview any witnesses?"

"No. All my information has come from the written materials, police reports, witness statements, that sort of thing."

"And the only part of the trial you've attended was when Dr. Q. testified?"

"Yes."

"He forms the major part of the material that you have on which you formed your opinion, doesn't he?" And so on.

The prosecutor's contention during my cross-examination was that Deborah was a legally sane, manipulative person who lied continuously and who murdered her daughter and son as a premeditated act of revenge against her parents. Throughout my testimony, under defence and prosecution questioning, I tried to make the opposite clear. But if Deborah had lied about having breast cancer and winning the lottery, could she be lying her sexual abuse, and what she remembered or did not remember about the homicides?

Deborah's request that her parents not be contacted concerning the alleged childhood sexual abuse had to be respected because it is the legal right of the accused to conduct his or her own defence. So I was questioned about whether or not the abuse had occurred or, more specifically, whether or not Deborah had been telling the truth.

Sometimes during testimony, I feel like I'm giving a mini-lecture, and this was one of those times.

"Getting at the truth is obviously very important. But in the psychiatric analysis, what we are concerned with is, what is a person's mental state? What does she believe? What is going through her head at a certain point in time?

"We all, in various ways at various times, distort reality, and we operate based on what we come to believe, rather than what the world truly is. Most of us do it in minor ways, but some mentally disordered people do it in major ways. And what drives their behaviour is what they believe. So the important thing is not so much whether the sexual abuse occurred, but whether she believed that it occurred. It affects her view of herself, of her parents, of what would happen to her children and so on.

"Anger against her parents was certainly a significant part of her state of mind, as is clear in her suicide notes. But if it were the main motivation, a more likely behaviour would be to get revenge by making them suffer and being able to watch: laying complaints against her father, disallowing access to the grandchildren, even shooting her parents. She hadn't seen any of these options." She had seen nothing but a hopeless future for herself and, without her, the same for her children.

The prosecutor tackled the issue of amnesia compared to lying. But I responded:

"There are a number of things that people can do in a situation where they have lost their memory. The most common is simply to say, 'I don't remember.' However, circumstances can occur where there is a desperate psychological need for a person to make sense out of something that has happened in order to explain some horrible event that has befallen them or someone else — like a murder. Their mind will then create an explanation that the person can face, that they can tolerate, that is at least not as awful as what happened. Psychiatrists refer to that as 'confabulation.'

"You see it after serious violence and you see it in people with alcohol brain damage. You can ask them questions and they give all sorts of answers — and they actually believe the answers — but the answers are part of something the mind has involuntarily manufactured, to fill in a blank spot. It is rare in the general population, but common in these two circumstances."

But, the prosecutor wanted to know, if Deborah could remember her name, address and date of birth not long after she regained consciousness, was she really amnesiac?

"When a person suffers an insult to the brain, its effect on memory is the strongest for recent memory and less for more remote memory. When someone has received a blow to the head, in an accident, for instance, he may not remember the accident itself, or even a few hours after that, whereas his memory of who he is and other past events would normally be unaffected.

"In Ms. LePage's case, I think it is most likely that there is genuine amnesia for the event, probably caused by carbon monoxide and the psychological effects of the homicides."

I had imagined Deborah, her mind tortured and reeling as she wrote the letters, fired the cataclysmic gunshots, tried for some time to light the fire, inhaling gas fumes until she finally got it to go, swallowed what she believed was a lethal dose of medications, then gathered her dead children to her and lay down to die. Not long afterwards, she partially comes to, in the heat and the smoke. Sounds and memories are swirling around in her head; then voices, breaking glass, a man's silhouette, blood on her children, and perhaps an undefined feeling that something is wrong. She has a fleeting thought about rescuing the children, but wanders back into the smoke, into the living room strewn with photos and cigarettes, and collapses on the floor. Moving in and out of consciousness, she is carried out past the youngsters lying on the grass surrounded by emergency personnel and flashing vehicle lights. What a nightmare of images. She is unconscious upon arrival at the hospital, where her blood shows a 39 percent carbon monoxide saturation, enough to cause unconsciousness, and she is treated for a drug overdose.

"I think it would be quite remarkable if a person with that level of carbon monoxide alone had an intact memory afterwards, and her blood readings were obviously something she couldn't fake," I said on the stand. "I think that the amnesia would have been caused by that, combined with the psychological effects of the incident. And the story of the intruder? A confabulation. Again, that's an involuntary mental creation to explain something that is so awful it demands an invention so the person can cope psychologically. I can't be certain of that conclusion, of course, but I think it is the most likely one. The story of the intruder could represent a lie, but confabulation seems to follow along the lines of some of the other sort of fantasy thinking she did, and it would be typical of someone in these circumstances."

"But assuming that she intended to kill herself and her children, and assuming that she was taken to the hospital unconscious and woke up there, there's not an awful lot of time to make up a good story, is there?"

"No, that's true."

"If she had won the lottery, did you form an opinion whether she would have found it necessary to kill herself?"

"I haven't considered that possibility."

"And the fantasies, what you refer to as fantasies, could be lies?"

"Yes, that's certainly a possibility, and indeed I hope it is not taken as my opinion that this woman is somehow incapable of lying. What I look at is the overall pattern of her statements, which, for someone of her level of intelligence, wouldn't represent a normal pattern of lies. It strongly indicates to me that at least much of the time she actually believed in what she said."

"And you would agree with Dr. Q.'s remark that this was a complicated assessment of extraordinary difficulty?"

"Certainly."

"And her own psychiatrist never made the same assessment as you and Dr. Q.?"

"I don't know what his opinion is on the matters now before the court."

"And Dr. Q. did a big report, and another psychiatrist, and a psychologist did reports, and all those people, plus the support staff at the Psychiatric Institute, put all their information into making this big report, right?"

"Yes."

"And the decision was that she was fit to stand trial, right?"

"Yes. And I point out, of course, that that's an entirely separate question from what we're considering here now."

"Of course. And as I understand from your earlier testimony, you're saying she would have known she was shooting the children?"

"Yes."

"She would have been able to put the bullets into the gun, she would have been able to take the gun and point it at the children and know that pulling that trigger was going to cause their deaths, or very likely to cause their deaths?"

"Yes."

"And it was your opinion, Doctor, that the course of action that she took was the only option in her mind that she had?"

"Yes."

"And she never said that to you?"

"No."

"Being emotionless and flat — after such an event as Ms. LePage experienced — is a normal response to grief?"

"It's certainly one of the common responses, yes."

"Drug abuse could cause panic attacks and depersonalization?"

"Drug abuse cannot cause these symptoms. What drug abuse can do is worsen panic attacks and worsen depersonalization. It's clear that she had panic disorder. In her case, I would not see drug abuse as being a fundamental cause, but probably an aggravating factor."

He went back again to get me to confirm that before my conversation with Dr. Q., both he and I did not have conclusive opinions that the accused had a mental disorder defence.

"Doctor, you deal with people. You must like people?"

"Most of them."

"And you consider yourself a compassionate individual?"

"Much of the time."

"And it's hard not to have compassion for Deborah LePage in the situation she faces today; would you agree with that?"

"That's true."

"Those are my questions, My Lord." He did not call upon the psychiatrist he had retained to audit the trial in my place.

The next day's newspaper featured this headline, in bold type: "Docs sympathetic to deadly mom, Crown says".

In the prosecutor's closing address to the jury, the story quoted, "The doctors' compassion, in all likelihood, interfered with their final judgment. They appeared to stretch every psychiatric term to the absolute limit to somehow find a way to include Deborah LePage, and save her from the criminal justice system." That would have appealed to the jury's natural revulsion towards a mother who would kill her children. Dr. Q. and I had gone by the contrasting psychiatric rule of thumb that mothers who kill their children are presumed insane until proven otherwise.

The jury convicted Deborah of two counts of first-degree murder and she was sentenced to two concurrent life terms with no possibility of parole for twenty-five years. The maximum.

Within weeks, because of her poor mental health and continuing suicidal urges, she was transferred to the Forensic Psychiatric Institute and held there in strict custody.

Three years later, a new lawyer for Deborah obtained a second trial on appeal, on the grounds that the original trial judge had mis-instructed the jury. The two trials were a study in contrast.

For the second trial, I was able to interview Deborah twice, but found it did not change my original assessment of her mental state at the time of the homicides. I submitted an updated report to that effect to the court, as did Dr. Q. Deborah's family physician and her psychia-trist submitted strong statements supporting the defence.

A psychiatrist who had not been involved in the first trial, Dr. N., made his assessment, was adamant that the case deserved an NCRMD defence, and outlined his reasons in terms of Section 16 wording. If an NCRMD defence was not accepted by the prosecution, Dr. N. said that a mental-state opinion would still be essential in seeking a reduced charge.

Dr. N. also pointed out that Deborah had now been three years in a custodial therapeutic environment, with clear boundaries and a reason-able framework for her, which had contributed to her current relatively stable mental state. But even with this degree of environmental control, her symptoms still required pharmacotherapy — a full clinical dosage of an antidepressant and lesser amounts of two other drugs — and she remained highly stress vulnerable.

A forensic psychologist, Dr. D., also new to the case, concurred with the essential diagnosis of mixed personality disorder of high severity, major clinical depression, panic disorder and some drug abuse "likely culminating in a steady, insidious deterioration in her mental function-ing and coping ability."

Dr. D. also commented that it was "rare to find so many experienced clinicians in general agreement regarding an accused person's mental state at the time of a criminal act."

The Supreme Court retrial resulted in a verdict of Not Criminally Responsible on account of Mental Disorder. Perhaps they got it right the second time because there was no jury. Perhaps it was the weight of medical evidence, all in agreement. It had been one of those cases in which many "grey-area" issues and the sheer complexity of the psychia-try would inevitably result in some subjective judgments. My recollec-tion of the jury was that its members often looked bewildered.

In addition, the adversarial element had been virtually removed: the new prosecutor said, in court, that the Crown believed an NCRMD ver-dict, advanced by a new defence counsel, was appropriate. In the first trial, we had seen the adversarial approach full-blown: we had two sides.

In the second trial, operating under the same set of rules, we had a cast of people intent on a reasonable outcome, and that was the result.

For four years, Deborah had been in a sort of medicolegal limbo. She had been hospitalized for most of that time, but her status as a remand patient awaiting an appeal had limited her long-term treatment planning. She had been receiving drug dependency counselling and individual psychotherapy, and expressed a desire to receive counseling for childhood sexual abuse.

I interviewed her once more about a year after the second trial and was impressed with the marked improvement in her mental state. She said that although she did have bad days, they were mostly good, the shaky times usually involving some reminder of her children, such as their birthdays or Christmas. She was adamant about continuing her psychotherapy. It had helped her accept responsibility for the homicides and deal with her own grief.

Most optimistically, I learned that Deborah had been gradually weaned off medications, although she knew that a medical need for some of them could arise in the future. She acknowledged that the true test would be to live drug-free with the normal stresses of life in the community, and that the highly structured setting in which she now lived had contributed greatly to her treatment success so far.

She had taken some creative writing courses and was enjoying writing poetry and fiction. I read one of her stories, a contemporary take on an old fairy tale. Universally adored and admired, Ms. Snow White is attacked by mean Mrs. Queen, then rescued back into a perfect life by a kiss on the lips from the hopelessly-infatuated Mr. P. Charming.

Ten years after the fire, following a very gradual re-entry program, Deborah was living in the community under continuing care, including psychiatric counselling, and was subject to regular Review Board assessment. I wondered what themes she was writing about now.

A case very similar to Deborah's came up six years later. I was asked by the police to interview Carey Branko in custody the morning after she had strangled her 5-year-old daughter. Carey, alternately distraught and emotionless, readily admitted killing Emily, saying that she "just lost it," and then, "I did it for Satan."

There were many parallels to the LePage case. Both women had experienced childhood abuse, had been in abusive relationships with men, and had been devoted single mothers determined to be the good parents they never had. Carey was an alcoholic. Because of that, she had been unable to hold a job, and depended on social assistance. She had had suicidal feelings. Two years before the homicide, she had been admitted to hospital after overdosing on acetaminophen and vodka. She said that she had taken the pills in preparation for punishment by Satan because she had been thinking about God. She also said that she had been anxious about the possibility of losing Emily because of her lifestyle, and felt that her life was going nowhere. A year later, she developed cancer but refused treatment.

In the year and a half between her arrest and her trial (a disgraceful but common lapse of time), she was not held in custody, but while out on bail was hospitalized three times for attempted suicide.

Like Deborah, Carey suffered from serious borderline personality disorder. Hers was characterized by occasional, stress-related paranoid thinking and severe dissociative symptoms. (In a dissociative state, a person may feel detached from her own body and mental processes, as if she is observing someone else in action. Instead of working together as a coordinated team, that person's consciousness, memory, identity and perception of her surroundings get out of sync.) Family and friends described many episodes of Carey "disappearing into outer space" for long minutes, and of telephone calls from a frightened Carey worrying about witches.

Unlike Deborah, Carey recalled, with chilling clarity, the act of killing her child while the little girl cried out, "No, Mommy, no!" She felt totally removed from the act (she was dissociated), and she felt that she was carrying out a command issued by Satan (a sign of psychosis). Carey had once seen demon wings on the back of Emily's father as he was beating her. Remembering this vision convinced her that she had created a child for Satan, that Emily belonged to Satan, and so it was right to give her back when Satan ordered. There were other signs she was the devil's child, including the fact that Emily supposedly sometimes slept with her eyes open.

Carey had not belonged to any satanic cult. She had developed her own set of ideas, and they clearly went into the range of paranoid psychotic symptoms. Some of these connections had occurred to her in the two weeks preceding the murder. The year before, she had prayed to Satan to be his bride, "and it really scared me. But I started doing it again a few months ago." Notes handwritten by Carey, referring to witches and warlocks surrounding her building and wanting to kill her, were found in her apartment after the homicide.

I testified in court on behalf of the defence. This was, again, an accused person who could have been seen as lying and manipulative or simply showing the effects of substance abuse, rather than suffering from a mental disorder. And again it was someone who had to be described in terms potentially troublesome to a layperson: "borderline personality disorder." Coincidentally, Dr. Q. had been called as an expert witness in the case, this time by the prosecution. He spoke against an NCRMD, saying the weight of evidence was overwhelmingly based on what Carey herself had said. He claimed that there was no psychiatric way of separating psychotic explanations from angry explanations (or even from alcohol withdrawal symptoms) for what she had done. It surprised me when he said he had trouble finding any evidence that Carey hadn't known what she was doing was wrong. I felt it differed little from Deborah LePage's belief that her children were safer dead than alive.

Dr. Q. did admit that not having been able to interview Carey put him at a disadvantage, and he allowed that she *could* have a major mental disorder; he just couldn't see a clear basis for an NCRMD defence. I was in the favoured position this time: I had been able to interview Carey within a day of the homicide, when her reactions and memories were fresh. Dr. Q. had been frustrated by the defence refusing to let him talk to the accused at all, even three years later.

Dr. Q. pointed to the "shaky evidence" in my own report to the court, making the valid point that, lacking a clear window into the accused person's mind, we could only offer our best educated guess in a case such as this.

Dr. Q. and I expressed our opposing opinions quite firmly. When we're in disagreement, there is an implicit questioning of each other's intelligence and competence — done through the mouths of cross-examining lawyers. Each of us knows that our own views and suggestions have helped shape the lawyers' challenging questions. It is gratifying that our out-of-court friendship has survived years of this kind of testing.

The judge (there was no jury) accepted the opinion that Carey had killed her daughter while suffering an acute psychotic episode with delusions, and found her Not Criminally Responsible on account of Mental Disorder. She was immediately hospitalized, and psychotherapy began for her post-traumatic stress disorder and alcohol and drug abuse, along with medications to stabilize her mood and reduce her suicidal thinking. Carey will have a long road to travel to recovery, but at least she was able to start along it sooner than Deborah had, because she received a correct verdict the first time.

"Correct" sounds smug and arrogant. I have to admit that — horrible as the death was — my heart went out to this sobbing young woman when I interviewed her the morning after the killing. I worked hard to stay objective, once more brought up short with a reminder how personal bias, often unconscious, can influence outcome in "grey-zone" cases.

CHAPTER SIX

NOT A SIMPLE CASE OF ROAD RAGE

At 10 o'clock on the last night of May's long weekend, the stars were just popping out, like fireworks at the end of the festivities. On the two-lane northern Highway 97, people were heading home after the holiday.

Hilda McBrandt was easing the family sedan through the curves when a van, approaching from the opposite direction, suddenly swerved into her lane, coming straight at her. Hilda pulled her car hard out of the way and stopped, her heart pounding, at the side of the road.

"What the hell was that about?" her husband exclaimed, "Someone playing 'chicken'?" Looking back, he saw the van return to the proper side of the highway and carry on.

Rob Nino's SUV was forced off the road a minute later, his two passengers shaken. The van wasn't even speeding, he noticed.

Barry Scholten saw the van cut over into his lane, and he just made it onto the shoulder. Then he pulled a U-turn and followed the van, intending to catch up and read the license plate. Just ahead of him, he saw the van pull the same trick on a big 18-wheeler, but the trucker was able to get his huge rig out of the way, sending up a cloud of dust and gravel.

The van pulled over twice, to let Barry pass; when he didn't, the driver turned into a farm driveway. Barry's wife cell-phoned the license plate number to the RCMP. An officer was attending an accident two minutes ahead of the van, she was told, and he would intercept it. Just after they turned back home, the Scholtens saw the van pull out of the driveway and back onto the road, this time with its headlights off.

Milos Pappas saw the van swerve at him just in time. He jerked his car hard right, startling his girlfriend, who had turned to look at the baby in the back seat and hadn't seen the vehicle come at them out of the dark. Milos turned the car around in hot pursuit, and was closing in, just as the still-lightless van swerved over the line once more. This time it drove head-on into an automobile approaching over a rise in the road.

Milos pulled over and ran to help. He hadn't thought either vehicle had been going fast, so he wasn't prepared for what he saw.

Reaching the van first, he saw the driver slumped over the wheel. Expecting to find "some drunk guy," he was shocked to see an apparently sober woman, conscious, alert and with no visible injuries. He told her to sit tight, and he turned to the occupants of the sedan — and choked at the carnage. One passenger had been thrown partly through the windshield and was lying with her head and shoulders on the hood of the car. The driver appeared to be jammed into the steering wheel, and another passenger was just barely visible under the dashboard. All three young people were unconscious. He tried to take the pulse of one, but couldn't find it. He thought they were all dead, and the two he could see were friends of his.

"What happened?" he cried out to the van driver.

She shrugged, no sign of dismay on her face.

"You just killed three people!"

"Good," she responded. "Call the police." She was still sitting calmly behind the wheel. The passenger from the other vehicle lay bleeding across the car hood, a few feet away from her.

Police, passersby and ambulances were arriving. The RCMP officer questioned the van driver. "Shit happens," was her only explanation, "Can you drive me home?"

The officer said he would, once the road had been cleared, and at that, she got out of the van and, uninvited, walked over and got into the back seat of the police cruiser. Ambulance attendants pronounced her uninjured. The constable detected no signs of impairment: no slurred speech, no lack of coordination, no odor of alcohol.

"The only behaviour that seemed abnormal," he reported later, "was her seeming total lack of concern for the accident and injuries. She appeared to be disassociated from it all."

Selena Collins was taken to the nearest RCMP detachment and booked for dangerous driving. She was released with the warning that the charges might be upgraded, depending upon the severity of the victims' injuries. The police officers reported being taken aback by her casual attitude. To detachment staff and the neighbour who came to pick her up, she described the accident as inconsequential. "I've had a little fender-bender," she said.

In the automobile hit by Selena, one woman died and another woman and a man were severely injured. Other drivers soon came forward to report having been run off the road. Selena was re-arrested and charged with one count of criminal negligence causing death and two counts of criminal negligence causing bodily harm. She spent several days in a women's correctional centre, then was transferred to the Forensic Psychiatric Institute on "Psych Remand," which meant that she would be held in custody for thirty days while a psychiatric assessment was conducted.

She was tested and observed, and tentative inquiries were made into her background. People who go out and kill seem to have in common a sad, bad history.

Selena's mother is a paranoid schizophrenic alcoholic who had six children with six different men. Three children were placed for adoption, but Selena and two younger sisters had been kept, to lead what can only be described as chaotic childhoods. She never knew her father, and through the revolving door of stepfathers came a stream of alcoholics and drug addicts, some more abusive than others. Fights broke out often enough that the sight of a squad car pulling up wasn't unusual. Selena learned not to trust men.

She learned about paranoia and delusional beliefs from her mother, Maggie, whose illness was a constant with which her daughters coped. Maggie had the common paranoid conviction that she was being followed, as well as some ideas of her own, loosely tied in with Jehovah's Witnesses' ideology. She had a birthmark that she said was a sign that God had selected her as one of the few who would never face death. She also had a web of beliefs around telepathy that related specifically to her.

Her daughters, and sometimes Mag herself, recognized these thoughts as irrational, but usually let them flow. Every so often, though, the children were frightened enough to take their mother to the hospital when her illness or substance abuse got out of hand. And when Mag made one of her frequent suicide attempts, an ambulance would take her away. Selena was in and out of foster homes during these episodes.

Living was hand to mouth. Selena's mother never worked, and wasn't great on cooking. Mag went on benders, and took tranquillizers in between. Her idea of a good evening was to swallow a handful of pills, have a few drinks, then head for the bar with like-minded friends. "Still, she was a good mum," Selena said.

Mag didn't object to Selena's regular shoplifting of shoes and clothes, which the girl had started at nine or ten years old. Nor were there any disciplinary consequences when Selena's gang burned down sheds and fences, poured milkshakes into mailboxes, harassed neighbours or stole candy. Other kids were intrigued with the house with no rules.

Schooling was a casual affair. From Grade 1 on, Selena and her sisters would fake illness and skip school once or twice a week. Mag played along because she wanted the company. Selena did all right academically, although by the time she reached Grade 8, she had attended eleven schools in various places. Mag was always moving, trying to get away from ex-boyfriends and imaginary pursuers. In fourth grade alone, they moved to Edmonton and back sixteen times.

"I never make plans," Selena said, "they never work out."

At 14, Selena was a hard-driving bundle of energy who had dropped out of school, left home and was working in a take-out pizza place. She was smoking marijuana as well as drinking, the beginning of a stimulus-seeking career. "You name it," she would say about drugs, "I've done it."

At 15, she moved in with Ray Lisgard and married him at 17, the year of her first conviction, for marijuana possession. They had a son, Cody. She started doing cocaine and claimed she spent up to $1,000 a week on it, for years. She said coke made her "very, very paranoid," and friends corroborated, saying she would cower in the basement, hiding in case the police were coming. After nine years with Ray, she left him "because he was picking on Cody." It had been an abusive relationship, but she had stayed because he was always contrite after he beat her, and besides, she knew he had had a hard childhood.

Selena took up with Trent Walker and fell in with a group that scared her friends and family. "Under-belly people," was how one person described the men and women who frequented the house. Oh, she knew lots of skid-road types and bikers, Selena agreed; but she added that she always lived out in the country, as if that kept everything wholesome. She started shooting heroin, used morphine and speed. She was convicted of possession, then trafficking, then possession, then careless driving, and then served a short sentence for possession and trafficking of a narcotic. She had a baby girl, Desiree, who was born addicted to morphine. Once in a while, she and Trent would stay awake for days at a time, stoked on amphetamines, driving across three provinces, getting morphine prescriptions filled while the children slept in the back seat. To support these expensive habits, Selena grew marijuana and sold or traded it for other drugs in Vancouver. She occasionally trained dogs.

When Cody was 15, Trent fed him LSD. No one who heard about the incident was surprised. It was well known as a hard-partying house.

About six months before the highway accident, things started coming unglued. Trent had been having an affair with a stripper and fellow intravenous drug user, LuAnn. Selena was diagnosed with Hepatitis C, and believed LuAnn had been the source, via Trent.

To Selena, it seemed that Cody was siding more and more with Trent and moving away from her. Then Desiree, now a year old, was apprehended by Social Services and given in temporary custody to Selena's cousin Terri. Selena entered a detox program for opiate addiction, stayed four weeks and left early.

More losses accumulated. Selena and Trent broke up after seven years together. Selena always said that her children and dogs were very important to her, but she had never loved a man. Still, she had been dependent on Trent's practical support, and LuAnn had apparently stolen Trent from her, which was a blow. Selena's life hadn't given her the capacity or discipline to hold a job, and it was doubtful she would last long in the drug-dealing business if she tried on her own to go up against the serious male dealers dominating the trade. Seemingly insurmountable survival problems loomed without Trent to support her family — and to keep her in the drugs to which she was addicted. Trent had even less motivation to provide for them with his daughter taken into foster care. Then her aunt died. A favourite dog died.

Terri gave Desiree back to Selena, contrary to the court order, but because it had to be kept quiet, Selena couldn't apply for social assistance. She, Cody and little Desiree moved into a trailer and lived in poverty until a friend of Trent's, Lee, and his young son moved in to share the rent for a while — until Selena accused Lee of sexually abusing all three children.

About ten days before the accident, police went to investigate a 911 hang-up call placed from her number, but an angry Selena refused to come out and speak to police. The next day was Mother's Day. There was no food in the house, so Cody went out and bought some groceries, along with a flowering plant as a gift for his mother. Selena hurled the groceries into the river, took scissors to the plant and began beating on Cody. Neighbours who heard the boy shouting, "Let me go!" came over to find Desiree sitting sobbing on the kitchen floor, and Cody outside, crying and scuffing his feet in the dirt. Selena ordered Cody to leave. He managed to get himself on the bus to Vancouver and went to stay with Trent.

The following afternoon, two police constables and a social worker went to a local "party house" following up on a call from the owner. The man, Josef Petit, told them that Selena and her kids had been hanging out there, more or less, for a couple of weeks. Josef described how Selena had seemed OK the first week or so, then became "very detached." She would laugh at everything, she wasn't even paying attention to the baby. When Desiree fell and banged her head, Selena had laughed and said, "We're all going to die." When the police arrived, she was feeding Desiree moss covered with ketchup.

They found a suspicious substance in Selena's possession. They arrested her, and once more, apprehended Desiree. The police described Selena as "vague and abusive." Josef said he thought she had been into a lot of mushrooms lately.

When the social worker spoke to her in the RCMP detention cells, he also felt Selena was abusive — but carefree as well, perhaps uncomprehending of the seriousness of her situation as Desiree's parent, and without any apparent remorse. Police saw her again about a week later. She had been at a party the night before, and the following evening she was still refusing to leave the party house. She was flippant and completely unconcerned about invading the privacy of the hosts, whom she didn't know. When the police escorted her out, they observed two malnourished dogs sitting by her van.

Selena slept until evening, the day of the accident. When she awoke, there was no marijuana in the house, so she set out for Lee's house to get some. Lee said later that she had been "schizo, out in left field" for a couple of weeks, and seemed to be equally bizarre whether she was doing mushrooms or not. She had talked of Social Services or the police plotting to kill her, and of her having some kind of transmitter in her tooth, and having "her mouth swept for bugs." Selena had outright accused Lee and Trent of abusing her kids. But she had been aggressive with the children, too, which Cody said was totally out of character.

"Well, you're grumpy." Selena left Lee's house without scoring so much as a joint, and drove out onto Highway 97.

She was mad, and she needed to fight their plot to get her out of the way. She thought the van had been acting up. She was sure that Trent and Lee had tampered with it. If it exploded and killed her, "It would bring them in line ... I'd be dead and then I would be everywhere." Her spirit would be able to move about freely and protect her children.

She started playing "chicken" with the van.

If people in the car didn't get out of the way, they must have done something wrong. "God will sort it out. It was an accident. They were abusing my children."

Shit happens. And high tragedy. The psychologist who would later assess Selena at FPI said that the offense "could have been a wail of despair from an overwhelmed person who wished to end it all or to advertise that she would no longer cope."

Selena, booked, fingerprinted and released, left for home — to all outward appearances without a care in the world. A few days later, Social Services told her that they would be seeking a permanent custody order for Desiree. Selena showed no emotional response to the news, as if this, too, were a trivial event. She took her re-arrest and commitment to FPI equally in stride.

Selena Collins was a challenge to FPI staff. She toyed with some of the psychological testing procedures and attempted to manipulate some of the results to indicate she was psychotic. "Is that crazy enough for you?" she asked at one point. Yet she showed genuine symptoms of mental disorder in areas where the testing could not be faked.

Her behaviour was perplexing. She seemed fully aware of her surroundings and her legal situation. They felt her speech was normal and her memory intact. She claimed not to remember the accident happening, although she believed the other car hit her, so she was not to blame, and also that her car had been tampered with. She treated assessment interviews as a game, a breezy conversation during which the doctors should consider her their equal in matters of mental-health knowledge. She refused to do parts of some tests, and she portrayed herself in a flattering light wherever possible. She said she felt "great about herself" and that she was "pretty happy right now, very content with whatever happens" — nothing in her life needed improvement at the moment.

Selena, confusingly, appeared able to will herself in and out of a psychotic state, lapsing into illogical paragraphs about some persecutory belief in the middle of a rational conversation on another topic. It was hard to tell delusion from acting — and if she was acting, what was her motivation? It seemed evident she hadn't considered the consequences of anything, and she said her lawyer was "another bad guy," so play-acting didn't appear to be motivated by any rational legal strategy.

Was she malingering — intentionally and consciously faking symptoms? Had she learned how to appear psychotic from her mother and was now simply imitating her? Or had she inherited the mental disorder from her mother and was genuinely psychotic now, or at the time of the accident? Was what the psychologist described as her "breathtaking nonchalance" about the accident a sign that she really didn't care about it? Or did it suggest that she really was psychotic and had been operating in a state of desperation, under a genuine belief that she was doing something that had to be done? Was she lying about not remembering the accident itself, or was she truly confused?

One of the psychiatrists, Dr. B., who had moved to have Selena certified when she first entered FPI, reversed his opinion and came down on the side of malingering. A psychologist and I independently came to the opposite conclusion. We each sought outside corroboration — people who knew Selena before and around the time of her offense who could give us a bigger picture. Her sister, two longtime female friends, and Trent and Lee were interviewed separately. Enough common views among them gave the clear impression of someone who, like her mother, would slide into paranoia under stress (or cocaine use), as some sort of coping mechanism.

There was universal agreement that following Desiree's first apprehension, Selena started a downhill slide, progressively ignoring her own health and appearance, her surroundings, her dogs and eventually, the children.She stirred ashes of her dead dog into her orange juice and drank it. With Desiree's second apprehension, all of Selena's anxieties seemed to have ballooned into delusions. Cody had been given LSD, so she extrapolated that both he and Desiree had been fed drugs, then that they were being sexually abused, then that they were being used in pornographic films.

Both Trent and Lee said that she was suspicious of police and Social Services, and that she had started talking about being under surveillance and "being bugged." It would have been unnatural for a drug dealer with several convictions under her belt, and whose child had been apprehended, *not* to want to avoid these agencies. But she must also have felt that without them, and with no family or marital safety net, she had nowhere to go for help, no one to turn to. Her religious fatalism told her there was only God. Perhaps He would help her stop the conspiracy. As usual, it wasn't her fault. It was part of God's strategy.

Psychological testing had indicated that her narcissism and antisocial behaviours were covering up major fears of abandonment and aloneness. "Drug use," the report states, "alternately soothes and worsens such anxieties."

In addition to all that, Selena was struggling to get off narcotics after years of use. She had been trying to execute her own program, substituting a heavy intake of "natural" drugs — mostly marijuana, magic mushrooms and cider — for heroin, cocaine and speed, while hard drugs continued to circulate among her friends. At the time of the accident, she claimed she was suffering from withdrawal; she had not had any marijuana, and although she may have consumed some mushrooms, that could only have been an aggravating factor, not a cause of the crash.

When I first interviewed Selena, three months after the accident, I concluded that she was psychotic then and — from the evidence, statements and reports that I was able to obtain — I decided she had been psychotic at the time of the crash. If not, the mishap had to have been either an accident, or an intentional collision as a result of "sane" motives and behaviour.

It was clear from witnesses that the collision had been intentional. The motive could have been suicide; but in her case, the motive would necessarily have been based on paranoid delusions, which puts it back in the "insane" category. In any case, she could have committed suicide by driving into a wall or off a cliff. Instead, Selena chose to involve another vehicle, indicating that part of her motivation had to be to harm the occupants of another car. She believed that she would be guided by supernatural powers to run into the exact vehicle that contained the culprits who had been sexually abusing her children. Again, that thinking would have had to be based on her psychotic paranoid delusions. Another belief she held was that if she herself was killed in the accident, her spirit would be free to protect her children more effectively than she could as a live person.

At the time of my first involvement, Selena was no longer certified, and was up for re-evaluation, raising the possibility that she might be released pending her trial. Dr. B. (the psychiatrist whose opinion differed from mine) and I each sent off recommendations against her release. We were both concerned about public safety, if she were dropped unsupported into a community where both drugs and vehicles were available to her. I also felt that she should be receiving intensive treatment for a psychiatric condition that must have been building up for years.

The trial went poorly.

A person whose anti-social behaviours have been allowed to develop unchecked, and whose shell of aloof disdain has been a reasonably successful tool for survival through a turbulent childhood, does not necessarily cut a sympathetic figure. Selena's lawyer made a good move in keeping her off the stand.

The prosecution decided not to call Dr. M., the psychologist who had made, to my mind, the most comprehensive and probing assessment of the accused. They said that if the defence were to call upon him, they would take the position that "as a psychologist, he [was] not qualified" to give an opinion, because he was "not a medical doctor ... and his area of expertise is necessarily limited to the observation of human behaviour." Psychologists frequently testify as expert witnesses, so he did here, supporting a diagnosis of Brief Reactive Psychosis and an NCRMD defence as an expert witness called by the defence.

I, too, testified quite strongly that Selena had been psychotic before, during and after the accident, and that she met the Section 16 insanity defence criteria in all respects. Unfortunately, the defence called no witnesses who could have offered evidence that Selena had been increasingly psychotic in the weeks leading up to the accident or that she had been psychotic at other times in her life. Perhaps it would have been too difficult to get people like Trent or Lee to come to court and testify, or perhaps they would be messy witnesses whose credibility could be undermined.

The Crown produced Milos Pappas, who described the swerving game on the highway, the human wreckage of his friends, and Selena's apparent callousness after the accident. Dr. B. testified that Selena had faked her symptoms and had an anti-social personality.

Part of the reason for this disagreement in opinion among psychiatrists and psychologists revolved around the fact that there are no standardized procedures for making such legal-based diagnoses, and perhaps not enough standardization in testing.

The judge rejected my and Dr. M.'s opinion, stating that it was more likely that Selena had lied to us and mimicked delusional symptoms to advance her case. This was no surprise, since the lack of Trent and Lee's corroborating evidence left only a wobbly basis for the defence's expert opinion, and, under law, the facts on which an expert opinion is based must also be proven to the court. He pronounced her guilty of manslaughter.

She received a short sentence, no psychiatric treatment, and is now back in her troubled life and, perhaps, on the road again. She almost certainly spent less time in custody than if she had been found NCRMD, and was released into the community without mandated treatment or supervision, thereby posing a greater risk to herself and others.

After the trial, that feeling of unfinished business, of a job not well done, stuck with me.

From a medical point of view, I was sickened by the outcome. Why couldn't the psychiatrists and the psychologist have gotten together, thrashed out the issues and come to a reasonable, professional conclusion which we could have then presented in such a way as to ensure that the judge completely understood? The answer is because the system isn't designed to work that way.

Sometimes, in spite of itself, it does, as my next case showed.

CHAPTER SEVEN

MURDER AT THE B&B

Keiran Marks and two guests met the police at the big, carved wood door of The Cedars Bed and Breakfast. Upstairs, the officers found the body of Glen Kosan on the floor, his face covered with a towel. He appeared to have been dead several hours. There were no signs of a struggle, no blood, no obvious wounds. The guests appeared shell-shocked, but were willing to describe the past twenty-four hours as they saw it.

The Cedars caters to a gay clientele, and Matt Shreck and Corbin Green had arrived in town two nights before, staying with Matt's brother the first night. They had known Glen and Keiran, life partners and owners of The Cedars, for a decade or so. Corbin remarked that they had seen a decline in the couple's relationship over the preceding two years. The four of them had gone out for dinner that first night; Glen and Keiran had arrived at the restaurant in separate vehicles.

The next day, Matt and Corbin moved into The Cedars, and everyone described what followed as a relaxing summer afternoon and evening by the pool. Several beers, some kind of light tequila drink Matt was mixing, a little marijuana, a barbecue dinner. No one seemed particularly high, and they slipped easily through Glen's steak-and-salad supper. After sunset, Corbin remembered floating in the pool, looking up at the sky and remarking to Glen that there were a few bats swooping around. Matt and Keiran were in deckchairs nearby, talking. First Glen, then Keiran and, not long after, Matt and Corbin went to bed; it was about 11 o'clock.

About 7 a.m., Corbin got up to use the bathroom, and saw Keiran across the hall, sleeping in a chair in the basement TV room. Corbin went back to bed, slept for another hour. When he got up, Keiran was still sleeping in the chair. Corbin went upstairs to the kitchen, poured two cups of freshly-brewed coffee, and came back down to find Keiran awake.

"Where's Glen?" Corbin asked.

"I don't know. I think something may've happened to him, because we had a fight last night."

"Have you been sleeping in that chair all night?"

Keiran didn't respond, didn't move from the chair. Corbin sensed something was wrong. Keiran had been naked when he went to bed, now he was fully clothed. He didn't know where Glen was, and he seemed, well, not quite with it. Corbin went looking for Glen, and found him on the master bedroom floor. He called Keiran upstairs and confronted him.

"I don't know, I don't know," Keiran stammered, distraught and confused. "We got into a fight last night. I — well, I guess I'd better call the police and turn myself in." He went down to the kitchen and picked up the telephone, tears streaming down his face.

After Keiran's departure with the arresting officer, Matt told the police he had had an odd conversation with Keiran the previous evening. Glen was somewhere else in the house and the other three had been looking at old photographs. There was music on, and Matt commented that it was a pretty good stereo system.

"Oh no," Keiran had said, "there are only two speakers hooked up. The wires for the other two are disconnected back here. I was getting big shocks from them."

Matt thought, "Well, you don't get a big shock from speaker wire," but he let Keiran go on. He said he was getting shocks from other things in the house that "someone had rewired." And he didn't want to eat at home anymore because he felt that he was being poisoned.

Matt remembered some friends who had come to stay at The Cedars, but left after a few days because Keiran had been so unpleasantly strange. He had been turning artwork upside down, kicking Glen whenever they passed in the hall. He had been convinced that Glen was sleeping with everyone who came to stay, and had tried to get even by coming on to the guests.

"So this is what they meant," Matt had thought to himself, "He's really paranoid."

The next morning, I presented myself at the city police cells to interview Keiran. After a homicide, the sooner you can reach the accused the better, in terms of your ability to assess him or her while the situation is still "hot." He remembers the event probably as well as he will ever remember it, and his reactions to questions are usually genuine and natural. Still, the person's own tendency to distort his own memories for his own psychological reasons, as well as to contrive conscious lies, are important and frequent problems.

The watch commander briefed me about what had happened, and offered some background information. There had been violence at the house before. Both a neighbour and Glen's son had said that Glen had told them he was afraid of Keiran. Glen owned the bed and breakfast, and it was up for sale. There had been talk of Glen and Keiran splitting up when the venture was sold. Glen's son had been worried for his father; he had been especially concerned about Keiran's reaction should the sale go through. An offer to buy had been faxed to Glen the day of the homicide.

My interview started with the usual vital statistics chronology, and when we got to the part where they had started to renovate the building to convert it to a B&B, the floodgates opened. Keiran began a long monologue on how there had been so much work building it, doing the gardens, running it nine months a year, and how he did much more of the work than Glen, he still did. According to Glen, though, Keiran did everything wrong. Even when guests complained he had done something wrong, Glen would never take Keiran's part, and it got worse over the years. Six years ago, he had gone to the hospital because he was a nervous wreck. He believed he had been getting threats to his life from guests and other people. He had been hearing people talking, but could never see who it was. "Am I hearing things? Is my mind going?" he had asked himself.

He was still hearing voices, seeing things. "I know I'm in bad shape."

I asked him a question he didn't answer. Instead he said, "I look around, I feel dizzy and it knocks me to my knees. I don't know where the shots are coming from. Then I get nailed with more electric shocks from another angle and I spit up blood. I don't know how they're doing it. I can't figure it out.

"The house is like one big magnet. I was very careful, cleaning the light switches, taking off the plugs and cleaning inside the wall, but the dirt and film would come back."

Keiran talked non-stop, rambling off in different directions, starting a sentence on one topic, finishing it on another, although he could always be brought back on course, even if only momentarily. I wanted to know more about his voices.

"It's like people telling me to do stuff, like a bug or recording in my head somewhere. At a friend's place, in his office, I felt a sharp prick to my back, like a needle. Since then, whatever I say is recorded. A couple of years ago, I was really constipated and the doctor said not to eat spicy foods, but then Glen made everything extra spicy, and I got worse."

Whose voice is inside your head? "Not anyone in particular. It says, 'Do it this way, do it that way.' It's like déjà vu. I can go to the bingo hall and see someone there, then to a restaurant and see the same person, like they were following me. I went downtown once and called home and the telephone company told me my number was out of service. I kept calling and it finally rang through. I thought that they were hooking up a separate phone system and somehow calls were getting routed somewhere else. I called my sister, but it sounded like someone pretending to be her.

"The car has been booby-trapped twice. All the shocks were disconnected. I don't know if Glen did it. The car is kept in the garage, but the garage is always unlocked, and people come and go. There are three staircases in the house, so people can go in and out and you never see them. Just shadows. I'd hear noises up and down all the time. I couldn't sleep because of all the voices. And the clocks all had different times. Glen wouldn't let me set the clocks.

"Lately Glen has been trying to sell the house. Our friends came and one said, 'Keiran, you don't look good at all.' She'd noticed changes. The other time, Susan came and saw me crying my eyes out. That was when I turned myself in to the psych ward. I think the treatment was just talking. Glen came in and brought a bouquet of scented condoms with dried opium pollen. He said, 'Enjoy the flowers.' But all I could smell was burnt rubber. I couldn't figure it out. Only burnt rubber. After a few days, I just left the hospital. Glen needed the help at home. He put tons of cayenne pepper in my food, and when I said I shouldn't eat it, he told me I didn't know anything, just eat it. Then I felt really sick.

"I've been double-imaging. I saw two people on the living room couch, but when I looked in the mirror by the hot tub, I couldn't see my face, only the two people on the couch. I can't understand how that works. There must be some trick being played on me.

"Over the years, just when I'm getting it figured out, something comes along and bonks me again."

I interrupted the flow. "Who do you think does this, Keiran?" I asked.

"Glen and his cohorts. Whoever is involved, it's just such a big sea of people. I tow the mark or they'll kill me. They're into drugs — well, mostly marijuana — art and porn. There's so much art in the house, but it keeps getting moved, taken down, changed. I haven't seen them making the porno videos. They must do the filming while I'm out or asleep. But there are always guys posing around the pool, moving the planters and so on.

Keiran believed he knew about Glen's infidelities with other men in the B&B. He had just never been able to catch them. Certain of Glen's friends had been condescending and some had threatened Keiran, and probably cut some of the wires. One had left his bathing suit behind, just to torment Keiran. Worst of all, Glen was constantly accusing him, Keiran, of being a slut, of wanting to sleep with people he just enjoyed talking to. Glen was always on him about something.

"Things were wired to different fuse boxes and would get disconnected. I'd hear noises in the night and Glen would always say, 'Go to sleep, you're just imagining it'. He would know they were there, but he denied it. I kept taping up the connections, but they would get changed again.

"A few days ago, I got such a shock from the telephone by the pool that I had to pull out all the wires from the box. Glen called the repairman from the store. I was really afraid that day. I thought they were going to get me. I thought I was going to get killed that day, because the voices told me to hide and keep away from the telephone guy and Glen. They told me to hide in the corner of the garden away from the pool, where there were grasses and vines, and to think of a colour like blue. I was just vibrating. The phone guy had a tool pouch; he could have had other things in it, like a gun.

"Sometimes the voices tell me to do things and I don't know if they're going to help me or harm me. Once I was extremely constipated and I finally passed something when I heard a voice from the floor saying, 'Give it to me, I want it.' I thought maybe I had got rid of the bug or the implant."

With all these hallucinations and delusions circulating in his head, how would Keiran describe the day of the homicide, and the act itself? His account up to bedtime coincided with the one Corbin and Matt had given the police, with a few exceptions. Keiran said he had been insulted by Glen, who had called him a "stupid fool" when he couldn't find more beer, and he had been zapped twice. Looking at the red raw steaks, he had felt weird. Recently, seeing red had triggered weakness in him, he didn't know why. He had been feeling tired and groggy lately, and had gone to his family doctor and asked for a complete check-up. The physician hadn't found anything wrong. Keiran had insisted on further blood tests; the results weren't in yet.

So when they went to bed, and Glen had wanted to make love, Keiran had been reluctant because he was afraid he might be ill. But he was feeling high on the drinks, so they had sex and then he might have fallen asleep. Or maybe not, it was just a blur. Sometime, an argument started. Glen didn't like Keiran sleeping on the bedroom couch, but Keiran said Glen thrashed about in his sleep and was always hitting him or scratching him with his toenails, so he preferred to sleep on the couch. Glen accused Keiran of not wanting to sleep on the bed so he could sneak downstairs with "the boys," and Keiran had said he wasn't going to do anything like that, they were a couple and he wasn't attracted to either of them.

Was that what started the dispute? Keiran told me he had tried and tried, sitting in his cell yesterday, to piece it together.

Arguing, they had started to wrestle, he thought, or grabbed each other, then he didn't know what took place. Were they choking each other? Was Glen trying to kill him? He just couldn't get it together in his mind. Voices in his head kept saying, "You're wrong. You're wrong." He thought he had been zapped during the fight, but when did it happen?

Usually, after he and Glen had had an argument — or simply to avoid one — Keiran would go outside to clear his head. Sometimes he had slept in the garden, on a lounge chair. This time, he went for a drive. He couldn't recall where he had gone, but it wasn't far. He came back to the house, thinking, "This is stupid." Did he make coffee, he wondered? Anyway, he fell asleep in the chair. He had no thoughts that he had killed Glen, none at all until Corbin called him and he touched Glen's cold foot, and thought, "My god, my god, have I done something really ...."

Bewildered, Keiran began to weep again. He did not believe he was even capable of doing such a thing.

"I don't wanna hurt the guy. I love him. He pushes me around and I push him around once in a while, I mean, but, Jesus, I'd rather take a beating than give one anytime. What have I done?"

An autopsy revealed manual strangulation as the cause of Glen's death. Keiran was charged with manslaughter. I had recommended that he be given a complete thirty-day psychiatric assessment, and he was subsequently transferred to the Forensic Psychiatric Institute on remand.

At FPI, background checks and interviews with several relatives and longtime friends indicated that Keiran had lived most of his life as the dependant, mild-mannered individual he appeared to be. He was the youngest of eight children who had been abandoned by their mother; he had left school after tenth grade, and had worked steadily as a cook, painter or handyman. He had had a fifteen-year relationship with an older man, who had died about two years before he met Glen. Glen was a retired university professor who had "come out" in his 60s, amicably leaving his wife of thirty years. He, his ex-wife and children had remained close.

For the first three or four years together, Glen and Keiran seemed extremely happy. They moved west and set up the bed and breakfast, with Keiran doing most of the brute work and Glen the creative and management things. It wasn't perfect. Keiran always said that Glen was much smarter than he was, and they had had an argument because Glen controlled the whole operation. As a result, Glen bought Keiran out, and things settled after that, for a while. The business went well and they would fly off to Hawaii every winter. But Keiran was always jealous, and friends described scenes of Keiran getting petulant when Glen appeared to be the centre of attention and he felt neglected.

A few years back, people began noticing that Keiran's stress levels tended to escalate over the summers. Their friends said he would "get paranoid" during the B&B's busy season. He began accusing people of conspiring against him, and more recently had started making asides about the electric shocks he was getting, or the poisoned coffee. Both Keiran and Glen drank, if not excessively, at least regularly. While Keiran would go outside to get away from domestic disputes, Glen would have several drinks to chase the problem away. They recognized that their relationship was in difficult straits and, each in his own ineffectual way, tried to fix it.

Keiran's tests showed no cognitive, neurological or physical impairment. He was described as having a dependent personality disorder: someone who has a strong need for closeness, is willing to be compliant and submissive in order to meet that need, and requires excessive reassurance and care. Somewhere along the line, his intense fear of losing the relationship, and his suspicions that he was losing control of the situation and becoming more helpless, developed into paranoia.

Six years before the homicide, he had begun hearing voices. When he checked into the hospital, he was diagnosed as having an acute psychotic reaction to what he perceived as the extreme level of stress in his life at the time. Released from hospital, he continued to build on his repertoire of persecutory delusions and hallucinations, which always peaked during periods of high stress, and waned slightly in the off-season.

Keiran was completely consistent in his descriptions of his beliefs and delusions, whether he was being interviewed by the police or by doctors, and family and friends corroborated his stories. To the psychologist and two psychiatrists who examined him, it was clear that Keiran was certifiably mentally disordered — and had been for a long time — and that he needed psychiatric treatment. That was the medical position. Determining his legal position — whether he might be Not Criminally Responsible on account of Mental Disorder — was another story.

The other medical consultants and I agreed that he was suffering from a psychotic mental disorder at the time of the homicide. But the death might have occurred during the course of a "non-bizarre" or "sane" domestic conflict — during which Keiran knew what he was doing, and actually intended to kill Glen. Given Keiran's apparently genuine lack of complete memory for the event, and the additional complication of his having been intoxicated to a degree, it was extremely difficult to determine which of these factors had the upper hand at the moment when Glen was killed.

There were significant causes of rational friction between Glen and Keiran. Both men felt that the division of labour at the bed and breakfast was unfair, and each thought the other was not pulling his weight. The sale of the bed and breakfast was another live issue. According to Keiran, Glen had vacillated between saying that Keiran would receive a "fair share" of the sale's proceeds and threatening to cut him out completely. Keiran claimed to be unaware of the offer that had come in that day, although one of the guests testified that Keiran had known about it.

Finally, the relationship had been increasingly rocky and, while they had mutually agreed to sell, it was unclear whether they would stay together after they left the B&B. Both partners regularly expressed jealousy and accused the other of infidelity.

There was ample evidence to suggest that any of these issues could have triggered a "sane" argument that resulted in a "sane" homicide. However, there was no specific evidence or witnesses to link any of them to the killing.

Similarly there was insufficient evidence to say for certain that the homicide had occurred purely as a result of Keiran's paranoid psychotic thinking. It did seem highly possible that Keiran could have thought that this was the moment when Glen was actually going to kill him, as he believed Glen had planned.

Another line of reasoning suggested that even if the argument started out on the basis of a "sane" disagreement, Keiran's paranoid psychotic thinking could have consequently intruded and driven him to homicide. For instance, if the topic of the B&B sale had arisen and Glen had made a negative remark concerning disposition of the proceeds, Keiran could have interpreted it as part of Glen's plan to kill him, so Glen could keep all the money. There might also be the possibility that alcohol and/or marijuana had aggravated Keiran's already psychotic thinking.

The best these arguments could do, I felt, was to swing the odds in the psychotic-versus-sane analysis to about 70:30 in favour of a psychotic mental state at the time of the killing. As I said in my preliminary assessment to the defence lawyer, this type of analysis was far more speculative than one would wish under such serious circumstances. Oddly enough, the same lack of information regarding Keiran's mental state in the killing that made my assessment so uncertain had also, in a way, added to its confidence. The fact that Keiran had not tried to link his own mental state or motivation in the killing to his paranoid psychosis convinced me that he was truthful and was not trying to concoct a psychiatric defence for himself.

I made a few comments in my court report about the comparative outcomes of Keiran's being found either guilty or NCRMD.

If he were found guilty, he might receive a short jail sentence and be released. Then, without any legal hold on him and therefore likely to be without any treatment, his psychosis would probably worsen, posing potential danger to himself and the community; he might find himself in this situation again. If he did receive treatment while in custody, given that Keiran himself had no insight into his delusions, it was unlikely he would voluntarily continue any treatment upon release. The prison option seemed to point inevitably to a future mental deterioration.

On the other hand, if he were declared NCRMD, he would receive an indefinite mandate for psychiatric treatment and close supervision, subject to Review Board determination. In this scenario, both Keiran's and society's interests would be better served, and likely for much longer. I also recommended that the defence allow the psychiatrist retained by the prosecution to assess Keiran.

To my relief, but not surprise, Dr. Q., called by the Crown, came out more strongly than I had in confirming Keiran's severe mental impairment at the time of the crime. Dr. Q. stated that although Keiran's amnesia created an unavoidable gap in our knowledge of the event, he was comfortable saying that the accused was likely psychotic at the time and provided a reasonable match with the legal criteria of Section 16. An odd form of disagreement: Dr. Q. seemed to think my opinion was more valid than I did.

"To put it another way," he wrote, "I would say that the available information would make it nearly impossible to offer an opinion that Mr. Marks was not psychotic at the time of the killing, that he could appreciate the nature and quality of his actions, and that he did know that his actions were wrong." In court, Dr. Q. said that there was more reliable background evidence here than in most of the hundreds or so cases of homicide he had investigated. He also echoed my opinions concerning disposition.

What was anticipated to be a two-week trial ended after three days, with the exceptional circumstance of both sides being more or less in agreement.

I did wonder if Dr. Q. and I, in our enthusiastic support for one another's opinion, had provided an amusing moment for the judge. He had presided at the earlier case, when we had spurned each other's assessment with great passion. He might have thought "if even these two rascals can agree, their opinion must be valid." Dr Q's opinion, even though he was retained by the Crown, was more strongly pro-defence than mine. But I hoped that this demonstrated that most of us are not hired guns, willing to say anything that will please those who pay our fees. I should add that Crown prosecutors are not usually bloody-minded about the heaviest possible conviction; most feel bound and are willing to accept a compelling pro-defence argument and do a fair and just deal with the defence.

The judge ruled Keiran Not Criminally Responsible on account of Mental Disorder. The prosecutor suggested that a disposition hearing be waived, and Keiran was remanded to FPI on an indefinite basis, subject to regular Review Board evaluation. This humane and sensible outcome was, I thought, a good example of the legal system actually allowing justice to be served. A win-win.

That said, the homicide itself was "a real tragedy all-round," as the prosecutor commented afterwards. Like most of those involving a mentally disordered perpetrator, it was a death that could have been prevented "if only …" The judge remarked that, "neither the accused nor the victim took the matter [of Keiran's delusions] seriously enough to insist on treatment," with this disastrous result.

Keiran himself wholeheartedly believed he was being persecuted, with no notion of being mentally ill. When he first began hearing voices, he had gone to the hospital with that suspicion, but spent only a few days there. He had been diagnosed as having a psychotic episode, and given some antipsychotic medication to take at home. He soon dropped the medication, though, believing he was well, and, because there was no really effective follow-up, he continued down a six-year slope of mental deterioration.

He saw his family doctor, but never told him about his hallucinations and delusions. In recent years, he had gone in occasionally to "just talk" about his and Glen's relationship. He always viewed their relationship as the problem, never considering that he might be experiencing any mental disorder. The physician had recommended couples' counseling and offered to set it up, but Glen had rejected the idea: "Why should I go? You're the crazy one."

Keiran had called 911 twice in the preceding years, but the first time the police had told him to leave the house, and the second time he believed he hadn't been able to get through because of the scrambled telephone system Glen had installed. He figured the police were in cahoots with Glen, anyway, so he never knew where to turn for protection. When friends suggested he see a doctor, he interpreted their solicitousness as concern for his fatigue or his stress from overwork. Either that or they were bound in with the conspiracy somehow. So he kept getting more and more psychotic.

Recently, Glen's friends had talked to him about Keiran's "paranoia or whatever," even warned him that they would lose all their B&B business if Keiran kept up his talk of Glen trying to kill him and being electrocuted, and his jealously kicking guests out of the house. Glen kept saying he had to make it work; he couldn't just turn Keiran out. At the end of the busy season, things would calm down and they'd go off to Hawaii. But two days before the murder, Glen had called Keiran's brother back east, hoping his family would make him seek treatment; he couldn't do it himself.

One of Glen's children had warned his father that it was unwise to be living with Keiran unless he was in treatment. "Dad agreed, but he didn't know what to do or was incapable of acting," the son said. "He was concerned for Keiran's welfare. He just wasn't going to show him the door."

Glen's family's reaction to the verdict was insightful and compassionate. They issued a statement expressing appreciation that the evidence had gone uncontested in court, "confirming our perception that Keiran suffers from a mental illness," and they thanked the press for its calm reporting.

Like everyone else involved, the family wondered why more couldn't have been done to prevent the tragedy. "But," they continued, reflecting a kind of universal regret in such calamities, "each of us possessed only fragments of the unfolding story ...."

The death was not prevented. But when the whole story did come together and was presented to the court — in its entirety, in a non-adversarial atmosphere — it came to the most just legal and medical ending possible.

Chapter Eight

Can I Take You for a Ride?

As evenings go, this one was nasty, brutish and prolonged.

Three low-level drug dealers bought, sold and consumed a large amount of cocaine among themselves, then had a disagreement about who owed money to whom. One shot the other dead. The sum in dispute was $90.

Dealers Bobbi and Carl, and Carl's wife, Corinne, had spent most of the day doing magic mushrooms and cocaine, and drinking vodka. Bobbi had made a few trips to the street to sell small amounts of cocaine. By evening she was drunk enough to be creating a bit of a disturbance. She had repeatedly been calling one of her clients, Anson Reese and eventually got him to agree to buy an 8-ball (one-eighth of an ounce, or 3.5 grams) of cocaine, which she would "middleman"- that is, buy from her supplier, then deliver and re-sell to him. She proposed to Carl that he front the cash needed for the 8-ball, in exchange for his money back plus a cut of the cocaine when she delivered it. Carl agreed and they took a cab to Bobbi's supplier, scored the drug and carried on to Anson's house.

Anson had been reluctant to do a middleman number with Bobbi. He usually did his own deals, trading marijuana he grew himself for cocaine, and often buying extra coke in order to middleman to "friends." He had purchased an 8-ball earlier that day from his regular supplier, exchanging it for a $500 pistol, which was more than the value of the cocaine, thereby also securing some advance credit on his next purchase. He had freebased about half a gram when a couple of friends dropped in unannounced. He shared some of his cocaine with them, and after they left, he carried on until the 8-ball was gone. Soon after, Bobbi called.

She had been persistent, telephoning several times over an hour, until finally he agreed to buy, although he was suspicious that what she really wanted was part of the cocaine for herself. When she arrived with someone else in tow, spilled some of the coke on the floor, and the deal seemed to be that all three of them share the 8-ball while he paid for it, Anson balked. But he continued to let them think he was going to buy, and cooked up about a gram, saying they would go to his bank machine when they'd had a few tokes. In the background, Carl made Bobbi a sexual offer she apparently could refuse. The first batch gone, Carl cooked up some more and again they shared, although Anson claimed Carl used most of it.

After about three grams, Anson offered Carl $60, which he figured covered the mere "six good hoots" he had smoked. Carl claimed they had agreed on $170. Anson retorted with a few choice words, then ordered Carl out of the house, saying he might have to call the police. They were both angry and the rocks were gone.

Still, all three of them got into Anson's car and drove Carl home.

Anson and Bobbi then stopped at Anson's bank machine, picked up a second 8-ball, took it back to Anson's house and consumed it. This time Anson got most of the cocaine; he felt good and his usual paranoia left. Carl and Corinne telephoned several times. Carl felt he had been ripped off, Corinne reported on the last call, and had left to come over and get his money.

Carl arrived back at Anson's "very pissed off and agitated." He demanded that Anson give him $90 immediately or else Anson would owe him $500 at the end of the month. Bobbi was drifting in and out of the kitchen, looking for something to eat. Anson told her that he "wanted to beat the fuck out of Carl," and that he wanted to call the police because Carl was threatening him. Bobbi dissuaded him, pointing out that there was a considerable amount of drugs in the house, including his marijuana grow operation. Anson assured Carl that he would call another dealer and get the money he owed him, and got up and went into the bedroom.

There he pulled a handgun out of a cupboard and told Bobbi: "I'm going to fucking kill him." Bobbi told him to "Just be mellow," and went back into the kitchen.

Anson removed the safety lock on the gun, walked up behind Carl, who was sitting smoking on the couch, and fired one fatal shot dead-center into the back of his head. The hollow-point bullet spread widely after entry, causing an exit wound that amounted to a large portion of Carl's face.

Anson then removed the burning cigarette from Carl's hand, extinguished it safely in an ashtray, found a plastic bag, put the gun and the ammunition box in it and took it next door to hide. Gordon Black, his neighbour, was sitting in the bath when he heard his young daughter tell someone at the front door to come back in ten minutes. But it was Anson, and he entered anyway, saying, "It's okay, I'm just your neighbour."

"What's up?" Gordon called out.

"I just killed someone in my house," Anson said, "He was threatening to kill me, so I popped him." Gordon saw Anson step into his back storage room, then leave again by the front door. Gordon's children said the man had been carrying a purple bag when he came in, and told them it was carrots. They thought he must have left the carrots in there.

After shooting Carl, Anson had told Bobbi, "I'm going to go away for a long time for this. I'm sorry." Bobbi, terrified, had wailed, "Please don't kill me." On his way out the door, Anson responded, "No, no. I'll drive you home. Please don't rat me out." Bobbi ran into the back yard, where she called 911 from her cellphone. The police arrived and arrested Anson as he emerged from his neighbour's house.

As with most homicide cases I am involved in, no one disputed who did what to whom; the key was to determine the perpetrator's mental state when the killing occurred. When Anson Reese pleaded not guilty, his lawyer offered the jury a choice of defenses: cocaine psychosis (which could produce either a complete acquittal or a verdict of manslaughter, depending on the jury's opinion of how unaware of his acts he had been) or cocaine-aggravated schizophrenia (which could result in a NCRMD verdict). Third and fourth options, of course, would be guilty of first- or second-degree murder.

With alcohol, the more you drink, the more you need to drink each time in order to get drunk. To a certain point, experienced drinkers develop an increased ability to "hold their liquor." With cocaine, the opposite is sometimes true: sensitivity to the drug often increases with frequent use. Chronic cocaine use sometimes induces a temporary schizophrenic-like paranoid state, which can be weakly present even when the addict is not under the influence of the drug. When the person does consume more cocaine, the drug intensifies the paranoid psychosis. This is cocaine psychosis, a deliberately induced mental state produced by a combination of both chronic and acute cocaine use.

Cocaine-aggravated schizophrenia, on the other hand, results when a person who already has schizophrenia uses cocaine. The cocaine intensifies the schizophrenia, pouring fuel on the fire, by aggravating the brain chemical imbalances that are a key feature of schizophrenia.

The degree to which an individual is affected in either of these two situations varies considerably. It depends on how much cocaine the person uses, has used and can personally tolerate; if schizophrenic, it depends whether he or she is very mildly schizophrenic or quite disabled by the disorder, and so on. Counsel for Anson's defence was hoping that a jury would conclude that he was a victim of one of these states, and let him off lightly.

I was asked by the Crown prosecutor to interview Anson Reese, prepare a report and be ready to testify as an expert witness at his trial for Carl's murder. This meant that the accused and his lawyer had consented to my interviewing him and that Anson understood my role, accepted the complete non-confidentiality of the interviews, and knew that he had the right to refuse to answer any questions, or to pause to confer with his counsel, or even to terminate the interviews at any time. I am legally obliged to be sure the accused understands all this, and if I have any doubt that the person I am interviewing is not clear on her or his decision to be interviewed, I will abort the interview.

Had I been called upon by the defence lawyer, almost the opposite would apply. In that case, because I would be acting as an agent of the defence lawyer, I would advise the accused that there is absolute confidentiality in what he or she tells me. Whatever is said will remain between me, the defense lawyer and the defendant, covered by solicitor-client privilege, unless the accused agrees to its use in court.

While most interviews take on a life of their own — and this one certainly did — there are some consistencies in format and style. The most common format I use is to do the interview in at least two installments. The first session goes over most of the necessary material in a friendly, non-confrontational way. I'll start by confirming the accused's personal and psychiatric history, and anything else that forms a background to the offence. Easing into the crime story helps me bring out the maximum amount of information spontaneously, allows me to build rapport in a non-threatening manner, and to establish a sort of baseline for the person's style of communication, "touchiness," level of intelligence, and so on.

In the second phase of this first interview, I'll start asking about the crime, taking great care not to use leading or suggestive questions in most cases, but general, open ones, with such follow-ups as, "And what happened next?" Another thing that requires strict attention is advising the accused to distinguish, carefully, between his own clear memories and inferences he might have made about what had happened or what must have happened, and information he had picked up from other sources (friends, witnesses and so on). As time passes, memories can become contaminated. It was now ten months since Carl's death, so I reminded Anson of all these things, not only at the start of each interview session, but several times during each session.

Between interviews, I usually go over the first conversation and compare it with other documents — the accused's previous statements, police reports, medical history, witness statements — looking for discrepancies and connections. I develop a list of more pointed questions.

The second interview is more like a cross-examination, as I probe for important details and explore discrepancies in the defendant's account of the offence or past history. Sometimes I will be very aggressive if I think there is a chance of getting more information, or if I have become reasonably convinced that the person is intentionally withholding or distorting information. I might use a technique familiar to anyone who remembers the 70s television detective, Columbo: I'll scratch my head and say, "I'm really puzzled by all the information I have, because you've told me one thing, the police report tells me another thing, and witness statements tell me yet another. Can you sort it out for me?"

If I sense that the accused is taking some ghoulish delight in the details of the killing, I might implicitly convey fascination for what I am being told: "Wow, really, you did that?" If I sense that the person is resisting telling the truth because he or she is ashamed of their act, I will move in closer, speak in lower tones, anything to indicate a non-judgmental empathy that will make it more comfortable for them to be frank. If I am with a hard-boiled, tough character, I might jump straight to the point, "So what happened, how did you waste this guy?"

Or I might use shock value to get past a block — showing the accused some grisly photos of the crime or autopsy, or downright accusing the person of lying to provoke a reaction. If the accused has some memory of the killing and is claiming a mental disorder, or claiming to have been in some way "out of it" because of alcohol or drugs, I might even suggest highly improbable symptoms to see if they agree.

Smoking out faking is extremely difficult, even for forensic psychiatrists. Some tools and techniques work better than others. One study says that it is easier to detect lying by listening, rather than looking. Hearing only the audio portion of a video-taped interview with a dissembler is apparently better, because people are more inclined to use visual rather than verbal devices to mislead others. Reading a transcript of the same interview provides the second-most-accurate lie detection. Watching the full videotape comes in third. Sometimes, when I suspect

I am listening to someone lie, I stop looking and fix my eyes on my notepad in order to reduce their ability to mislead me with body language and facial expression. Typically, though, instructions to the jury concerning assessment of witness credibility only suggest taking into account the witness's demeanour and actions.

This may sound as if I watch too much television but, with experience, I've learned that interviewing homicide perpetrators is often manipulative, although not outright dishonest. Training and time have made my use of some techniques instinctive, rather than self-consciously deliberate, but a bit of acting ability is a must, if only to keep my own feelings in check. I can usually remain unemotional when conducting an interview, concentrating on treating it as an intellectual chess game. If I am upset about a case, I work hard to deal with that before and after the interview, so I can remain clear-headed during it. The bumps and turns of some interviews can even be funny in retrospect. During the interview, however, it's harder to find the humour, because you're always aware that someone has died.

The initial interview with Anson Reese unearthed no new truths. He remembered little about his childhood, he said, but he graduated from high school, and had started in on booze and marijuana at age 13, cocaine at 15. He became an alcoholic, but four years ago quit cold turkey. He used about a gram of coke a day, he stated, and he smoked about a quarter of the marijuana he grew. He supplemented with heroin. He used a tranquilizer to sleep, and had dabbled in speed, crystal meth and a few other drugs.

Now in his mid-30s, he had been living in the same Vancouver house he grew up in, but said he only had two friends. Those two were interviewed by the forensic psychiatrist for the defense and each confirmed that Reese had no other friends; people were turned off by "his weirdness." He never really had a girlfriend.

After high school, he alternated between casual, low-level jobs and social assistance. His father, with whom he had issues, had died and his mother lived in a care facility. Each month he would cash her $2,000 pension cheque, give $700 to the facility, and live on the rest plus his drug transactions. He told me he spent $500 to $800 a month buying drugs for himself, but from what he said at other times, that must have been a gross underestimate. For a long time, it seems, all his activities had simply revolved around doing drugs.

Anson had no formal psychiatric history before being arrested. He avoided doctors in general, he said. Mel, the older of his two friends ("I was like a father figure to him"), felt that Anson was schizophrenic. Mel thought he recognized in Anson the same symptoms displayed by his schizophrenic wife. Anson wouldn't discuss hearing any voices, although Mel had seen him talking — even shouting — to himself. Mel described a few instances of Anson's paranoia, and said a couple of times that he "didn't know if it was the drugs or schizophrenia" with Anson. Mel made a point of avoiding anyone who used drugs or alcohol, so their contact had been irregular.

His other friend, Alan, described many episodes of Anson hearing voices, always when he was intoxicated on alcohol or drugs. Once he'd had a few beers, there might be minor violence. He'd shouted some threats and grabbed a few people when drinking, but no real fight came of it. Often, both Mel and Alan volunteered, Anson wouldn't remember the morning after what he'd said or done the night before.

Anson agreed with everything that had been said about him, and our interview proceeded beyond history and into the evening of the homicide. He had started doing cocaine about 4 p.m. When he had worked his way through an 8-ball, he said, he'd become "paranoid as usual," covering the windows with towels and blankets and keeping the lights low so it would look like no one was home. When he was "paranoid" he started hearing voices and worried that it was people outside trying to look in. Could it be that he was worried about his marijuana plants being discovered? I asked. Didn't you usually cover the windows so the blue grow-lights couldn't be seen? Well, yes. But this particular evening, he heard people out on his driveway and thought they were acquaintances who had come to share his cocaine with him. He wasn't afraid; he just didn't want to share.

After we'd been talking for a while, I began to focus some concern on his credibility. He seldom volunteered information. He agreed with almost everything I said, but if I questioned some answer he had given, he would readily revise his opinion. I decided to suggest some highly improbable psychiatric symptoms to see whether or not he would agree to having experienced them. I was careful to suggest the possibilities in ways that left him free to adopt them or not.

"Sometimes when people hear voices, they hear them reciting children's nursery rhymes. Did you hear that?"

"Yeah, yeah! That's exactly what it was like," Anson answered. I asked him if he recalled which songs he heard. Pause. He wasn't sure, but maybe "Ring Around the Rosie" or something like that.

"People sometimes hear Christmas carols."

"Yeah, that's what it was, Christmas carols."

"Christmas carols."

"But maybe it was just singing, not Christmas carols specifically."

"Just singing?"

"Singing with nursery rhymes. Yup."

"Singing with nursery rhymes, for sure?"

"Singing 'Ring Around the Rosie,' that's it."

By the end of the first 8–ball, he said that the singing had subsided and he had started the deal with Bobbi. He described the sequence of events leading up to the murder essentially as he had told it before, more or less in congruence with Bobbi's statement. When the coke she and Carl brought was gone, he said, he wanted them both out of the house, but Carl refused to leave, and that was when Anson gave him the $60. By the time he and Bobbi returned to the house, it was early morning. His "paranoia" had gone. As they finished this 8-ball, he felt high, he said, and his mind seemed detached from his body, like he was outside his body, watching from up on the ceiling.

"Sometimes when people see themselves from outside, they see themselves not from the ceiling, but from up above the house — above the roof — and can see themselves right through the roof. Did that happen with you?"

"Yes, that's what it was like, I was seeing right through the roof, but not seeing the roof or the yard or anything."

"Could you see anything in the attic?"

"No. I could just see that the roof was transparent and I could see through it. It was like my soul had left my body."

I asked if he was hearing any voices or feeling paranoid, and he said that there were no voices, but he was a bit paranoid that his neighbour would find out he had been doing cocaine, and he didn't want Gordon Black to think badly of him. He certainly wasn't afraid of Bobbi. He really had no fears at all. I asked more about seeing himself from above the roof.

"Some people in this position see themselves in black-and-white, rather than in colour" I knew this was not true, but: "Oh, yes," Anson replied, "It was just black and white for me, too."

"Sometimes the image of themselves rotates, turns around ..."

"Oh, definitely."

I continued offering ideas that he could reject or accept, about the turning direction, heights of "flight," and relative speeds.

Within a relatively short time, he said he'd been looking down on his body, seeing it (in black and white) right through a roof and ceiling, swooping up and down from eight to twelve feet above it, while his lower self was slowly spinning beneath him — spinning clockwise, faster as he swooped down, slowing as he rose back up.

117

No voices, though. And when Carl arrived, the ride came to a halt.

Carl started threatening him right away, Anson claimed — demanding his money now or $500 at the end of the month, threatening to kill Anson at the end of the month, or to kill Anson's dog. That last one really got to him, Anson said.

While I was wondering, without saying anything, why Bobbi had only reported the "$90 now or $500 later" threat, Anson made a point of telling me that Bobbi would not have heard everything that Carl said.

As Carl was threatening him, Anson said that he began to hear an unknown male voice coming from inside his own head, saying, "This man is going to kill you." It was like a transmitter in his ear, or maybe like between stations on a radio. Could it have had a metallic robot or computer-generated-type voice? Yes, yes. He adopted that "memory" as enthusiastically as the rest. "He's going to kill you, so you'd better kill him first," the voice added.

I then asked if he might additionally have heard quieter or childrens' voices chanting, "That's right, that's right" and "Better do it now, better do it now." Anson greeted this bolder trial of his memory with another positive confirmation. Had the voices said anything about how to kill him? "Shoot him in the head, shoot him in the head," they said. Any directional advice? "Shoot him from behind." We then went through it again, and when I asked him to clarify the nature of the sound of the voices, he affirmed that the main voice had a computer- or robot-like timbre and that the background voices were those of children.

How long had Carl gone on threatening him? About fifteen minutes. And could you see yourself from above during this time, I asked? Yes. When people see themselves from above, I told Anson, if someone else is in the room, their point of observation will sometimes be underneath the ceiling, as opposed to above the roof when they are alone. Yes, when Carl was there, Anson too was just below the ceiling. Are you sure? Yes.

By then, Anson said, Carl was "really freaked out. I figured he's there to kill me."

"Were you afraid he was going to kill you right then?"

"No. I wasn't afraid of being killed then. I figured he would turn up some time before the end of the month and get me."

"So you didn't fear for your life right then?"

"No. I wasn't afraid. But I was sure he would kill me some other day. Then he went over the line when he threatened to kill my dog. That was when I made the decision to shoot him."

Anson said that he went into the bedroom where he kept the hand-gun, fully loaded and ready to protect his marijuana operation.

I inquired if he was still hearing voices or seeing himself from above when he was in the bedroom, and Anson answered that he had heard the voices, but only saw himself from overhead when he was in the living room. Then he described walking back into the living room and shooting Carl in the back of the head.

I suggested that when people shoot, they sometimes see an image of a target directing them, and he agreed that he had seen a target. What shape was it: concentric rings or a cross? He said it was a cross. I sketched two crosses, one like the letter x, the other like a plus sign. He chose the latter. Thick or thin lines? Thin. Colour? Reddish orange. Was the colour uniform? It was red in the centre and more orange towards the ends of the arms. Was the cross steady, or did it pulsate? It pulsated back and forth between Carl's head and the gun, about two feet, and, he volunteered, suddenly, that the cross flashed on and off until he had the gun perfectly aimed, at which point the cross would glow steadily and he would know when to pull the trigger. Had this ever happened before? No, but then he had never shot a gun before when on cocaine. The target would have been there because of the cocaine. It reminded him of a video game target he had seen, he added.

I then asked why he had taken the gun to his neighbour's house, and he stated that he didn't want the police to find it, but really, he should have just driven away. He put the gun and ammunition in a bag, so no one could see it — especially his neighbor's little kids; he didn't want them to panic. He told me about the other precautions he had taken: removing the cigarette from Carl's hand so the house wouldn't catch on fire; putting the spent shell and the five live shells in his pocket, then dropping them into an old boat alongside the house because they would be incriminating if he were caught with them; telling the police that there had been other people in the house when Carl was shot, to throw the cops off his trail and make them think there were other suspects.

Was he still hearing his voices at that point? No, the loud bang of the gun had stopped them.

Had he ever heard of cocaine psychosis? Yes, he had learned a bit about it, from his fellow inmates in jail. They told him that it was like having schizophrenia, having the same symptoms — "they hear voices and have hallucinations." His friend Mel had a wife who had schizophrenia.

"I'm probably a schizo myself," he offered. "I have lots of weird hallucinations, even when I'm not on drugs."

119

He volunteered that he had an occasional "radio transmitter voice" in his head. Did he think there was a possibility that a transmitter had been inserted in his head? "Yeah, well, it could have happened at the dentist or something." Had he had it checked out by a doctor — x-rayed or anything? No, he never went to doctors.

It was a male voice, like his father's. Sometimes when he was stressed out, it said, "You're going to be all right." Mostly it told him to say bad things, like the time he called a girl a "skank." He usually had control over whether or not to obey the voices. There had been many times he hadn't called women the bad names the voices commanded. And when it was important, he didn't obey. Like the time he was standing on a balcony holding someone's baby. He heard a voice telling him to throw the baby over the rail, but he hadn't done it.

I asked Anson if he had ever been interviewed by a psychiatrist before, and he confirmed that he had, by the doctor who had been called by the defence. I inquired if he had told Dr. Q. the same things he had told me, and he said, "Pretty much, yes." I went through the list of hallucinations, the images and patterns, including the target image. For each one, he replied that no, he had not told the other psychiatrist about them: "I didn't think they were important."

In our third session, I spent some time going over everything we had talked about and reviewing Anson's previous statements, questioning discrepancies.

"In your first interview with the police, you said you didn't recall anything about the homicide. Do you remember saying that?"

"Yes."

"Why did you say it?"

"I didn't want to incriminate myself."

"When did you cock the gun?"

"As I was walking down the hall towards Carl."

"Here, in your second statement to the police, you say you had 'blanked out or was in a fog' concerning the homicide."

"I didn't want to incriminate myself."

During the interviews, Anson spoke in a logical, goal-oriented manner, and evinced no distortions, logical or psychotic, in his thought patterns. He did not appear to be suffering any psychotic symptoms, including delusions or hallucinations. He seemed of low-average intelligence. His emotional state was even and stable. Conceivably, this mental state was the result of antipsychotic drugs he had been given in custody. He showed hardly any emotion, even when we were discussing difficult or dramatic material, such as the blowing apart of Carl's head.

By this point, I had formed a clear opinion that Anson had been fabricating information about his mental state, particularly in relation to the killing. To be fair to him — and to give him the opportunity to correct himself — I confronted him.

"Mr. Reese, I believe that you've told me some things that weren't true. Can you think of anything you've said in our interviews that you would like to change?"

"No." A flush was starting in his cheeks. It looked like some emotion was at last going to surface.

"When I asked you about hearing nursery rhymes, and you said you heard them, had you actually heard 'Ring Around the Rosie'?"

"Yes!"

We went through the different "improbables": the video-game target, the black-and-white out-of-body experience, above the roof or below the ceiling. Red-faced and anxious, Anson angrily denied fabricating any symptoms or in any other way providing dishonest information.

"When we talked about your seeing yourself from above, swooping up and down while your body was spinning beneath you, did that actually happen, or did you agree to it because it was what you thought I expected to hear?"

"You asked me tricky questions! I didn't make up nothing!"

I agreed that I had posed tricky questions, and said so. I had asked certain questions for the sole purpose of hearing whether or not his answer would be truthful. But part of my evaluation task was to assess truthfulness, I explained. The interview ended shortly afterwards, with Anson adamantly denying that he had fabricated any information.

In court, I gave my opinion that Anson Reese had extensively fabricated psychiatric symptoms, both in relation to the killing and in his claimed past history of cocaine psychosis and schizophrenia.

I described my methodology of making improbable suggestions in a deliberately neutral fashion, rather than trying to promote them. Had he adopted just a few of these symptoms, it could have been put down to confusion or difficulty in remembering. But he had not only adopted many of them, but had elaborated enthusiastically. He had chosen the symptoms and provided details, rather than parroting my words.

He had also made some claims that didn't fit with "textbook" cocaine psychosis, including his statement that his psychosis terminated the instant he fired the gun, about half an hour after his last hit of coke; cocaine psychosis tends to persist at least several hours, and often several days, after the last ingestion of cocaine.

Also, none of the behaviour observed by Bobbi, neighbour Gordon or the police was specifically indicative of a continuing cocaine psychosis. He had been flushed and agitated, but those symptoms were not helpful in discriminating among cocaine psychosis, schizophrenia or a simple state of anger and emotional arousal. His psychiatric records since the killing suggested the possibility of symptom fabrication, although this was not conclusively settled. If he had suffered from any mental illness before the killing, it had not been severe enough to bring him to medical or police attention.

Combining these observations with Anson's admission that the notion of cocaine psychosis was suggested to him by others and he then set out to learn about it, it seemed unlikely to me that his statements concerning his mental state at the time of the killing could be honest, accurate or reliable, but must be opportunistic fabrications calculated to absolve him of guilt in a courtroom.

If he had lied about his mental state, could we believe anything he had to say about the killing? Yes. He gave a general account of the events that was consistent with other reports, most particularly with that of the witness, Bobbi, whose statements had been recorded without the possibility of corroboration with Anson. He did not claim any amnesia (after admitting he had twice lied to police about it). This suggested that, despite being under the influence of a significant amount of cocaine, his mental state was clear enough that he was aware of events as they were occurring, and his mind was functioning well enough to record them as reasonably accurate memories. His descriptions of the amount and timing of cocaine consumption were consistent with other information.

He was clear in his decision to kill Carl, and in the reason for it: not because he felt in immediate danger, but as a preemptive strike to avoid debt collection or possibly violence at a later date. Although he said that voices told him to do it, this claim is inextricably bound in with the fabricated symptoms and so may be unreliable; there is no certain way of resolving this contradiction.

He made a covering remark (he was going to call someone to get the money Carl wanted) when he went into the bedroom to get the gun. He told Bobbi what he was going to do. He operated the gun knowledgeably, carrying off an execution-style killing that indicated he was neither under immediate threat nor acting in self-defence. After the shooting, he admitted to Bobbi he had done a wrong and illegal thing — "I'm going to go away for a long time for this. I'm sorry." Then he proceeded to carry out several activities designed to cover his tracks. He hid the gun and ammunition in a bag, he got it out of his house, he lied to his neighbour about stashing it (although he told Gordon that he had killed someone, indicating that he was very much aware of what he had done), he hid the shells, he attempted to mislead the police into thinking there was someone else in the house.

All these activities occured in an organized and thoughtful fashion, consistent with wanting to kill the victim, and then consistent with wanting to avoid the consequences. None of this behaviour suggests disordered thought processes, delusions, hallucinations or any other indication of psychosis, whether substance-induced or the result of mental illness. Appalling judgment? Yes.

I testified that there did not seem to be any credible basis for either the presence of cocaine-induced psychosis at the time of the killing, or for the killing being the product of schizophrenia aggravated by cocaine intake. Instead, it appeared that Anson Reese had a sane motive for killing Carl, based on a disagreement over money and possible threats. His poor judgment and impulsiveness were caused in part by intoxication with cocaine, but there was no credible evidence that his perception of the circumstances and his options were fundamentally distorted by drugs or mental illness. He was aware that he was killing the victim and intended to do so. Even if we were to believe all the symptoms Anson claimed, there is no reason to doubt his ability to appreciate what he was planning to do, the intended effect on the victim and that he knew his behaviour was wrong. In my opinion, Anson's mental state at the time of the murder provided no credible basis for any psychiatric defence based on mental disorder, cocaine intoxication or any combination of those factors.

As expected, I was accused, on the stand, of tricking or entrapping Reese. I agreed, but justified it as an entirely appropriate and ethical tactic under the circumstances. Interviewing murder suspects is no Sunday School exercise. Many of them do their best to mislead and deceive, so you have to apply countermeasures to draw out the truth and catch the fibs. It would be absurdly naïve and unprofessional to take everything an accused person says at face value.

The report of the forensic psychiatrist, my friend Dr. Q., who was called by the defence, contained an interesting sentence. When asked if he could explain a discrepancy between two of Reese's statements, Dr. Q. stated that "when questioned [and unable to recall the incident he is being asked about], he gives an answer that seems like a reasonable one to him."

Then Dr. Q. described me as "mesmerized by Mr. Reese's endorsement of strange and absurd symptoms." Up to a point, he was right — catching a liar red-handed is a very satisfying experience that can easily lead to throwing out the baby with the bathwater — being truly insane

MURDEROUS MINDS ON TRIAL

doesn't make you incapable of lying, and many accused parties with legitimate defences may be tempted to gild the lily. After all, Anson was on trial for a homicide, not for lying to a shrink.

It was indisputable, Dr. Q. said, that Anson had been intoxicated by cocaine and genuinely frightened for his life, which "raises questions about his ability to think clearly, appreciate his situation and make voluntary choices." The pivotal question, Dr. Q. said, was whether or not the accused was also suffering overt psychotic symptoms at the time of the killing, which might make him eligible for a mental disorder acquittal. "If we believe Mr. Reese, he was. If we believe his friends who say he gets paranoid and hears voices when he is intoxicated, it's not a stretch to accept that, under a genuine threat, overt psychosis might emerge. If we believe, based on Dr. Semrau's evidence, that he was faking it, we have no evidence of overt psychosis."

A very black picture had been painted of Carl, the big, bad, biker drug-dealer, so when Anson took the stand, perhaps he elicited some sympathy from the jury, I don't know. He seemed inarticulate and unbelievable to me. But he is small and kind of harmless-looking. I'd seen borderline cases before where appearances tipped the scales — one way or the other. Perhaps that's what happened.

Or perhaps the jury saw me as a predator — "He tricked me. I didn't mean to lie to anyone." Or perhaps they just couldn't make it over the balance-of-probabilities barrier to a full conviction. The verdict was Not Criminally Responsible on account of Mental Disorder.

If Anson Reese actually had mild schizophrenia, and if the doctors who are now treating him diagnose him as such, he will receive the proper medication for it, which is good. But I suspect that he will carry on fabricating new symptoms until he either finds himself subjected to a full complement of medications with their often-distressing side effects, or he is disbelieved and eventually discharged.

II

The Intoxication Defence

Whose is the misery? whose the remorse?
Whose are the quarrels and the anxiety?
Who gets the bruises without knowing why?
Whose eyes are bloodshot?
Those who linger late over their wine,
those who are always trying some new spiced liquor.
Do not gulp down the wine, the strong red wine,
when the droplets form on the side of the cup;
in the end it will bite like a snake
and sting like a cobra.
Then your eyes see strange sights,
your wits and your speech are confused;
you become like a man tossing out at sea,
like one who clings to the top of the rigging;
you say, 'If it lays me flat, what do I care?
If it brings me to the ground, what of it?
As soon as I wake up,
I shall turn to it again.'

— Proverbs, Chapter 23, *New English Bible*

CHAPTER NINE

POOR CHOICE OF MOVIES

He'd pick up a goddam video, that's what he would do. Whenever things got too tense between him and Teena, they'd hang out in front of the tube, and over the course of a movie and a couple of six-packs, the mood would ease up.

To what? Damned if he knew. One day Teena would tell him she loved him, the next she'd be telling him to fuck off, it was all over. Then he'd hear, from someone, that she'd been downtown looking for him, worried he was in some kind of drug or booze trouble — so he'd go hunting for her. But when Raymond caught up to her at home, she'd refuse to let him in, saying she didn't want him around the house when her kids were there, he was too angry all the time, they'd had enough of that.

"Dangerous" and "unhealthy," that's how she had described their relationship to the couple's counsellor a few days ago, when, right there in the office, she'd told Raymond she was breaking up with him, again. Hah! He knew that they'd go on like this forever. Sure enough, on about the twelfth phone call today, she had agreed he could come over. So, he got a video, picked up a case of beer, then rolled into a convenience store to call a cab to take him to Teena's.

"What the fuck are *you* lookin' at?" An uptight grocery clerk had been watching Raymond use the pay phone and then jitter around the shelves searching for something edible. Confident the old man was more frightened than suspicious, Raymond slid a few candy bars into his pocket and defiantly tossed a buck for the jelly roll onto the counter, looking straight at the clerk, ready to pop him one if he objected. He didn't.

Outside, waiting for the taxi, pacing, his thoughts were of Teena. She was still around after countless fights, even after the assault conviction that landed him back in the pen. Hell, he hadn't even remembered hitting her that time, he was so drunk. Teena always came around, let him back in. His other girlfriends had never lasted long before they took off or turned into bitches and had to be straightened out. His own mother had only stuck it out with him nine months. From then on, his life had been all shit and abuse.

Teena had had a tough life, too, been knocked around. Like him, she was in AA. No big drugs or hard time, though. And she had none of the anger that kept him charged up like a relentless bad trip. Whenever he got hauled into court, he admitted to the lawyer or shrink or whoever they got to grill him that he knew he had to deal with his rage. They always reacted with interest; you had to give them something. In between times, he didn't do a whole lot of thinking about it.

Once, they put him on a prescription drug of some kind, but when it ran out, he went back to booze, coke, whatever he could get. It was easy enough to buy the stuff; he could make fast cash doing B&Es or selling coke — much more money than at the legitimate jobs he'd had washing dishes. He had been doing drugs, alcohol, assault, theft, fraud, jail and, occasionally, dishes since he first ran away from home at 14.

The taxi was hot and airless, and it took Raymond back to summer days when he was a kid, all heat and mosquitoes and endless battles with his foster family. He remembered shouting and beatings and accusations. Trouble in school, until he left after ninth grade. Trouble out of school: detention homes, then graduation to the penitentiary. Maybe the counsellor who "supported" Teena needed to hear about his abusive childhood. He'd show them whose fault it was that his anger ran to violence. He cracked open a beer, and with a glare stopped the cab driver's incipient protest.

His friend Karen understood about abuse. He'd met her at the AA meeting where she had told her story: abused by alcoholic parents, then by two husbands, having her brother murdered, having a bad, bad time giving up drinking, but that very day being five years sober. Some button in him got pushed, and he had cried like a baby at the meeting, then gone up and introduced himself, drawn to Karen as if to a sister.

He had searched her out the night he'd gone ballistic six months ago, after shooting up cocaine on the heels of a lot of booze. He made her promise to stay with him while he was bad, and she did, although he moved so fast she sometimes had to run to keep up. He imagined that people were threatening him as they drove by, so he had hurled threats right back. He boasted loudly that he could get access to guns and knives and do in anyone he wanted, but he remembered feeling frightened at the same time. Karen tried to tell him that no one was threatening him. She urged him off the street into a coffee shop to settle down.

Karen and Teena shared the same AA sponsor, and he'd insisted that Karen call Teena to "see if she was okay," and finally she did. He didn't tell Karen that Teena had broken up with him earlier that day; he just wanted to make sure she wasn't with some jerk.

Karen never told Raymond, but Teena had told Karen that she was scared of him — afraid to keep seeing him and afraid to break up with him. Teena knew that Raymond had told one of his buddies that he would kill her if she dumped him.

When Karen returned to their table from the telephone, she simply reported that Teena was all right — but he kept raving. When Karen said, "You can't go over there now," that only brought on more fury and frustration. When two outreach workers pretending to be friends of Karen's pulled up chairs and mildly asked Raymond a few questions, he had threatened to kill everyone in the coffee shop.

Eventually Al, his own AA sponsor, had turned up. Raymond had sat with Al and Karen and slowly wound down.

He arrived at Teena's place untroubled, and they settled into the pre-dictable routine. The video proved to be mutually distracting. Some shots of rum combined with the beer made Raymond feel relatively laid-back.

But one of the female characters in the film was portrayed as sorrowful, and the turning point of the evening came when, an hour into the story, she revealed a history of sexual abuse.

"Quit your whining! You're just a fucking sexual anorexic," Raymond sneered at the actor on screen, "Isn't she, Teena?"

At his words, alarm bells went off in Teena's mind. She too had been sexually abused as a young woman, and she had made it clear to Raymond that she couldn't stand insensitive remarks about sexual abuse, ever. And now here he was, insinuating ....

"Oh, hell, you're takin' it too personally," he accused, attempting to dismiss her reaction. But an argument ensued. After a long, hostile exchange, Teena stomped out of the room. He heard her pick up the bedroom telephone and call her friend Coral.

"It's just so typical of him," Teena replayed Raymond's comments to Coral, "It really is the last straw." Their conversation led to the inevitable conclusion that Teena should tell Raymond to get lost once and for all.

Raymond later stated that he recalled Teena ending her telephone call and coming back into the living room. After that, he testified, he remembered nothing.

Two telephone conversations partially fill in the gaps. Coral's phone rang again about fifteen minutes after she and Teena had hung up. This time, she heard only voices that Coral recognized as Raymond yelling and Teena sobbing — then the line went dead. Ten minutes later, the local RCMP detachment received a call through 911 from Teena's number, in which a clearly upset Raymond says over and over, "I think I stabbed my girlfriend ... You've got to come and help ... Send the police and an ambulance." With persistence and patience, the operator managed to get him to give his address so she could dispatch assistance.

The police found Teena dead on her back on the kitchen floor, with multiple stab wounds to her chest and abdomen. Several more wounds to her arms and hands were classed as defensive wounds, indicative of efforts to ward off blows from a knife. The table had been slammed into the wall, chairs knocked over, and a bloody knife was on the floor. Also in the kitchen were a dozen empty beer bottles, a half-empty bottle of rum, and Raymond, agitated and unsteady, speech slurred and eyes bloodshot.

Raymond told the police that he didn't know what happened, but his girlfriend was dead. He showed them a superficial laceration on his abdomen and said that Teena had stabbed him. Almost immediately, the officers arrested him and read him his rights. Thereafter, he refused to make a statement and refused to take a breathalyzer test.

Raymond was charged with first-degree murder — he had previously threatened to kill Teena if she ended the relationship, and she had decided to end the relationship minutes before her death. The defence chose trial by jury, and the plea Not Guilty, on the basis that the accused had been too intoxicated at the time to be able to form the intent to kill.

By the time I met Raymond, at the request of the Crown prosecutor, several months after the killing, I had sorted through the background baggage of his criminal record and previous assessments — which meant I had many unanswered questions, some contradictory reports, and the resume of a sorry life.

As an infant, Raymond had been placed with the Albertson family and had stayed with them until he was 14. In various reports, he had described each of his foster parents as "alcoholic psychopaths" and claimed a long history of physical and emotional abuse by both. When he was 7 or 8 years old, he told one psychiatrist, he was beaten so badly by his father that he suffered "dozens of fractures." In a subsequent session with a different psychiatrist, he made no mention of those beatings, but said that when he was 5, he had been tied up by his mother and sexually molested "about twenty times."

Interviewed by a psychiatrist for one of these assessments, Mr. and Mrs. Albertson were described as "a very caring couple who feel a great deal of guilt for Raymond's present troubles, and for him having gone astray while under their care."

Raymond and the family had long been estranged. They accepted his infrequent collect telephone calls, but would not see him again until after he had received the psychiatric help they believed he badly needed. Their natural children described the parents as being afraid of Raymond now. To the Albertsons, Raymond was a very aggressive, resentful, manipulative person, continually lying and thieving.

"He would promise the world, but could never refrain from stealing," they said. "He absolutely refused to accept any blame for his actions." The Albertsons told how they, school officials and social workers had all worked over the years to try to elicit positive changes, but by the time Raymond left home and school, his behaviour was totally uncontrollable.

Alcohol and drugs were what did take control, and he parlayed his inauspicious beginnings into a career of crime, substance abuse, violence and despondence. By the age of 21, Raymond had racked up thirty convictions — mostly robberies to finance his drug habit — and was starting a five-year penitentiary sentence for four counts of armed robbery and possession of a concealed weapon. By 32, he had been gainfully employed for less than two years in his adult life. The remainder of the time he had spent either in custody or working his way there.

In the reports from medical people, social workers and corrections officers, Raymond was consistently described as insincere and uncaring. He always confessed that he needed help keeping his temper under control, and giving up substance abuse. Despite that, he either wouldn't commit to participation in any treatment program, or he attended but made no effort and hence no significant progress.

The counsellor who had been seeing Teena and Raymond noted that while she had become more assertive, he had paid scant attention, hadn't seemed to change. Always in good physical health (addictions excepted), he was reported to suffer from no thought disorder, and his intelligence tested about "average."

Alcohol was a perpetual theme. Raymond admitted to being violent when under the influence, and, chillingly, ten years before this charge, told a psychiatrist that "if I drink too much I might kill somebody."

At the time of his arrest, he had been on probation. As a condition of his probation he had been forbidden to consume alcohol. There was also a restraining order in effect against his contacting Teena.

All the reports described a profoundly dysfunctional relationship between Raymond and Teena, punctuated by break-ups and re-starts, despite Teena's evident appreciation that the situation was toxic for her. The break-ups had always been instigated by Teena, who appeared to be growing more assertive in her attempts to terminate the relationship. I wondered if Raymond had recognized this and felt threatened.

All the physicians who had assessed Raymond had reached negative conclusions, ranging from "antisocial personality disorder" in his younger days to "undoubtedly psychopathic."

My job, however, was to provide an opinion on his mental state at the time of the murder. His history, or as much of it as I had been permitted to know, offered a source for some questions, to help determine if his actions that night fitted any consistent pattern of behaviour. Raymond claimed that he was acting in a dreamlike state — that is, not responsible for his actions and certainly too drunk to be capable of deliberately killing someone. My purpose was to critically evaluate his claims in light of his personality and history, keeping in mind his strong motivation to pull the wool over my eyes.

The sullen young man entering the interview room appeared not to notice my absurd, spontaneous greeting of "Pleased to meet you." He just accepted a handshake, sat down and waited, expressionless, for me to begin.

It was a long, hard slog. I would pose a question, a considerable pause would follow, then a brief, guarded, slow-spoken response and a look that said "So what?" would be followed by another silence until I asked another question.

I asked about his relationship with his foster family.

"It's all in there, isn't it?" he gestured at the file.

"Some of this stuff is pretty old," I ventured. "How do you feel now — about your father, say?" Pause. "Lousy."

"What's he like?" Pause. "Moody." Pause. "Mean," then "A fucking drunk." Stories of beatings and emotional abuse unfolded slowly.

When we've exhausted all he's going to say about that, we move to his mother. "Moody." Pause. "A drunk. Psycho." More references to abuse. What about his three foster siblings? "Fucking racists." (The family was Caucasian; Raymond was not.)

Girlfriends? "About ten, I guess." None of them, except Teena, for as long as a year. What ended the relationships?

"Well, usually I got put in the slammer, eh?" What for?

"B & E. Robberies. Or sometimes I got a little rough with them."

How did he get along with other inmates? Shrug.

"OK. Mighta got hauled up a few times for fighting." With a smirk: "Self-defence."

Raymond was open on the subject of his alcoholism and substance abuse. He had been a "hard drinker" since the age of 18, and at the end of his last prison sentence, three years before, had moved to the big city to "get away from a coke-abusing" lifestyle. When I asked what he had been doing in the city since then, he replied, "Drinking and trying to figure out where to go in life." He averaged, he said, about a dozen beer a day. After about six brew, he "feels real good," but after about ten he says he does not remember events, and over the years he's had many blackouts as well as "the DTs" (severe alcohol withdrawal episodes, which often feature vivid and terrifying hallucinations).

He declared he had never come close to committing suicide. He did portray himself as slightly paranoid. He said that once he believed that a hair stylist had put a curse on him. His account of the evening with Karen matched her own report, both saying he had been both drunk and high on coke at the time.

Otherwise, the varied details and apparent contradictions between his versions of events and those of the professional and other witnesses, probably make it impossible to say what his real, full story is. Raymond struggled with expressing or even recalling his feelings, or what emotional state he had been in at significant times. As a result, it was hard to know how reliable the information he provided was — including what happened during the killing — which put me in a less than ideal position to make this assessment.

However, it was clear that Raymond was drawing from a huge reservoir of anger. During our time together, he was tense, on-edge, taking offence many times. Often I had no idea why some innocuous question had insulted him, and I had to work hard at re-building enough rapport for the interview to continue.

I waded as far as I could into a discussion of his anger, which, he declared with certainty, sprang from his childhood and prison abuse. Sometimes "the anger just builds slowly" until he erupts in some kind of violence. Other times, he'll fly into a sudden rage, finding himself fighting without thinking or intending to. He can sometimes restrain himself, but other times he carries on relentlessly until his opponent is "beaten." But before this killing, he said, he'd "never even put anyone in the hospital," a doubtful claim, given his record of serious assault convictions.

His relationship with Teena had been "OK, the way I saw it.". For four years they had been "breaking up and getting back together"; that was just how they were. He had assumed they would always go on like that. He denied any form of obsession with her, although the word had been used by several other people to describe his feelings, or lack of them, towards Teena. Yeah, she was probably afraid of him. She was always accusing him of threatening her, shouting and waving his fists around. Yeah, he had assaulted her earlier in the year, and yeah, he had threatened her at other times, including once with a hatchet.

Begrudgingly, he acknowledged that any argument between the two ran the risk of ending in violence or threatened violence against Teena. From what he was telling me, *anyone* getting into a confrontational situation with Raymond ran the risk of meeting up with violence. Although surrounded by security people, I felt the possibility myself. He could easily do a lot of damage before guards responded.

After a recent split with Teena, Raymond said he had gone on a binge, but a week or two later, they were back together. He had then resumed his routine of alcohol, marijuana and cocaine abuse. He repeated that he "never" felt threatened that any time could be their last time together, that Teena would actually end it — certainly not on the night of the killing, when he had been sober two weeks. Well, he had "just started drinking again that day," he said.

That evening he thought things had been pretty normal. His mood had been sort of up and down, and he had felt the urge to run off and get drunk and shoot up coke, but that was nothing out of the ordinary. He did not feel angry. He did not feel paranoid. They were just sitting there watching this movie about a sexual anorexic, and he asked her a harmless question about that and she took it too personally. An argument started. They didn't argue about anything else. She never told him to get out, or that she wanted to break up, or anything of that sort. She had the telephone conversation with Coral, came back into the living room, and after that, "it's a blank." He denied experiencing any fear, paranoia, hallucinations or any other unusual mental phenomenon. He remembered nothing after she came back from the call until several hours after he had been taken into custody.

He was almost tearful talking about the killing:

"I couldn't have done such a horrible thing, doc. The fucking booze must have taken over after she just pushed me too far."

I had to agree with past assessments. He fit the mold of a typical psychopath: smooth, selfish and assigning blame everywhere except himself. I believed he was capable of intentionally killing Teena. I did

134

not believe his claim of complete amnesia. But none of this would matter when we got into the courtroom.

Opening day of the trial, about a year after the killing, was as hot and muggy as the murder day itself, and the poorly-ventilated courtroom soon cast the jurors in a haze of drowsiness and irritability. Their six-hour day was punctuated by two short breaks and lunch. Each time they returned to the box, the loosening of ties, mopping of brows and surreptitious attempts at fanning began again.

My scan of the jury suggested a full range of ages among its members and, I guessed with less certainty, probably also of education and income. There were eight women and four men, and, although the accused was a First-Nations Canadian and the community had a relatively high aboriginal population, there was just a single First Nations juror. These gender and ethnic imbalances could not be redressed. Historically, jury assembly by random selection has satisfied everyone as offering the best chance for a fair decision. A sweet-faced old lady can turn out to be vengeful and adamantly biased, the young man who looks like an angry redneck can be the voice of reason that keeps the jury objective and on track. There is some leeway for lawyers to reject prospective jurors — mostly if it appears the candidate has prejudged the case or has a potential cause for bias, such as a significant relationship with the victim or the accused — but straying from the basic principle would stretch out the selection process interminably and lead to regular, perhaps justifiable, accusations of rigging.

The prosecutor, who had called me to testify, was a seasoned veteran of the criminal courts, a successful defence lawyer who had "lost the stomach for getting people off," and idealistically switched sides to work for the Crown. This plainly cost him more than a drop in personal income; government staffing budgets had left him working this trial without any assistance from junior counsel.

His first witnesses were the police. Several officers took us step by step through the murder scene, beginning with Raymond's first contact with 911. The recording of his telephone call crackled out over the courtroom and the jury strained forward to hear. Not all his words were discernible: "I think I stabbed my girlfriend ... You've got to come and help ... Ambulance and police." After she finally extracted his address, the operator kept talking to keep him on the line until the police arrived.

The police had documented Raymond's spontaneous comment as they came in the door about not knowing what happened but his girlfriend is dead, as well as his claim that Teena had stabbed him. By now the prosecutor also had hard evidence to prove that Raymond was lying about his wound — that it had been self-inflicted, a calculated cover-up tactic.

But Raymond's opening remarks to the police would never be heard by the jury. The defence successfully objected to their admissibility as evidence, on the grounds that they were made before the accused had been read his rights, and while "his mental state was too intoxicated and agitated" for him to have been considered to make the statements voluntarily. (The 911 recording was admissible because it was a spontaneous act initiated by Raymond and made not "to a person in authority" — one of those abstruse legalities .) The police *were* permitted to say that immediately after having been read his rights, Raymond refused to speak or to take a breathalyzer test. They were allowed to describe his appearance, including (without comment) the minor abdominal wound, and his "distraught" state.

They described the murder scene: the wreckage of furniture, the beer and rum bottles, the bloody knife lying on the floor beside the victim. Examination of the knife by forensic technicians had disclosed Raymond's fingerprints, but none belonging to Teena. The police then gave their observations of the victim as they found her.

I can understand why there are so many television cop shows, and sometimes I feel like I'm in one of them. Police work and mine share the same inherent drama, but theirs has the added dimension of rules and procedures that make their job seem almost pre-scripted — and easily imitated. In this courtroom, the RCMP officers' polished, careful presentations were made standing stiffly erect in full uniform.

Testifying officers are well-schooled in the potential implications of what they say, and they answer questions in a precise, cautious manner, scrupulously avoiding expressing an opinion or drawing an independent conclusion. (By law, only the jury and judge — and expert witnesses — may make inferences.) The testimony that makes me think of this was, "The victim's chest area was covered with a reddish-brown substance which appeared to be blood."

I hoped that kind of description might at least dilute the more graphic evidence for Teena's family, who were in the gallery. Her parents, a sibling and her 12-year-old son attended almost every day of the trial, showing obvious distress at some of the evidence, but for the most part sitting quietly as though — and they probably were — still in shock. I looked at the boy and wondered where this child would take *his* pain and anger.

The police maintained their form under cross-examination. Defence tactics were to focus on trying to get the police to portray Raymond as being as deranged as possible at the murder scene.

"When you arrive at the victim's apartment, the accused is there, he makes no attempt to leave. But he can't tell you what happened. Would you agree that he was staggering around, more or less 'out of it'?"

"His gait appeared to be unsteady, that is correct."

"Would you agree, Officer, that the accused didn't seem to know what he was doing — that he was confused, disoriented?"

"I'm not a psychiatrist, sir, so I can't tell you what's going on in his mind. I can only tell you that I observed his speech to be slurred.." The defence seemed to make no headway in steering the police witnesses in that direction.

The prosecution called Coral to the stand. Here was someone with an insider's view of the history of the relationship. She could provide evidence that Raymond had often threatened and frequently beaten up Teena, and about the times Teena had told Coral she was fearful of Raymond's violence.

Wrong. The jury would never learn about any of that, either, because of standard legal doctrine: evidence of past violence of the accused directed towards the victim (other than convicted offences) would be prejudicial to the rights of the accused to a fair trial, because the jury might just think, "Oh, there he goes again," without properly considering the unique merits of the current charges. Nor could the Crown put the character of the accused in issue. However, the witness was instructed that she could testify to prior conversations in which Teena had said she was seriously considering dumping Raymond and Coral had encouraged her to be strong and do it.

Under the questioning of the prosecutor, Coral recounted the two telephone calls from Teena the evening of the murder, the second abruptly ended by Teena's scream and the disconnect.

The more senior of the two defence counsel is good with words; Coral was no match for him.

"Now, Ms. Webb, can you truly tell me that it was Teena who brought up the idea of breaking off the relationship with the accused during that conversation? You say you had talked about it before, could it have been you who brought it up this time? Are you saying your memory is perfect on this telephone call?"

"She said she was going to dump him."

"But she had invited him over, they'd just watched a movie, maybe had a few words, nothing serious — could it be she had no intention at all of breaking up until you brought up the idea?"

"She was always trying to break it off."

"But can you tell me under oath that this was her plan and not your idea in this particular conversation?"

"I don't know who brought it up, she said she was going to dump him and I said, 'good.'"

"And how did the conversation end? Did she say, 'OK, I'm going to tell him we're breaking up? What did she say just before she hung up?"

"Hell, I don't remember exactly. Geez."

And so on. Coral grew more defensive, less co-operative, even argumentative, as the cross-examination continued. By the time she stepped down, her credibility as a witness seemed to be seriously undermined.

Raymond's friend Alvin had made a statement to the police describing a conversation in which Raymond had said he would kill Teena if she tried to dump him, so the Crown called him as a witness. He'd obviously regretted his words. Alvin was the sort who was likely to do future prison stints, and that culture is decidedly intolerant of "rats." It took a great deal of effort on the prosecutor's part to drag out even a watered-down version of the conversation for the jury.

"Well, like, he's my buddy, you know. I don't know for sure he went ahead and did it, so maybe he was just kidding, you know?"

Cross-examination by the defence painted this witness as a fairly degenerate character (criminal record, abuser of drugs and alcohol), and the lawyer questioned him adroitly, until everyone in the court had a clear picture of two pals in a pub, engaged in a drunken, rambling conversation of exaggerations and boasting.

The Crown's last witness was the forensic pathologist, who gave a dry, detailed and technical analysis of the number, location and severity of the victim's wounds and the resulting massive haemorrhaging, mainly in her lungs and liver, which caused her death. He noted that the wounds on her hands and forearms were consistent with someone trying to ward off blows. Finally, he described the small wound on Raymond's abdomen and gave his opinion, based on the angle and depth of the wound, that it had been self-inflicted.

I suppose I shouldn't have been surprised when the defence counsel's cross-examination actually played up the suggestion that the wound had been self-inflicted. While it seemed clear to me that this injury had been an attempt by Raymond to mislead the police into believing that Teena had stabbed him, the defence seized upon it as a symptom of his wild grief, of his being deranged.

The Crown didn't call for any psychiatric evidence at this point because, just as an individual is presumed innocent until proven guilty, so in law he or she is presumed sane and to have intended his or her acts until proven otherwise. The Crown cannot tender psychiatric evidence that the accused's character made him capable of committing the offence. Because of his plea, the onus was on Raymond to prove that in his intoxicated mental state he was incapable of forming the intent to kill Teena. The prosecution, therefore, saved its psychiatric witness (me) to rebut the psychiatric evidence the defence would present.

Karen was first witness for the defence. How relevant could her testimony be? I wondered. She couldn't testify about the violence in the relationship nor that Raymond had been under the influence of cocaine, as well as alcohol, during the strange street episode she had described in her statement to police. She was calm, straightforward and believable on the stand, and there was no legitimate reason to challenge her. But what Karen really did was provide the defence with a dramatic, successful opener in the form of a graphic characterization of Raymond as a crazy man, deranged and irrational when intoxicated.

Now Raymond himself was called to the stand. It's always a touchy strategy question for the defence. The accused is not obliged to testify, and there is always a possibility that he will do himself more harm than good up there. But if he doesn't appear, the jury can take that as a sign of guilt. Juries are specifically instructed not to hold it against any accused who fails to testify, but in practice, that must be difficult for jurors. The defence lawyers decided to play their Raymond card in the hope that he could paint an indelible picture of himself as a helpless victim of a wretched childhood — and the murder would be seen as just another instance of the uncontrollable, irrational behaviour to which his background had driven him.

"Mr. Albertson, where were you born?"

"Finster, Manitoba."

"Tell me about your parents."

"Dunno. Got put in a foster home when I was a baby."

"How long were you there?"

"Till I was 14, maybe. Kept running away."

"Why did you run away?"

"Couldn't take it. [Pause.] Beatings. Broke my leg."

"How did you break a leg?"

"Father. Broke it for me. Always on at me."

"Always?"

"Nothing but trouble, hitting on me, sex things, yelling. Even when I was a little kid. I was always crying, hiding."

"Sex things?"

"Both of them at me. [Pause.] I can't talk about it no more."

139

"That's all right, Raymond," solicitously. "Once you got away from your foster home, were things OK?"

"No, man. I was completely screwed up by all that shit. Kept drinking to get it off my mind. Kept doing stupid stuff I didn't mean to."

"Like what?"

"Dunno. Half the time I can't remember. Buddy says to me the next day, 'You know what you did?' Hell, I can't help it somehow. Tried AA. Keep tryin'. Can't stop."

"Have you been able to work at a steady job?"

"Couldn't handle a real job. Concentrating. Always have to get out for a while, go have a drink, relax and forget."

And so on. The defence counsel avoids Raymond's criminal history and avoids any mention of his record of violence. When he asks about Teena and the killing, Raymond startles me by breaking into grief-stricken sobbing. The jury is spellbound. "No, no. I would never, never want to hurt her." He rocks forward in the chair, head down, moans.

He can't recall anything after she came out of the bedroom. He has no memory of getting the wound on his abdomen.

"Could you have put it there yourself, Raymond? Could it be that you were so distraught when you realized that Teena was dead, that you wanted to kill yourself?"

Quiet weeping. The audience respectfully awaited his response. He nodded. "I could've. I was just out of it. I don't remember anything. Teena ...."

I watched him try to maintain the same emotional level under cross-examination. Although he flagged somewhat, I was impressed by his wariness — almost caginess — in dealing with the prosecutor. Raymond had been coached, for he apparently recognized the prosecutor's strategy (a common one) of trying to irritate him in the hope that he would flare up and make it easy for the jury to imagine him lashing out and killing someone out of simple anger. Raymond rose only slightly to the bait. The prosecutor asked if he had ever, as his buddy had disclosed in his sworn statement, said he would kill Teena if she tried to break up with him. Raymond waxed indignant. He didn't remember ever making such a claim, and the thought never occurred to him. That would be totally out of line with what he felt for her. Of course he wasn't "obsessed" with her or "dependent on her." And he never felt that the last evening was his last chance to keep the relationship together.

The court never heard about his earlier assaults on Teena, the fact that he was on probation, with a restraining order against his contacting Teena the night he went to her house and killed her. When Raym,ond stepped down, the defence lawyers exchanged "high-five" looks.

The defence called two expert witnesses, a toxicologist to provide an estimate of Raymond's probable alcohol level and degree of intoxication at the time of the killing, followed by a psychiatrist to testify concerning his mental state.

Expert witnesses are the exception to the evidence law that says only the judge and jury may draw any conclusions from the evidence presented at trial. The opinion of an expert witness is both called for and admissible when there are facts that are essentially too technical for the judge and jury to draw their own inferences from general knowledge and personal experience. If someone qualifies as an expert witness, that person may testify and give an opinion only within his or her area of expertise. At the beginning of the witness's testimony, a process of questioning establishes the expert's qualifications and area of expertise.

Thus the toxicologist was able to report that she had performed the technical task of taking the information she had been given about Raymond's alcohol consumption on the day in question and estimating what his blood alcohol level would have been at the time of Teena's death. Given police evidence, the accused's own statement of how much had been consumed, and taking timing into account, the analyst came up with a figure of approximately .15 percent, corresponding to the general category of "moderate intoxication." (For comparison, vehicle drivers with anything above .08 percent are legally impaired in Canada.)

"Can you describe for us the symptoms that a person who is 'moderately intoxicated' might exhibit?"

"Usually, you could expect their speech to be unclear or slurred, they wouldn't be able to walk a straight line, and their judgment and self-control would be impaired."

"I will read you the police description of the accused when they encountered him at the death scene, from their report: '... slurred speech, unsteady gait ...' Would you say that this is consistent with someone who is 'moderately intoxicated,' as you have calculated?"

"Very definitely."

"What effect would a blood alcohol level of .15 percent have on a person's ability to be aware of his acts, on his ability to form the intention to do something?"

This question had crossed the limit of the toxicologist's area of expertise. The Crown objected successfully, because the witness had no mental-health training or experience and was therefore not qualified to give an opinion on anything other than the physical effects such an alcohol reading might produce.

Now the defence psychiatrist stepped confidently up to the stand.

He methodically reviewed Raymond's personal and psychiatric history, highlighting his series of alcoholic blackouts and agitated, paranoid episodes, to portray Raymond as someone only minimally in control of his behaviour, particularly when under the influence of alcohol, and highly disordered in a general way. He lumped all Raymond's incidents of drunken mishaps together, without discerning between types of intoxication, circumstances or consequences.

"Under stressful conditions with alcohol intoxication, he lost all awareness of his actions and had very little or no ability to make decisions, to intend to do things, or to control his actions." — a tailor-made conclusion dropped by a qualified expert into the laps of judge, jury and defence counsel.

I believed he was dead wrong.

The prosecutor attempted to expose the main flaw in the psychiatrist's testimony: that Raymond's behaviour could not be characterized as unthinking, random or purposeless.

"Dr. A., do you consider thirty stabbings — thirty separate acts of raising and lowering the knife while the woman he claims he loved presumably screamed and struggled against him — a random, unthinking act? Surely throwing a toaster at a sofa is a random act, but taking up a knife and attacking a person thirty times is not random?"

"He was simply too drunk to know what he was doing. It indeed could as easily have been the toaster that went. He was out of control."

"Let's review the sequence of events as we know them. He got a large knife out of a drawer. Then he backed her into a corner, knocking chairs over, pushing the table aside, and he stabbed her, not once, not twice, but thirty times. And you propose that this was behaviour without any purpose, that this was, in effect, an accident?"

"I don't believe you understand the meaning of the term 'profoundly deranged'. His mental state was such that he was incapable of forming any intention to kill ...." and so on. The defence psychiatrist wove around the prosecutor's questions, eschewing details, keeping to generalizations and failing to provide a direct answer to the challenge that the murder represented an example of goal-directed behaviour. He wandered into jargon-loaded, technical digressions that the jury was unlikely to understand, and he maintained an air of calm, so there was no negative note of irritability or over-defensiveness. He simply ignored any suggestions that Raymond had acted other than totally out of his own control.

"Dr. Semrau." I took to the stand hoping to re-direct the jury's attention to the nature of the act related to Raymond's intentions. I stated that he had been in an abnormal mental state, but that out of the huge universe of possible behaviours he could have undertaken in that situation, he specifically chose to select a lethal weapon and apply it repeatedly to the victim, and this indicated that his behaviour was purposeful and could not be explained on any other basis than intent to kill the victim.

"In order to carry out such multi-staged, prolonged acts, you must be able to observe what you are doing and to be aware of the effects. And the fact that you continue with a series of repeated stabbing motions — as opposed to a single impulsive act — means that having seen the results of one stab, you continue on with more to complete your task."

"So you are saying that Mr. Albertson had the intention to kill the victim, as opposed to being unable to control what he was doing?"

"His ability to control his behaviour may have been extremely limited, but his *intent* was not limited by his intoxication."

"Mr. Albertson claims he remembers nothing of the events of the evening during which Ms. Teena Rondeval was killed. What does this tell you about his ability to have formed the intention to kill?"

"The claim of amnesia is actually irrelevant. Carefully controlled research studies have shown that many claims of amnesia for violent crimes are faked to avoid responsibility, and that even those people who were really intoxicated — to the point of not remembering afterward what they did — were still somewhat capable of understanding and following directions and carrying out intentional activities while highly intoxicated."

"Dr. A. has told the court that there have been many similar agitated, paranoid episodes during Mr. Albertson's life. Does this tell you that this is a generally out-of-control, mentally ill defendant?"

"The only way the mentioned episodes could be linked to the fatal episode is by pure speculation, because Mr. Albertson claims he has no recollection of his mental state during these prior episodes. In any case, only one incident has been specifically discussed, during which Mr. Albertson spent an evening in the company of the witness, Ms. Karen Muller. He was then under the apparently heavy influence of both cocaine and alcohol, yet, despite that, he remembered events in detail when I asked him to describe what happened that night. His recall was essentially identical to that of the witness who was with him, and who was not under the influence of any drug or alcohol."

Did any of that get through to the jury? I felt hobbled. I was unable to talk about Raymond's past violence with Teena or other women, because such background history would be prejudicial. And I was unable to give my carefully documented assessment of him as a psychopath with a low threshold for violence, because "evidence of bad character and predisposition" can only be presented by the prosecution as rebuttal — that is, if the defence has first tried to portray the accused as a person of good character, incapable of the crime.

My frustration only grew during cross-examination. Defence counsel simply put before me a series of examples of Raymond's deranged mental behaviour before and including the murder, and had me agree that each represented quite significant mental malfunction, which was true.

The very specific and legally central question of whether or not Raymond was capable of intending to kill his victim never arose. Their strategy was to try to broaden the definition — in the jury's mind — from not guilty of murder by reason of intoxication to something like a general quality of mental derangement. Thus they never did question me on anything that came close to my core assertions that Raymond's behaviour in killing Teena demonstrated awareness and intent, and their questions to me were so narrow and carefully structured that I couldn't include my opinion in my responses.

In closing arguments, both sides reviewed the evidence they had presented and repeated the opinions of their respective psychiatric experts. The prosecutor tried to get the jury focussed on the legal issue of intent; the defence counsel avoided that issue and underlined the broader evidence for general mental derangement. After summarizing the collective evidence, the judge told the jury they could accept or reject any of the evidence, including that of the experts.

He told them their verdict options were first-degree murder, second-degree murder, manslaughter or acquittal. He advised that a first degree conviction was unlikely because, although Raymond had talked about killing the victim beforehand, such talk fell well short of anything you could call planning and deliberation. A second-degree conviction, he continued, required that the jury be satisfied beyond a reasonable doubt that the accused had intended to kill the victim (the prosecution's argument). A verdict of manslaughter was appropriate if the jury believed Raymond had committed wrongful acts that caused Teena's death, but that he was too intoxicated to have the capacity to form the "specific intent" to kill her (the defence argument). Complete acquittal was not truly an option, because the defence had admitted the accused had killed the victim. The jurors retired to make their decision.

What would I have concluded, if I had been on that jury? I would have homed in like an eagle on the intent issue, and understood and agreed with the clever expert witness for the prosecution — me — that getting out a big knife, holding an adult down and stabbing her more than a couple of dozen times was not a sloppy accident by someone too drunk to think.

But if I *had* been a juror, I would have heard repeated incantations that the accused was a pathetic, demented man driven by forces beyond his control, tortured by society since he was a small child and still haunted by those terrible memories. A person who drinks to forget, and is controlled by what alcohol does to him; it makes him do strange things he can't remember afterwards. He clings to the one person he loves and who sometimes loves him. He thinks her friends are trying to make her leave him, and that makes him drink even more, so much he can't talk properly, he staggers, he doesn't know what he's doing.

Then the accused (but isn't he really a victim, too?) comes out himself to testify, and tells about his sad, abused childhood, and breaks into heart-rending tears. He didn't know what he had done, still can't believe it. Why would he kill someone he loved? he pleads. Next a doctor testifies that the accused was, indeed, too drunk to know what he was doing. He and the lawyers go back and forth using a lot of technical medical terms, but the psychiatrist insists that Raymond was too intoxicated to really mean to kill anyone. The prosecutor's psychiatrist then agrees Raymond was in a highly disturbed and intoxicated state — but he says that he could have controlled his behaviour more, and that, even though drunk, people can carry out intentional, goal-directed tasks, and this is what *he* thinks happened. Still, the defence goes on painting Raymond as an out-of-control, mentally disturbed individual hounded by life to this dismal act.

We, the jury, must make our decision based only on what we have heard in court.

A few hours into their deliberation, the jurors emerged with a question for the judge: can the accused be found guilty of second-degree murder if he doesn't remember killing the victim? The accused's memory is not the legal issue, the judge responded, the legal issue is his intent at the time he killed her. The question sent a chill down the prosecutor's spine, he told me later, because it sounded as if the jurors were off on a tangent and didn't really understand the criteria for choosing a verdict. They hadn't heard my testimony about the irrelevance of amnesia, either, I thought.

A day and a half later, they brought down a verdict of manslaughter. The judge subsequently gave Raymond a mid-range sentence of six years; he could be back out on parole in two. A conviction on second-degree murder would have called for a minimum of ten years without parole.

The winning verdict in this case was largely brought about by skilled courtroom tacticians and a legitimate defence based on an obsolete assumption about how alcohol affects the operation of the mind.

The intoxication defence is guilty of aiding and abetting more responsibility-dodging than anything else I've seen in court. At the root of it is the old saw that "he was so drunk he didn't know what he was doing" — that is, didn't intend to do it. It has long been scientifically proven that alcohol can reduce inhibitions, erode judgment and exacerbate existing feelings (such as anger and paranoia), but it virtually never removes intent or motivation.

If a drunk person stumbles and falls, that's accidental, caused by a decline of physical competence. But if he tries to bribe a traffic officer or points a gun at someone, that's intentional, the result of a thought process. The behaviour is clearly purposeful, goal-directed and would be extremely unlikely to occur as the random, bad-luck product of a non-operating mind. The fact that it is still potentially accepted in court that a person can be "too drunk to form the intent to kill" keeps allowing cases to be decided based on misinformation. And unfortunately, the opinion of any expert witness who claims an accused is "too drunk" is more likely to be accepted by non-expert jurors if only because the court, by allowing this category, legitimizes it. Opposing views will be less readily accepted, given that psychiatry comes to the courtroom disadvantaged: much psychiatric evidence is considered "soft" data, whereas "hard" statistics, photographs, and perhaps even tears are easier to believe.

Many crimes involve perpetrators who are under some degree of influence of alcohol or drugs. Some people drink to bolster their nerve in order to carry out their intentions. (The term "Dutch courage" came from the seventeenth-century habit of taking a tot of Dutch gin before going into battle.) Some drink to relieve themselves (even subconsciously) of some of the responsibility of their acts. There is tremendous scope for bogus claims of innocence as long as it is believed that intoxication destroys intent and, as a corollary, that individuals are not responsible for the outcome of their behaviour when drunk.

The amnesia issue also seemed to muddy the waters. Alcohol does impair memory and chronic alcoholism can lead to chronic memory loss — but not being able to remember what happened bears no relation to what actually happened. That is, at the time, you had the intention to do something and you did it; whether or not you remember later is irrelevant, even though many people, including jurors, assume that absence of memory goes hand-in-hand with absence of awareness and intent at the time of the crime.

Another issue this trial raised concerns the rule against the prosecution revealing past history (other than criminal record) which might be prejudicial to the accused. The rule is inherently sound and fair, as when it protects victims of rape. In this case, unfortunately, the rule worked in favour of the killer. Because I'm a doctor, not a lawyer, that may sound like pouting, but it is incredibly frustrating to see a jury decide a case while it is kept blind to relevant facts, such as an impressive string of prior spousal assaults.

There were other issues that may have affected the outcome, and shouldn't have. The defence seemed to want to plant an underlying assumption in the jury's collective mind that if Raymond were generally mentally disturbed, they could assume that his illness caused him to kill Teena — or at least removed his responsibility for her murder.

Mental illness rarely causes violent behaviour. A John Klevchin (see Chapter 1) who hears divine commands and acts upon them is far different from a basically violent person who is well aware that his violent behaviour is illegal and harmful.

CHAPTER TEN

JUST LIKE DAD

It started out as just a regular working day for Dennis Young. He planned to do two or three scams to get the money, then pick up some cocaine from his dealer and spend the rest of the day freebasing. Tomorrow would be the same.

He approached the first house cautiously but confidently; he was very good at what he did. As usual, he had chosen a lower-middle-class neighbourhood — fewer alarm systems and a greater likelihood of cash and valuables being left in obvious places. Dennis picked an out-of-sight basement window, slid the hunting knife in at just the right place and angle, and the aluminum frame popped out. Within five minutes he had the window back in, and ninety dollars, a gold chain and a traveller's cheque in his pocket.

The next home was even easier. He found an unlocked patio door, with a cookie jar full of coins just inside. Some kind of mop dog followed him from room to room, not barking, but at his heels continuously, looking up at him expectantly. He took a watch and a bottle of whiskey. Before leaving, he went into the refrigerator, took out an opened can of dog food, and fed the mutt.

The third house, locked up tight, presented more of a challenge, but Dennis was inside within a few minutes. He pulled a hundred dollars out of a sock drawer, lifted a gold watch and ring from the bedside table, and was gone without leaving a trace. He figured he had about $400 now, so he headed downtown. Since his regular cocaine dealer wouldn't be open for business for another couple of hours, Dennis hit the usual spots but had no luck finding any coke on the street. He had run into a young woman selling magic mushrooms. He didn't do shrooms often — they had severely upset his stomach a few times — but the price was right and he could always trade them for coke. He handed over one of the watches and some cash for a three-gram bag, and stuffed a few in his mouth.

A few nights before, he had left a backpack at some guy's place in the "party district" near the Sagebrush Hotel. He thought he'd go retrieve it and maybe score some coke to tide him over. As he was calling a cab, the phone booth started to look like it was melting around him, the paint running down the sides in big drops. The mushrooms were kicking in. He felt a bit queasy, but forgot it during the cab ride to Pine Street. Later, he remembered that the driver's face had looked like a dripping mask.

Brandon wasn't home, but whoever answered the doorbell told Dennis to check a townhouse in the complex two blocks away. Brand was there, and two other people Dennis knew: Ardel, whose place it was, and Cher, an ex-girlfriend of his. Brand wasn't ready to leave to get Dennis's backpack, so Dennis got out his mushrooms. A few people took some, one asking Dennis, "Aren't you going to have any?" He had several then. He didn't want them to think he had sold them stuff he wouldn't do himself.

His coke dealer didn't have his cell phone on yet, so Dennis asked Cher to set him up with her dealer. Together they cabbed to the Sage, scored half a gram of cocaine from the dealer and returned to Ardel's. They went to the basement and freebased. Dennis always wore two pairs of socks; he kept a bag of baking soda and a spoon between the pairs. A pipe was produced, and Dennis cooked up the cocaine. Ardel and Cher each had a toke and Dennis did the rest.

They returned upstairs and hung out for a while. Brand kept brushing Dennis off when he suggested they go for the backpack. Finally, Dennis reached his dealer, who told him to start walking along Pine Street. About ten minutes later, he picked Dennis up, drove around the block while he sold him a half-gram, and dropped him off across the parking lot from the townhouse complex. Dennis got out his paraphernalia, "rocked up" his cocaine and finished the whole thing before going back to Ardel's. Nothing much had changed there. Everyone was sitting around talking, drinking, smoking marijuana, in various states of intoxication. Brand told him to chill out; they'd get to his backpack all in good time.

He was starting to "jones." On a cocaine binge, an addict keeps wanting more cocaine, and if the supply runs out, the desire for it grows more intense as time passes. If it isn't satisfied, the craving becomes almost unbearable, and the addict will do almost anything for coke; this is known as "jonesing." Sometimes it can occur just after a hit of cocaine, which is what happened to Dennis following his solo freebasing of half a gram. He shovelled a handful of mushrooms into his mouth to drive off the jones, and called his dealer again. They met at the same place, and Dennis bought two half-grams. Dennis had run out of money, so the dealer, with whom he had a longstanding relationship, fronted the $80 worth of coke. Dennis could pay him back the next day, which was Welfare Wednesday.

As he re-entered the townhouse, he noticed a man who looked familiar. The man got up from the couch and followed Dennis into the kitchen.

"Hey, don't I know you," he asked. "Peters, from —"

Dennis remembered. They had been in prison at the same time. 'Skid' Peters had been dealing heroin inside. Dennis didn't know why Skid was doing time — jailhouse courtesy: you can ask a fellow prisoner how long he's in for, but not what his crime was. They talked some more, briefly, but Dennis wanted to get down to the basement, to the coke.

A toke each for Cher and Ardel, and the rest for him. Going upstairs again, Dennis noticed the railing was wavy, which he recognized as a regular mushroom hallucination. Ardel said something about going to the liquor store — Dennis had sold her the rest of the jewelry, and she had turned around and sold it to Skid.

Dennis went outside. Skid came out, and Dennis asked him if he would drive him home because he was feeling sick. The mushrooms might be upsetting his stomach, he said afterwards, and he had almost given up on getting his backpack from Brand. Skid said no, he was taking Ardel and Brand to get some booze. After they left, Dennis found some marijuana and papers on the coffee table, so he rolled and smoked a joint, and talked to Cher. When the others returned, Dennis refused a drink. There were now eight or nine people drifting around, partying.

Skid went upstairs to the bathroom. A minute later, Cher and Ardel were sitting in the kitchen when they heard a noise like someone tripping and falling. They laughed, assuming that Skid was so stoned he was stumbling. Then came the unmistakable sound of someone falling down stairs, followed by a groan, and Skid calling, "Ardel, help!" Skid came flying out of the stairway and into the living room. Dennis was following and dived right on top of him, attacking.

Ardel jumped up and went after Dennis. She only realized he had a knife in his hand when he brought his arm back to stab Skid. She got hit by a backswing so powerful it knocked her across the room. Dennis stabbed Skid again and again. Cher threw a vodka bottle that hit Dennis hard on the head, but it didn't seem to affect him at all, and he kept on stabbing. Everyone else was frozen, horrified, and probably stoned. Ardel ran out the front door for help.

Police and ambulance arrived together. Dennis was spotted hiding in a bush two blocks away, and made an unsuccessful run for it. As the officer handcuffed him, he told them he had a broken arm. He was covered in "what appeared to be blood." A dagger-like knife, also bloodied, and a bag of "a white powdery substance," later confirmed to be about $1,700 worth of cocaine, were found in separate bushes between him and the townhouse.

Travelling to police headquarters, Dennis suddenly began to shout and roll his head against the seatback. He soon calmed down.

When they arrived, Dennis was booked and searched. A hunting knife was found tucked into his waistband, and a small bag of a different "white powdery substance," the baking soda, between his socks.

At this point, Dennis appeared to lose control once more. He yelled, screamed, flailed about, and banged his head repeatedly against a door. Two police officers attempted to restrain him, a tough task in light of his considerable strength and the additional problem of his injured arm. He was strait-jacketed and taken to a cell. Half an hour later, he was removed from his cell, charged with Skid's murder, read his rights. He promptly contacted a legal-aid lawyer, and subsequently refused to talk further with police. He appeared unsurprised by the charge, and didn't ask any questions, but when a doctor later inquired how he fractured his arm, he said he didn't know, he had blanked out.

The business of "blanking out" and his "berserk" episode helped turn the case into a less-than-straightforward proposition. Dennis claimed not to remember anything from the wavy stair rail until the police took him to his jail cell. So, while there was never any question about who did it, Dennis's mental state at the time of the killing became an issue.

The prosecution viewed the homicide as an intentional, planned murder for the purpose of acquiring the victim's supply of cocaine. The accused was motivated by an extreme craving for coke and a lack of cash, and he knew the victim was a cocaine dealer with a large amount of the drug in his possession. Two of the seven witnesses to the killing testified that half an hour before the attack, they heard Dennis say he was "thinking stupid ... thinking about killing Skid and taking his cocaine."

Dennis further knew that it was common practice for dealers to "crotch" their supply. (Would-be thieves are less likely to attack someone's groin area, especially if the intended victim is a large man like Skid.) The dealer's one vulnerable time would be when everything was unfastened — in the toilet, where Dennis may have begun his attack. Skid's pants were still open when the stabbing stopped and Dennis fled. Cher also said she had seen Dennis grab Skid's coke as he left.

The prosecution felt that Dennis's behaviour following the homicide continued to be appropriately goal-directed: running away, hiding, ditching the cocaine and the murder weapon, and attempting to escape arrest. His state of intoxication had, perhaps, impaired his judgment and self-control to some degree, but his behaviour remained rational, deliberate, knowing and fully intentional. It also seemed in character, considering his lengthy criminal record and his known abilities as a street fighter.

The defence took the approach that Dennis was extremely intoxicated — primarily with cocaine and magic mushrooms, a combination he was unfamiliar with — and that he was suffering from a severe mental disorder at the time of the killing. The nature of that disorder could not be clearly known, largely because of the accused's amnesia, but might be some combination of intoxication, delirium, dissociation, panic or psychosis. The conclusion the defence hoped the court would arrive at was that the homicide had no rational motive, but was the product of a disordered mind. Dennis, therefore, could not be held criminally responsible because his ability to be aware of, understand, appreciate, control or intend his acts had been seriously impaired. The defence felt his actions had been out of character compared to his usual handling of cocaine and his self-proclaimed restraint against fighting except in self-defence.

So there we were again, lacking clear and direct evidence as to a defendant's mental state at the time of a killing — that very mental state being the key factor in the outcome of the trial. Again, I fantasized about the convenience of having a little black box that would give us a read-out of the accused person's mind at the time of the killing.

I was retained by the defence, and one thing I was sure of, entering the case, was that no expert could reasonably claim to provide a definitive and confident analysis of the major issues. Dennis's amnesia left an unfillable gap in the information, and the memory blank itself proved nothing useful to either side, unless it could be shown that he did remember and was lying. Eyewitness and police evidence were strong, and favoured the prosecution. To get his client off, defence counsel would have to hope that something indicating mental disorder would come out of his psychiatric and psychological testing and assessments, and/or that a strong case could be made blaming the quantity and combination of drugs Dennis had consumed.

No matter what triggered his attack on Skid, Dennis had spent half his twenty-six years training to make sure he would win such a fight. Early on, he had had troubles in school and troubles at home. He did poorly academically and had few friends. Slightly overweight, he was teased with the inevitable "Dennis the Menace." but he seldom provoked tussles, perhaps because he never expected to win. His father, a big tough ranch hand, strapped him regularly and bullied him incessantly. Because of his mother, he never showed his anger, but it would build up until it exploded in a fit of temper at school, where he generally misbehaved.

When he was thirteen, he learned that his father was actually his stepfather. His biological father, Eddie, contacted him out of the blue, and Dennis took off, leaving school for good, and went to live with his new-found parent.

The move took him into hell. His real father was an habitual criminal, a substance abuser and a wife beater. He introduced Dennis to marijuana, cocaine, heroin, and his new stepmother, a heroin addict and prostitute whom Eddie forced the boy to have sex with. Dad believed in on-the-job training: he took Dennis along as a lookout to "keep six" while he robbed and beat an acquaintance.

And most critically, he used fighting — the no-rules, street kind — as a disciplinary technique with his son. The first time Dennis antagonized him, Eddie took him out in a fist fight, knocking him out cold. Then he started teaching Dennis how to win. While he was hammering Dennis, Eddie drilled into him the necessity of fighting back, and, more important, of "striking first and striking hard. The first strike counts the most, because the winner is almost always the one who strikes first" ... and, "You put the guy down and you keep him down for the count" ... and, "It's not a crime unless you get caught."

Dad figured Dennis would follow him into a life of crime and wanted him to be able to fight hard, and not to get caught. One time, he and Eddie went back to back against six others in a parking-lot dispute. Dennis got to be a very good street fighter, strong, fast, aggressive, and tough as nails.

But his relationship with his father consisted almost entirely of fighting and drugs, and eventually, there was a blow-up. Dennis, at 15, moved to a town in central B.C. and lived on the streets. For a while, he was a prostitute, but then, posing as a student, he landed a summer job in a parks crew and stayed on for three years afterwards, living on welfare during the winter. Intermittently, he lived in the parks, but he kept up his street contacts, and one evening the police stopped the car he and three friends were in and arrested everyone for possession of stolen property. Dennis proclaimed his innocence, and the charges were dropped, but not before he lost his job.

He quickly settled back into street life, started doing drugs heavily and joined the criminal subculture, just as Dad had predicted. He moved in with a buddy who was dealing cocaine and was soon himself both a dealer and an addict. He supplemented with shoplifting, and break-and-enter jobs. He did get caught, though. For the next seven years, Dennis was in and out of prison, and racked up a lengthy criminal record for theft, trafficking, assault and one jail-break.

Released from his latest incarceration four months before Skid's murder, he had walked out the prison door and taken a cab straight to his cocaine dealer. His life was focused entirely on getting and consuming cocaine. He loved the intense high of freebasing and found enough of a thrill in crime to resist any change to his life.

After he was charged with the murder of Skid Peters, Dennis was tested and assessed by psychiatrists and psychologists. They came to similar conclusions, despite receiving dissimilar stories from him concerning some aspects of his life.

He denied being a prostitute at any time, although there were records proving he had been; it apparently didn't fit with his self-image as macho street fighter. He denied being a violent person, although he had been convicted of assault, recently accused of sexual assault, had a medical history of fight-related injuries, and frequently boasted about his fighting prowess. Every altercation had been a question of self-defence, he said, although he repeated his "strike first" rule like a mantra. It was a question of "knowing" the person who was about to attack, and he saw himself as highly perceptive. Once he had apparently struck first at a window.

Concerning the night of the homicide, to one interviewer Dennis said it was only the second time he had done mushrooms, but to another person he said it had been about the fifteenth time. He told one psychiatrist a multi-incident story of defending a friend who had been threatened at the party; he didn't mention the event to any other medical people. He told one interviewer he had asked Skid for a ride home because he was feeling sick from the mushrooms; he told another he wanted a lift because it was raining.

He admitted that he was "wired to react" and always on the defensive, and that if Skid had threatened him, he probably would have responded "Kill or be killed." He was absolutely consistent in his claim that he, remembered nothing of the time around the murder. Most of his "guesses" about what might have happened seemed to place the blame on the victim, on Skid making some kind of threat or move that necessitated a self-defensive strike. Weeks after the death, he uttered a few words of regret, but by that time, his sincerity was considered questionable.

154

Testing and interviews concluded that Dennis had a substance abuse disorder and a severe antisocial personality disorder. He placed very high on a psychopathy scale with what is termed aggressive narcissism: self-centered to an extreme, with total disregard for others, refusal to accept any responsibility for his actions or feel remorse for them afterwards, and a manipulative personality. Someone, in short, who could intend and commit murder and not think twice about it.

I agreed with the other clinicians who categorized Dennis as a psychopath, but as usual when dealing with a psychopath who has murdered, it gave me pause for reflection. We know that there are genetic and environmental factors that put people at risk for antisocial personality disorder. I suspect that one day we will find an organic cause for psychopathy, and the full horror of someone like Dennis getting a double whammy in life will be revealed. First he comes into the world cursed with a cluster of psychopathic genes just waiting to dominate, then he suffers a dreadful upbringing that enhances and channels his bad heredity into ultimate tragedy.

But Dennis's diagnosis as a psychopath only increased the *probability* that he was capable of intending to kill his victim, and his addiction to cocaine only increased the probability that there was a rational motive. We had to narrow in on his mental state at the time of the homicide.

He claimed to remember up to a point not long before the murder, when he was coming upstairs from his coke break and the railing appeared wavy to him. I asked him if he knew, at the time, that it was a hallucination, and he said, yes, that it was a typical magic mushroom visual effect and he had known it was "not real." I asked if he noticed any different or unusual effects that could be specifically attributed to having cocaine and magic mushrooms together, as opposed to separately, and he said no. Thus, for the period of time Dennis could recall, the effects of the mushrooms, or the combination, were not creating a mental state that could be regarded as directly causative to the killing.

I questioned him on his activities and timing immediately before the wavy stair rail, and his memory was fine. He knew how many tokes everyone had taken, how long between tokes, and a number of other details that were corroborated later, indicating that his memory and time acuity at that point had still been sharp. He also indicated a pretty usual pattern of cocaine effects throughout the evening, but with no paranoia or psychotic symptoms, although substantial intoxication.

Moving ahead to his early time in police custody, I was convinced Dennis was suffering then from a drug-induced delirium, a serious toxic reaction to drugs (often multiple drugs) characterized by a cyclical "scrambling" of mental processes that produces flailing, purposeless, aimless behaviour. I rejected the possibility of cocaine psychosis, given that there were no hallucinations or delusions, and that cocaine psychosis would have lasted over a longer period of time. Similarly, I felt that Dennis would not have been suffering a paranoid delusion attributable to cocaine psychosis at the actual time of the killing; it was unlikely that it would have come and gone so fast.

Between the wavy stair railing and the toxic delirium, we have a period of about an hour and a half for which the accused claims he has no memory. He enters this time frame in a state of substantial intoxication but exhibiting none of the effects that might produce any specific mental process that would explain the killing. The homicide occurs, which, according to witnesses, involved focused activity: pursuit down stairs and twenty-five well-placed knife wounds. He follows the stabbing with a series of purposeful actions: grabbing the cocaine, fleeing the scene, dumping incriminating evidence (the knife), attempting to stash the stolen coke, attempting to escape capture by the police. During this flurry, Dennis's last intake of mushrooms could have been kicking in to produce the toxic delirium that began in the police cruiser. Forty-five minutes later, it was over and Dennis was discussing his rights with his lawyer.

Much of my opinion bordered on speculation, and was hedged with limitations and reservations, leaving the defence psychiatric evidence rather weak. Defence counsel didn't lean on me to produce something stronger. Another tactic employed "against" forensic psychiatrists and psychologists — by lawyers who recognize that negative psychiatric findings against their client are inevitable — is the "preemptive shrink strike." I'll get a call from defence counsel asking me to take a look at their case. I read all the material, and respond by saying that there's really nothing useful or positive for the defence that I could find if I did a report — say the accused is a callous psychopath with no mental disorder and there are eye witnesses who corroborate his homicidal intentions. So defence counsel says, OK, thanks anyway, having known all along how I would answer. Then I hear from the prosecutor in the same case, for whom my report and rebuttal testimony would have considerable value. But I have to turn him or her down, because I have already been shown confidential material that may be used by defence.

In Dennis's case, the defence could only postulate the possibility of his carrying out the killing in a psychotic state because of the combination, unique for him, of magic mushrooms and cocaine. A pharmacologist, however, testified that there was no available information concerning the specific interaction of the two drugs — nothing that would reasonably predict what would happen when they were taken together. A second expert, a toxologist, agreed with my own rationale of the progression of their effects over the evening. The defence's second claim was that Dennis's violent reaction was unlike his usual, relatively calm handling of large amounts of coke. However, this would be mitigated by his record of violence in other areas.

I suspect it was the party guest's testimony that Dennis had told her he was "thinking of doing something stupid" (even though he denied saying any such thing) that swung the jury. Their verdict was Guilty of Second Degree Murder. Given a vote, I would have gone that way, too.

CHAPTER ELEVEN

BAD SPIRITS

It's an all-too-frequent sequence on the bleak side of town: young people in twos and threes, wandering from bar to bar, increasingly inebriated, stopping on the street to share a bottle, or a toke, or an invitation to a party house or hotel room. Some of them are under age, so the older ones make the booze purchases. Friends wander apart, meet up again. When the body or the wallet can take no more, some will fall asleep or pass out in a corner, a shooting gallery or a friend's room. The fortunate ones will make it home. Sometimes the money runs out but the thirst lingers, and thirsty intoxicated people do foolish and dangerous things.

On a rainy night in March, a 19-year-old Paul Wolf had been to the liquor store, the pub, a friend's basement suite, back to the pub, then back to the liquor store. At one point, he was so drunk he had been unable to walk without his buddy holding him up. He had been with his younger brother, his brother's girlfriend and three friends at various times over the evening. One of his friends left at ten to meet a curfew. About midnight, the other two went back to the pub. Paul downed another cooler, sitting on the curb outside the pub. Sometime after that, the brother and his girlfriend watched him stagger off into the night under his own steam, alone.

At three in the morning, Paul's father, with whom he lived, woke to the sound of a car crashing in the alley behind his house. He got up and looked out the back window, but could see only an unfamiliar grey vehicle. The car looked beaten up, but as there were no signs of a driver or any activity, he decided he must have imagined the crash, and went back to bed.

By 8 a.m., the alley was crawling with police. A disabled man living in an old house on the edge of town had been murdered, and the grey vehicle belonged to him. Two officers conducting neighbourhood inquiries came to the door and spoke to the father, who then led them to his sons' bedroom. At the knock on the door, Paul's younger brother mumbled a "come in." When the police said they were investigating a murder, the older sibling sat straight up in bed. The two denied any knowledge of the car, and the constables left after taking a few notes.

"I think I mighta killed the guy." Paul Wolf turned to his brother, "I think I ran over him. Twice." "I flipped the car." Paul jumped out of bed and searched through his clothes on the floor.

"Jeez, look at this," he held up his jeans. There were spots of blood on the legs. He threw them under the bed, started getting dressed. Dan was staring at Paul in disbelief. Their sister walked in.

"Like, what's going on?" She had heard them scrambling around after the cops left.

"Somebody died last night," Paul told her.

"What are you talking about? Someone I know?"

It came out slowly: "I just met him. I don't know how I ended up at his house .... We're sittin' there chatting, you know, and he wanted some cigarettes and I was gonna go get them .... And his car keys were right next to me and it was really tempting to steal the car. So I tried to sneak out, but he musta got there first. I thought I ran over a log, but it was the guy .... So I took him back into the house. Then the next thing I know I'm flying down the road. And the car flipped. But then I got out and I guess I went to bed."

Gloria began crying. Paul handed her a bunch of coins, "Here, keep these," and left the house. Dan was right behind him.

"Where are you going?" Paul didn't answer. They crossed the park to the bus stop. Paul fished a bunch of bills out of his jacket and thrust them into his brother's hands. "Paul, what are you doing? Where ..."

"I dunno, to the canyon maybe."

"What for?" Dan beseeched. "Paul, why?"

"I just feel too guilty, man." He was looking far away. "I can't believe I took someone's life. I just wanna kill myself." The bus door closed behind him and the bus took off, leaving Dan in fright and confusion.

The pay phone. Pray it was working, for once. It was.

"Cassy! Where's Leon?"

"I dunno. Around here. Why?"

"He's gotta get down here. No — he's gotta go to the canyon, right now! Paul's going there to kill himself, he says. Says it's because he killed a guy last night." Now Dan was weeping.

"OK, OK, Danny, I'll get him. You at home?"

"Yes. Well almost. He has to go after Paul, now!"

He had just reached the house when his cousin Leon's big pick-up pulled in. "Where's your dad?" Leon didn't wait, but burst through the door, then back out, Dan's father, Jesse, in tow. "Oh Jesus, Leon!" he was saying, pulling on his shirt, "Not Paul." They jumped into the truck and were gone.

Meanwhile, the police were re-constructing the story of the murder, and it was uglier than his family could have imagined.

The grey car had actually crashed into a garage, then bounced high — "airborne," the projected trajectory indicated — until it was stopped by a utility pole across the lane from the Wolf house. The garage owner had called police, and they determined that the vehicle belonged to one Cyrus McIlroy. The keys had been left in the ignition. While Paul slept, passed out, in his room, a pair of officers examined the car and its surroundings, then one of them set off to find its owner. A routine stolen car incident, he figured. It hadn't been reported stolen, so the owner probably hadn't missed it yet.

At McIlroy's house, a straight one-mile run down the street from Paul's, the officer received no response to his knocks. He tried the door, found it unlocked, and opened it slowly, calling out, "Mr. McIlroy?" He almost stepped into a pool of blood just inside the door. He could see more blood ahead, in the hall and living room, and an overturned chair.

The pajama-clad, blood-soaked body of Cyrus McIlroy, a near-paraplegic in his 30s, lay on the floor of his home office, hand clasping a telephone cord. He appeared to have suffered massive head injuries. A bloodied cane with a carved wood handle lay nearby. There was blood everywhere; forensic experts would be called in to make sense of the red trail.

A wallet lay in the hallway and a VCR covered with bloody fingerprints sat by the front door. Stereo components were partially disconnected and left sitting in the middle of the family room floor. Drawers in the bedroom had been overturned.

The police suspected that the killer had made his getaway in the stolen car, so had sent a team into the crash neighbourhood right away. They hadn't come up with anything helpful, so after going over what they had, the officers went back to talk to the Wolfs.

Leon and Jesse had hiked up a familiar path and spotted Paul sitting on the edge beside the top of the forty-foot falls. He was staring down into the water, rocking back and forth.

"Paul," Leon called softly. The waters were running too swiftly and must have drowned him out, so Jesse called, louder, "Son!" and this time Paul turned his head and gave them a look filled with anguish. He was crying.

Leon, not much older than his cousin, brought all his skills as a community counsellor into play as he inched closer to Paul. We don't want you to do this, he said. I know this isn't the way you want to end your life ... I know you've done something wrong, but let's see what we can do here to help you ... Jesse started speaking quietly, too, about Paul's mother, about her committing suicide with an overdose, and all the anguish it had brought on the family. This isn't the way, he said, I don't want you to go like your mother. For twenty minutes they went on like this, until they were close enough. Jesse grabbed one of Paul's shoulders, Leon the other, and they sat down on either side of him.

"I know you must think you've done something wrong, Dan told me what you said, but let's see how we can help you," Leon began. Paul started crying again.

"I can't live with myself, that's why I wanted to kill myself," he said. Leon again said they could think how to help him, and then Paul began explaining. He had been at a man's house that night and an accident happened and he rolled over the man in this vehicle ... and he had brought him back into his house . And then he panicked and decided to make it look like a break-and-enter and so he did a few things in the house, he couldn't remember what. He was so freaked out he took the vehicle and wanted to kill himself, and he went speeding down the road until the car spun out of control and he ended up crashing. When he woke up with the police in his room, he was still drunk. Now he knew he had done something really wrong, and he was terrified.

Leon and Paul went way back. Paul had got caught doing a few B&E's in his mid-teens, then had fallen into the pit of alcoholism. Leon had helped pull him out with counselling. It had been hard for Paul, but now he was in the Pathways program for First Nations youth, had seriously taken up art again, and until last evening had been clean and sober for two months. Ever since his nineteenth birthday.

"I know there's a good guy inside of you, a real quiet kind of guy. I don't see you as a violent kind of person at all," Leon reassured him, "You know I can get you a lawyer, and then we'll go on in and talk to the guys who are investigating ...." And Jesse was backing him up, telling Paul he loved him and he wanted him to come home. Gradually, they got him away from the cliff.

Leon dropped the other two off at home with the understanding that they would all go to the police later. But Jesse left soon afterwards to spend a few minutes with his mother, who was in her eighties and had heard rumours. Before he returned, the police arrived, and Paul denied everything: denied knowing anything about the car, and said he would certainly tell the police if he found out who it was. Yes, he would even turn a friend in, because he had just got his life back together and "I don't want nobody to take that away from me."

Leon called, and when he heard what had happened, he protested, "Well now, you know what we talked about doing ...." Paul said he had just been so scared, and besides, he heard they had already arrested someone for the murder, so maybe he should just leave it at that.

No one got much sleep, and the next morning Leon felt palpable tension in the community and on the streets where he worked. Cyrus McIlroy had been fairly well known for his work as an advocate for the disabled, and somehow word was out that First Nations people had had something to do with it. Leon could see the bridges crumbling that they had worked so hard to build. Paul *had* to report the homicide, and explain it was an accident, or it would soon tear his family apart, as well as the community.

Once the police even suspected Paul, they would be talking to Dan and Gloria and Jesse, and put them in a terrible position: tell the truth about what they knew, and rat on Paul — or lie. Leon called Paul. No answer. He called his wife, Cassy, who said that his mother was with her, and that they had been talking to Granny, who was upset and taking it really hard.

Leon drove over to Granny Marie's house. Paul was there. He had been to see an uncle who had seen some big trouble years back, and had turned his life around; but Paul wasn't saying anything about any advice he might have received. He was just sitting there with Granny, and she was saying, "You know, it's your life, son, but you better let them know what your involvement is." And to Leon: "We have to tell what happened, what we know. And son, you know we can't lie." And then they talked about how five years ago a cousin was murdered downtown, and all the struggling and grieving and anguish their family went through, until Leon said, "You know we'll all drown, so we gotta do this."

Paul weeping, nodded. Leon phoned the police, told them the basic facts, and said that Paul would come in. The family talked for another half hour, until Leon said, "I'm going to walk you down to the station, Paul. I said I'd support you, and things that have happened here are pretty bad and you've got to resolve it."

While Paul was making his statement to the police, Leon contacted the others and told them that Paul was confessing and that they should tell the police whatever they knew.

Having arrested him, the police commended Paul for coming in on his own. He replied, "It was either this or kill myself."

During the course of his first statement, Paul gave three versions of what he remembered happening the night of the killing. He had left a bar and met the man somewhere — was it at the man's house? — and he asked the man to lend him some money for cigarettes. And he took the car keys, and instead of hitting the brakes, he hit the gas, and didn't see the man. He thought he ran over him. He packed the man back into the house. He didn't remember doing any of it until he dreamt about it the next night.

How did he get into the house in the first place? He just walked in, and the man asked him what he wanted, and Paul said something about partying. He got the cigarette money and took the keys and got into the car. He saw the man come behind the car, maybe trying to stop him from stealing the car, but he hit the gas instead of the brake, and the man's head went down, bang. No, he didn't actually see him, he felt him. He guessed that he then got out of the car and carried the man into the house. After he carried the man, he was so totally scared, he ran out and drove off. But before he left, he thought he'd make it look like a B&E job, so he threw some stuff around and stole a few things. Well, he guessed he didn't steal anything, because when he got home, he had nothing. He wanted to drive home, and he just remembered flying down the street and the car flipping over, and he thought he was dead. When he woke up, he thought it had just been a dream, but the cops were standing in his bedroom.

He basically didn't remember anything else after about midnight. Before that, he remembers going from one place to another, drinking rum, drinking beer, drinking coolers, just a lot of drinking. His brother told him that he had been staggering and falling-down drunk most of the evening. Paul began to cry when he said, "I hadn't had a drink for eight weeks."

When he went off on his own, he had been at this pool hall, and there was more drinking, and after that he thought he went to a party. Everyone the next day told Paul he had been places he didn't remember being. He only recalled staggering and falling all over the place. He "was in a state of blackout." He couldn't tell what was real or part of a dream.

He had tried to bring it back while he was sitting on the cliff yesterday. He thought when he put McIlroy down, laid him down on the floor, the man had started to bleed profusely, and Paul had tried to pick him up but couldn't. He thought he sat in a chair for a long time, then got up and went into the bedroom, and then the bathroom, looking for something to wrap up the wound, and then he sat down and cried. Then he might have remembered talking to the guy and getting this idea to steal his car, because the keys were sitting right beside him. Then he tried to make a getaway, and he didn't see McIlroy behind him in the garage, he was so busy trying to get the thing in gear. He remembered falling as he struggled to carry the man, and trying to get him up off the floor by levering him with some kind of pole, but nothing worked. He had some notion of trying to get McIlroy to the hospital. He remembered picking up the VCR, swaying with it, then putting it down again. He didn't touch anything else. Except the dresser drawers. The whole thing was about fading in and out, staggering around and just being completely wasted.

Before long, the autopsy had been done, forensic experts had made their reports, and Paul's friends and family had given statements to the police. Much of what became known contradicted Paul's statements, so police confronted him.

The victim had died of severe head injuries caused by a beating with his own carved-wood cane. A blood splatter analysis showed where in the house he had been hit: he had been attacked in the front hallway. There was no evidence that anything at all had happened to him in the garage. The injured victim had been able to move about, and had gone into the laundry room, picked up a towel, and made it back to his office, where he was attempting to telephone for help as he collapsed and died. An antique coin collection had been opened up and the victim's wallet, found open on the floor, was empty. Although Paul had told the police he hadn't taken anything, he had given his sister the coins, then later that day had taken them back, saying he didn't want Gloria to get into trouble. He had given the bills to Dan.

Paul's reaction was, "I don't remember anything. I can't explain it, what took over my body and just shut my lights out." But he knew enough to tell them some things that were accurate.

"I don't know what happened. I dreamt about it next day. I could see myself inside that house like I was standing outside, my spirit standing inside." He insisted that he packed McIlroy into the house from the garage, and the police insisted that the car never hit McIlroy. He said the coins he gave Gloria were collectors he had bought himself. He didn't remember the bills, or giving them to his brother. He remembered rummaging in the bedroom for a head bandage, then coming out and seeing McIlroy, he guessed, dead, after which he ran out and, finding the keys in the car, drove off. He remembered flying through the air in the car. He remembered deliberately leaving handprints and fingerprints all over the house, and he didn't know why he had done that. Then he said he and McIlroy initially sat and talked about football, until McIlroy got out a pole or something and asked Paul to kill him. He couldn't remember exactly where he was when he was carrying McIlroy.

He really only remembered two things, carrying McIlroy and leaving fingerprints, He did not remember killing him. If he had killed him, it was just his body that did it, it wasn't him. His spirit had been outside his body.

And: "Um, I basically lied to you guys last night, because I don't remember what happened. I just don't. When they said it must've been an accident, I just started thinking of the car, and maybe I ran over him with the car. And at the falls yesterday, I just had a vision of me carrying him and then the fingerprints.

"I don't remember doing half the things I did last night. People told me, man, you were like the harsh alcoholic, just drinking everything .... And I drove a car home? I don't even know how to drive, I never had a licence. Man, I don't know how I could have done any of that, I was just so wrecked."

Wrecked indeed. Paul had consumed as much as half a forty-pounder of rum, six whiskey shooters, a six-pack of tall beer, an undetermined number of one-litre vodka coolers, and four or five "powerful hits" of marijuana between 7:30 p.m. and midnight, which was when his friends observed him to be falling-down drunk. He then struck out on his own with a mickey of rum in his jacket and went to the pool hall to drink more. After that, he somehow got to Cyrus McIlroy's house.

Paul was charged with second-degree murder. To be found guilty of second degree, the accused must be proved to have committed the act and to have intended either to kill the person or to cause serious bodily harm, knowing that death would be the likely result. If it was an intentional assault, but it cannot be proven there was any intent to kill or create a serious risk of death, the accused can be convicted of manslaughter, rather than murder, and receive a lesser sentence. If the accused can be proven mentally disordered at the time of the homicide — and by meeting the criteria of Section 16 can be proven incapable of appreciating what he was doing or knowing the act was wrong, he or she can be found Not Criminally Responsible on account of Mental Disorder. If the accused was intoxicated on alcohol or drugs, a can of worms is opened. Can someone be "too drunk to kill"? And should they be held responsible for what they did in a self-induced state of drunkenness?

In Paul's case, forensic blood and fingerprint analyses alone were sufficient to prove he had killed Cyrus McIlroy. But the question remained whether or not his state of intoxication (or less likely, a mental disorder) rendered him unable to intend to commit murder. Ten months after the homicide, I was called upon by the prosecution to provide an assessment. The defence agreed to my interviewing Paul.

There was nothing in Paul's history or demeanour to suggest a hardened criminal capable of premeditated murder. By all accounts, he had had a relatively happy, normal childhood. His mother had died of an overdose when he was four, but he thought he had been too young to be badly affected. Right afterwards, he and his younger siblings had been sent to live with an aunt for a year; he recalled that year as a "really fun time." Then they came back to live with Jesse, and his father had "always treated him well." He didn't learn until much later that his mother had had booze and drug problems, or that his dad had quit cold turkey when his wife died.

School had gone well — he was into sports and art, and he even skipped a grade. But in Grade 10, he fell in with a bad crowd and smoked a lot of marijuana. He lost all motivation and, ultimately, he was expelled from school, earning "The Big Scold" from Jesse. His friends were older and badder. One time they got him to be lookout while they did a B&E. He got curious, went inside the house, and they were all caught. He got deeply involved with alcohol, did a lot of coke and marijuana, and had a couple more B&E convictions when he was 17. Neither Paul nor his friends ever recalled his being violent. Once, intoxicated, he had grabbed the sweater of a guy who had made a racial comment, but that was the beginning and end of it. At 18, he decided "the illegal stuff wasn't for me." He joined Pathways and, with counselling, started working his way out of addiction. It wasn't a steady progression, but the day he turned 19, the legal drinking age, he stopped, and stayed stopped two months, until the night of the homicide.

What made him relapse? It started with one friend dropping in. It's Saturday night, he said, let's go party. Naw, said Paul. They played video games and drank iced tea for a couple of hours. Another friend came by. Hey, I missed your birthday, Paul, gotta buy you a legal drink. No thanks. But the second guy had come equipped with a big bottle of rum. OK, maybe one shot. OK, maybe another. Now a third buddy arrives. Paul had just been paid for work he had done, so he offered to go get some beer. He walked over to the beer and wine store, picked up two cases and a half-sack of tall ones. On the way out, he ran into a couple of friends and stopped in the pub for five shooters. He drank a tall beer en route home. Back there, he and the others played cards for a while; he finished the half-sack of beer and had five more hits of rum. Now he was ready to go partying. One of the guys had more rum at his house, and some marijuana. And that's how it went.

Paul remembered staggering with his friend holding him up, remembered feeling woozy and drunk, had a flash of being in the pool hall, and after that remembered only being in a car, rolling back and forth, maybe crashing. He told me that when the police came in the morning and afterwards, he found some money in his jeans, he thought, "Maybe I ripped someone off," then later, "What if I did it?" He said he worked at remembering but couldn't. He made up the stories about talking to the victim, going to get cigarettes, stealing the car, running over McIlroy, carrying him, searching for a bandage, fingerprinting the VCR. He had no real memories of the man or the house. He had wanted to commit suicide the next day because he felt he had killed someone, even if it had been an accident. He went to the police to prevent killing himself.

Why hadn't he just told the police what he knew instead of making things up? He didn't know. He just followed their lead, their clues, and the story built up. Why had he told his brother, his sister, his father and his trusted cousin "made up" stories? He didn't know, but he made himself feel better when he had a story to explain what happened.

One of the things we did in my interview was look at police photos of the McIlroy house. He said the exterior looked familiar, but he could have walked by it sometime. He studied the interior photos intently and at length, but in the end said nothing at all looked familiar.

He had a general air of puzzlement as to what had occurred that night. He said again that he spent a lot of time trying to remember, and he began to wonder if someone else could have been involved, because he couldn't believe he could do such a thing.

Sifting through the contradictory and incomplete statements he had made to me, his family, friends and the police — to come to some kind of conclusion about Paul's mental state at the time of the homicide — was a challenge. What were we to make, for instance, of the fact that many of what Paul claimed were "fabrications" jibed with police evidence — stories he had told his family before the police had had a chance to talk to him, let alone tried to prompt the same stories from him? Standing, swaying, holding the VCR and knowing he was leaving his fingerprints was one "lie"; but his bloody prints were indeed found on that equipment. Was he lying about not remembering — or did he truly remember nothing and had followed everyone else's lead in making it all up? I felt that the truth lay somewhere in between, but there was no clear way of resolving these uncertainties based on Paul's statements alone. I had to take into account the statements of others and the crime-scene evidence, to assess his mental state during the homicide.

167

His history, statements from those who knew him, and my own interview with Paul provided no evidence of any mental disorder before or after the night of the killing. It was evident that he had been substantially intoxicated. It was possible, if not probable, that he had partial amnesia for the events between the pool hall and waking up in his own bed. He could have remembered some things vaguely, almost as if they had been parts of dreams, and forgotten others; amnesia is a relatively common occurrence following severe intoxication. However, it says nothing about how he was thinking during the homicide, only that he didn't remember it all afterwards. What he did remember appeared to be a mixture of reality-based and confabulated material — it partly agreed with known facts, but partly appeared to be things he'd imagined as part of the process of filling in memory blanks in an attempt to make some tolerable sense of the confusion.

The reports of his behaviour up until midnight indicate that while he was certainly heavily intoxicated, he did not behave bizarrely or confused as to his circumstances or events. Evidence at the victim's house indicated that he carried out some purposeful, goal-oriented activities there: the television was disconnected and stereo components disassembled, the bedroom had been searched, a wallet had been emptied, he had stolen a car and made his getaway. His level of intoxication did suggest that he was at the point where he had impaired judgment (as in his actions with the VCR and his going off drunk in a car he couldn't drive) and self-control (as in a normally non-violent person over-reacting to a perceived threat). His ability to form the intent to kill might also have been compromised.

Taking all the evidence and my interview with Paul into consideration, and despite some details that would remain unclear, it seemed to me highly plausible that the overall enterprise had been a robbery attempt. The victim had possibly caught the accused in the act and was beaten, because he threatened Paul, or resisted him, or was a witness to the crime. Afterwards, Paul decided to leave suddenly. Maybe he heard McIlroy try to call the police, or maybe McIlroy had already died and Paul became aware of that. In any case, except for the money, he left the items he was probably preparing to take, and fled.

Given Paul's history of break-and-enters, there would be nothing particularly remarkable if, judgment impaired by alcohol, he again did a robbery for the sole purpose of getting some money; he had exhausted his funds on liquor and marijuana that evening.

Nothing in his background suggested brutal aggressive violence, even if intoxicated. So it seemed unlikely that he would have premeditated the killing, more likely that he would have reacted impulsively in the context of unexpected circumstances. The fact that he had never before engaged in major violence when intoxicated was no guarantee that it didn't or could not happen. Unique circumstances will often produce unique and unexpected behaviour. Paul could have encountered unanticipated resistance from McIlroy, who could have been aggressive himself towards this intruder, and with his judgment and self-control impaired, Paul may have acted violently to defend himself, primarily against being caught and arrested, but perhaps also against injury.

Did he intend to physically assault the victim? I believe he did, given that the actions involved were specific and goal-directed, in hitting the victim in a vulnerable place in the body with an effective weapon. He would have had to see his victim in order to take accurate aim at his head several times, and he would have seen McIlroy stumbling or falling (particularly as McIlroy depended on the cane, which must have been seized for the purpose of beating him), and bleeding profusely.

Did he intend to kill McIlroy? It is possible that he did, but there is considerable doubt, insofar as it might not have been obvious to Paul that the beating would result in death. Beatings with a stick are less likely to be lethal than a shooting or stabbing. Given his impaired judgment and perceptual powers, Paul might have administered the beating with the intention of disabling or subduing the man, which he did. But McIlroy was able to move from one room to another and then into the office. Because he did not die immediately, Paul was able to see him while he still showed substantial signs of life, yet did not continue to attack after first beating the victim in the hall.

A cold sober person administering such a beating might be accused of assaulting the victim in a manner reckless or indifferent as to whether or not death might result, largely because the attacker could appreciate the effects of the blows he was inflicting. I could not say for certain whether Paul's intoxication would have impaired his ability to judge the effects of the beating he was inflicting, but I believed that his judgments and perceptions were so clouded, as a result of intoxication, that he was unable to accurately perceive the risk of death and therefore unable to be reckless or indifferent to the outcome.

My assessment, then, stated that I thought that Paul definitely intended to beat the victim, not necessarily to kill him. The Crown prosecutor informed me that he disagreed with both my conclusions and my reasoning. He went on to suggest to the defence counsel that she might want to call me as a witness. Defence did. So, jilted once more, I switched "sides" just before the "game." At almost the same time, a second

169

psychiatrist called by the defence weighed in with an opinion virtually identical to mine. Serendipitously, the defence counsel's allowing me to interview Paul as a psychiatrist called by the prosecution paid off; it resulted in two psychiatric evaluations that essentially supported the defence. The fact that I had initially been retained by the prosecution, presumably to bolster their case, and yet had instead been convinced by the merits of the defence case, likely added to my credibility as well.

Again I found myself regretting the inherent lack of cooperation in the justice system. Occasionally, defence and prosecution will agree that justice can only be served by agreeing on major issues — before they approach the court. More often, the sides will fight to win. Sometimes, the prosecution will use a strategy, aimed at the jury, that intoxication is a trumped-up defence, one that can be used to get guilty people off the hook.

Sometimes the defence will take advantage of the different rules for prosecution and defence. The prosecution has to reveal all their evidence to the defence, even if it hurts their case, including turning over turncoat witnesses like myself. The defence doesn't have to reveal any information unless it uses it as evidence in court, and some defence lawyers will only reveal it at the last moment, effectively "ambushing" the prosecution. Keeping your cards close to your chest can provide a tactical advantage; but the more open and straight-shooting breed of defence counsel is more likely to get a break from the prosecution in the grey areas.

An intoxication defence gets us into the controversial business of determining degrees of guilt or innocence, degrees of responsibility. It is rarely proven that an accused person was so lacking in intent, because of voluntary intoxication, that he or she deserves a complete acquittal. More often, a reduced conviction of manslaughter (and accompanying lesser sentence) results when a judge or jury is convinced that the accused was so intoxicated that he or she lacked the capacity to form a specific intent to kill. Such a decision should follow a rigorous examination of the accused person's behaviour and mental state before, during and after the killing. Sometimes that is done, but the jury doesn't hear it — as in Raymond Albertson's surprising manslaughter decision.

In Paul Wolf's case, the jury's decision was a reduced conviction for manslaughter. No ending to this tragic story could be a happy one, given the death of Cyrus McIlroy. But after a few years in prison, there is a chance that Paul could be paroled and, given the support that surrounds him, return and start his own long, tough climb back.

III

AUTOMATISM AND PROVOCATION DEFENCES

Automatism is a term used to describe unconscious, involuntary behaviour, the state of a person who, though capable of action, is not conscious of what he is doing. It means an unconscious, involuntary act, where the mind does not go with what is being done.

— Supreme Court of Canada ruling

Automatism assumes the dichotomy of mind and body. When it is said that the accused functions as an automaton, it is meant that the body acts independently and separately from the mind. Such an assumption is erroneous. The behaviour and the function of the body is always governed by the mind, whether normal or disordered.

— Canadian Psychiatric Association Brief to the House of Commons Standing Committee on Justice, 1992

(1) Culpable homicide that otherwise would be murder may be reduced to manslaughter if the person who committed it did so in the heat of passion caused by sudden provocation.

(2) A wrongful act or insult that is of such a nature as to be sufficient to deprive an ordinary person of the power of self-control is provocation for the purposes of this section if the accused acted on it on the sudden and before there was time for his passion to cool.

— Section 232 of the Criminal Code of Canada

CHAPTER TWELVE

THE NEIGHBOUR FROM HELL

Harrison "Clark" Kent attended church that Sunday, stayed to conduct his regular Bible studies class, went home and made lunch for his wife, spent a happy hour with two of his six children watching Canada win an international hockey match, then went outside and shot his next-door neighbour three times.

Everyone who lived near the Kents' neighbour, Eldon Low, had probably entertained similar notions of shooting him, but no one dreamed that Clark, of all people, would have taken it on.

Clark was regarded as an upstanding citizen in the Ontario community where he had lived all his life. Like his namesake, Superman's mild-mannered reporter, he was known as a person of integrity with sound moral values, although not someone who was pushy about it. He was clearly intelligent, a voluminous reader, a Grand Master in chess. He had held the same job for twenty-eight years, as a technician with a forest products company. About fifteen years ago, Clark had tried going into business for himself, but found it didn't leave him with enough time for his children, so, a devoted family man, he went back to his old job. Every aspect of his life seemed to be fine until two years ago, when Eldon and May Low moved into the house next door.

The Lows hadn't been in their house two days, when Eldon appeared at the Kent's door, complaining about the noise the Kent teenagers had made saying goodnight to friends the evening before. Sorry, Clark had said, I'll talk to them.

The next day, Eldon was back. There were bicycles and toys in the Kents' driveway and alongside the house. It made the whole neighbourhood look run-down, he said. Clark got the kids to put their stuff away, and he took extra pains to ensure the lawn and garden were kept up. But the moment the basketballs and bikes started to creep back, Eldon returned, calling the place a pigsty.

Eldon took to making grunting and oinking noises whenever he saw one of the Kents, upsetting and frightening the younger children especially. A Kent boy cut across the corner of Low's grass one day, and Low shouted that he would sick his German Shepherd dog on any youngster who set foot inside his property. A few times he pretended to release the dog to attack, laughing loudly while whichever Kent was the pretend victim ran into the house. They had to take his threats seriously. The dog could be vicious, and like many people in that area, Eldon had a rifle. He had threatened to "pick off" various members of the family, and, a few times, had performed pseudo-marching maneuvers with his gun where the Kents could see him aim at their house.

Clark's wife, Mary, had once made the mistake of sunning in shorts on their back deck. The Lows, too, had a back deck, about fifty feet away. Eldon must have decided that Mary was insufficiently clothed for his standards, because after that, he began making obscene gestures to her, and calling out, "Yo! Slut!" whenever he saw her.

Eldon saw Clark's company service vehicle parked outside the house on three separate daytime occasions, and each time, he called the firm to report that Clark was truant from work. Clark's supervisors were mystified.

Eldon did succeed in getting Clark into trouble with City Hall. Mary's mother had lived in a basement suite in their house for the last six years of her life. After she died, the Kents rented the rooms to a friend, to help make ends meet, without thinking that doing so changed the suite's status. Eldon reported that they had an illegal suite, and he kept at it until inspectors were dispatched, and the Kents were forced to make expensive renovations to meet municipal standards for rental space.

Thefts and small acts of vandalism occurred frequently on the side of the Kent house facing the Low home. Three garden hoses were stolen; Clark saw one disappear into the garbage truck along with the Low trash. Cars were scratched, flower heads were lopped off, plants trampled, sprinkler heads broken, raw eggs thrown at the garage door. The sort of thing that might happen to anyone occasionally, but not weekly.

Clark decided to plant a cedar hedge, to separate and screen his house from the Lows'. He was careful to plant it well on his side of the property line. He even thought Low might appreciate not having to look into their driveway. But Eldon blew his stack and came over as soon as he saw the hedge, yelling obscenities and going on about sunlight or views being blocked. Eventually the two men came to blows.

"Don't think this is over yet," Low shouted as he went into the house to call police. "You don't know what I can do!" When the police arrived, Eldon was meek, polite and innocent. Clark felt "suckered in."

After that incident, Clark said he realized that no attempt at peace-making was going to work with Low. He hadn't been able to have a single conversation with Eldon in which the man made sense. The Kents talked to a lawyer, and on his advice, they reluctantly listed their house for sale. They had owned the house for twenty years, they had put a great deal of work into it, their children had grown up in it, and for them, it had been the ideal home in the ideal neighbourhood. Now they felt they were under siege, unable to leave the house without a threat or obscenity following them, unable to use the deck or garden for fear of Low bringing on some new aggravation.

The market was down, and they received no offers on the house. The barrage of insults from next door continued unabated. The Kent's 12-year-old unfortunately sent a ball flying through a Low window. Eldon told the boy to tell his father that he was "going to blow up the fucking house and kill you." This time, Clark called the police, but he got the impression they thought it was a trivial affair.

Clark felt trapped. Low seemed to escalate the hostilities at every turn. Clark could see that confronting him would only make it worse, and there didn't seem to be any way the law would protect his family. In short, there was no prospect for peace.

Clark's traditional values held that it was a man's responsibility to provide for his wife and children, and that the family looked to him to protect them. Yet he had done nothing, and apparently could do noth-ing, to keep them from experiencing this abuse at the hands of their neighbour. He had seen the shock on both Mary's and the children's faces whenever they had been subjected to an attack of obscenities and threats. They were almost speechless, and often weeping. None of them, including Clark, could understand why this was happening to them. He had hoped the very idea of their selling the house and moving might result in Eldon cooling off, but so far it hadn't.

They were going into their third year with the Neighbour From Hell, but on this particular Sunday, Clark hadn't thought of Low for most of the day. A dedicated and enthusiastic hockey fan, he had settled in to watch Canada play their biggest rival, and it was an exciting match. His youngest son and daughter were caught up with it, too and when Canada won with a beautiful last-minute shot on goal, they were ecsta-tic. The kids went downstairs to re-play the game on their Foosball table, and Clark went to refresh his coffee.

As he neared the kitchen, he heard Mary say to their tenant, Glynnis, "Did you see what that Low just did to me?! He gave me the finger, then he shook his fist at me like this, and he was yelling, 'Go fuck yourself, bitch!'"

Clark put down his coffee mug, turned around and walked down the hall, thinking to himself, "She can't even stand in front of her own window without being harassed." He went to the cupboard and pulled out his shotgun, then got some shells. He went to the TV room to look out the window, to see where Low was, but a child had slipped into the room, and he didn't want her to see him with a gun, so he put on his boots and went out the front door.

A two-sided conversation was going on in his head. One side was saying, "This guy is not going to quit, and you've got to do something, because nobody can stop it but you." The other side argued, "You can't stop it this way, you'll only make it worse, you can't accomplish anything good through this." Then the first side said, "I'm just going to scare him," while the other asked, "Then what are you taking ammo for?" "It has to look real, or it won't scare him. He'll think I'm just faking." He described it afterwards as "a real conversation. I just listened and recorded, floating along."

He spotted Eldon Low coming towards him pushing a wheelbarrow. "This isn't happening," he heard in his mind, "Please say this isn't happening."

"Cool as a cucumber," he would later say, "I could see my body reacting, as if I was somewhere behind it, an observer, like in a dream." He loaded the gun, then "the gun went up to my shoulder." "This isn't right, it's not legal, you can't do this," came to him. Low continued towards him, raising his finger to point at Clark, saying, "You're in trouble now."

The safety came off, Clark's finger pulled the trigger. He heard a bang. Low kept walking toward him. Clark held the gun steady until he and Eldon were face to face, the muzzle of the gun against Low's cheek. They just stared at each other for a few seconds. Low suddenly pushed the gun muzzle away from his face, groaned, and ran towards his house.

"He's scared, keep him running," Clark's voice said twice, and each time he said it, the gun fired, aiming just to the right of Low, to show him Clark was serious. Then Clark walked across the road and into the woods and slumped down to the ground.

He didn't know how long he sat there but, afterwards, the first thing he remembered from that time period was wanting to kill himself. He had put the rifle muzzle into his mouth, but the barrel proved too long: he couldn't reach the trigger while the gun was at or near his head. When the police arrived, he called out to them, "I'm here. I'm not armed." The unloaded gun was propped against a tree a couple of yards away. "I don't know how I could have done anything so stupid," he remarked to police as they led him away.

The day after the shooting, I was asked to do an in-custody psychiatric assessment, , so I interviewed Clark at the RCMP detention unit where he was being held on a charge of attempted murder. Low had received a serious wound in his right shoulder/chest area and graze wounds on an arm and a leg.

I found Clark Kent rational, charming, intelligent, articulate, and fully aware of his circumstances. He described the shooting in a logical and coherent fashion, as the outcome of the accumulated stress of his ongoing conflict with Eldon Low. He was somewhat anxious and agitated, but that was appropriate.

He was deeply regretful, and somewhat confused in that he couldn't understand how he could have actually shot someone. He had no history of psychiatric problems, and I could detect no signs of mental disorder now. I recommended follow-up counselling and anger-management therapy. I could see no barrier to his being released on bail, but only under the strict condition that he have no contact with Low, even indirectly through either family, and that he must not live in or even visit his own residence. Given the impulsive nature of the offense, I recommended that Clark should avoid being in any situation where he might somehow perceive himself as being provoked by the victim, even by hearsay.

Clark was released on bail, awaiting trial, and about ten days later, he asked to see me. He had moved into his eldest son's apartment and was receiving a great deal of support from friends and family. He had been given the opportunity to return to work the following week, and was keen to do so. He was still a bit anxious and "down," but only to the degree one would expect, given the circumstances. I wrote a letter to his employer saying that he was fit to return to work. I explained that he was currently in good mental health, not a danger to co-workers or the public at large. The incident with the neighbour was out of character for him, I said, and while alarming, didn't reflect any general tendency to be violent. Clark returned to work, happier being a responsible employee and provider for his family again.

Seven months later, the prosecutor in Clark's trial telephoned. She asked me to do a psychiatric assessment and provide an opinion concerning his mental state at the time of the incident. The defence had decided to plead not guilty, claiming automatism. They would have to prove, to the jury's satisfaction, that Clark had been acting in an involuntary and unconscious manner when he shot Low — what amounts to temporary insanity.

The defence of automatism (or, more formally, non-insane automatism) is less common than the other mental-state defences, which plead mental disorder or intoxication. But it is more common than it should be, because a successful plea results in complete acquittal: the accused will walk out of the courtroom a free person. An attempted murder conviction, on the other hand, brings with it a sentence of life imprisonment — with as much as twenty-five years before parole eligibility, at the judge's discretion. There is no minimum period before parole eligibility, though, and I guessed that Clark, with his clean record and extenuating circumstances, would probably get about five years if he were convicted.

The automatism defence is a good example of how the law has not kept up with medicine. The precedent-setting Rabey verdict was based on a simplistic view of the mind that said that a person can carry out complex, goal-directed behaviour without any conscious awareness or control. That makes as much sense as saying the body's actions are directed by men from Mars.

In 1977, Wayne Kenneth Rabey, a university student, became infatuated with one of his classmates, and thought she felt the same way about him. Unfortunately, Rabey came across a letter she had written to a friend, in which she wrote about being attracted to someone else, and referred to Rabey as a "pathetic loser." The following day, Rabey ran into the young woman on campus, thumped her twice on the head with a large rock he had carried from geology class, then tried to choke her, until someone came along and intervened.

Rabey's defence against an attempted murder charge was based on "psychological blow automatism." The shock of reading the young woman's letter and learning her true feelings sent the spurned suitor into a dissociative state, a defence expert claimed, and therefore the assault was the unconscious and involuntary act of an automaton. A psychiatrist called by the prosecution, however, claimed that Rabey had attacked her in a state of rage — an uncharacteristic state of mind for Rabey, but not an abnormal one in terms of awareness of reality and one's actions. He could therefore have formed the intent to kill or cause serious bodily harm, and must have known by the amount of blood alone that he was striking her, and that he had badly injured her.

The defence of automatism succeeded, and Rabey was acquitted. However, the verdict and a number of related issues remain controversial today. Automatism is, in my opinion, the flakiest of legal-psychiatric concepts. The idea of a mind unaffected by illness or injury having no idea what its body is doing has no basis in modern psychiatry, psychology or neurology.

We can't say that the mental state of killers or would-be killers is normal. People in a state of rage focus narrowly on their immediate situation and can act on short-sighted impulse, doing things they would never do when calm, and which they deeply regret afterwards. But some substantial part of their mind is still executing intentional acts.

The Canadian Psychiatric Association is on record with the House of Commons Justice Committee as recommending abolition of this defence. "When it is said that the accused functions as an automaton," the 1992 CPA brief said, "it is meant that the body acts independently and separately from the mind. Such an assumption is erroneous. The behaviour and the function of the body is always governed by the mind, whether normal or disordered .... The concept of ... a factor 'external' to the mind affecting the mind, cannot be supported."

But the defence still stands, and it remains attractive because of its potential for complete acquittal. Paradoxically, we wind up basing the most extreme outcome (freedom if the defence succeeds) on the flimsiest of concepts and evidence. Most medical experts approach a claim of automatism with skepticism.

Clark Kent's lawyer called upon my colleague Dr. Q. and forensic psychologist Dr. F. to test and assess the accused. Both found him — as I had — open, honest, intelligent, sociable, aware, conservative, respectful, and eliciting no signs of any mental disturbance. They felt that he had been slightly depressed in the months leading up to the shooting, with feelings of helplessness and lowered self-respect in the face of the hostile aggressiveness he was subjected to from his neighbour.

They concluded separately that Clark had been in a dissociative state when he shot Low. Normally, several mental processes operate simultaneously to give us our functioning idea of reality: our memory, consciousness, identity, and perceptions of our environment. If one of these is not working integrally with the others (is "dissociated"), we would feel detached from our mind or body. Our reality becomes distorted, depersonalized. Dissociation is one of the least understood mental states, making it virtually impossible to determine, retrospectively, if someone was dissociated or not at the time of committing a crime. Even if we could diagnose it reliably, we still couldn't say that the person didn't know what he was doing, or didn't intend his acts.

Clark's dueling voices and the feelings he had described of being apart from the activity, including his depersonalization of his actions ("The gun went up to my shoulder", "I heard a bang"), were given as evidence that he was not acting in a rational, conscious manner. Dr. Q. stated that several factors were consistent with an episode of dissociation. The aggression was totally out of character for Clark; he was experiencing extreme stress (the harassment had additionally produced family and marital tension); the onset was abrupt; his focus was limited and selective during the incident, and his memory afterwards was sketchy. Dr. F. went further in his assessment, stating that he believed Clark had not had the mental capacity to have formed the intent to kill, given his dissociated state.

In his report to defence counsel, Dr. Q. said that he couldn't find any basis for a defence of Not Criminally Responsible on account of Mental Disorder, nor could he find any clear connection between a psychiatric finding of a dissociative episode and any specific legal finding; however, automatism was the closest match.

I considered these two assessments, then went back to interview Clark for the third time. He readily understood my new role in his case, and I found him unchanged, still open and truthful, a pleasant and thoughtful man who had done something he profoundly regretted. After going over his personal history as well as the history of his war with Mr. Low, though, I felt that he had not been on automatic pilot when he shot his neighbour.

For virtually all his adult life, Clark held himself back whenever he was angry or frustrated, to the point of over-control. His strategies in dealing with situations like the one he faced with Low were avoidance and passivity. Rather than attempting any kind of confrontation, he would almost always try to think out the problem or rationalize it away. He had slapped his wife once, in the early years of their marriage, but she had made it clear it wasn't to happen again, and it hadn't. He considered himself a disciplinarian as a parent, and had spanked a few of his kids maybe once, but admitted that now he was actually lenient. He felt strongly that he should protect his wife and children, but had refrained from any overt showdown with Low, hoping the conflict would resolve itself.

This self-control fit with his beliefs and self-respect. But while it made Clark feel as if he were doing the right thing generally, in his relationship with his neighbour it left him frustrated — feeling inadequate because the problem had not been solved in any way — and full of pent-up anger. In the cedar hedge incident, he had released some of his negative feelings, and demonstrated that he did have some capacity for aggression. He had taken the first swing.

That episode left him feeling more angry, more frustrated, more inadequate. After the house went up for sale, he thought things would cool down, when Eldon realized he had won. The day of the shooting, there had been nothing for a few days, and Clark was feeling hopeful. After the hockey game, he was a bit wound-up, happy and excited with his team's victory. He had had no alcohol or drugs, had exhibited no abnormal behaviour or emotion. But when he learned that his wife had been insulted again, he allegedly turned into an automaton.

The defence claimed that he acted unconsciously and involuntarily. Yet he had been aware of, and recalled in detail, where he was and what was unfolding, from beginning to end. After overhearing his wife's comment, he turned and went to a certain cupboard, removed the gun, picked out the ammunition (the three shells required to fully load the weapon), went towards the television room, but changed his mind about going in when he saw his daughter. He turned to go out the front door, stopped and put on his boots but not his jacket, walked towards his neighbour, loaded the gun, released the safety, fired, realized Low was continuing towards him, kept the gun raised, remembered the dramatic eye-to-eye stare, then Low pushing the gun away, saying "Ohhh," and running towards his house. He recalled shooting at Low twice again, stumbling into the woods, trying to get the gun muzzle into his mouth and realizing it wouldn't work (and "it wouldn't solve anything anyway") and being arrested.

He had characterized his mental state during the event as "dream-like" and "detached," which is actually a common subjective description used by people in the heat of violent, dramatic incidents. He talked about sitting stunned in the woods, and of not remembering his wife's name at the police station; he was simply, proportionately, shocked at what he had done.

He remembered the internal conversations he had had, arguing for and against what he was doing. Which of us hasn't stood at the top of a tough ski run, or thought about proposing marriage, or prepared to ask a boss for a raise without the "Should-I, shouldn't-I" dialogue running through our head? Part of it indicated that he not only appreciated the conflict in its present context, but was thinking of the past and future,

181

too. This, I told the court, was an individual with an operating mind, carrying out consistent, purposeful behaviour. There were no random or incongruous actions, no hallucinations, no indications of confused mental processes.

Clark's conduct showed every sign of being willful rather than involuntary. He testified that he never meant to kill Low, but that he had gone out with the gun specifically to scare the man. He expected after the first shot that his neighbour would promise not to harass the Kent family any more. Clark was surprised when instead, Low appeared to ignore him. Then, when Eldon shoved the muzzle aside and ran away, Clark was convinced he had not frightened him at all, so he fired twice more. The second and third times, he had told me — but not the court — he wanted to hurt Low physically: "My intent was to cause him pain."

Everyone's day-to-day activities include some involuntary and partially unconscious behaviours. They can be purely involuntary or reflexive (such as removing your hand from a hot stove or braking from the passenger's seat), or part of highly habitual and learned behaviours (such as brushing your teeth), or more complex and learned behaviours with a substantial unconscious component (such as driving to work). In more complex or novel situations (doing something new or travelling somewhere), we operate almost entirely on the conscious, voluntary end of the spectrum. There is no scientific evidence that we have a hidden, separate part of our mind that enables us to carry out novel or complex acts outside our awareness, such as deciding and carrying out the task of shooting our neighbour. Although doctors do sometimes see symptoms that suggest automatism, science isn't yet sophisticated enough to prove it. Our best analyses come from looking at the person's behaviour and any reliable mental state information we can gather.

You won't find "automatism" in the index of the psychiatrists' diagnostic bible, the *Diagnostic and Statistical Manual of Mental Disorders*. As Dr. Q. noted, the closest relatives are dissociative disorders, conditions in which there is a disruption in the usual integration of functions of consciousness, memory, identity and perception, the most extreme example being multiple personality disorder. About half of all adults may have a single brief episode of depersonalization, such as Clark Kent claimed to have had, usually under circumstances of severe stress.

However, depersonalization is not a disorder unless it greatly interferes with functioning, causes acute distress for the person, lasts a long time or recurs repeatedly. Self-induced trances that are part of religious or cultural practices, for example, are not disorders unless they meet these criteria, which would usually be when the trance or depersonalization starts occurring involuntarily. None of these criteria applied to Clark. So although he may have experienced some dissociation, it did not appear to have prevented him from acting consciously and willfully during the shooting. Too bad, I thought, but he seems to be guilty.

Too bad, the jury apparently thought, but we have to acquit him, on the basis of automatism. The facts, as they saw them, must have left the jury with a reasonable doubt.

The defence had had a major resource of drama on its side, and had used it well, making a blatant play for sympathy. The psychologist came up with the media-attractive term "battered neighbour," relating Low's treatment of Clark to spousal abuse. Clark's own nice-guy testimony was bolstered by that of other neighbourhood witnesses, one of whom Low had also threatened to kill. Although I have never had a truly troublesome neighbour, I had no trouble putting myself in Clark's shoes, and many others in that courtroom must have thought to themselves, "There, but for the grace of God, go I."

Although automatism was a dubious defence for Clark, his behaviour was a textbook example of "over-controlled hostility" in which a decent upstanding citizen repeatedly suppresses his growing anger. If the relief valve on the pressure cooker doesn't let enough steam off, it blows sky-high, and everyone is amazed that the peaceful guy who never seemed to react suddenly goes on a rampage. Contrast this with "under-controlled hostility", the more usual pattern of an antisocial personality or psychopath who uses his fists with the slightest of excuses, frequently, doing mild to moderate damage frequently, but not usually exploding big-time.

A year later, I found myself testifying in a murder case in which the issues were almost identical to the Kent case. The three expert witnesses, Dr. Q., Dr. F. and I, even resumed the same positions and repeated approximately the same opinions. This time, it was the accused who had an Eldon Low personality. He did things like dropping into his ex-wife's apartment, via the balcony, by breaking into the suite above, in order to surprise her in bed with her new lover. On the fatal day, he came to her not-easy-to-find office for the first time, asked her a question — "Do you love me?" — then, not liking her negative reply, stabbed her to death. He claimed these and other complicated maneuvers were carried out in a state of automatism. The jury didn't go for it, and convicted him of first-degree murder.

Why was one man acquitted and the other convicted? I wondered if a thoroughly irrelevant factor could have coloured the juries' perceptions: one accused was likable and sympathetic, the other aroused no feelings of compassion.

Clark Kent has resumed his life, and I would be astounded if he stepped off the straight and narrow again. Although he and his family did sell their house and are now living in another part of the city, he is still not free of his former neighbour. Eldon Low is suing Clark in civil court for assault causing bodily harm, physical disability, pain and suffering, and loss of employment income. Such a suit could succeed (in the way the civil case went against American O.J. Simpson), given that only a balance of probabilities (at least 50% likely true) rather than "beyond a reasonable doubt" standard of proof is necessary.

Chapter Thirteen

"Is He CRAZY?!"

The two men had just sat down on the park bench when they saw the truck go flying by, right through the stop sign, not ten feet away. It was making some kind of mechanical sound that the old man would later refer to as gears grinding, and his grandson would describe as high revving.

"Whoa!" Randy jumped to his feet. In seconds, the truck had gone through the intersection, angled onto the wrong side of the road, then onto a sidewalk and crashed with a loud bang into the cement-brick wall of Bigfoot's Boot Warehouse. Randy was off and running before the truck had bounced down, settling in a cloud of dust, front fender buried in the building. He ran to the driver's side, just as the man raised his head from the steering wheel. The driver's head had been down on the wheel when he roared past them, Randy was positive; Grandpa said his head had been partway up and looking to the side. They agreed that he sure wasn't paying attention to the road. Now he had blood all over his face and a completely blank expression.

"Are you okay?" There was no answer.

"Are you hurt?"

People were starting to gather. Randy saw a woman come out of the Tribal Council offices next door, look at the front of the truck and go back inside.

Randy tried opening the driver's door, but it was locked or stuck. "Open the door," he suggested. The driver reacted slowly, trying to put a shoulder into it, but it didn't budge. Someone on the opposite side called, "Come out this door." The driver crawled along the seat and someone helped him out. He looked dazed and he still hadn't said anything. He just kind of stood there, blood running down his chin. The woman Randy had seen before, Laurie Joe, came back out of the office just as Randy was coming around the back of the truck. Somebody yelled, "Call the police and ambulance!" Laurie and two people with cell phones called back at almost the same time, "I already did!"

Laurie began talking to the driver, "Come and sit down, you really should take it easy for a while. The ambulance is on its way. You'll be okay, you'll feel better if you sit down." The man, a big burly guy in mechanic's coveralls, let the small, motherly woman guide him onto a street bench, where he sat quietly.

It was then that Randy saw the crowd at the front of the truck, and the man lying partly under the front fender. Oh God, a pedestrian had got in the way. Raw bone was protruding from the man's legs, and a woman was kneeling next to him, trying to find a pulse. A man was holding his head, trying to keep radiator fluid from dripping onto the injured man's face, talking to him, telling him help was coming. Someone put a blanket over him, someone else grabbed a hard hat from the truck and put it under the drip, like a bucket.

"Does anybody know CPR?" "Don't move him." Everyone seemed to be talking, wanting to help, but Randy guessed the poor guy didn't stand a chance. Where was the ambulance?

Suddenly, there was a roar.

"Never mind him! Who's going to fix my truck?!" Randy turned, and came face to face with the truck driver, on his feet, waving his arms and looking like an enraged, dangerous grizzly.

"Hey, no, it's okay, insurance will cover it," Randy began, thinking to calm the man down, but apparently having the opposite effect. He wouldn't remember afterwards what the driver, Torval Mander, said, but he found himself being backed away down the street by the shouting man, who was looming over him, shoving and swearing and — this was so weird — laughing. Randy failed to see the parked car behind him until Mander had backed him right onto the hood, grabbed him by the shoulders and dropped him again onto the car.

Bystanders had followed the pair down the street. Mander took a swipe at one of them, hitting him squarely on the jaw, then started back towards his truck. Laurie was there, and said something; Mander socked her hard on the side of the face. Two men grabbed him, but he shook free and walked up to the injured man. To the crowd's astonishment, he reared back and attempted to kick the victim.

The guy holding the injured man's head quickly moved his back around and took the blow. The woman beside him, who had also been trying to render first aid, shouted, "Somebody get this guy away from here!" When she turned back to the victim, Mander punched her on the back of the head and tried again to kick the critically injured man. Randy and a man who had been trying to re-direct traffic to clear the way for an ambulance managed to position themselves between the victim and Torval. Mander had just slugged Randy for the second time when two police vehicles pulled up.

Torval Mander gave the officer a shove on the chest with his bloody hand, and when asked his name, simply swore. He allowed himself to be handcuffed, but first shouted, "What are you doing?" — then laughed.

"The most sinister, bizarre laugh I have ever heard," a witness would later testify, "totally out of context and very chilling." It took all four officers to force Torval into the rear seat of the squad car.

He sat in the car, unmoving, while the police dealt with the ambulance and talked to a lot of eager, angry and righteous witnesses. It was later reported that the 911 operator had received more than thirty calls for assistance from the accident scene and nearby shops and offices.

When the officer returned to his vehicle, he spoke to Torval and was astonished at the change in the man. The look of combativeness had disappeared, replaced by a weary and confused expression. When told he was arrested on charges of criminal negligence causing bodily harm and read his rights, Mander responded that he understood, but he asked no questions — almost, the constable thought, as if he hadn't a clue. Torval sat unmoving and quiet all the way to the station.

The arresting officer re-read Torval his rights at the station, telling him he was charged with criminal negligence causing bodily harm or death to one Percival Jack. The brief interview was videotaped, and I was able to see it later. A look of shock and despair came over Torval's face when he heard the first charge.

"Perce is a friend of mine," he whispered.

The officer added that assault charges were also possible, that witnesses at the accident scene had claimed Torval had taken a few punches at them.

"I don't remember a thing," was all he said.

Later, the arresting officer asked him where he had come from and where he had been going before the accident. Torval said he had driven thirty miles into town from work. He was a heavy-duty mechanic. "I was going to Trico for a part, and I don't know what happened. I was on Sixth Street going towards Seaview and I don't know what happened." The constable had not been able to detect any signs of alcohol or drug use, but he asked the questions anyway, as well as whether Mander was on any medication. The answers were all "no."

An hour after the accident, Torval saw an emergency-room physician to have his injuries checked. He had a laceration inside his cheek and a bloody but unbroken nose. He showed no signs of concussion or shock, and his blood sugar was normal. The doctor asked him about alcohol, drugs, medications. All negative, except he said he had smoked a joint very early that morning. She noted that he was oriented as to time, place and identity, but that when she asked him what had happened, he told her he couldn't recall the accident, only just driving his truck. She reported his mood was "sad." She discharged him, and he was returned to detention cells.

Next morning, they told him that Percy had died, and that five people had filed assault charges against him. Twelve witnesses, most of them indignant, had come in to make statements, and several others had spoken briefly to police at the scene. The majority thought it had been a blameworthy case of drunk driving and drunken belligerence afterwards. Or maybe he was stoned on some kind of drug. One person postulated that Torval and Percy could have had a major disagreement and Torval had deliberately run Percy down. Others were totally puzzled. This last group included the police, Torval's boss, Torval's wife and Torval himself.

Several people had seen the truck as it went through the stop sign and intersection, and the consensus seemed to be that the driver was then either slumped over the wheel or had his head bowed and was not looking ahead. They were sure he was speeding. There was sound, something like a roar or a transmission out of gear, but no one heard brakes or saw brake lights come on at any time before the truck hit the building. "I know one thing," a witness said, "there wasn't an inch of rubber on the road." The truck must have slowed down when it jumped the curb; engineers determined that it had been travelling at between 23 and 32 kilometres per hour when it met the wall. Police had the truck thoroughly examined. There had been nothing wrong with it before the accident.

Had there been something wrong with the driver before the accident? Not according to Walt Peltier, owner of the company Torval worked for. He said Torval had arrived at his usual time, 5:30 a.m., just before everyone else, and worked steadily all morning on a backhoe that was due out the next day. Torval had worked nine years for Walt.

"What kind of worker is he? How would you rate him?" asked the police officer interviewing Peltier.

"Right in the top," came the immediate reply.

"He's dependable?"

"Very."

"Shows up on time?"

"Always."

"Capable at what he does?"

"Extremely capable."

His co-workers spoke highly of Torval, he was cooperative, and Walt couldn't remember any confrontations, let alone Torval ever having been angry. There were five of them plus Walt, and they were all independent, in and out of the shop all the time, working on individual vehicles.

Just before lunch on the day of the accident, Walt had walked past Torval's backhoe and a broken hose caught his eye. He pointed it out to Torval, the two looked at the piece together and decided Torval should go into Trico and purchase a replacement; this particular type couldn't be repaired in their own shop. "He wasn't upset or anything," Walt offered. "He just said, 'If I gotta go, I gotta go,' happy enough." Since it was a forty-minute drive at best, Torval could pick up a few other things and save Walt a trip. Forty minutes later, Torval's truck was stopped by the cement-brick wall.

"Would there have been time for him to have stopped, or to have made his purchases and then gone and done anything else?"

"Oh no, it's partly a gravel road, so you have to go pretty good to get to town in forty minutes."

A preliminary hearing was held, during which it was decided there was enough evidence to proceed on the charges, and some time later, I was called upon by the defence counsel for an assessment. I interviewed Torval at length, then a few months later, I talked to him and his wife together.

There was nothing in his upbringing or young adulthood to suggest he might turn into the bad guy portrayed by the accident witnesses. He came from a fairly close family. There had been no alcohol, drugs, violence or abuse, and he described his mother and father as "really good parents." His three siblings were "doing well" with no histories of substance abuse, mental disorders or legal problems. Torval had been an average student, more interested in his after-school job and saving his money up to buy a dirt bike. There were no youthful skirmishes with the law, although once he and another 14-year-old managed to buy a six-pack of cider from a bootlegger, and drank "some of it."

He left home after high school, and worked steadily, operating various types of heavy equipment until he got his mechanic's ticket, which he'd had twelve years. He married "too early" the first time, and had been with his second wife, Megan, four years. He'd had two or three speeding tickets in his life, and two years ago had been cited for an unsafe lane change.

He had drunk too much beer between marriages, even getting caught in the middle of a bar fight once, but when he hooked up with Megan, he stopped going to any bars, and only had maybe a few beers a year. When his second child was born, he made a conscious decision to be a good role model. He's a quiet, unaffected man, and he talks naturally of things like being a good role model and a responsible employee.

Concerning marijuana, Torval said that until the accident, he'd have a couple of joints a month, always with friends, and never at work. His job was too dangerous — working on and operating the big equipment — to take that kind of chance. He didn't remember telling the emergency-room physician he had smoked that morning. It was unreal, he said. Like all of it.

As for anger, Torval described himself — and his wife agreed — as slow to get mad, usually very calm. When he was really ticked off, he would swear, at most. Once, he kicked the furnace when he couldn't get it to work. Even during that bar-hopping year, he would always try — and almost always manage — to avoid any kind of confrontation or argument.

His health record was clean, with no significant illnesses or injuries. At 16, he had been knocked out briefly when he fell off a motorcycle, but recovered quickly, and hadn't bothered to see a doctor. He hardly ever had to see a doctor.

In addition to the head injury Torval received in the motorcycle accident, there were two other incidents that may or may not have provided clues as to whether or not he was conscious during the accident and what triggered his behaviour afterwards.

About three years past, he had been driving home from work one sunny summer afternoon, when he suddenly became aware that his truck was in a ditch, and someone was asking if he needed help. He didn't recall it happening, he wasn't injured and was able to drive the truck out, so the episode was never investigated. There had been no alcohol or drugs involved, and he hadn't even felt sleepy, although falling asleep was the only possibility, however remote, he could come up with to explain how he landed in the ditch.

Four days before the fatal accident, Torval had been working underneath a vehicle when the heavy wrench he was using slipped and fell, landing on his face. He didn't believe he lost consciousness at the time, although he felt a bit dazed, but he said he was unsure because he was lying down anyway. He had a headache that evening, which was unusual for him, and took some aspirin, but the headache persisted for a couple of days. He attended a junior high school graduation ceremony for his older child, and afterwards his father-in-law remarked to Megan that Torval had been speaking rapidly and somewhat oddly. Megan agreed that he had been highly talkative all evening; he was usually a quiet guy. Torval himself later said he had felt quite ordinary. Megan noticed that, in addition to the bruise under one eye and a nose cut, he now had blood in the white of the eye. She thought he should see the doctor, but Torval said he was fine, it was pretty well better, and left it at that.

These two episodes pointed to avenues that medical people should explore, but on their own, they weren't legally significant. The issue in court was whether or not Torval was at fault through negligence or an intention to cause the accident, and whether or not he intended to harm the spectators he assaulted.

His family physician and a neurologist conducted extensive testing. Everything, including electroencephalograms (EEGs), a CAT scan, MRI and glucose levels showed normal. Essentially, the three of us agreed that he almost surely had no pre-existing or chronic seizure disorder (such as epilepsy), blood-sugar disorder or mental illness. The neurologist and I submitted our reports to the defence counsel.

Defence took the position in court that Torval Mander was in a state of Automatism at the time he committed the offences; that is, he was acting unconsciously and involuntarily.

Although one witness claimed that Torval looked at her, several said he was slumped over the wheel or had his head down as he went through the stop sign. He had gone right through a stop sign without so much as slowing down. The strange engine noise could not be connected with anything provable. (I privately guessed that Torval's feet had gone down on both the clutch and the accelerator at the same time.) In the last block before the intersection, there had been no signs of braking, no swerving to avoid a collision (nor turning deliberately towards someone or something), no horn. That Percy Jack was a good friend of Torval's was just a tragic coincidence, not a murder. Virtually everyone in the community knew the families socialized, and that there had been no ill feeling between the two men.

Immediately after the crash, Torval had appeared, to all accounts, dazed and confused, with his eyes looking right through people. Then, he became highly agitated, violent, striking at people, including the victim, making inappropriate comments, smiling and laughing bizarrely, and all the while having a "glazed" or see-right-through-you look in his eyes.

191

Within ten minutes of the accident, the driver was sitting quietly in a squad car, fully alert to his surroundings, but totally bewildered because he had no memory of what had happened between then and when he had driven past the Dixie Freeze drive-in two blocks back. As he heard accounts of the event, he reacted with horror and disbelief.

His memory of the next twenty-four hours would prove patchy. He remembered arriving at the police station and being in cells, but not being interviewed there. All he remembered of the hospital was having a drink of water; he didn't recall speaking to the doctor. He vaguely remembered seeing Megan through a small window at the station. His brother picked him up the next day and took him home; the brother described him as frightened, indecisive and tearful. His memory returned to normal and was fine for events after that day. There was no indication that he was feigning any memory lapse, though you can never be sure.

The neurologist, Dr. E., and I separately concluded that Torval had not been in control of his vehicle when the accident occurred, and that the most likely cause of his behaviour had been a seizure with post-seizure confusion. I testified in court to that effect.

Simple loss of consciousness from some form of fainting, hypo-glycemia, or merely falling asleep were ruled out because none of these could account for both the rapid onset and Torval's post-accident behaviour. Dr. E., however, reported that he had seen many patients exhibiting agitated, violent behaviour following a seizure. Generally, he said, the violence is not directed, but if confronted, the person will often strike out.

As a psychiatrist, I could extend the explanation. Torval's actions in attempting to kick the victim and in lashing out at bystanders in an almost random fashion make no sense whatsoever from a rational point of view. There could be no rational or even irrational purpose it could serve for him.

On the other hand, this behaviour is definitely consistent with a confusional or delirious mental state in which an individual does not understand what is going on around him, and behaves in a somewhat chaotic and aggressive manner. He perceives his surroundings and other people to be threatening. But he doesn't know how or why they are a threat to him — so he lashes out indiscriminately, without discernible motivation or logical purpose. It seemed clear to me that Torval's mental functioning was profoundly disordered from shortly before the crash until he found himself in the police car. During this time, which includ-ed the eruption with the victim and bystanders, he was unable to understand his own behaviour or to adapt it properly to the circumstances in any rational or meaningful manner.

What causes such a mental state? Typically, some sort of serious insult to the normal functioning of the brain. A number of diseases can produce it, but the rapid onset in Torval's case — who was driving along feeling normal one minute and in the next was severely impaired — reduced the options, probably to a "petit mal" seizure or complex partial seizure. In either of these types of seizure, the person suddenly becomes unaware of his surroundings and can't interact, purposefully, with his environment at all. (The victim does not experience grossly abnormal body movement, as in the better-known "grand mal" seizure, which often includes a flailing of arms and legs.) Brain activity during the seizure is completely disordered. Thus, Torval would have been unable to control himself or the truck at all, let alone drive.

Following most types of seizure, there is normally a delirious period in which the person generally becomes more aware of his surroundings, but is extremely confused and has great difficulty focusing or reasoning appropriately.

In Torval's case, this mental state would have been combined with the alarming and provocative situation he was in. He would have seen that his vehicle had just been damaged or involved in some kind of collision, but he would have been unable to understand or explain it. He might also have seen his friend horribly injured and similarly been unable to put anything about him together in his mind. The people who attempted to calm him seemed very threatening to him, again in a way he couldn't understand. The type of chaotic and purposeless violence that he subsequently demonstrated — in attacking what were in reality non-threatening individuals — was highly consistent with a post-seizure confused state. It is also typical that it would last the length of time it did, subsiding as he sat in the squad car.

As the post-seizure confusion retreated, its place was taken with the emotional effects of being in a great deal of trouble without a proper understanding of what had occurred, followed by the added shock of learning that the victim, who was his friend, had died. He was overwhelmed.

Torval's seizure, like all seizures, was probably triggered by some factor. Most people who suffer seizures have an ongoing seizure disorder, which means they suffer multiple incidents over time, if not properly treated. Tests had ruled that out, except for the slimmest possibility. (The ditching incident may or may not have been the result of a seizure, but the lack of subsequent incidents makes it doubtful.) But isolated seizures can, and do, occur under some unusual circumstances when the functioning of the brain is irritated in some manner. For instance, occasionally someone will experience a seizure as a consequence of fainting, for whatever reason.

Looking at Torval, it could be that there was some limited focus of brain irritation as a result of the head injury he had received from the falling wrench several days before the accident. The injury had produced headaches and nosebleeds and was followed by some unusual behaviour. An additional factor may have been lowered blood-sugar levels. Torval had gone to bed at his usual time, before 10 p.m., but the day of the accident he woke up late, too late for him to have his regular, large bacon-and-egg breakfast and still be on time for work. So he left without eating. He took his lunch — always a generous one — with him, but he left it behind when he went to town. At the time of the accident, this normally big eater would have been about fifteen hours since his last meal. His lowered blood-sugar levels at that point could have compromised his neurological functioning to some extent and precipitated a seizure, in combination with the lingering effects of his recent head injury. The fact that his blood-sugar level tested normal an hour later can be explained by the effect of shock-induced adrenalin boosting the glucose level back up.

Not having been in the truck to see, we cannot absolutely prove that Torval Mander did have a seizure followed by a post-seizure confusional mental state caused by these factors. But given the many observations, examinations and history, it was an entirely plausible explanation. And no other explanation fit. I could find nothing to support a diagnosis of any mental disorder; Dr. E. could find no neurological disorder; and there was no motive or rational explanation for the crash and homicide being deliberate. There was nothing to suggest intoxication was a factor; there was no evidence of alcohol or drugs. In the unlikely event Torval had smoked a toke many hours earlier that morning, it would not have produced the sort of behaviour he exhibited after the accident. Alcohol and marijuana take effect slowly and wear off slowly, which was not what happened. As for picking fights, laughing, and attempting to assault the dying victim, the notion of any kind of rational intention being behind these actions is inconceivable.

The prosecution did not put up much of a fight. There was no contention that the collision was deliberate, only an emphasis on the need for the judge, in order to convict him, to be satisfied beyond a reasonable doubt that Mr. Mander drove negligently, rather than in a state of mental dysfunction, and that there was intention to assault the various bystanders. The prosecutor raised the fact that Torval had been driving in control for some time before the accident, that one witness stated he "looked right at her" while speeding through the stop sign, that he was rational enough to get out of the car and to recognize the police officer, and that he appeared oriented to the emergency-room physician afterwards. The prosecutor claimed that, if not guilty of criminal negligence, the call should be Not Criminally Responsible on account of Mental Disorder. However, he did not call any expert witnesses from the medical field, or put forward any evidence in rebuttal to my or Dr. E.'s opinion.

In a small town, the position of Crown prosecutor in such a case is a decidedly delicate one. The prosecutor may see that the proposed defence is legally sound, the evidence is strong (particularly after having done the usual due diligence of obtaining a second psychiatric opinion), and fighting it is clearly hopeless. But to many of his or her law-abiding fellow townfolk, psychiatric subtleties in testimony can come off as just so much psycho-babble brought to the case by a glib big-city shrink. In this case, they had just witnessed their good friend and neighbour snuffed out by an apparently enraged culprit, who then tried to kick the victim while he was down and attack those coming to his aid. That was the reality, and no matter what the high-priced outsider psychiatrist had to say, someone had to be held responsible for the evil that had occurred. So the prosecutor walks a fine line, putting up just enough resistance to the defence not to seem a wimpy pushover in the public's eyes, making the defence fight back, and yet not inviting disgrace in the court's eyes by being too obstructive either. Wise defence lawyers and judges understand this, and assist the prosecutor in getting the job done properly, without a lot of unnecessary theatrics.

The judge in Torval's case felt there was ample evidence to support the defence contention that the accused had likely experienced a seizure followed by a confusional state. The difference between a verdict of NCRMD and full acquittal on the basis of Automatism, he felt would rest on whether the seizure was part of an underlying, recurring disorder of the mind or had been an isolated occurrence. Dr. E.'s note that up to 25 percent of all epileptic conditions may not be caught by EEG testing — and my statement that there was a very slight possibility that the previous ditching incident had also been the result of a seizure — were "negative considerations rather than positive evidence" of a recurring mental disorder. She was satisfied that this case was, in law, an instance of automatism.

Had the prosecution proved that Torval had committed the offences willfully? The judge's statement said, "There is not a shred of evidence that this act was intentional, or that there was any ill will between [Torval and Percy] .... All the evidence is to the contrary .... To be guilty even of an offence where the mental element requires only negligence, rather than an advertent or intentional guilty mind, the act must be volitional. You must be capable of being aware of your actions." On the basis of the evidence — almost entirely uncontradicted — the Crown had not, in the judge's opinion, proven beyond a reasonable doubt that the offences had been a voluntary act. The judge concluded that Torval had been in a state of automatism, and completely acquitted him of all charges.

I found this a satisfying conclusion to the court case, really the only just legal conclusion that could have been reached. So while the automatism defence generally makes little sense — serving better as a legal strategy on which to take a flyer than as an explanation of an accused person's behaviour — we need to be careful not to discard the valuable principles when we think about doing away with it. There is no other defence in law today that could have been put into play to defend this innocent man, victim himself of a medical anomaly.

To say a just conclusion was reached in the courtroom is not to imply a happy ending. The trial judge observed that Torval, on the stand, appeared neither evasive nor nervous; rather, he seemed to be (a year after the accident) "in a state of shock or emotional withdrawal throughout the proceedings .... He simply seems to be living with the knowledge of having been involved in a terrible event which had tragic consequences, which he can neither remember nor explain."

Torval kept his job, but no longer drives any kind of vehicle. Megan takes him to and from work. The community itself seemed not to have come to terms with the tragedy at the time of the trial, and some dissatisfaction was voiced with the verdict, even mumblings about vigilante justice if the court didn't see fit to do its job properly. Percy had been well liked, and, in a way, the acquittal left friends and family with no one to blame. I made a public offer to counsel or explain as much as I could, to groups or individuals, but there was no response. I hope they have come to some kind of peace among themselves.

CHAPTER FOURTEEN

A TALE OF TWO LITTLE OLD LADIES

If you were up that early and saw them coming down the street, you knew it was seven o'clock. Abby Dixon would have been up and over at Effie Gerhard's house in time to give Effie her morning pill, then the two of them would take their dogs down to the beach. It was a nice flat beach, easy to walk, even for an elderly person or a small mutt, unlike the rocky coves on some of the other islands. The women would pick up pieces of driftwood for their stoves, then walk slowly back up the road to Effie's place. They were sisters-in-law, neighbours for forty years, and the best of friends.

Effie and her brother, George, had grown up on a farm in Manitoba, with a small town separating them from the farm where Abby was raised. Abby's mother had died when she was a young teenager, and there was no question but that Abby just went to work in the fields and barn alongside her father and brothers. She did morning chores, filling the woodbox, carrying water from the well, then went to school, came home, did housework and more chores. The pace was set: Abby would work hard all her life. When she left school at 16, she took the place of a full-time man outside, milking cows, pumping water, clearing forest for farmland, pitching sheaves at harvest time. It was the "Dirty Thirties," on the heels of the Great Depression, and times were tough, as they said countless times.

Abby and George Dixon met and fell in love at a dance in the town's Grange Hall. They married and moved to their own farm, acreage formed by combining George's parents' homestead with the smaller farm of Effie and her husband, Morton Gerhard. George's parents moved to the coast, settling in the Gulf Islands. The Gerhards went at the same time, Mort finding work as a logger.

Abby and George tended a mix of farm animals, and vegetables, and had three children, doing it all without benefit of electricity, running water or any means of transportation aside from horses. After ten years, with three school-aged youngsters, and still scrabbling to make a living from the farm no matter how hard they went at it, they made the bold and scary move west. They bought a small house with lights, a wood stove and cold running water, just across the road and around the corner from Effie and Mort, and not far from the elder Dixons' trailer. The brothers- and sisters-in-law were together most of the time, and became well-liked in their island community. Money was still "scarce," but George worked more or less steadily as a labourer. Abby worked steadily with her children, her enormous vegetable garden, and with whomever needed a hand. Particularly after their children were grown and gone, Abby and George were known as the "caretakers of the community."

"If you decided to clear out your blackberry bushes, Abby would jump in with her clippers and shovel to help, unasked. If you got sick, George would just come over and mow your lawn for you," their good friend Cath recalled. "Abby was the one person in the neighbourhood who always asked how so-and-so was feeling, always remembered a gift if someone's child was getting married, always noticed if someone could use a hand."

Abby picked up new family chores as she went. Her mother-in-law lost one leg to a blood clot, then developed Alzheimer's. Abby nursed her until she died. "She is a very pleasant little woman," was all Abby would say if people remarked on her devotion. Not long after, George's father, Dick, suffered a debilitating stroke. Abby continued to go back and forth between the two homes. Then one day, Dick came to their house for lunch and decided to stay. Abby took care of him, helping him dress, get to the bathroom, eat, everything. She wouldn't hear of anyone outside helping, or of moving him to a nursing home. Then he fell ill with something that made the doctor say, "I think you'd better come into the hospital for a while." Abby ferried over to visit him every day. His leg turned gangrenous — Abby could still remember the awful smell. They had to amputate Dick's leg, but in the end, they couldn't save him. Abby had watched her mother die, and now she had seen George's parents go, both suffering greatly.

Then Mort suddenly died, of a heart attack. Now there were just the three of them, Abby, George and Effie, doing everything together. Both houses were heated by wood, so they gathered their fuel every day, lugging it by wheelbarrow to the woodpiles. Both houses still had huge vegetable gardens, which all three worked. Effie had an apple orchard, which had to be tended, pruned and harvested. Abby quilted and sewed on a treadle machine, selling what she could. At 65, George retired and turned to doing odd jobs, pruning, cleaning gutters and window washing. Often Abby would share the tasks. "We liked to work," Abby said. They had always lived frugally, the two families sharing a wringer-washer in the Dixon basement, and a bathtub in Effie's house.

When the Dixons were both 71, and Effie 77, George developed emphysema. He had to slow down and finally stop working. First he just didn't have the breath, then his legs started giving him trouble. Abby took up the slack on the wood-gathering, pruning, vegetable-growing and other outdoor jobs — and added one more project: Effie. Alzheimer's, or something like it, had crept up on her.

Effie began wandering. Neighbours would meet her on the road, and she couldn't remember if she was going to the beach or was on her way home. She frequently didn't know if she had eaten or if she had remembered to take her daily thyroid pill. Abby worried about her sister-in-law's safety, and she began checking regularly to make sure she was safe at home. Eventually she was also taking Effie's pill to her every morning, and making an extra dinner and trundling it down every evening. Sometimes Effie wouldn't eat the meal; she would have seen it was 6 o'clock, and say, "Well, I must have had supper already." She became argumentative and demanding.

George's emphysema grew worse, and his legs broke out in ulcers that had to be bathed and re-bandaged two or three times a day. George refused to have anything to do with doctors, so Abby played the role of nurse again. She tried to talk him into seeing a doctor, but he said "no." He was her husband, so she carried on.

If the strain of nursing two people and being responsible for housework, yardwork and the wood supply for two houses was too much, Abby never complained. Her patients were family she loved dearly. If George wouldn't see a doctor, well, that was "just how he was made up. He's my man." If Effie bossed her around or disparaged George because he didn't "get up off his butt and go for a walk" — when he was sometimes so sick he couldn't get out of bed — she just told herself that Effie didn't know what she was saying. She felt hurt, but not angry. Anger never solved anything. If Effie called her a "stupid bitch" when Abby wouldn't follow Effie's order to pick some pears from a neighbour's tree, Abby reminded herself that Effie had never in her now 81 years used such a word before, and that she only did it this one time because her brain wasn't right.

The two white-haired ladies still had happy times together, still spent most of their days in each other's company, gathering driftwood, gardening, grocery shopping, reminiscing about the old Manitoba days. The path between their houses ran through a small bush area, and Abby, mindful of Effie's failing eyesight, would fill any holes in the pathway, and keep sticks and overhanging branches trimmed back. Abby did all the work, but she was younger and stronger, and Effie didn't seem to notice that it was Abby who kept her house clean and comfortably heated, her refrigerator stocked with bread, milk and garden produce, her clothes laundered. Abby said it was a terrible thing to put an old person into a home, and for probably five years, she made it possible for her sister-in-law to stay on her own. If you asked Effie how she was, she'd say proudly, "Never an ache or a pain!" Neither George nor any of the neighbours ever heard a cross word pass between them.

Through the spring of that fateful year, Effie's mental health deteriorated. Once she had to take a thyroid test that required her to fast for ten hours before. Abby knew Effie would forget and have something to eat, so she sat up all night at Effie's kitchen table, making sure she didn't get up to the fridge in the night or have breakfast in the morning. Effie began refusing to wash or bathe, and became careless about her toilet habits. Abby would have to persuade her to let her wash her hair or take a sponge bath.

If Effie had "a bad or restless day," Abby would come and check on her constantly, even in the middle of the night. At home, she fretted over George, haunted by visions of his father losing his legs. She was getting about three hours of sleep a night, sleeping "with one ear open" for fear that George would get up and perhaps fall. Later, she described herself as "running entirely on nerves." Finally, she called her elder daughter and told Lynette she couldn't handle it.

The Dixon kids lived away with their families: two in the Okanagan, one in Langley, near Vancouver. It was a close family. They all regularly offered to help or to get help, but any suggestions that their parents might be experiencing hardship were rebuffed by Abby. When George couldn't do any more roof work, their son insisted on coming down periodically to clean the chimneys, and when it snowed, he would turn up to shovel off the roofs. They felt their mother was being run ragged, and each offered to come down and help with their aunt, but the most Abby ever said was, "Well, when I get things in order I'll give you a call."

Among themselves, like most adult children of elderly parents, they discussed taking over, but worried that their mother would think they were interfering, and would be upset that they thought that she couldn't handle what she obviously felt was her responsibility, her "job." Now when she told George that she had telephoned Lynette, George said, "You shouldn't have. They'll worry."

Lynette and her husband arrived the next day. First priority was getting George to accept some medical care for his ulcerated legs, second was to get some help for Effie. George told Lynette that Abby had agreed that Effie needed — well, sometime — to go into a home. The first evening Lynette was there, her mother returned from Effie's house looking hurt. Lynette said, "How did Aunt Effie like her dinner?" and the reply was, "She fed it to the dog." "Oh, Mom. How nasty." "No, dear, she's to be pitied," was Abby's compassionate response.

Next morning, Lynette and Abby paid a visit to their family doctor and explained the situation. George had refused to come, but the physician proposed a house call, and once Dr. N. was there, George allowed himself to be examined. Arrangements were subsequently made to have a community nurse come in and tend to his legs twice a day, to provide some relief for Abby. The physician next paid a visit to Effie. Effie didn't recognize any of them. ("I don't remember a darn thing anymore!" she said cheerfully.) She said it was October when it was June, and gave a lot of incorrect and untrue answers to the doctor's questions. As a result, Lynette was able to make an appointment for the following month to have Effie evaluated as the first step towards having her placed in long-term care. This didn't seem to have much of a calming effect on Abby — perhaps, thought Lynette, it was because of the time delay, or maybe Mom was thinking of the protests Effie would undoubtedly raise.

Lynette's brother, Ross, and his wife arrived for the weekend. They observed that Abby seemed to be having trouble concentrating, probably because she was so rundown and anxious about George, and practically beside herself with worry that Effie would wander away or hurt herself. They offered to stay on, or to leave an older grandson behind for a week or so, but Abby said, no, no, she could take care of things. She gave them all hugs as they left and thanked them for helping so much.

Three evenings later, Abby fell asleep on the sofa at 6:30 p.m., after taking Effie her supper. At midnight, she was still sleeping so soundly that George covered her with a blanket and decided to let her sleep on while he took himself to bed.

At 4 a.m., Cath and Willis across the street were awakened by someone banging on their front door. Willis jumped out of bed, and called out as he opened the door, "Cath, it's Abby!" but as he spoke, Abby collapsed forward into his arms, and he had the devil of a time keeping her upright. Between Willis and his wife, they got her into a nearby chair, where she flopped over to one side, mumbling incoherently. She was as white as a ghost and shaking uncontrollably. They pulled her upright again.

"I killed her. I killed Effie," she said.

They didn't believe her.

"Abby, what's wrong?" Cath kept asking. Abby was crying and muttering at the same time. They couldn't make out what she was saying until she handed Willis a piece of cardboard that she had been clutching.

"Take care of this," they thought she said, "Get them to come." Willis recognized the names and telephone numbers of the three Dixon children, in Abby's handwriting.

"Poor George," were the only other words they could understand before the ambulance and police arrived.

While one constable tended to Abby, Willis directed the other to Effie's house and waited outside. The officer found the front door wide open, but no lights on. Stretched out in the bedroom doorway was Effie's body, a gaping slash wound running the length of her back. She had twenty-nine other knife or stab injuries to her stomach, chest and arms. The broken-off blade of what appeared to be a long kitchen knife had been left lodged in one of the wounds. Forensic examination of the body later showed that because there was no bleeding at the sites of two large wounds, including the slash along her spine, those had been inflicted after her death. The victim had been killed on her bed, then the body dragged to the doorway. Police found blood-coloured shoe impressions and hand marks in various places throughout the main floor.

The house had been ransacked: plants tipped out of pots, a few drawers pulled out and overturned, the refrigerator left open with food spilling out, a deep-freeze open and bags of frozen foods strewn around the rooms. The bedding was in disarray on the floor, and the mattress had been removed from the bed and tipped up against the wall. A pile of loose change was found near the body. A search of the area surrounding the house produced a change purse, credit cards and identification belonging to Effie scattered in bushes along the pathway. Either there had been an attempted robbery or someone wanted it to look that way. The examining officers were confident that the ransacking had been staged after the murder.

The many bloody hand smudges were found to have been made by household rubber gloves, and the footprints had come from rubber boots, both with distinctive patterns. That afternoon, as Ross Dixon comforted his father at home, the police paid them a visit and asked George to show them the shoes Abby usually wore, and the clothes she had been wearing when he saw her the evening before. He pointed out Abby's rubber boots by the stove, then observed that his old leather jacket was missing and, actually, his own boots were gone, too. Police said they believed that they had retained both these items when Abby was admitted to hospital that morning, and they added that she had also been wearing jeans and a plaid shirt. George thought she had on a flowered shirt last night. The officer asked if someone could have a look around to see if any clothes had been left out, and Ross came out of the bathroom a minute later holding a green garbage bag. Inside it were Abby's flowered shirt, jeans and a pair of rubber gloves, all with blood stains.

Abby was still in the hospital. She had been having trouble breathing, and it had taken two paramedics, one on either side of her, supporting her, to walk her to the ambulance. Before they left Cath's and Willis's house, the police had placed her under arrest for assault and read her her rights. She had understood, and when they asked her if she wanted to contact a lawyer, she replied, "I don't know anybody. I just want to go to sleep."

On the hour-long drive and ferry ride into King George Hospital, Abby lay with her eyes closed. Every now and again, the accompanying police officer would ask a question or two, but the answer was always, "I can't remember." While the admitting physician was examining her, the constable asked Abby, "What happened tonight?" The answer came, "I can't handle it anymore. Oh, poor George, poor George."

The doctor found her to be disoriented and amnesiac, noting that she was hesitant to respond to any questions, and that she kept her eyes closed. He called for a psychiatrist, and shortly after Dr. W. arrived, he advised the officer that Abby was in no mental condition to be interviewed by the police, and that she should stay in the hospital's care for now.

She spent the rest of that day and the next, lying with her eyes shut or staring at the ceiling. Lynette, Ross, their sister Marlene and their spouses had arrived by afternoon. When Lynette, Marlene and Ross's wife, Ann arrived at the hospital, Abby's eyes were barely open, and they stayed that way during the short visit the women were allowed.

"Mom, can you hear me, it's Lynette, I'm here. And Ann and Marlene." Lynette put her arm around Abby, and Marlene and Ann held her hands. After a few seconds, Abby responded. She asked if Ross was there, and her sons-in-law. Lynette assured her that they had all come.

"Oh, what have I done?" Abby whispered slowly. "I've ruined all your lives. This will take every cent we have. Just let me die."

"No, Mom ..."

"Is Ann here?" Ann was still holding her hand. She squeezed it now, and Abby seemed reassured, but still didn't open her eyes fully.

"Mom, we know it wasn't you, not really you ..."

"Try to explain to your father why I did this," Abby said softly.

"He knows, Mom, he knows this isn't you ...."

"All the evidence is at the house." They could barely hear her. "I'm so tired."

A nurse appeared, signalling that they shouldn't stay.

"I want you to get some sleep now, Mom. We're all here, we'll stay with Dad. We know it's not you. Try to sleep and take care now. We'll be back." It took a couple of minutes, but Abby seemed to relax and gradually drifted to sleep.

The following afternoon, Dr. W. found her more alert, but still essentially immobile, with eyes half-shut. They had tried getting her to walk, but her knees had buckled beneath her. When she was taken for tests, she had to be lifted onto stretchers and wheelchairs and didn't assist in any way. She had apparently clearly told the nurse, "I don't want any breakfast," but while she responded to Dr. W.'s commands to move various body parts, she "couldn't or wouldn't" repeat even her name to him, and responded to all other questions with, "I don't remember." She fumbled with the glass and straw when offered a drink, and didn't manage to get much in her mouth; when helped, she swallowed some, then let the rest dribble out of her mouth. Later, Dr. W. found her sitting in a chair with dinner in front of her.

"I got a little down," was her first sentence to him. But she said she didn't remember her children visiting her, nor even how many children she had.

When one of the children arrived for a visit, she had put her finger over her mouth, then pointed at something in the ceiling, "Shhh," she said, "They're listening." Another time, she asked Lynnette if she had "found the clothes." Lynette answered that they had, and had given them to the police.

"They're trying to trick you," Abby warned.

Their family doctor came to see her, and she told him she had been having nightmares about her family, but was vague about when or how long. The answer to all his other questions was, "I can't remember." When Abby and Lynette had seen him the week before, Dr. N. had understood immediately that there was another patient involved, not just George and Effie, and had diagnosed "severe caregiver burnout" for Abby. They had discussed Abby's slightly elevated blood pressure, and her concern that she, too, might be getting Alzheimer's, then set the wheels in motion to take some of the load off her.

The fourth day after the homicide, Abby took a turn for the better. She saw a lawyer and was able to discuss his role with the psychiatrist, and consent to having her medical records examined by police and copies retained. She was able to answer questions about her family. She indicated she had reasons to be anxious, but they didn't discuss anything related to the homicide, and the psychiatrist, Dr. W., felt that she should not yet be aggressively questioned.

Following the homicide, the police had interviewed Abby's neighbours. Without exception, they described her as kind, helpful, cheerful, hard-working, supportive and friendly. Almost everyone had a story about some kindness Abby had done. Her friend Cath said, "I can't in my wildest dreams imagine she could have done this. Never! She's a kind, generous woman. She'd do anything for anyone, and never mean-mouthed a soul. She's just a good woman." The police asked everyone how they would feel if Abby were released back home into the community. To a person, they said they would be happy with that; many expressed the hope that she would return because they wanted to provide her with care and support.

Her family was blown way.

"She's just about the biggest-hearted person in the world," George said. "I've never known anyone who knew her who didn't like her, going way back to when she was a kid."

Cath was allowed to visit briefly, and she brought cards and messages from the neighbourhood. The family was in and out. Abby started taking an interest in things, began eating and drinking ("My daughter says to eat, so I eat!") was pleasant and smiling to the nurses, and returned to talking in a normal voice. She was able to get around slowly on her own. Occasionally, she would get tearful.

The sixth day after the homicide, she was discharged with the understanding that she would undergo a evaluation at the Forensic Psychiatric Institute within thirty days. Her final diagnosis in hospital had been severe reactive anxiety to her sister-in-law's death, dissociative amnesia, caregiver burnout, and possible but not yet investigated early Alzheimer's. Dr. W. noted, "Her differential diagnosis [the range of possible diagnoses to be explored] has to include malingering to evade facing possible charges related to her sister-in-law's death."

At the Forensic Institute, she was given a battery of tests. One session had to be cancelled when Abby began weeping. "I'm scared. I will die here." She said it over and over again, then, "I just broke. I needed help for a long time, but no one knew what to do until I broke. I don't remember what happened ... but I'm going to die for something I didn't do."

Abby told the psychologist that she couldn't remember being in King George Hospital at all, or any of the circumstances around Effie's death (which she claimed to have learned about for the very first time during her second interview with the FPI psychologist) and only "bits and pieces" for weeks before that. She said that otherwise her memory had been fine until she came to FPI, and she denied having had any difficulties with her sister-in-law, or that she had been overly burdened taking care of Effie and George. One day, she appeared to have a stroke, losing her vision and hearing, developing paralysis on her right side, and seeming unresponsive. However, after she was rushed to emergency, no indication of a stroke or neurological damage could be found. The psychologist concluded that Abby's memory problems concerning the homicide did not appear to be related to any cognitive or neuropsychological damage, but were more likely to be psychologically or emotionally related.

The FPI psychiatrist who assessed Abby felt that she was suffering from delirium when she arrived, which had since been resolved by time. Dr. R. also diagnosed major depression, which had probably been building up before the homicide; Abby was responding very well to antidepressant medication in FPI. The psychiatrist found no severe mental disorder, and saw that Abby understood the ramifications of her situation and the machinations of the court process, so recommended that she be found fit to stand trial.

And so a trial date was set. Now Abby would be examined and assessed yet again. I was called upon by the Crown, and the defence retained a psychiatrist, my buddy Dr. Q., and a psychologist, Dr. R.

This was the third set of mental-health professionals to vet Abby, and each set had different objectives. At King George, the physicians' and psychiatrists' job was to diagnose and treat her acute, immediate condition. At FPI, it was to diagnose and treat her continuing or current condition, and to evaluate her fitness to stand trial. Now, our task was to assess her mental state at the time of the homicide.

In her contacts with all these people (as well as the police), Abby gave varying versions of her recollections before and after Effie's death, but concerning the actual killing, she was absolutely consistent, through hours and hours of separate interviews, and right through the trial. Her only answers to questions bearing on what happened were, "I don't remember," "I can't remember," and "I don't know."

The defence chosen was not guilty on the basis of automatism. Once more the claim was that the accused had committed the homicide in an unconscious and involuntary state. Once more the tactic was to link the automatism defence (a strictly legal term) with a dissociative state (a medical term for a mental process) experienced by the accused. And again the accused person's claim of amnesia (for the event) threw up an insurmountable barrier to reliably determining the truth of what had happened.

Both the psychologist and the psychiatrist called by the defence confirmed, on the stand, what they had said in their reports: that they believed Abby Dixon had been in a dissociative state when she killed her sister-in-law. Dr. Q. allowed that dissociation was "a theoretical construct, not a scientifically proven phenomenon," wherein, under stress, a fragment of a person's mind, rather than the whole mind, directs that person's behaviour. Examples were given of people in a severely dissociative state: combatants in war, the girl who is being raped by her father and "who removes herself to somewhere else in the room" while the assault is taking place, and sleepwalkers.

Abby was felt to have been particularly vulnerable to dissociation: first, because she was under great stress; second, she was terribly fatigued (in addition to her heavy work load, it had been months since she had slept more than three or four hours a night); and third, because of her personality — she was so stoic and over-controlled that she could not admit ever having felt anger, let alone expressed it. Family and friends said, many times, that she always refused help, never got mad, was always under control. Something (and it could have been something very minor) tipped the scales that night and overwhelmed her psychological defences, Dr. R. testified. Dr. Q. conceded that it is not easy to draw the line between behaviours motivated by an intense emotion such as rage, as opposed to behaviours based on a dissociative state, and that one couldn't say that she had no awareness or no consciousness at all of what she was doing; it was a matter of degree. The psychologist and the psychiatrist were agreed that Abby's total and dense amnesia was an indicator of her having been in a dissociative state, with no conscious memory of the homicide to fall back on.

The prosecution took the position that the homicide had been a case of repressed anger and resentment that had exploded in rage, like a pressure cooker that builds up until it finally blows its top. After interviewing Abby and Lynette, and reviewing the voluminous amount of material that had been gathered over the past year, I felt sure that the most plausible explanation for the amnesia — assuming it had not been malingering — was a psychological repression of the memories of the homicide. Rather than resulting from the incident itself and her unconscious role in it, the amnesia came about as a result of Abby's emotional reaction to the homicide and her processing of those memories and thoughts. The thought of what she had done became unbearable, so it was repressed out of consciousness.

The amnesia was first noted as a symptom only after she left Cath's house. She had gone to her friend's place knowing what she had done ("I killed her. I killed Effie.") and prepared for the consequences. She wrote down her children's contact addresses, asked Cath and Will to call them to come, made references to her husband and told them she had killed Effie. She was thoroughly distraught, but at that point she had some substantial memory for what had happened. In the hospital, in acute distress that manifested itself in severe physiological impairment, she anguished that she had ruined all their lives, that she would cost them a lot of money; she referred to "evidence at the house," and asked if Lynette had "the clothes," presumably meaning the clothes she had changed before going to Cath's. The period for which she was amnesiac then expanded, so that by the time I interviewed Abby, it included weeks before the homicide. She could not remember Lynette's or Ross's or Dr. N.'s visits having occurred, or interactions with neighbours, or shopping with Effie. Consciously and unconsciously, she had been processing what she had done. The more she processed and was devastated by it, the more memories she repressed.

As for the dissociation idea, I saw no clear basis for that diagnosis in terms of Abby's behaviour or mental functioning. Her amnesia did not present itself as a prior symptom, and she had no prior history of dissociating. Her claimed dissociative vulnerability was not indicative that she had actually dissociated. Her stress, fatigue and personality were risk factors for something happening, but not necessarily dissociation. (Someone with a couch-potato lifestyle who eats too much butter cannot be presumed to have heart disease.) Additionally, there are no clear, objective criteria for diagnosing dissociation on its own, and Abby did not fit any of the dissociative disorders except dissociative amnesia. Since the amnesia did not arise until after the killing, as I argued, such a diagnosis was not relevant to what was going on during the killing. In any case, amnesia for an event does not indicate that the person was acting unconsciously or involuntarily during the event, only that he or she does not remember it later on.

There is no reliable scientific evidence to link dissociation with a lack of awareness or control of one's behaviour. Even if we granted that some cases of dissociation can involve a lack of awareness or voluntary control, there would have to be direct evidence that this particular accused in this particular homicide was acting unconsciously and involuntarily.

The evidence seemed to be all to the contrary. Abby had left her house sometime in the middle of the night, carrying a large flashlight, and made her way to Effie's. We don't know what transpired between the two women; Effie might even have been asleep when Abby arrived.

We do know that Abby went into the kitchen and got out a long knife. She may have put the rubber gloves on then, or she may have put them on later. Why, if she was acting unconsciously, wouldn't she have used whatever was closest — the flashlight, or her hands, to attack Effie?

She then stabbed Effie twenty-nine times, plus two long running wounds to her back, apparently inflicted after Effie had died and been turned over. Dr. Q. suggested that dramatic overkill is often a sign of unconscious behaviour, but I believe there has never been any study to prove that, and am convinced that it is more likely to occur deliberately, while the perpetrator is enraged. Following Effie's death, Abby dragged the body over to the hall and ransacked the main floor of the house. She was wearing rubber gloves, which appeared suspiciously as though the intention was not to leave fingerprints. I don't know much about the methodology of ransacking, but apparently the forensic experts saw a pattern that told them the vandalism had been staged. The defence would claim that this was a sign of a disorganized mind, but I had little doubt that it was part of a series of puposeful, goal-directed activities. There was a pile of loose change by the body, and the empty change purse and wallet cards had been tossed into bushes at the side of the pathway, where they could easily be found.

After the killing, Abby returned home, removed her boots and put them in their regular place by the stove. She took off her bloody shirt and jeans, and put them in a garbage bag along with her gloves and flashlight. She wrote down the names and addresses of her children, put on her husband's boots and jacket, and went over to her friends' house and told them she had "killed Effie." Blood and print analyses later connected the clothes, boots and rubber gloves to the scene.

There were other clues (not proof) that Abby's actions could have been fuelled by rage. According to neighbours, family and Abby herself, Effie had become an extremely difficult person to care for, contrary, stubborn, spiteful, and even physically threatening. Abby had felt, for months, that she couldn't do anything right in Effie's eyes; everything she did was wrong or not good enough. Once Effie had yanked on the ladder Abby was standing on, almost knocking her off from ten feet up. Another time, while Abby was chopping kindling, she had turned around just in time to duck as Effie came towards her with a heavy piece of wood raised to strike her. Effie was angry that Abby felt she had to "supervise" her medications. Abby didn't clean the kitchen properly. Effie didn't need a bath, Abby did. And that husband of hers was just lazy. Abby was hurt and frustrated, exhausted and stretched to the max, but she kept it bottled up tight, almost to the end.

At this point, the defence took a flyer and raised the issue of sleep-walking. Sleep-related violence occupies a special niche in the law, another example of the legal system running behind medical findings. The closest defence is still automatism, although sleepwalking itself has become, in a variety of forms, a recognized mental disorder since the law on sleepwalking originally developed; it should therefore fall under the Not Criminally Responsible on account of Mental Disorder defence. The whole issue has always been controversial. A sensational Canadian case roused public furor years ago, when a man claimed to have got in his car, driven many miles and murdered his in-laws in their home, all while he was asleep.

People can do many things in their sleep, but generally, these are unsophisticated activities. A sleepwalker may urinate, go down stairs, eat, respond to simple commands or carry on a conversation. It won't be much of a conversation — a response or two — and the sleepwalker's motor actions are usually slowed down. Activities are usually of low complexity. Although cases have been reported of people operating machinery while asleep, it is very rare. As for violence, it may sometimes occur as a sleepwalker tries frantically to escape a nightmare threat of some kind, and he or she may even lash out to ward off an imagined attacker, but the motions are likely to be feeble.

Could Abby Dixon have been sleepwalking when she killed her sis-ter-in-law? No. Her actions were too complex, required too much strength and too much time, even for her to have sleepwalked through the murder itself, then awakened afterward and carried out the cover-up activities. It is also highly unusual for a person to have a single episode of adult sleepwalking, and Abby had never done it before. Dr. Q. and I were in agreement on the unlikelihood of that having happened.

The prosecutor inserted money as a final possible motive for the killing. George and Abby were the sole beneficiaries of Effie's will. However, the Dixons said they only learned about that after Effie's death, and their years of frugal living had allowed them to accumulate two hundred thousand in their own bank account. While Effie's money could have made things more comfortable for them, there was no evidence that Abby had planned the killing in the mistaken belief they would gain the inheritance as a result. And Abby herself ruled out euthanasia as a merciful deliverance from Effie's Alzheimer's. "No one but God has that right," she said firmly.

The jury was out quite a while, and I couldn't blame them. To my surprise, they came back with a verdict of Guilty of Second Degree Murder. A legally correct verdict, I felt, but one that carried an unfair sentence: life imprisonment, with no chance of parole for between ten and twenty-five years. The judge picked ten, the least she could. Abby Dixon would be in her mid-80s when released, having missed critical years with her husband, and posing virtually no risk of re-offending; that she was living in deep remorse was obvious. How much more humane if Abby could have pleaded guilty at the outset and received a sentence, with the judge being allowed discretion to go well below the statutory minimum of ten years. She and her defence team wouldn't have had to mount a trial — with mental-health professionals debating whether or not their square peg (dissociation, and perhaps sleepwalking) fit into the round hole of a non-medical defence (automatism). In the present system, the defence has to shoot for the lowest possible sentence regardless of the facts, and if it is clear that a plain Not Guilty won't do it, then the lawyers have to fight hard for the closest match to it. Murder is *not* a humane act, and leading an otherwise noble, self-sacrificing life does *not* entitle you to "get away with it." There just has to be a better way to resolve individual cases.

Abby was the image of everyone's grandmother, including mine, a "salt of the earth" type who had conducted her life based on a strong sense of morality and hard work. Rarely have I felt so uncomfortable — and even a little dirty — despite my intellectually honest testimony.

Chapter Fifteen

A Sort of Frantic Night

At the Orca Bar, the staff were taking the usual Welfare Wednesday precautions. Servers had been warned not to serve patrons who were obviously intoxicated, and to let any altercations be handled by the manager, Reg Holman, or the doorman. The lights had also been turned up a little brighter than normal so they could see better what was going on. Known to outsiders as "the Orchid", the pub had a regular clientele — "98 percent male, 97 percent gay," as Reg described it. But it was a big room in a rough part of town, and the day the social-assistance cheques came in, more than the usual crowd would turn up. Things could get out of hand if staff didn't enforce the rules.

Reg, who presides over the bar with authority, swears (along with many hospital emergency-room workers) that the worst problems arise when Welfare Wednesday coincides with a full moon. There was nearly a full moon this particular evening, and the Orca's patrons kept Reg and his servers active, squelching squabbles that threatened to turn into fights. "It was kind of frantic," he said the next day, "but under control. We're almost always able to protect people, physically, in the bar.

"But," he added ruefully, "we can't stop them from taking trouble home." In fact, he had done his best that night to prevent one of his regular patrons from leaving in the wrong company.

As he and the assistant bartender moved from table to table, they had come across a pair of drinkers long banned from the Orca. "C'mon, you guys, you know you're not allowed in here," Reg told Gus and Rainbeau. "How about just leaving quietly." But the two were inclined to stay, and they had a few friends who agreed. Soon the four of them were on their feet arguing with Reg. The assistant bartender had to leave to put out a fire at another table, but Reg felt he was on the verge of solving the problem when an unfamiliar fellow with bleached hair burst in, claiming, "Leave these guys alone. I'll deal with it."

"This doesn't concern you, " Reg had told the interloper quietly, "go sit down." In response, the man wheeled on Reg and pointed a threatening finger at him, saying, "I can take you out, man," then, to the server who had come up to the table: "And I can take *you* out, too." He then walked away, put a barstool against the wall, leaned back and stared intently at Reg.

The banned pair saw something intimidating about the man that Reg had missed, and they allowed themselves to be escorted peacefully to the door. On his way back to the bar, Reg stopped to greet someone he recognized, and as he did, the obstreperous character got off his barstool, came over and grabbed the man's beer. The surprised patron demanded the return of his glass, and the stranger slammed it down and returned to his seat. Reg was about to go for the doorman, to have the man removed, when the bartender leaned across the counter to warn him: the troublemaker was wearing brass knuckles.

The manager called the police. It's what you do if there's someone in your bar with a dangerous weapon. He studied the man as he described his appearance to the operator, and his stare was returned. Reg was chilled by the look. There was something more to it than drink or drugs, he thought.

"You didn't have to call the police," the man told Reg on his way to the Men's room. When he emerged and headed towards the exit, a departing regular nicknamed "McHappy" said to the bartender, "You don't have to worry about him. He's going home with me." The bartender relayed the comment to Reg. Shocked, Reg hastened outside to warn McHappy. He tried to do an end-run around the man using a side exit, but arrived out front just in time to hear him ask McHappy, "Are you going to South Bay? Can I share a cab with you?" They got into the taxi together and left.

Reg called the cab company dispatch, gave them the number of the vehicle, and asked them to monitor the ride because their driver was carrying a passenger who had been reported to police and could be dangerous. He followed up with a call to the police to tell them where the man was. Now it was out of his control. He looked at his watch; it was almost closing time.

As he was leaving the locked pub an hour later, two police officers arrived in response to the call concerning the man with the brass knuckles. Reg related the sequence of events, including his conversation with police reporting the cab number. Yeah, maybe nothing had happened, he said, but you can't be too cautious around people who are drinking.

At four in the morning, Reg sank into bed at home. His last thought before sleeping was of McHappy, a jovial but meek type. If Reg had known his real name — Bill something? — he could have telephoned. Naw. It was definitely none of his business. Besides, he'd hear tomorrow if anything unusual happened to one of the regulars.

Over in South Bay, Ruby Lee was having a nightmare. A heavy sleeper, she seemed to be involved with drums and loud chanting, which evolved into shouts, bangs and thuds as she gradually came to. It sounded like a fight, and it seemed to be happening right above her. Things were hitting the floor in the apartment upstairs, and now she heard a man shouting an obscenity. She lay transfixed, too scared to move a muscle. The bumps subsided. Maybe they had all gone home, she reasoned sleepily.

Now she heard the sound of running water: someone was having a shower. No, it was closer. Was her toilet running? Resentfully, she got up and shuffled down the hall. The first thing she saw was a waterfall on one wall, water coming out of the ceiling and spilling down to the floor. Now it was turning red. A waterfall of blood. Ruby let out a scream just as the fire alarm sounded, and she thought she was losing her mind. *Wake up*, she told herself, *get help*. She ran out into the hall, wailing the apartment manager's name.

Tony was already racing to the electrical room to determine the source of the alarm, and she followed him, crying about blood on the wall, and fighting. A water leak on Ruby's floor had set off the alarm. At her apartment, the manager took one look at the red flood, said, "William!" and was gone up the stairwell.

He knocked, unlocked the door, pushed it half-way open, calling out the tenant's name. He could see blood all over the hall walls, wet carpet, something metal on the floor, perhaps a knife.

A man appeared at the end of the hall. He simply stood there, shirt unbuttoned, hands hanging at his sides, looking at and through Tony. "Who are you?" Tony demanded.

"He tried to rape me." The man said the words without emotion, in a tone so glacial it frightened Tony. He pulled the door shut, holding it closed. Other tenants had gathered, some peering out of their doorways. "Get into your suites, lock your doors and call 911 NOW, "he ordered everyone.

One old man two doors down didn't appear to hear. Tony released the door handle. In almost the same motion, the door opened and the man inside came through, brandishing an industrial-weight toilet plunger up high, and heading right for Tony. Tony ran to the old man, shoved him ahead into his suite, and slammed and locked the door behind them. He heard the heavy metal fire-exit door open, and then footsteps running down the stairs.

Within five minutes, the police had arrived. Tony let them into William's apartment and the two constables entered, guns drawn. He heard one of them make an exclamation, and within minutes they were back out.

Was William in there? Was he okay? The officer allowed that they had found a dead male approximating Tony's description of William, with what appeared to be multiple stab wounds. Could he go in? Tony asked. William had been a friend as well as tenant.

"It's not something you want to see," the constable said gently.

There had been an explosion of violence between two men: a fight that had taken place in various rooms, and involved six knives and a pair of brass knuckles. William "McHappy" Bogner had died, naked and hemorrhaging on a flooded bathroom floor, after being stabbed more than sixty times.

Mike Mallory was soon reported to police, by a passerby who called about a suspicious, shirtless man staggering near Bogner's apartment building, carrying a plunger. (When details of the murder were released in the media, a few days later, someone called to say he had seen a plunger being tossed into a dumpster by a similar-looking person. The plunger was never recovered, but a bloody shirt was found nearby.)

Nevertheless, Mallory managed to make it across town to the house he shared with half a dozen other young people. All of them were welfare recipients, and all but two had gone out partying the night before and either hadn't returned or were too "out of it" to hear Mike trying to get in at 4:30 in the morning. The whole house had spent the afternoon beer-drinking (they had headed out the moment the cheques arrived in the mail, as was their custom), with pills and marijuana for snacks. Mike's best friend, Miller, had declined on the evening club crawl and stayed home reading comic books, while his girlfriend, Mia, smoked dope. They had popped a few Valium and gone to bed early. Miller got up and opened the door for Mike.

Mike pushed past into his room, got some cash and ran out to pay a cab. When he came back in, he fell apart, "crying and freaking" as Miller put it. Between sobs, Mike told him he might have killed a guy.

"He fucked me up the ass! He told me I could shower alone, then he fucked me!" There was blood on Mike's pants and chest. "I stabbed him. There was so much blood!" He talked of turning himself in, but he was scared shitless of going to jail. "He raped me! I need an AIDS test. I'm dirty, gotta wash it off." And over and over: "My god, I think I killed someone!"

Miller grabbed Mia's car keys and took Mike for a drive to calm him down. It didn't work. The cops stopped them for not wearing seatbelts, of all things. Miller didn't possess a driver's licence, so the police gave him a ticket and called a tow truck as well. Meanwhile, Mike, still shirtless, was being belligerent and uncooperative, refusing to give his name or provide identification: "I don't have to give you that. He's the driver, I'm just the passenger, so you got nothing!" The officer noted he was unsteady and perhaps slurring his words. Miller had enough cash with him, so the car got towed home, while Mike and Miller rode in the truck.

As soon as he saw the police flash their lights, Miller had grabbed Mike's arm and told him to pull himself together, to stop crying. When they left the tow truck, Mike fell apart again, and Miller had to half-carry him into the house. Mia wasn't too happy about her car being towed, but she got over it when Mike's story emerged between crying jags. For a few hours, she consoled Mike; they smoked, wept and talked, but remained confused. Mike removed his bloody clothes and shoes, and left them sitting by his bed. Finally, he said he had to get out of there, so they got back in the car, Miller driving again, somewhat aimlessly. Mike eventually had them drop him off at a midtown intersection, but didn't say where he was going from there. When Miller and Mia got home, the police were interviewing their puzzled housemates. Mike's wallet and underwear had been found at the crime scene. Mike turned himself in the next day.

Mallory was originally charged with second-degree murder. The defence wanted a complete acquittal, or at least a lesser conviction for manslaughter, arguing that the accused had committed the homicide in the heat of passion as a result of provocation, heightened by intoxication and a "homosexual panic reaction." This was a grab-bag of defences and excuses, including the legal defence of provocation, which deserves to be abolished. No matter what label it would wear to court, Mike's defence was based on a claim that he lacked any intent to kill because he was acting, temporarily, totally out of control. I was called by the Crown to make an assessment.

That Mike had been intoxicated that evening seemed clear. By his own account and those of his friends, he had cashed his cheque at noon, then gone to the bar. There he drank beer and played pool for three hours, when he bought a few cases of brew and went home. Someone in the house had "found" a big jar of Valium in a pharmacy dumpster, and someone else had locked onto a "huge" source of marijuana, so he and his housemates, who got along well, sat around smoking pot, listening to music, drinking beer, and popping pills until eight or nine in the evening. Mike and some of the others then went club-hopping. He claimed a fuzzy memory for part of the evening, but knew that at one point he had been in an infamous drug area, smoking marijuana from a pipe because he was "too drunk to roll his own," and tossing back Valiums without anything to wash them down. He admitted that, lately, if he went without Valium for more than about three hours, he would get irritable, but that finding a supply never seemed to pose a problem.

Somewhere around 1 a.m., his friends were "starting to annoy" him, so Mike went off on his own. He tried to get into a fairly upscale club, which he described as "a good place to meet hot women," but the bouncer turned him away. He went down the street to the Orca, where he had at least two drinks in a short time (and tried to swipe another). He then left, he would claim, with William promising him beer and pot at his place. Two and a half hours later, after the murder, he was observed by street witnesses as well as the police to be staggering and slurring his words. It couldn't be clearly proven that he was still intoxicated at that point, but there was a good case for intoxication having influenced his judgment and memory up to and including the time of the homicide.

Mike's memories of the substances he had abused during the evening corroborated testimony of his friends and other witnesses, drawing a picture of a definitely intoxicated person by 2 a.m., and who was probably still significantly so at 4:30 a.m. (The murder took place at about 3 a.m.)

His general drinking patterns and criminal record suggested that when intoxicated, he could become obnoxious and aggressive, with poor judgment and self-control. By his own account, he had above-average violent tendencies, and at the time of the homicide, there were outstanding warrants for his arrest for robbery, aggravated assault and assault, as well as past convictions on similar charges.

He told me he always acted in self-defence, in full control, and never initiated a fight. This may or may not have been true, but I rarely encounter anyone who admits to starting fights, despite the obvious truth that somebody usually does. In the Orca Bar, Mike seemed to have been spoiling for a fight, and in that frame of mind I believe he would have had a very low threshold for responding to any perceived threat or insult with aggression or violence.

Then there was the defence postulation that Mike was an innocent heterosexual who had suddenly found himself in a threatened position by a homosexual and had gone temporarily psychotic: the "homosexual panic reaction." I was dismayed to see that old chestnut brought up. The term was floated by Freudians in the 1920s, referring to a terror, perhaps going as far as temporary insanity in the form of a psychotic episode, felt by a repressed homosexual when he or she acknowledges the threat of being tempted by homosexuality. A favourite example is the macho football player who allows himself to be seduced by an older gay man, then in a fit of rage suddenly lashes out and kills his seducer.

The term hangs on, although the definition was never precise. It first leaned heavily on Freud's contention that everyone is a latent homosexual. It has since been expanded by some to include the sudden, intense fear that one is homosexual, or the fear that one would act out closet homosexual impulses. Over the years, "homosexual panic reaction" came to rest on a broader base, sometimes being used to describe a state of anxiety or neurosis without the usual eruption of violence.

"Homosexual panic reaction" was coined and used while homosexuality was considered a mental disorder. North American psychiatrists generally cast this biased categorization aside more than twenty-five years ago, tending to believe that most people have latent or limited openness to homosexual conduct, however unconscious. An apparently purely heterosexual man, particularly when intoxicated, may experience some homosexual feelings when an advance is made to him. These feelings will, however, be ambivalent, conflicted or uncomfortable according to the degree of discomfort that the individual has with homosexual feelings. In our still partially homophobic society, however, a negative reaction to any kind of homosexual encounter is as likely to be caused by homophobia as it is by fear of one's own homosexuality.

There is no good reason to separate out violent consequences of "homosexual panic reaction" and give them a special classification. They are acts of violence towards another person, bearing the same legal responsibilities as any other assault, and today are usually treated as such. (Unfortunately, some accused assailants blame their victims, for having "asked for it," much as heterosexual rapists sometimes still do.)

The evening did raise a number of questions concerning Mike's sexuality, and it is impossible to answer all of them. Why, for instance, had he gone into, and stayed in, an openly gay bar? Usually, men go to the Orca if they are either gay, or with gay friends or acquaintances. Mike went alone. Perhaps he drunkenly chose that bar because it was the only nearby place to get a drink, given that he had been refused down the street.

Or perhaps he was a psychiatrist doing research on a case. I found myself in that area one night not long after I had interviewed Mike

Mallory, so I made a detour on the way back to my hotel. In the late evening hours (the same time Mike had paid his visit), there were no women, a gay clientele clearly predominated, and overt homosexual flirtation abounded. Posters in the entranceway advertised male strippers, gay events and AIDS support groups. It was unmistakably a gay bar — very difficult even for someone intoxicated, I thought, to miss its character.

Although there was apparently some contact between Mike and William inside the Orca Bar, another indication that Mike was aware of what he was doing is that he seemed to take the initiative by asking if he could share William's cab specifically to South Bay — a district on the opposite side of the city to Mike's home. So he went to William's, where they smoked marijuana and Mike fell asleep watching television. When he awoke, he was — his own words — "grinning and feeling a bit giggly." William made a mild pass at him by putting his hand on Mike's thigh. Mike said he wasn't feeling at all threatened at that point. In fact, instead of leaving, Mike asked if he could take a shower alone, then proceeded to do so, presumably without locking the bathroom door. None of these actions proves anything about Mike's sexuality, although they suggest a possibility of openness, even if unconscious, to homosexual contact. We could also indulge in pure speculation: that Mike picked William as a mark whom he planned to rob of money or drugs and was leading up to that with a pseudo seduction.

On one hand, we have Mike's professedly unthreatened attitude towards someone he knows is a homosexual; on the other hand, we have Mike's childhood.

He was the only child in a house full of animosity, where nothing got talked out. His alcoholic father sometimes punched him, but mostly put him down with words like "worthless" and "dummy." His mother was also abused, "a nervous wreck," and seemed to take her anger out on Mike by yelling and hitting. He quit school as soon as he could, at 17, and had lived on welfare and as a street musician for the ten years since.

He talked fairly easily about his background, and about his sexual relationships as an adult. Nothing unusual, going out with girlfriends, sometimes casually, one for as long as two years. He had never had a sexual relationship with a man. He said he had nothing against homosexuality, "to each his own, just don't try to impose anything on me." He hadn't even been curious about it as an adolescent.

His only experience that way was with his uncle.

He found it painful to talk about. Our conversation slowed right down, as he wrestled with the memories, visibly tortured, at times in tears. It had been a sunny winter day, the first time, and he was about five years old. His father and his uncle had been drunk, but they had all gone skating on a pond. Without warning, the ice had split beneath Mike's feet and he dropped into the frigid water. There was momentary fright and confusion, but then he was pulled out, rescued by his Uncle Bing. Uncle Bing wrapped Mike up in his big coat, bundled him into his car and took him home, where he showered with him to warm him up, soaped, washed and dried him, and rubbed his big erection between Mike's buttocks. Mike remembered not liking it, but not knowing it was wrong, especially since Uncle Bing was the big hero of the day for saving him. He had a vague memory of the man stroking a plunger handle. (Was he trying to turn the little boy on — or had the boy got that mixed up in his memory?)

About two years later, there was another incident. By then, Mike had figured out that his uncle's family was even worse than his own, because Uncle Bing yelled even harder and hit his daughters harder and drank harder than Mike's parents. He had come to hate the guy. One weekend, Uncle Bing took Mike fishing, just the two of them. Wasn't that nice of Uncle Bing, his mother said. In the car, he unzipped his fly and told Mike to "grab it." The boy felt apprehensive, but his uncle insisted, and Mike "felt he had to do it." He wasn't fearful, he said, it was pretty calm. Again, he didn't tell anyone about the episode. He knew what his parents' reaction would have been.

In his teens he learned that Uncle Bing had raped his daughter, one of her friends and his disabled niece. There were never any charges laid, although his wife divorced him, Mike said. His own anger at the man seemed to grow and grow. He couldn't get rid of the hate, sickness and disgust at what had been done to the girls and to himself. Just before he left home for good, his uncle shot and killed Mike's dog. The dog was ill and Bing's gun was cheaper than a veterinarian's needle, but nobody consulted Mike. He felt like killing his uncle.

When he was about 10 years old, he found a man masturbating while he stared at Mike through a hole in a public washroom stall. The police were called, and Mike was first frightened, then angry about the invasion of his privacy. He took to using "fag" as his major epithet with other boys at school.

After talking to Mike, I reasoned that two troublesome emotions had probably collided just before the murder: one reflecting his possibly unconscious and conflicted receptiveness to William; the other his strong, longstanding homophobia. In the situation that led to the fight, they evoked a powerful reaction exacerbated by Mike's intoxication and his propensity for violence.

Mallory said he had no recollection of being in the Orca Bar, of actually stabbing William, or of anything between the fight and the following day, when he woke up at a friend's place. But he did remember some events, and although there were gaps in his credibility as well as his story, he was for the most part forthcoming with me. A great deal about the actual crime had also been learned from apartment witnesses, police who examined the scene, blood-splatter analysis and the forensic pathologist who provided the autopsy report.

The picture shapes up like this. According to Mallory, Mike "snaps awake" sitting on the sofa beside William, the television on. He looks around and grins. William smiles at him and puts his hand on Mike's thigh. Mike vaguely recalled saying, "No — I'm not like that," nonchalantly, in a good mood, not feeling threatened. He got up, but his head started to spin and he felt a bit nauseous. He asked William if he wanted to go to an after-hours club, but couldn't remember the reply. He then asked William if he could take a shower "alone" — because he felt sweaty and had drooled in his sleep, but mostly to clear his head and wake up.

When he pulled back the shower curtain to step out, William was there, naked, with an erection, saying, "I know you want it, you little bitch." He was holding the toilet plunger in one hand and stroking it up and down in the other. Mike let out a wordless scream, and next recalls wrestling in the bathroom, falling backwards in the shower.

The fighting went on and on. Mike yelled, "Fuck!" and "Fuck off!" a lot and very loudly. They went round and round. He had only one foggy recollection of a knife: while they were circling in a bear hug, he thought he remembered slamming William's back with a knife in his hand. William didn't seem to want to stop wrestling, Mike said, and he was stronger. Mike didn't feel he was getting anywhere. The next thing Mike remembered was being dropped off near Key Park (not at a midtown intersection) by Miller and Mia; then there was a gap until he awoke next morning.

William's upstairs neighbour, as well as Ruby Lee, confirmed the shouting and banging in the protracted struggle. The police and pathologists had uncovered much more. A total of six knives and one knuckle duster had been used. The attacks had left large pools of blood in the bathroom, hall and on the bed. There was blood spattered throughout the apartment, on walls, furniture, windows and appliances, indicating that the fight had indeed travelled. The toilet tank had been smashed, which was the major source of the flooding. How the knives came into play, we don't know. Two had broken blades, presumably snapped during the fight. At some point, a bloody hand retrieved additional knives from a kitchen drawer.

William's stab wounds were grouped in critical spots on his body: in and around his heart (one or more of which caused his death), in his throat and the back of his neck (severing jugular veins), and in his chest and abdomen (puncturing his lungs, stomach, liver, diaphragm and kidneys). Some of this grouping suggested that the hits had been made while there was little relative movement between the fighters. Lacerations were, however, scattered over most of the body, showing that at one time or another, there had been considerable movement. One group of stab wounds had resulted in hardly any bleeding into the adjacent tissues, which suggested that those wounds had been inflicted after the victim's death. Abrasions on the forehead were consistent with having been hit by brass knuckles. Knife cuts on the arms and hands were consistent with defensive wounds caused while the victim attempted to ward off blows from his assailant.

Mike Mallory had volunteered to show the arresting officers his own wounds: some scratches on his back, perhaps fingernail marks, but not caused by a weapon; fabric abrasions, possibly caused by knocking against items in the apartment, and a black eye.

Given the lack of eyewitnesses, it was not a simple matter to sort out the mental state of the accused at the time of the homicide. Mike himself claimed not to remember crucial points of the evening, let alone the fight and subsequent death. It's possible this was true, as he could have had amnesia as a result of over-imbibing or as a psychological reaction blocking out the trauma of the event. It could also have been untrue, because he described, to me and to his friends, remembered portions of the evening, and because he was not always credible or consistent in what he said.

For example, he told the apartment manager, the first person he spoke to after the homicide, "He tried to rape me." He told his friends in graphic detail he had been raped. And in his interview with me, he described the fight in considerable detail, but gave no indication there had been any or sexual contact whatsoever — or sexual overtones, except for William's opening line as Mike stepped out of the shower. The mystery of his avowed innocence in finding himself in the company of a gay man remains. And in a telephone conversation some time after the interview, he made a point of telling me that he had never worn or owned brass knuckles.

Because we cannot be sure of Mallory's mental state from his own account of it, we have to look at his behaviour. Putting all the evidence together, I felt that there may have been three phases to his mental state. In the initial stage, at the time of the confrontation outside the shower, he may have felt fright, shock and panic. Certainly, William's comment and appearance there had an intense emotional effect on Mike. During the struggle, his feelings may have developed into a mixture of fear and anger. Finally, simple rage and a desire for vengeance may have motivated him during last of the stabbing and then the "overkill" stage, when he continued to inflict wounds after it would have been obvious that William had died. It was impossible to sort out the relative contributions of each of these emotions.

There was nothing to suggest a mental disorder or substantial mental impairment. Mike's apparently goal-directed actions, his own recollections — although limited — his straightforward, if emotionally upset, recounting to his friends, and observations of him by the building manager suggest the presence of accurate awareness. His explanation, as he told Miller and Mia, combined with the great many sequential, coordinated and effective physical acts (involving several weapons that resulted in a rather one-sided and extreme pattern of lethal injuries), disallow any conclusion other than that there was awareness and intent for the killing, at least in the later stages of the struggle. His intoxication may have added to his aggressiveness and reduced his judgment, but his capacity for awareness and intent remained; an intoxication defense would have relied on the absence of that capacity.

The issue of provocation remained. If the court found that a sudden wrongful act or insult had occurred (sufficient to deprive an ordinary person of the power of self-control), and that the accused had acted suddenly, before there was time for his passion to cool, they could decide that he had been provoked into killing. A successful provocation defence could reduce the charge from murder to manslaughter. This is legally different from a defence of automatism, but conceptually similar, with the idea of a "psychological blow" — being able to push someone over the edge into a total loss of control, a temporary insanity of sorts.

Provocation is a loose and facile defence, particularly when the killer's goal-directed actions seem to prove intent and awareness. It's pretty much an aberrant anachronism, originating in a patriarchal version of social-justice policy, including property rights to wives, which allowed a husband to come home unexpectedly, find his wife in bed with another man, terminate the pair and get off lightly.

Provocation defence is based on the notion that an ordinary, reasonable person would have lost control in the situation that brought about the killing. How do jury members go about determining if this is what happened? Essentially they have to create an artificial conception of such a person in their minds and decide how the person would have behaved — an almost impossible task. Thus although there is meant to be some kind of objectivity to this provocation defence test, in practice it is extremely subjective and ill-defined. The task becomes even more difficult when we consider that the particular personality and the psychological vulnerabilities and circumstances in the crime are unique, and must be factored into jury members' efforts to put themselves in the accused person's shoes.

And how do you draw the line between the factors the provocation defence is meant to consider and a tendency to be over-excitable, over-reactive or violent?

From a psychiatric point of view, this is difficult to deal with because there is no established means of assessing capacity for self-control. How do you establish the difference between someone who cannot control himself and someone who chooses not to control himself? Darned if I know. You can't do ethical psychology lab experiments in which you provoke people to the extreme and see if they try to kill your poor research assistant. Behavioural science has very little light to cast on this provocation issue. In fact, because psychology and psychiatry pretty much believe, at least implicitly, in complete behavioural determinism (that is, that completely free choice is an illusion), almost by definition we can't help discriminate between inability and unwillingness to control your anger.

If a provocation defence is successful, we wind up rewarding, with a lesser conviction, lack of ability to control one's anger — a strange act of favouritism, compared to the way we deal with other motivations for killing. For example, Robert Latimer, who euthanised his extremely disabled and pain-ridden daughter, cannot get the same break because his avowed motivation lay in caring for his suffering child, as opposed to having uncontrollable anger.

Unfortunately, following a three-year federal justice department review of the defence, Canada decided, in 2001, to keep provocation on the books. Public ire — but apparently not enough — had been raised after several cases in which men who murdered their wives got off with light sentences after claiming they were provoked. As there was when the defence was first used 110 years ago, a good deal of implicit gender bias is still at work here, as men are far more likely to react with lethal violence in situations where their "passions haven't cooled." Most victims are women, and it's particularly problematic when you consider that imbedded in the defence is some implicit allocation of responsibility to the victim, who supposedly triggered the passions in question.

At the other end of the spectrum, in terms of the rights of women and men, the battered-spouse defence gives wives and husbands greater leeway for lawful self-protection, and offers an example of what some argue is positive social-justice evolution in the law.

The battered-spouse defence is an extension of the self-defence defence (quite a mouthful). Essentially a spouse (in practice, almost always a woman) is allowed a pre-emptive lethal strike if certain conditions can be shown to exist with regard to herself and/or her children. There must be a history of severe physical battering, often with credible death threats, and a history of psychological and material domination (such that the woman effectively lacks the will and/or means to leave safely without undue risk of serious physical harm and/or death from enraged/vengeful hubby). All that says is that she is cornered, and in her view she has no realistic options other than to endure and perhaps be killed. In a state of learned and/or real helplessness, the woman has credible reason to fear serious physical harm or death in the near future, so is permitted a first strike before she gets into a situation where her spouse acts first and she has no way out.

Legal scholars, misogynists and some feminists criticize the defence for different reasons: scholars, because it seems to stretch self-defence law too far; misogynists, for its perceived favouritism to women; and feminists, because it characterizes certain women as weak and helpless.

But I have digressed. In the Mallory case, with its provocation defence, I came to the conclusion that an unwanted homosexual advance to a heterosexual with a background of abuse and entrenched homophobic feelings, particularly if he was raped, could meet the legal test for provocation. And considering the rather frantic and tumultuous nature of the fight, it could well have been that there was not "time for his passion to cool." All this assumes, of course, that there was at least a moderate degree of accuracy to Mike's account of an unwanted sexual advance or attack from William.

It troubled me greatly to be unable to oppose a defence which I felt was based on a bad piece of law, but in the courtroom, we often have to play by rules we disagree with. It's better than living in a country where the law is disregarded by those in the system.

By the time the case reached the courtroom, the prosecutor had accepted a plea of manslaughter from the defence, because the prosecutor said he could not disprove Mike's claim he was provoked into the killing. Mike Mallory was given five years. This struck me as a very unsatisfying outcome on principle and a rather light sentence, but arguably the best that could be done under existing homicide law.

What started as a "too intoxicated to mean to do it" case had taken a few twists and turns, defence counsel trying various defences before settling on what turned out to be a successful one. The Mallory case shows how difficult it can be to separate out the number of possible psychological states that can lead to a homicide, to say nothing of the subtle and interesting interactions between these mental states and alcohol and drugs. For all the stresses and demands of forensic psychiatry, I'd never say my work is boring.

IV

VERDICTS AND SENTENCING

"No! No! Sentence first — verdict afterwards."

— Lewis Carroll, *Alice's Adventures in Wonderland*

CHAPTER SIXTEEN

A JEALOUS WIFE

"Beef Sale!" Vonda leaned over the meat counter. Chuck steak? Short ribs? A T-bone would give the dogs something to gnaw on afterwards. No — ground beef was good enough. She sighed, picked up a package and headed down the aisle towards the Hamburger Helper. "Not *again*," Tom would complain, but at least it was something she didn't burn or mess up.

Outside, it was hot and muggy and she wished Tom had thought to pick her up after work; but he never did, and she never remembered to ask. It was only a few hours of cleaning at the rec centre, but she was tired. Lugging bags of groceries up the road, Vonda felt a stab of resentment when she caught sight of Tom's pick-up in front of the house, looking just-washed and shiny — at least compared to all the other junk parked in their yard. He must have come home early. Out of work again, she guessed. They'd be back on the dole.

It was quiet in the house. Tiptoeing, in case he was sleeping, she heard a sound in the living room and looked in. Tom was there, all right. On the couch. With *her*. With his pants wide open, and his big thing stiff, and his tongue rammed down Diane's throat.

Shee-it! That was the fucking limit. Vonda kept going, right through the kitchen and out the back door, sat down on the grass, pulled a bottle of day-glo wine out of one of the bags, unscrewed the cap and took a good suck. She was so furious, so jealous, so mad she could kill him.

And Diane. She could almost swear Diane had seen her and given her a sort of friendly look. Hah! Well, once she had thought Diane was *her* friend, at the beginning. Vonda had brought Diane and her sister Cleo home one afternoon when she worked at the bar. She was excited about the two new arrivals — they lived in such a small community — but right away Tom had begun flirting with both of them.

"So, Diane, you must be Princess Diane with that blonde hair. Doesn't she have nice silky hair, Vonnie?" And, "Cleo, sexy Cleopatra, eh. I remember Dad drooling over Elizabeth Taylor in that movie. Even as a kid I thought she was hot."

Vonda, who owed her name to some uncle who claimed he made it up when no one else could think of one, had tried but failed to come up with an actor or a major babe named Vonda. Sometime later, when she and Tom hadn't made love for weeks, she put heavy black makeup around her pale blue eyes, put on her best attempt at something filmy, and in her most seductive pose, asked Tom what he remembered about Cleopatra/Elizabeth Taylor that made her so hot. Well, he got excited all right. He insisted they call Cleo and Diane right then, just to see how they were.

Vonda decided she would skip the Princess Diane impersonation. She was pretty sure it was "Diana," anyway, and it would have been hard to disguise her own long and decidedly unsilky hair.

Now here was Diane, making out with her husband, in her house. Vonda thought about storming back inside, but took a second dose of wine instead. What was she doing wrong, and how could he prefer Diane over his own wife? For months, Tom had been paying less and less attention to Vonda. They had had arguments about it, but it always wound up with Tom telling her she was being stupid. Maybe they had hooked up with each other simply because, living in this isolated town, they had run out of choices. If you weren't sleeping with a particular "townie," it was probably because you had in the past and it hadn't worked out, or you were related, or both. Most people here drank a bit, did the odd drug, and lived fairly aimlessly, scrabbling along the poverty line.

Instead of just shacking up, though, she and Tom had got married. And when you're married, you're supposed to have sexual relations with your wife, only your wife, that was the deal. But now she wasn't getting any sex, and he seemed not to care how she felt about his fooling around with Diane, and probably Cleo. And they weren't the only ones he messed with. Oh, no. But Diane was his favourite.

Last weekend, while they were watching TV — Vonda, Tom, Diane and a few others — she stole a sidelong look and caught Tom feeling up Diane. And Vonda could tell he was getting more aroused than she had been able to make him lately. She sat there burning with anger and frustration, then got up and quietly exploded into the backyard, pounding her fists on the very tree she was slouched against now. She tried to think of a way to show the bastard, to get even with him, but she couldn't. What she needed was a smart idea to get him to stop all this.

Hearing the front door slam and footsteps going down the stairs, she rose slowly, went into the house and started making dinner. Half an hour later, Tom came bouncing in, all grin and energy, "I just took the dogs for a walk." She didn't mention what she had witnessed earlier.

Somehow this evening she cooked far too much food, but she put it out and Tom ate it, then announced he was going for his nap. Soon he was stretched out on the couch sound asleep in his usual after-dinner position, head thrown back, arm over his eyes, the television on with no sound. Vonda, as usual for her after the meal, was doing the dishes. Running Tom's infidelities through her mind, she absently sloshed the soapy water around in the basin, and eventually became aware of washing the same long knife over and over. She stopped and looked at it for a moment, dried it off carefully, then took it into the living room and slit Tom's throat from ear to ear.

When I was called to take on this case, I did a quick read through the background material. I prefer to go into the first interview fresh, then during the interval between interviews, review the material to make sure I haven't overlooked any salient factors and to check for discrepancies between the interviewee's story and other documentation. There's usually adequate time to follow up on any questions that arise.

So, wife kills husband for having affair; the accused is of below-average intelligence with little education; she has no history of violence or mental illness; comes from an inbred community rife with poverty and unemployment; poor relationship and work record. Is there any basis for a psychiatric defence?

When I met her, Vonda had been in custody for two weeks. Aside from the pallor and bad teeth that come with chronic undernourishment, she seemed in average good health and appearance for a woman in her late 20s. During my usual opening questions — vital statistics and personal history — she was slow on the uptake and not very animated. But she became livelier when I started asking about the murder.

"He deserved it! He was unfaithful, and he got what he deserved." She seemed pleased with herself. I thought she would have more to say, and she did.

"I sure fixed him. He won't do that any more."

"Had this been going on for some time, his being unfaithful?" I ask.

"About a year. All the time. They was always right there."

"Who?"

She snorts, "My ri-vals!" She stretched the word out sarcastically. "Right under my nose, he messed with them!"

So there was more than one other woman involved, and her husband hadn't tried to hide his activities. Her jealousy seemed justified, although not to the point of murder.

Could Vonda have been imagining her husband's roving eye? Intense jealousy or over-possessiveness can help flag a personality disorder, or in the odd case, a paranoid psychotic disorder with groundless delusions of infidelity. I would try to draw her out.

"Messed with them?"

"Kissed. Touchy-feely. Had *sex*. He wouldn't do it with me." She began to cry. She told me about her sad, futile attempts to win her husband back to her bed while his sexual drive seemed to be diverted elsewhere. A torrent of details started pouring out, more than I felt I needed to know.

"He put peanut butter on his dick and got her to lick it off. I wished she would *bite* it off. French kissing. He was always feeling them up. Stroking them. Pulling their penises ...."

"So he was bisexual?"

She looked at me puzzled, not understanding.

"He had affairs with males as well as females?"

"Well, yes, but mostly it was the bitches. Diane."

"Tell me about Diane."

She gave me that strange look again.

"Um, nothing special. A Heinz-57. I dunno. Friendly. Too friendly." The dawn of understanding started breaking over me.

"Sort of big. A nice coat, Tom always kept her brushed good. He took good care of them all." The tears came again.

Dogs. The family dogs. A wife kills her husband because he's unfaithful, and I expect to hear an angry story about some skirt-chaser and his floozy. I must have missed that most vital point in the police reports. And Vonda hadn't made it clear because, for her, the important thing — the real offence — was infidelity, not bestiality. She had been hurt and rejected, and was angry and jealous enough to kill. It didn't matter who, or what, her husband had forsaken her for; he had broken his marriage vows.

In rural, isolated and impoverished communities, animals often assume a more significant role than in places where there is varied, widespread personal interaction. But even in circumstances involving socially unsophisticated people in remote settings, most pets serve simply as constant companions and family members. It's unusual for a relationship to interfere.

Tom and Vonda had been married two years. Vonda knew he was fond of dogs when they married. He had two part-Alsatians, and from what she told me, he was then a responsible but ordinary pet owner, playful and broadly affectionate but not sexually involved with the dogs. At some point, he started to become more intimate with them, and concurrently his affections started to wander away from his wife. When they acquired a third dog, Tom had sent Vonda to her sister's for the weekend so he could "bond" with the new one, a shy adolescent whom he'd found shivering and hungry outside the bar. Slightly jealous of the dogs but not suspecting the depth of Tom's involvement with them, and hoping to "do something nice" to win back his attention, Vonda innocently brought home the two puppies, Diane and Cleo.

Now Tom became more and more open in his romantic involvement with the canines. Maybe he thought Vonda was condoning his behavior, because she had given him two more "girls." In any case, his sexual activities with all five dogs seemed to accelerate as his and Vonda's lovemaking deteriorated. Finally, she just could not spend one more evening watching *Married With ...* or whatever, while beside her Tom stroked and kissed someone else. So she had put an end to it.

My report to the court concluded that Vonda was without any basis for a psychiatric defence. She showed no signs of mental illness although she had "dull normal" intelligence, was uneducated and almost totally lacking in social awareness — attributes that contributed to her inability to see her husband's attraction to his pets as anything out of the ordinary.

A preliminary hearing was held, and following that, a guilty plea was entered, so there was no trial. I reiterated my assessment of Vonda in a psychiatric pre-sentence report.

Vonda had pled guilty to second-degree murder. There had been some evidence of prior intent, but not a full process of planning and deliberation to justify a first-degree charge. Vonda was given the minimum life sentence with ten years before she could apply for parole.

This was yet another case that argues for discretionary sentencing on humanitarian grounds. The prosecution had shown some leniency in accepting the second-degree conviction with minimum ten years' incarceration, using the small amount of sentencing discretion available in a reasonable manner. This slow-witted woman was clearly guilty of murder, but deserved some kind of break, I thought, and was given the best she could get in our system. I imagined her being persecuted immediately by her fellow inmates. Jail was not going to do anything but harm her. It would take far fewer than ten years for her to get the message that she should not repeat her crime, but long before that, the harsh criminal environment would damage her irreparably. Given her naive, unsophisticated nature, low intelligence and poor social skills, she could expect to be brutalized in prison, even in women's prison. Severe depression and suicide attempts would probably follow.

I faced a similar clinical scenario a few years later, and because any good book on homicides should include a crossbow murder, I'll relate some of it.

The accused, Rod Polbert, a young man of borderline intelligence, lived in a shack by the river. He did odd jobs in town and supplemented his larder with rabbits he hunted with a crossbow.

Rod had a girlfriend, also fairly low-functioning, who had moved in with him for a time, but left after a few months. Accompanied by four or five relatives, she returned a day or two after moving out to pick up some belongings she had left behind. While her family hovered protectively outside, she went into the shack with Rod. He apparently tried to talk her into staying, but she refused and started gathering up her things. Rod then slammed the door shut, locked out her relatives, picked up his crossbow and killed her with a series of well-aimed steel bolts at close-range.

Defence counsel at Rod's trial by jury opted for an insanity defense, arguing that the accused was so mentally deficient that he was unable to appreciate the nature and consequences of his act, or to know that it was wrong.

Brought into the case by the Crown, I was initially refused an interview with Rod, but was suddenly granted one in the middle of the trial. I found myself feeling rather sympathetic to the man, who certainly didn't understand why his girlfriend would leave him, and had just wanted to prevent her departure.

"How else could I stop her?" Of course, I didn't agree with his killing her, but I could see his bewilderment.

However, the prosecutor unearthed some information that seemed to indicate that Rod was more intelligent than he seemed — that he was reasonably skilled at "playing dumb" in order to make life easier for himself. Prior to the shooting, he actually operated at higher intellectual levels than portrayed by the defence. Faced with this new information, I had to admit to myself that I had been naïve in my assessment, accepting his apparent low intelligence at face value without the skeptical, hard-nosed examination I would usually have applied to a less sympathetic figure. So on the stand, I cited as a sign of the man's intelligence a claim that Rod had considerable prowess at the game of Monopoly. The defence lawyer, well prepared, pulled me up short on that one by producing a box of Monopoly and asking me to read part of the label aloud to the court: "Recommended for children seven years old and up." Well, OK. Although Rod seemed more intelligent than I had first thought, he was still well below average, and in the same league as Vonda.

The jury declared Rod guilty of second-degree murder, and — like Vonda — he received the minimum sentence of life with ten years before he could apply for parole. As she had, he got the same sentence as someone far more capable than he was of making a decision to murder, and would be dumped in for a decade of education with seasoned killers and psychopaths with voracious and indiscriminate sexual appetites. I wondered what his chances of survival were.

Both Vonda and Rod would have benefitted from a more flexible sentencing structure, under which they could have been given a shorter parole eligibility period and/or custody, specifically in a mental health facility, or some other combination of more-humane and constructive measures. Such options would be based on the diminished self-control capacity of such offenders, as opposed to the callous, predatory tendencies of psychopaths. They would also reduce the likelihood of the person's brutalization in the prison system, and improve prospects for him or her to be released back into society mentally healthier and less prone to victimize others in the future.

Our rigid sentencing choices following murder convictions actually came about initially in 1967, the year Canada abolished the death penalty, except for killers of police officers and prison guards, and then completely eliminated it in 1976. Minimum sentences for first- and second-degree murder — life with at least twenty-five and ten years, respectively, before parole eligibility — were introduced as a sort of soft landing to appease those who had been in favour of retaining the death penalty. The objective was to make sure that murderers, no longer facing execution, would nevertheless not get off with anything less than very lengthy imprisonment. This was true for first-degree convictions, but the pursuit of second-degree verdicts intensified because life with ten was seen as a pretty light sentence. For some convicted killers, like Rod and Vonda, however, the sentence isn't much better than the death penalty.

CHAPTER SEVENTEEN

SOMETHING SHE FORGOT TO MENTION

Born three months early, all two pounds of him struggling for life, Mackenzie Brockaw spent his first ten weeks in the hospital bringing his lungs, heart and weight up to speed. When they took their tiny son home, Marcy and Don knew he would be a high-maintenance infant for some time, but they took on the task eagerly and lovingly. When he was 9 months old, a thorough check-up confirmed what seemed obvious: Macky was a healthy, happy baby, developing well. His parents had done everything right. A month later, Macky would be dead, the victim of child abuse.

Marcy had delayed the start of her six months' maternity leave from her job at the bank until the baby came home, so she could spend as much time as possible with her first child. Don fell into the role of devoted dad, sharing duties with Marcy when he wasn't working; he was a self-employed electrician. Their social life took a dip, but they didn't care. Apart from the usual rigours of being new parents, they knew it was important to keep Mackenzie away from germs he could catch; he needed to stay healthy to give his lungs the best chance to develop.

He had only one minor cold during those early months. His frequent check-ups were invariably good. As with all premature babies, Macky remained behind others his age in development, but at 9 months, he was right in line with the 6-month-olds, as he should be, and everyone was pleased. He loved his Jolly Jumper and riding in a back carrier. Whenever he needed settling, in fact, Marcy or Don would pop Macky into the backpack and go for a walk. They carried a small mirror so that the person carrying the baby could look at him anytime. If he wasn't sleeping, he would smile.

About two months before Marcy's maternity leave expired, she started making enquiries about daycare services. One of her friends recommended an agency called FairChild. The agency would try to match their needs with a caregiver, someone FairChild would have under contract. Parents' could choose either regular licensed daycare situations, where several children would be cared for, or unlicensed daycare, where two or fewer children would be looked after in someone's home. While the latter didn't require a license to operate, the agency had stringent requirements and supervised its contractees closely. FairChild's manager suggested a woman named Miranda Clay, and arranged for Don and Marcy to meet her in her home, not far from theirs.

Miranda had two daughters of her own, one 3 years old, the other in high school. During the day, there would be just her younger child, Emma, and Mackenzie. Marcy and Don gave Miranda their son's whole history, and explained that they needed a caregiver with some patience, because Macky did need quite a lot of holding, and that they needed to keep him healthy, so it was important that he not be around sick children. The meeting went well. Their impression was that Miranda was a nice person, and she assured them that she had lots of experience in looking after children, and lots of patience. The agency gave them several letters of reference to check. Marcy's only negative was that there didn't seem to be an emergency evacuation plan in place, something they had been advised to ensure. They were satisfied on that concern before they agreed to start bringing Macky three days a week in November, the following month.

The first week Marcy returned to work, Don stayed home to care for Macky. It was a slack period at work, and he wanted to stay with the baby, so he took time off. Then FairChild called to tell them that Miranda's younger daughter had contracted the flu and was vomiting with a fever. Perhaps they would like to have Mackenzie go to another caregiver for his first week? No, they didn't want to switch him temporarily, because there were already going to be enough adjustments for him to make. Don took another week off.

Ten days later, a Saturday, Marcy and Don took the baby to Miranda's for two hours as a warm-up. When they came to pick him up, Miranda's husband was there, and he commented on what a happy baby Mackenzie was. Miranda said that everything had gone well. On Monday, Marcy took Macky to Miranda's for four hours, while she went to the dentist. And on Tuesday, Macky's first full eight-hour day, everything was fine.

When she came to pick up the baby, Marcy received the standard FairChild form, "What I Did Today," which Miranda would complete daily. It listed how many times the baby had been changed and fed, what he had eaten, how his mood had been, how many naps he had taken, and anything unusual that had occurred during his stay. Marcy chatted briefly with Miranda about baby food, and the usual stuff, and Miranda said Macky had maybe been a bit fussy once, but he was doing well.

Wednesday, it started to feel like they were settling in, and "What I Did Today" was again upbeat. Marcy had telephoned a few times during the day, and she didn't want to take up too much of Miranda's time when Miranda had her own family to get dinner for, so she took Macky and his empty bottles and went home without too much conversation.

When Miranda handed the baby to Marcy after the third full day, Thursday, Macky didn't really react to seeing his mother, as he always did. He was just waking up from his nap, Miranda said. Macky was quiet and solemn all the way home in the car, not babbling away in his usual fashion. Marcy and Don noticed that the late afternoon nap was not mentioned on the daily diary sheet, but everything else was normal, including descriptions of him as "happy," "playful" and "full of smiles."

That evening Macky nursed, would only take a teaspoonful of solid food, and went to sleep about an hour early. He woke three times during the night, and had difficulty getting back to sleep. In the morning, he wasn't interested in nursing or in eating breakfast, his favourite meal. They put him in the Jolly Jumper, but he gave a tentative push, then whimpered and wouldn't bounce any more, so Don took him out. While Marcy was getting ready for work in the bedroom, Don sat on the floor holding Macky and talking to his wife.

Suddenly, Macky threw up violently — what we graphically describe as projectile vomiting — three times, all over Don. It was the first time Mackenzie had vomited, ever. So, given his wakefulness, lack of appetite and listlessness, they thought he must have picked up Emma's flu.

They called FairChild, then Miranda, to say that they would keep Macky home that day. Marcy asked Miranda what Emma's symptoms had been, and what her doctor had said. Miranda said she had been told that the flu just had to run its course, and to give the little girl acetaminophen for fever. Macky didn't have a fever. Don stayed home with Macky, and Marcy called the family doctor from work but couldn't reach her, so she talked to a friend who was a doctor. The friend told Marcy that Macky could be just teething, although the symptoms were a bit odd. He agreed with Marcy that all the recent changes in going to daycare, and in going from breast milk to bottle might have been upsetting, or that the baby could be reacting to a new solid food. Probably the best thing to do was keep an eye on him, go back to breast milk and re-introduce solids one by one, generally keep the baby quiet, and if he didn't improve in a day or so, take him in to the family physician.

Macky did seem to get better over the weekend. He was eating a little fruit and napping longer, although he was wakeful at night, and more silent and serious than usual. He hadn't thrown up again. He still protested going in his Jolly Jumper, and being bounced, even in the backpack. Other than that, Macky seemed well enough to return to daycare Tuesday, after four days away.

"He's still not quite himself," Marcy told Miranda when she brought the baby back Tuesday morning. "If he's fussy and it gets too much for you, just call me and I'll come get him, no problem."

"Don't worry about it, everything will be okay," Miranda reassured her, "Just go to work and have a good day. We'll be fine."

Two hours later, Miranda telephoned Marcy at work. She was with Mackenzie in the emergency ward at the General Hospital. The baby had been very fussy that morning, so Miranda thought she would take Macky and Emma for a walk in the stroller to settle him down. She had lain Macky on the floor to put his snowsuit on, when he went limp and very pale, his eyes rolled up and his breathing slowed to once every five or six seconds. Miranda called 911 and the ambulance came right away.

"I'll be there as fast as I can," the young mother cried. Miranda told her to calm down. Marcy was impressed with Miranda's own calmness. She didn't think she would have been able to hold it together that well if it had been herself on the other end of the line. Marcy's boss drove her to the hospital while she called Don from her cell phone.

A nurse took Marcy into a room where Miranda was sitting with a social worker. Miranda looked somewhat distressed, so Marcy gave her a hug, feeling badly that Miranda had been forced to deal with this crisis. Miranda told Marcy the same story she had told her on the telephone.

"Oh, Miranda, I'm so grateful Macky was at your place, you're so close to the hospital," Marcy told her, and Miranda started to cry.

An emergency-room physician appeared, determined who they were, and asked Miranda what had happened. Miranda repeated the sequence of events. She had put Mackenzie on the floor to dress him in a snowsuit when the child went limp, his eyes rolled back into his head, he became pale, and his breathing slowed to every five or six seconds. Miranda had called 911 immediately and the paramedics got Macky on a mask ventilator and into the ambulance while Miranda ran next door to leave Emma with her neighbour. The doctor asked Miranda if the baby had been dropped or fallen, if he had been slapped, or had an accident of any kind. Miranda shook her head, replying, "No." He asked Marcy the same, if anything had happened at home, and Marcy also answered negatively.

Marcy and the doctor went over Macky's medical history, and just as they finished, Don arrived and they were taken to see their son. Dr. H., a pediatrician, came in, examined the comatose baby, asked more questions. He explained that Macky had been given an antibiotic in case an infection was involved, and medication to help relax his muscles. His arms and legs were stiffening intermittently, and because they suspected a brain injury, they wanted to minimize his movement or struggling against the ventilator; such motion could increase the pressure in the brain and lead to brain swelling. They had taken some fluid from his spine to examine, and they would be doing a brain scan as well as some other tests. He didn't give the parents a diagnosis, but said they were going to move Macky up to intensive care, and Marcy and Don could follow. Marcy suggested that she could go and tell Miranda she could leave.

Miranda was still there, still looking stressed; her husband had come over to join her.

"They don't know what's wrong yet, Miranda," Marcy explained, "But there's no point in your having to wait around. Why don't you go on home, and we'll call you when we know something."

"I guess we can't do anything here," Miranda agreed, and the couple left.

Medical staff came in and out of ICU, running tests on Macky while his parents waited anxiously, and seemingly forever. Finally, well into the afternoon, the pediatrician sat down with Don and Marcy and told them that everything the doctors had learned so far about Macky's condition seemed to point to shaken baby syndrome.

A distinct set of injuries and symptoms characterize shaken baby syndrome. The infant's brain is injured as a result of being shaken, which subjects the baby's head to rotational forces — back and forth, side to side and perhaps diagonally.

Babies (as opposed to adults and older children) are especially susceptible to being injured this way. First, their heads are proportionately larger and contain more water than adult brains, making their heads heavier, while their necks are relatively weak. (As an expert witness later described it: think of a tulip with a large head and a weak stem.) When you shake a baby, this weaker neck offers practically no protection to resist rotational forces; only the chest, back or shoulders stop the head's movement, when it hits one of them.

Second, an infant's brain hasn't grown big enough to fit its skull, so the brain can move around more freely when the head moves, like liquid in a partially filled jar. If the baby's skull moves quickly forward, the brain follows; but if the head stops suddenly, the brain bumps into the skull, and the same when it moves swiftly backwards or sideways.

Third, babies are more susceptible because their brain's nerve cells are not yet as well protected as adults' nerve cells. A substance called myelin, which sheathes the cells, hasn't yet developed.

Finally, babies are more susceptible simply because they are little and vulnerable, and they cry without understanding that some bigger people don't want them to.

Shaking can produce three different types of injuries to the brain. One, brain tissue gets bruised from the bumping against the interior of the skull. Two, nerve cells can get stretched or sheared between layers of the brain, because the layers travel at different speeds. Three, the small veins connecting the brain to the dura — the membrane just beneath the skull — can be stretched to the point where they start leaking or haemorrhaging.

The leaked blood fills space in the skull — which is effectively a closed box — preventing proper circulation of blood and oxygen to tissues in other parts of the brain, which damages and kills more brain cells. All the damaged brain cells swell, producing even more pressure inside the skull. With nowhere else to go, the brain may be pushed downward into the hole at the bottom of the skull, where the brain connects to the spinal cord. When the brain stem at the base of the brain gets compressed by this downward pressure, it cannot send out signals for vital functions to keep operating, and so the baby's respiration and heart may stop.

The clearest sign of shaken baby syndrome is the haemorrhaging inside the skull, usually evident in a CT scan. Commonly the haemorrhage is subdural (under the dura membrane) but it can also be subarachnoid (one layer down), or it can be inside the brain. This kind of bleeding occurs in virtually all cases of shaken baby syndrome, and is otherwise found only in severe accidents, such as a car crash or a fall from a height of two or more storeys. A second sign — found in most, but not all cases — is haemorrhaging in the back of the eye, the retina, or along the optic nerve sheath. A third sign might be broken ribs or other long bones, or bruises on the upper body, depending upon the mechanics of how the baby was shaken; but often — as in Macky's case — there are no external injuries.

Infants who have experienced a mild to moderate episode of shaking commonly exhibit such symptoms as irritability, vomiting, not eating or sleeping, disliking movement, and generally not being themselves. Unfortunately, these non-specific symptoms, without closer examination, can be mistaken for indications of teething or stomach flu. A baby who experiences a severe shaking will show symptoms dramatically, and almost immediately. The infant might go pale, might have difficulty breathing, might go floppy, might have a vacant, "out-of-it" facial expression, or might lapse into unconsciousness. In any case, it would be obvious even to an untrained observer that this was a baby in serious trouble. Immediately after even a mild to moderate shaking, experts tell us, it would also be clear to anyone present that the baby had been injured by the shake.

Ten percent of infants diagnosed with shaken baby syndrome die. *All* the others suffer irreversible brain damage resulting in some kind of long-term impairment. This can range from an inability to walk, speak or develop well intellectually, to the child who seems fine until he or she enters school, at which time cognitive and motor impairments start to show up, with difficulties in reading and writing.

The pediatrician, pediatric neurologist, radiologist and other doctors who were on Mackenzie Brockaw's team had identified the signs and symptoms of a severe shaking episode that morning, and suspected a previous, milder incident.

His condition was worsening. He had been having seizures, and the "soft spot" on the top of his head was becoming tense and abnormally firm, a sign of increasing pressure inside his skull. Medication was controlling the seizures, and a neurosurgeon would operate to relieve some of the pressure within his skull.

In the late afternoon, a pair of RCMP officers knocked at Miranda Clay's door. They asked Miranda to tell them what had happened, and she told them about the baby being fussy, not wanting his bottle or a nap and crying. She put him on the floor to get him into his snowsuit, and that's when he went limp and pale, his eyes rolled back and his breathing slowed to every six seconds or so. She called 911.

The detachment had received notice from the hospital that Mackenzie had suffered some bruising to the brain that could have happened because of a fall, a blow or being shaken. Sometimes these injuries turn out to be the result of something as simple as falling off a couch, one of the constables told Miranda, but they had to check it out.

Actually, there had been a fall, Miranda responded. Two falls, in fact. One that day and one the previous week.

In that morning's incident, Macky had been in his baby seat on the kitchen table, and while she turned away to get Emma some cereal, Macky had tipped out of the seat and onto the floor. He hadn't been buckled into the seat. He landed face up, and cried, but Miranda didn't see any cuts or bruises when she picked him up. About twenty minutes later, he went limp and that was when she called for help. Last week, the day before he got the flu, he had fallen off the family room couch. That time, he had been buckled into the same baby seat, and both Macky and the seat rolled onto the floor. Again, he had cried, but didn't seem injured.

Had she mentioned these falls to the doctors, the paramedics, Macky's parents? No, it was the first time she had told anyone, Miranda said. "It probably sounds irresponsible, considering what Macky has been through, that I didn't say anything." She showed the police where the incidents had taken place, and said they were the only accidents that had occurred. "I probably should have been more careful, especially because Macky is so little."

Miranda agreed to come into the RCMP office the next day, so a taped statement could be made. When she arrived, the officer informed her that, although she had not been charged, they could not say that she would not be charged, pending further medical developments. She should know that they were conducting a criminal investigation, and would likely have to determine whether Mackenzie's injuries had been the result of an accident of if someone had been negligent. She had the right to retain and instruct a lawyer immediately, and to remain silent if she chose. Miranda contacted a lawyer from the interview room, told police that the lawyer had advised her not to talk to them, but that she wanted to carry on with the interview, anyway.

She repeated the stories of the two falls, but in greater detail. In the first incident, she was in the other room heating a bottle, with Macky strapped in his seat safely on the couch, when she heard a "thunk," and she re-entered the room to find him on the floor. She couldn't tell if he had hit his head on the coffee table or not, but he didn't seem hurt. He soon seemed better, and even had a nap later on. Miranda didn't know why she hadn't mentioned the event to Marcy when she came to pick Macky up, but she guessed she had been scared by the fall herself and wasn't thinking clearly.

Concerning the second fall, she added a number of points: she had pulled a chair up close to the table to feed the two young ones, and she wasn't sure if Macky hit that chair when he fell off the table. He was crying in an unusual way when she picked him up, but after a while he settled back to his normal cry. He refused any of his bottle. Miranda laid him down for a nap, but he only slept ten minutes, so she got him up again, thinking they were "just going to have a fussy morning." That's when she decided to snowsuit them both up and go for a walk, she said, but then Macky suddenly went limp, terribly limp, and unresponsive. She made the 911 call. Miranda hadn't mentioned the fall to anyone before the police — although she had been with or talked to the paramedics, her neighbour, the social worker, the doctor, Marcy and Don, her FairChild supervisor, another neighbour, and her husband — "because of the panic and fear I felt."

Doctors continued to fight for the baby's life, but as early as the first day, after the surgery, they knew that the brain damage was so extensive that even if he survived — now just a remote possibility — Macky would endure life in a vegetative state. He died two days later.

Miranda returned to the RCMP detachment office next morning, and was informed of Macky's death. They would be interviewing her concerning a possible charge of Criminal Negligence Causing Death, and once more she was read her rights. She spoke again to her lawyer, but told police the lawyer had simply told her not to say anything, and no arrangement had been made for a meeting. She was puzzled by this, but did not call a halt to the interview.

One of the officers explained that the doctors had said that Mackenzie's injuries were not likely caused by a fall, but by being shaken, and that police now had to examine all the possibilities of who could have shaken him: Miranda, Miranda's husband or daughter, or Don or Marcy. They now knew that Miranda had withheld some information concerning two falls, from both the parents and the FairChild agency, contrary to FairChild's company policy, so they were perhaps a bit suspicious that she might have thought it was better to say the baby had fallen rather than that she got frustrated and shook him. Babies can be frustrating when they keep on crying, the constable offered. And sometimes people there are told to shake an unconscious person and call out to them, "Can you hear me?" Could Miranda have done that? Was it possible that you shook him?

"Yes, it is, but I didn't mean for this to happen," Miranda answered. "It was only once. I just said, 'Mackenzie, would you stop!' And it scared the daylights out of me because he just went limp."

She had been leaning over the baby, trying to put on his snowsuit, and he was crying, and all she had been hearing for an hour was crying, and she held him by the shoulders, and his head may have hit the floor; she didn't remember because she was so upset when he went limp.

"And did he ever fall?"

"Yes, the first time. From the kitchen table." Macky had not fallen the day she rushed him to hospital, and, she answered, he had never fallen off the couch.

She had gone to answer the door on the day when he tumbled off the table. Her husband was home, but outside. She told him about the fall, and he said she'd better tell Marcy, but Miranda didn't, maybe because she was feeling responsible for the fall, having forgotten to belt Macky into his seat.

She didn't tell a single person she had shaken the baby, and she was "absolutely sure" she only shook him once.

An autopsy revealed no injuries, even external, that would have occurred as the result of a fall or a blow. The cause of Macky's death was intracranial (within the skull) trauma, consistent with shaken baby syndrome. Miranda was charged with one count of assault causing bodily harm, for the first incident, and one count of manslaughter (based on intentionally causing bodily harm, which results in death, but without specifically intending to kill).

Ten days later, Miranda attempted suicide with an overdose of aspirin, a mild tranquilizer and an antidepressant (prescribed by her family doctor when she went to him feeling "overwhelmed" the day after Macky's death). Miranda told her husband what she had taken, half an hour afterwards, and he rushed her to hospital. She recovered quickly, but did have an apparent paranoid episode, during which she claimed that hospital staff members were involved in the criminal investigation against her and that television reports of her deeds were being broadcast. She was detained four weeks in hospital because of this, but the psychiatrist who discharged her diagnosed an adjustment disorder with anxiety and depressed mood, which he characterized as a not-surprising reaction to being charged with a serious offence involving the death of a baby.

"I think everyone would be better off without me," had been her explanation for the overdose. Miranda was seeking self-punishment, the doctor thought, and neither antidepressant medications nor hospitalization would resolve that. Her paranoia had remitted, probably as a result of a medication she had been given, which he would continue. He felt that she was competent to instruct counsel and to stand trial at that time, and he observed that during her hospitalization, her father had died, and she had coped with his death and funeral appropriately.

She returned to hospital three months later, having attempted to ingest another large quantity of various drugs. She had called her husband at work, and he had called 911. By the time she was brought into the emergency ward, she had vomitted up most of the overdose, and was on her way to recovery again. She had been released on bail, and, under the court's conditions, was living with her mother and seeing her children only if there was an outside chaperone present. When her mother went away overnight, Miranda had sunk into suicidal despair. It was difficult and stressful making arrangements to be with her family, and the hospital doctor said she was still totally locked into her guilt and the legal nightmare.

Discharged the next day, she agreed to keep seeing a psychiatrist, Dr. Y., on a weekly basis. She was still considered at risk for self-harm, but much less so with her mother back home and her acknowledgment that she could call her husband or talk to the psychiatrist instead of attempting suicide. (She had not mentioned to Dr. Y. — whom she had been seeing regularly since her arrest — that she had been feeling increasingly "down" for the last two weeks, as she told the hospital psychiatrist.)

To Dr. Y., she had revealed a history of undiagnosed and untreated depression. Six years ago, she had been in rough shape for nearly a year following her delivery of a stillborn infant. Her family confirmed this, saying Miranda wouldn't see a doctor about her emotional difficulties, although she received medical attention at the time of the birth. "I'm not one to ask for help," she told Dr. Y. after her second suicide attempt. "I thought I could handle it myself."

After Emma was born, three years ago, Miranda had appeared to suffer from post-partum depression. This time, on the urging of her sister, she went for five weekly sessions with a clinical counsellor; this was offered to all new mothers, as a free community service. During these sessions, Miranda told the counsellor that she had been abused as a child by her mother, who had once locked her in the unlit basement and another time threatened her with a baseball bat. Miranda said she worked hard to please everyone, but she had a "harsh internal critic," in addition to her mother's constant fault-finding, which demanded high standards. She didn't even like to go to parent-and-tot gatherings, because she thought that she would be judged as a "not good enough mother if Emma cried." At the end of the five free sessions, Miranda told the counsellor that she had learned enough to go it on her own, and since they were going away for the summer to help on her brother-in-law's ranch, that day would be her last.

Neither Miranda nor her family physician declared any background of emotional or mental problems on the forms they completed for Miranda's application to work for FairChild, including negative replies to questions such as, "Have you ever been under any psychiatric or psychological counselling for any emotional conditions?" Her family doctor never knew that she had seen a psychiatrist briefly, nor that she had been feeling depressed after both the stillborn delivery and her younger daughter's birth, nor that she had received brief counselling.

Miranda also chose not to disclose to FairChild that, the year before she applied to work for the agency, she had been the subject of a Child Protection Services investigation of allegations she had abused (including shook) two children under her care. The investigation went no further because the children's parents removed them from her care, but in a subsequent Child Protection assessment of the risk that Miranda would harm her own children, the allegations were apparently accepted as evidence of previous abuse of children.

A few months after her second suicide attempt, Miranda was deemed to have responded sufficiently to treatment that she stopped seeing Dr. Y., but remained in regular contact with her family doctor, who continued to treat her with antidepressant medication.

More than two years after Mackenzie's death, Miranda came to court, still insisting that she had only shaken the baby once. An international medical expert in shaken baby syndrome was brought in to testify at the trial, along with several pathologists, the doctors who had treated the injured Mackenzie at the hospital, and those who had cared for him during and after his birth. (I was not yet involved in the case.)

Copious medical testimony seemed to cover every aspect of Macky's short life and every micron of his fatally injured brain. A crucial focus was on dating the two markers of subdural haemorrhaging. The existence of older and newer haemorrhaged blood within his head proved that there had been two shakings. The last shaking could be shown to have taken place within two hours of Macky's arrival at the hospital , partly because of the freshness of the haemorrhaging blood in his skull and in the fluid taken from his spine. The older markers of subdural blood could not pinpoint the earlier episode with total accuracy, although they could narrow it to within a few days. However, one expert testified, clinical history is the most accurate indicator in assessing when a shaking has taken place, and that history favoured the day of the first incident. Miranda had admitted that an accident occurred on that date, although denying she shook the child. Macky's signs and symptoms that day and the following days pointed inexorably to a shaking, particularly in the absence of physical manifestations of any other kind of trauma, including a hit or a fall.

The jury accepted the Crown's evidence, and convicted Miranda of assault causing bodily harm and manslaughter. A hearing would take place before the judge decided her sentence.

A verdict of manslaughter. While lawyers have debated the issue for countless hours and from many angles to arrive at the present system, I am not the only lay person who remains uncomfortable with the different kinds of accountability we assign to killers, depending on the relationship between their intentions and the ultimate cause of the victim's death. How and why should we discriminate between a drunk driver accidentally causing death, a child abuser unintentionally causing death, or a stoned drug abuser stabbing someone to death? The first two homicides are categorized as accidental or unintentional, and the perpetrators are generally viewed as less blameworthy. But are they, really? The inebriate knows before she gets drunk and drives that she may have an accident and injure someone else, but she goes out and drinks and drives anyway. The child abuser knows before he hands out drugs or beats a kid that he may cause serious damage to the child, but he goes ahead anyway. They know their actions may lead to a death, but they don't go out intending to kill, therefore they are not deemed murderers.

There is no minimum sentence for manslaughter, so the verdict carries with it the possibility that the sentencing judge will "go easy" on the convicted person. Is this appropriate when there are such rigid sentencing requirements for first-and second-degree murder? Given the enormous range of circumstances in homicides of all types, why shouldn't *all* verdicts have the benefit of more flexible sentencing, either lighter or heavier? Individual sentences could reflect individual cases — allowing lighter or tougher sentences, and choices and combinations concerning incarceration and, where needed, treatment.

One reason to hesitate would surely be the inevitable outcry as the public imagines a worst-case scenario: "some bleeding-heart judge letting some serial killer off scot-free." Many people feel that where there is sentencing flexibility, as in a manslaughter conviction, it only flexes in one direction: towards leniency. How many times have we heard howls of protest when a drunk driver who has killed gets off with what seems like a slap on the wrist, although all the facts of the case aren't publicly known?

I entered Miranda Clay's case after her conviction, when I was called upon by the prosecutor to provide a psychiatric pre-sentence report on her. At such a time, the judge receives a number of submissions to give her or him additional information to use when deciding upon a sentence — often information that wouldn't or couldn't have come up during the trial. The judge had also ordered a pre-sentence psychiatric report and psychological testing. The main contribution of my report would be an assessment of the risk that Miranda might re-offend. Others providing reports included the corrections officer to whom Miranda had reported during her nearly two years out on bail; the Brockaws, who submitted victim impact statements, and Miranda's mother and husband, who expressed their support for her.

I was given reams of pre-trial reports, notes and statements, as well as transcripts of the preliminary hearing and the trial, and the other psychiatric assessment for sentencing purposes. I was denied an interview with Miranda herself, however. This put a severe crimp in my ability to assess her current risk for future violence — the chief reason for my report — let alone define what caused her to commit the offence, which would have helped determine whether she might do it again.

The question of why she had done it had not truly been addressed by anyone. It was not relevant for her trial; there was no mental-disorder defence. There were claims that she had been somewhat depressed at the time, and Miranda herself said that the baby had been crying continually that last morning. The descriptions of her pre-homicide depression were sketchy, retrospective and not backed by firm medical diagnoses. Her psychiatric and medical care after her trial and subsequent suicide attempts focused on acute treatment for depression and suicide prevention.

Dr. D., the other psychiatrist providing a pre-sentence report, felt that, while he couldn't say with certainty, Miranda seemed to have been overwhelmed by a mixture of chronic and immediate stressors, which led to her being "uncharacteristically impulsive" in shaking the baby. This impulsivity was expressed twice more when she attempted suicide. She told him she had been worried about money, tired because Emma had been keeping them up at night while she had the flu, that the demands of being a caregiver were stressful, and that, thinking back, she had been depressed. Except for the self-diagnosed depression, these are things most people worry about (money, insufficient sleep, work), and to the same degree she described, so I wondered how her situation upon release could be controlled so that this combination of factors wouldn't occur again.

One way, of course, was to ensure that Miranda was not permitted to look after children any more. Dr. D. recommended that prohibition firmly, although he felt that whether she was at risk to harm her own children was an assessment that should be made by the Ministry of Children and Families, who had more resources and were better qualified than he was to judge family situations and dynamics. Otherwise, his opinion was that she was of low risk to the community, including children with whom she might have casual contact. He believed she would be likely to comply with any conditions of her sentence, including a requirement to take an anger-management course and insight-oriented psychotherapy (his recommendations). He felt she was remorseful and accepted responsibility for her actions.

The psychologist who tested Miranda also thought that she had accepted responsibility, was genuinely remorseful, and presented a low risk of re-offending, as did the corrections officer.

Even though I felt greatly hindered by my inability to interview and assess Miranda for myself, I could not agree. For one thing, I felt her lack of credibility got in the way of everything these other professionals claimed in her favour.

Miranda had been issuing a steady stream of lies and committing errors of omission from at least the time she applied to work for FairChild right through her assessments by Dr. D. and the psychologist. She seemed to have worked hard to present herself in the best light in all circumstances and without regard to the interests of other people. She had omitted that she had been the subject of a previous child-abuse investigation in order to get the job. Although the allegations in that case were never proven, never went to court, I have to wonder, parenthetically, why she applied for an agency-supervised job as a child's caregiver; surely she must have known there was a chance this information could surface.

Miranda denied that anything at all had happened in the first incident, even though she would have known she had injured Macky, and that any kind of information (other than the misleading agreement that he must have caught the flu) might have sent Don and Marcy to Macky's doctor and aided his recovery. She continued to deny anything had happened then or at the second incident, until the police officer inadvertently offered her an excuse by suggesting that it could have been a fall. Quickly, she invented two falls. Even if, flying in the face of compelling medical evidence, the tiny baby had managed to propel himself out of his angled-back infant seat and onto the floor, why would she have told no one at the time? When he was in the hospital, why would she similarly deny point-blank that there had been any falls? Then, after Macky died, she changed the story again — disclaiming one of the falls and reversing the dates — and admitted to shaking the baby "just once." At some point, she admitted to shaking him for six or seven seconds.

Two years later, she gave two more versions to Dr. D. First, she said she shook Macky for five to ten seconds, during which his head hit the floor three times. A month afterwards, when Dr. D. questioned her reasons for giving different versions of events, she denied ever shaking the baby. As she was putting on his snowsuit, and Macky continued to cry, she said she lifted his head about half a foot above the floor and let it drop. She did this three times, and on the third time, the baby went limp.

Miranda prevaricated in relating her family history, giving different descriptions of her childhood to her counsellor, psychiatrists and psychologist, most often describing abuse from her mother — treatment vigorously denied by her three siblings as well as her mother, who described Miranda as "a loving, caring and sensitive person, but in need of psychiatric help now." In her first interview with Dr. D., Miranda referred to her relationship with her mother as "easy," and her corrections officer said her memories of her childhood and family were "strikingly warm and happy." When Dr. D. confronted her with her earlier stories of being locked in the basement and of being threatened with a baseball bat by her mother, she said she hadn't wanted to be portrayed by the court as some kind of unremorseful violent monster, which the court might assume, "knowing that abuse can be passed on." (Child abusers often do have histories of being abused themselves.)

The psychologist had to administer one part of her testing twice, after emphasising the need for openness and honesty to Miranda. She reported Miranda was defensive, self-protective, non-disclosing and showed aggressive tension, occasional leanings toward irritability that could result in insensitive action, and a susceptibility to stress. Nevertheless, she found Miranda capable of empathizing, in reasonable emotional control, genuinely remorseful and having accepted responsibility for her offence.

The corrections officer appeared to blame the death on Miranda's depression, which "went untreated with tragic consequences." He shifted part of the blame to FairChild, saying that as a depressed person, Miranda should never have been entrusted with childcare — even though Miranda herself had concealed any depression. And, of course, many depressed people have competently cared for children without killing them.

The corrections officer felt she was truly remorseful, because she was horrified at what she had done. What she had done that she regretted, she told him, was to shake the baby in the second incident, and to withhold information about the fall in the first incident. He said it was significant that this was the truth as she saw it, and that she was sticking to that story.

"But are you aware," the prosecutor questioned him during the sentencing hearing, "that this wasn't the first story she had clung to, which was that Macky had caught the flu? Or even the second or third story? This was, in fact, the fourth story that she was clinging to."

Yes, he responded, but many times he had seen accused people, when first confronted, make up stories and deny their actions. The thing was that she accepted responsibility for the baby's death. She felt horror for those two things, which she acknowledged had resulted in destroying two families, and she was telling him the truth when she said she was horrified.

Remorse in always difficult to evaluate, particularly from a remove, and it is hard to separate remorse from the regret that every offender who is caught must feel. Even face to face with an individual who weeps and says he feels terribly about what he has done, it's not easy to sort out whether he feels sorry for the victim and the victim's family, or whether he is sorry for himself because of the consequences he faces. It wasn't possible for me to determine how much remorse Miranda felt, but I do think that she did not show remorse when she misled Macky's parents and the medical people, when she lied to police, when she continued to deny shaking the baby, when she continued to revise her stories. While her legal strategy was her undisputed right to pursue, a remorseful person might have pled guilty and got it over with, for the victim's family's sake as well as her own. Her sentence might even have been lighter.

And even if she did state to the psychologist that "[her] actions had caused the death of another human being," it still wasn't clear to me that she had accepted responsibility. Certainly, she continued to claim that the shaking had never occurred. Once she had accepted that she had been depressed, she seemed to shift the blame to that: "I failed to take care of myself well enough to prevent a baby's death." Although depression was probably involved, the description of an adjustment disorder in reaction to the homicide seemed to fit better, and the two attempts at suicide were so speedily and efficiently aborted, they could have been plays for sympathy rather than cries for help, or any genuine desire to die.

I made these points in my report, but stated that I could not make an accurate risk assessment, given my lack of access and information in certain respects. I said that I believed Miranda's risk of further child abuse was neither low nor had been reduced, given two principles. One, if you don't understand in detail why a behaviour occurred, you are not in a position to predict its recurrence accurately. And two, if the internal, psychological factors and external circumstances have not changed, there is no reason to provide a low estimate of risk. In such a case, all you can rely on is that past behaviour is the best predictor of future behaviour. In fact, if the fallout from the offence exacerbates such risk factors as stress and depression, one would expect the risk to be elevated, if anything.

Most sentencing hearings are over in a day. This one took several days, stretched out over two months. First, it turned out that Dr. D. had made his first report without some of the information that had been given to me. Although he had interviewed Miranda, he didn't know that she was denying the first shaking, and she hadn't told him of any childhood abuse by her mother. So he was given the additional reports and time to re-interview her before submitting a revised assessment; his second assessment wasn't much changed from the first.

A clash of expert opinions, in which I played a role, also extended the sentencing process. Dr. D. objected to my objections to the testing methods he and the psychologist employed — I felt Miranda should have been tested for possible personality disorder, and that parts of one of the tests employed were not relevant to the case — and we took turns sniping at each other's interpretations of Miranda's testing, treatment, displays of remorse, and prognosis. Dr. D. fired off a counter-report to mine, and I rebutted. The psychologist also replied, and the corrections officer created a stir of his own. Statements from both Macky's parents and Miranda's family contributed to what was already an emotionally intense hearing, as the trial had been. Finally, both lawyers fought to the finish without giving an inch.

From my point of view, I found it hard to believe that Miranda's ongoing deceit was not factored into any opinion of her reliability, and that her compliant behaviour while out on bail and her favourable response to antidepressant treatment alone made her low risk for re-offending. It was almost as if everyone else looked upon her as a nice lady who would be all better now that she was being treated for depression, so let's just send her home. Although let's not allow her to look after other people's children. Dr. D. did say that *if* she were incarcerated for any time, she should be monitored by the forensic psychiatric clinic while on probation. The corrections officer, however, felt there was no need to incarcerate her at all to protect the community. Wait! Does anyone remember an offence that resulted in a dead baby?

The judge remembered. Miranda Clay was sentenced to seven years in prison for manslaughter and six years for the assault, the terms to be served concurrently. I have not heard of her since. As there was no legal requirement to do so, it is unlikely that the woman subsequently has been psychiatrically assessed to determine what her core difficulties are, and to initiate relevant treatment if needed.

What a shame that we must make either/or decisions when sentencing — prison or treatment. Miranda's case cried out for a hybrid disposition along the lines of Britain's Hospital Orders. There, people who are found guilty and are mentally ill, but don't qualify for a verdict of Not Criminally Responsible on account of Mental Disorder, can nevertheless have psychiatric treatment ordered as part of their sentences. In Canada, we have failed to recognize, in law, that people who murder are not necessarily all bad, or all mad, but that many are some of each. If we don't treat the mental illness part, but just punish the "bad" part, it's more likely that offending behaviours will re-occur when the prisoner is released.

CHAPTER EIGHTEEN

BIG BOY

When 8-year-old Tannis Fabro went missing during a hide-and-seek game in the park, the neighbourhood was galvanized. As soon as anyone was asked if they had seen Tannis, they offered to search. Jill Fabro, Tannis's mother saw Lincoln ("Link") Montgomery coming out of the woods. He had been part of the game, he told her, at first, but he hadn't seen Tannis. Then he agreed to help look for her. He spent three-quarters of an hour alongside Tannis's mother, searching the wooded area, and at one point he said that this was all his fault, because he was the last to see her. They encountered Jill's father, and Link said he would show him the last place he saw Tannis. He took him into the woods just off the main pathway and pointed towards a big fence on the park boundary. Eventually, they split up and went looking in different directions.

The police arrived and started collecting stories. They had called Search and Rescue, who organized a grid search of the park and neighbourhood. A bunch of young boys had gone into the bush looking for Tannis, and bumped into Link coming out. He was "looking sad, with tears in his eyes," and told the boys that he was mad at himself. He had been playing hide and seek with Tannis, and it was his fault she was missing.

"I'm sorry I ever did this," he apparently said, knocking his head, "I should never have brought her into the woods. I probably got her parents really, really worried."

To the constable, Link repeated the sad tale of hide-and-seek gone wrong. He showed the police officer where he had last seen the missing girl, by the fence. He was walking ahead of her when she said something about seeing a fort, but he said they should keep going, and when he turned around, she was gone. Link continued to cry and blame himself, and the officer took him to a police vehicle and put him in the back seat.

He was not being detained as a suspect, but as the last person to see Tannis, he might be able to provide more details that would help the search.

Two hours after Tannis had been reported missing, a Search and Rescue member found her, in an area of very dense bush, nowhere near where Link had indicated he last saw her. She was half-hidden under a fallen tree, her head coated with blood and what seemed to be off-white brain tissue exposed. The Search and Rescue man thought she was dead, but when she moved slightly, he began first aid, almost simultaneously radioing for help.

Tannis was taken to hospital. Then, her life hanging by a thread, she was air ambulanced to Children's Hospital in Winnipeg, where she underwent immediate emergency surgery to her skull and brain.

As the fire chief secured the area where she had been found, he noticed a shoe-sized stone covered in blood near the girl, and a trail of blood leading from her to a striped hair band, about five metres away. It looked as though Tannis had been beaten with the rock, dragged under the log in order to conceal her, and left for dead by her attacker.

Lincoln Montgomery, age 16, was arrested for assault. When his clothes were seized, there seemed to be fresh blood on his pants and shirt, so once the paperwork was completed, these and the rock were sent off for DNA analysis. Tannis's clothing was also submitted. Samples were also taken of Tannis's blood, and, eventually, blood samples were provided from Link.

It took three years before the case came to trial. Link fell under the protection of the Young Offenders Act, but was of an age (between 12 and 17) where his case could be transferred to ordinary adult criminal court, if it were deemed in the best interests of society and better serving the needs of the young accused person.

In terms of society's interests, the court wants to minimize the danger of the accused re-offending, holding the public's protection paramount, and to try to match the punishment to the crime. In youth court, the maximum penalty for first degree murder is 10 years, of which no more than six are to be served in custody. For second-degree murder, the sentence is seven years, with a maxiumum of four years in custody, with the balance of both sentences being served in the community for a maximum probation of two years. Recent amendments to the Young Offenders' Act mean that all 16- and 17-year-olds charged with first- or second-degree murder, manslaughter, attempted murder or aggravated assault are automatically transferred to adult court, unless a request comes from the accused, defence counsel or the Crown that the case remain in Youth Court.

After receiving such a request, a judge would have to make this evaluation before the facts in the case have been adjudicated, concentrating on the accused youth's history of offences (before the current allegations), and to consider what the ultimate possibilities for sentencing will be. Raised to adult court, and subsequently given a sentence of more than two years, a youth would be placed in a special regional facility until his 18th birthday, at which point he would be transferred to an adult corrections facility. This route includes the risk of his being victimized when he moves up to adult prison, but if he were kept in youth court and committed to custody in a youth facility, he would be the "top" of the pecking order and potentially a corrupting presence among younger offenders. Counsel for youths accused of offences such as murder may prefer going to adult court, where trial by jury is an option, and judges are more experienced in major crimes. If substance-abuse treatment is to be a factor, more comprehensive and longer programs are usually available in adult prisons.

Link was raised to adult court. His alleged offence was serious, although it could not be designated as murder. Tannis had survived, but she and her family had been plunged into a situation from which there was no recovery. The 7-year-old had been paralyzed in mind as well as body, and now saw life from a wheelchair and through the eyes of a 2-year-old, as the result of multiple skull fractures and brain damage. The charges against Link had been upgraded to one count of attempted murder, and one count of aggravated sexual assault.

Link's sixteen-year history presented a pattern of accelerating criminality. It was one of those troubled stories that involved many incidents and upsets — with a changing cast of caring but unconnected people and professional experts. In hindsight, Link simply kept heading for bigger and bigger trouble.

His mother had smoked and abused alcohol and marijuana throughout her pregnancy, and left Link and his father when her son was 3. Link carried the anger at this abandonment with him, and it no doubt affected his personality and emotional development. It may have been at the core of his hatred towards women, which seemed to drive some of his offences.

Link's father, Garth, struggled as a single dad with limited parenting skills. No stepmother appeared for Link, who started doing things like jumping off balconies into swimming pools, letting pet-shop animals out of their cages, and riding the outside of strangers' trucks, all before he was old enough to go to kindergarten. His behaviour made getting babysitters tricky. Fighting and rough-housing became a standard issue in school.

At 7, Link and his father followed a job to a town where they knew no one. Link was no good at making friends. He eagerly sought peer approval, but his immature attempts at gaining it annoyed and irritated other children his own age. He started hanging out with younger kids, and soon got into trouble for bullying. "Aggression" and "temper problems" appeared in school reports by Grade 3. At home, his father's frustration led to yelling and spanking, although the latter stopped when Garth took a parenting course.

Link slapped and punched a female babysitter, so she was his last. He rode a bike in his apartment building and dropped water balloons near passers-by. A few times, Garth called the police when Link got out of hand. Nevertheless, Garth defended his son all through his troubles, saying that Link was often accused of causing trouble when actually he was the victim. He was impulsive and "hyper," Garth said. Link was caught shoplifting, but that was dealt with, and he wasn't caught again.

By Grade 8, Link's academic achievement was poor, and he seemed unable to relate to his peers. His interactions with kids his own age often turned into conflict. He liked to bait people and play practical jokes. When his negative attention-seeking didn't produce a favourable reaction, he would ratchet it up. He began sending notes to girls about murder, rape and suicide. One note was turned over to a school counsellor, and that led to his being sent to an adolescent treatment centre, Tartan Hill, for assessment. He was diagnosed with attention deficit hyperactivity disorder and treated with medication for a while, but as often occurs, the symptoms of ADHD disappeared over time.

At Tartan Hill, the focus was on improving appropriate peer interaction and providing positive role modelling. Link focused, instead, on being a disruptive force. He ran away from the treatment center for ten days and lived on the downtown streets, which he later described as, "conning people out of change, scaring little kids into giving up their cash, breaking into cars, taking whatever wasn't locked down."

Upon returning home, he entered an alternative school program, which probably kept him in school two and a half more years. He got a job delivering newspapers, but was soon fired because he didn't deliver the papers when he didn't feel like it. He took a similar approach to his school's work-experience program.

A few months after returning from the treatment centre, Link earned his first criminal conviction, for break and enter with theft. He was put on probation for a year and required to do community service work. He completed the community work on time and reported faithfully to the youth worker. But he received his second conviction while still on probation, for assault with a weapon. He had been following two much younger girls home from school, when they became annoyed enough to tell him to go away. He then pulled out a knife, put his arm around one of the 8-year-olds to hold her and, waving the knife in front of her, "suggested" she come into the bushes with him. The second girl threw a rock that landed near Link's feet, startling him just enough that his victim was able to break free and escape.

He told the court that he had done nothing wrong. The girl had asked to see his knife, he said. He did admit being angry, and felt it was a reasonable reaction to fight or become violent when angered: "I give people a warning, then I'm not responsible for my actions." He was given three months in open custody and eighteen months' probation.

He was sent to Miller Place, a transition house in Winnipeg, for two months, where he was to live and participate in social-skills and self-esteem programs. Reports of Link's behaviour there said he was unable to relate to his peers or to age-appropriate activities, and that he was "sneaky." More significantly, he appeared to hate women, refusing to take direction from female staff and frequently swearing at female residents.

A few days after he finished at Miller Place, with sixteen months left on his probation, he received his third conviction, for assault. The victim, who had been hospitalized after the fight, testified that he had been attacked and had not been able to retaliate. Link agreed he had beaten the boy, but said the altercation was consensual, adding that once he started, he had gone wild punching and kicking. His probation was extended.

Months later, Link was convicted of making indecent telephone calls. In the first, he had laughingly stated that he would like to have sex "doggy style" with the man of the house. In the second, he wanted sex with the man's daughter. In the third, he said, "and now I want to fuck your lovely wife, Mona." Link claimed he was drunk and his buddies (although he was not known to have any) did the dialing and told him what to say. Link was given twelve months' probation and seventy-five hours of community service.

At 16, Link dropped out or was asked to leave high school. He had been in a regular program for Grade 11, with failing grades and poor attendance.

It was near the end of the school year, and he had no plans, so he just hung out. This did not sit well with the community. By now he had earned a reputation, and it was not positive.

Over the years, Link had been involved in cub scouts, church youth groups, judo, even briefly in a substance-abuse program when his father caught him drinking. Group leaders, teachers and parents learned to keep an eye on him, because he was always the one at the centre when a commotion erupted, the boy who caused fights, who deliberately killed a mouse on a field trip, who tripped a girl, and, worrisomely, who always gravitated towards the youngest members of any group. Parents who knew Link were suspicious of his activities with younger children, and kids between 7 and 12 seemed to be his only companions. He frequented playgrounds, and although there had been no formal complaints of any actions against children, it was later said in court that it was "common knowledge among many parents that his tendency to be attracted towards much younger children was not normal."

Parents in the neighbourhood were protective, and watchful. Several parents had observed Link at the playground with youngsters and had called their children home. Two mothers had talked about it together, and one of them, seeing Link with two little ones she didn't know, had got on her bicycle and made two loops through the playground to make her presence known, in the hope that Link would leave. Another mother had noticed Link help a young girl do flips so that her panties showed. She had gone over to the playground and retrieved her son and daughter, bringing the other girl back, too.

Somehow, though, Tannis and her friends Candace and Tara got into a two-against-two, hide-and-seek game with Link. He kept setting "home" farther and farther back with each game, until finally Candace and Tara were in the parking lot, counting, and he and Tannis must have started walking towards the woods. When Candace and Tara called out, "Ready or not," the other two were nowhere to be seen. They called and called, but Candace wasn't allowed to go past a certain spot at the edge of the trees, so they gave up. They went to Tannis's house and told her mother that Tannis had disappeared on them. Jill picked up her little son and went into the park, calling out for her daughter. She came home briefly to call her mother to come over to watch the 2-year-old, and the search that ended in Link's arrest had begun.

From detention the day following his arrest, Link telephoned Kimmy, a girl his age he had seen the afternoon before. The girl was developmentally delayed and slightly deaf, so his words came over a speaker phone and her mother transcribed them so Kimmy could understand. He said that he had "blacked out": he had been playing hide-and-seek with some kids and suddenly it was forty-five minutes later. Kimmy said that if the little girl "woke up," she could tell the police what happened. He replied, "I will never see you again," and started to cry.

"How do I make them realize I didn't do it, and if I did, I didn't mean to do it and I am really sorry." That was as close as Link would come to admitting anything.

He carried the story of the blackout into his trial, pleading not guilty, saying he remembered nothing. The only other witness to the crime testified not in the courtroom but by way of a video tape filmed at home. Tannis was barely able to talk, and while she identified "the big boy" as her assailant, it was brought out that she hadn't mentioned him until nearly three years later, and that her father had probably unwittingly tainted her memory by referring to Link. The judge stated that he could not truly distinguish between what Tannis recalled and what she had been told by other people, and that her evidence would therefore have to be considered unreliable. The case would have to be decided on circumstantial and forensic evidence.

The witnesses who placed Link in the area at the time of the offence — and the fact that he was, including by his own admission, the last person to see Tannis — weighed against him, but the evidence from the forensic lab was compelling. DNA testing had established that it was Tannis's blood on the rock, on the trail of leaves, and on Link's clothing. That is, they could not state with certainty that it was Tannis's blood, but the chance of it being someone else's blood was one in 3.8 billion. Bloodstain pattern analysis indicated that the blood on Link's jeans and t-shirt had landed there from a distance of less than three feet, and blood on the leaves had dropped there as Tannis's body was moved from where she was assaulted to where she was found.

Semen had been found on and in Tannis' panties and Link's underwear. It was Link's semen (the chance of someone else having the same DNA structure is one in 560 billion.) The experts giving this evidence were as usual cautious, saying that the DNA testing cannot positively identify an individual, it can only positively exclude someone.

The judge found that the Crown had proven beyond a reasonable doubt that Lincoln Montgomery was the offender, that he intended to commit the offence of murder, and that he attempted to murder Tannis Fabro by striking her forcefully several times with a rock. The blood-soaked rock, the visible severity of her head injuries and the attempt to hide her body contributed to the conclusion that Link had the requisite intent to commit murder. It was also clear that Link had sexually assaulted the young girl, and that while doing so, he had wounded or endangered her life. The verdict was guilty of both attempted murder and aggravated sexual assault.

While Link had committed a horrible crime, he had not committed murder. Rather than life imprisonment with no chance of parole for ten to twenty-five years, Link faced a potentially shorter sentence because of the fine line between destroying a life and ending one. The maximum for attempted murder and for aggravated sexual assault can theoretically be as long as life imprisonment, with up to fifteen years before applying for parole. However, there is no minimum sentence for either of these charges. With concurrent sentences, the possibility of parole at one-third of the sentence, mandatory parole at two-thirds of the sentence and inclusion of the three years he had already been in custody, he could have been released not long after the guilty verdict was declared.

The prosecutor decided to have a go at getting the longest possible sentence, by a different route. An application was made to have Link declared a Dangerous Offender. The decision would be made by the judge, who would then carry on to sentence Link, based on that decision. If classified as a dangerous offender, he would receive an indeterminate sentence, which could mean custody for the rest of his life. It's the nuclear weapon of deterrence.

Unlike most other hearings, a Dangerous Offender application must include at least one mental-health expert's report or evidence. Being obliged to make such a report puts us in a tricky spot. We are being asked to predict the likelihood of the offender's violent behaviour recurring — an uncertain thing even for forensic psychiatrists, and made more difficult because the underlying legal assumptions (for such a prediction) don't necessarily agree with what those of us in psychiatry or psychology think. We have to learn as much as we can about the legal constructs in order to provide relevant testimony, and not step beyond the limits of our expertise, even though the court asks us to do so in predicting future behaviour — namely dangerousness. From the court's point of view, determining the risk of future violence is necessary, and mental-health professionals are regarded as the people most able to do it.

A person may be declared a Dangerous Offender if he or she has been convicted of a serious personal-injury offence, and the party filing the application (the Crown) can prove to the judge beyond a reasonable doubt that the offender constitutes a threat to the life, safety, or physical or mental well-being of other persons, based on one or more of three additional factors.

One, the Crown must show a pattern of repetitive behaviour, of which the current offence is included, showing the offender's failure to restrain his or her behaviour and demonstrating a likelihood, through future failure to restrain his or her behaviour, of the offender causing death or injury to other persons, or inflicting severe psychological damage on other persons. Two — which further defined Link's case — if the serious personal-injury offence has a sexual component, it must be demonstrated that the offender's conduct in *any* sexual matter has shown a failure to control sexual impulses, and that there is a likelihood, through his future failure to control his sexual behaviour, of his causing injury, pain "or other evil."

These two factors are difficult to prove beyond a reasonable doubt, especially when the offender is young and has a short history. And while a chronicle of similar offences — sexual or not — *may* point to someone continuing to commit further similar offences, there is no real scientific basis for us to cite and say, "If x, then y." I wish there were. But we don't have absolutely accurate methods for proving that violent offenders will or will not commit the same crimes again in the future.

It is an extremely difficult thing to assess. For one thing, if we don't have a complete understanding of what causes the violent to offend, how can we measure the risk of it happening again? Other barriers to sorting it out include the great variety of experiences and influences that have been brought to bear on individual offenders, their individual characteristics, the uncertain effects of treatment and supervision, community and family circumstances upon release, and even the true intentions of the offender as revealed under assessment, which could involve self-deception, and deliberate deception.

We have not been able to devise a standard framework for appraising future dangerousness, so we combine approximate tests and extrapolate from past behaviour. The court says that "this likelihood for sanctionable behaviour in the future must be derived from past conduct" of the offender — yet requires proof beyond a reasonable doubt. It's not easy to sit in court and be asked, "Is there any scientific research to support this?" or "Can you prove that treatment rather than custody for sexual offenders reduces recidivism?"

The third factor, which the Crown had to prove in Link's case, was a history of persistent aggression, including the current offence, for which the offender had shown "a substantial degree of indifference respecting the reasonably foreseeable consequences to other persons of his behaviour." Lack of remorse raises the issue of antisocial personality disorder, in which indifference to others is usually present to some extent. That, in turn, can lead to the discussion of the different degrees of antisocial behaviour and loaded words such as "psychopath," with its lay image of the incorrigible villain, being bandied about in the court-room. This is not what the defence counsel wants to hear. He or she is usually dealing with emotionally laden testimony anyway, often including victim impact statements — in this case, from the mother of a permanently injured child.

For Link's dangerous-offender hearing, I was asked by the prosecution to provide an assessment, and the court called upon a forensic psychologist, Dr. T. Our disparate points of view turned out to decide the outcome.

Following his arrest and charges, Link had received a conditional release, requiring twenty-four-hour supervision. He encountered such hostility living with his father in his home community that he was transferred, within a month, to another town nearby, then back to Miller Place. While there, he maintained his former reputation for obnoxiousness, threatening another resident with a hunk of cement while offering to knock his block off, and causing enough disruption on a recreational outing for the event to be cancelled in the first half-hour. He had been following some little children around a wading pool, and refused to leave and join his peers.

Almost a year after his attack on Tannis, Link was placed in an provincial inpatient unit of Youth Court Services for a month-long assessment related to the application to raise his case to adult court. Detailed reports were filed by a psychiatrist and a psychologist.

Link told the psychologist that he had committed his first break-and-enter in order to be caught and sent back to the adolescent treatment centre, where he had met a girl he expected to have sex with. All the other charges, including the last one, were "bogus."

He had been "set up" by the little girl he had been convicted of threatening with a knife. The girl, he said, had slapped him, so he had shoved her — not mentioning that she was five years younger and half his size — and he had never brandished any knife. Next, he hadn't done anything wrong in the fight for which he had been convicted of assault; it was purely self-defence. Then he had blacked out and had no recollection of the indecent phone calls; it wasn't his fault, it was his buddies who set him up.

As for the most recent offence, he said the DNA evidence was "bull-shit." The so-called blood on his clothing was rust from the old barbecue he trashed in the woods, and the stuff on his shoes was pizza sauce. The police were trying to build a false case against him because they had screwed up.

The psychologist with Youth Court Services concluded that Link had no major mental illness, but a moderate to severe conduct disorder, psychopathic personality traits, and possibly pedophilia (having deviant sexual desires directed towards children). The latter was difficult to assess and would be difficult to treat because Link refused to talk about his feelings and denied both involvement in and responsibility for any sexual misbehaviour. The psychiatrist had similar findings, but he came out much more forcefully, pointing out that the fusing of violence and sexuality is seen by most psychiatrists as being virtually impossible to treat, a life-long condition that may be contained, but cannot yet be cured or even totally controlled. Link's "escalating violence," he continued, combined with his lack of remorse and compassion in his sexual assault and beating of an 8-year-old girl, rendered him a danger to society at that time.

Three years later, Dr. T. found him capable of being safely maintained in the community, citing Link's exemplary behaviour while under supervision in a series of wilderness camp programs, his ability to work as a casual labourer for the last two years, and favourable comments about him by a number of people who had come in contact with him. There had been no allegations or evidence of further offending. The four non-offending years since his arrest represented a fifth of his young life, and had marked his passage from adolescence to adulthood.

When I was brought into the case, I was refused an interview with Link. Still, the volume of information I was given, including the many extensive psychiatric and psychological reports, greatly mitigated the lack of personal contact.

I was looking at a life that apparently had only been steady and regularized during those last years when he was in custody under strict supervision. The preceding years had been full of bumps and disruption, most of it caused by his own behaviour.

He may have been born with subtle problems as a result of his mother's substance abuse during pregnancy. Then the family split up in discord, with his mother departing, leaving Link with an abandoned feeling that blossomed into bitterness that may have affected all his relationships with the opposite sex. When he and his father moved away from all their relatives and friends to another city, Link probably felt cast adrift again.

His father, Garth, even now his best friend and most fierce protector, floundered while trying on his own to cope with a boy who was increasingly off the wall and always in trouble at school. He tried spanking, and not spanking, and a few times, called the police. Link loved Garth, saying he would always let him do what he wanted and, "Ask my dad, he'll tell you I was framed." Starting in kindergarten, his father was called repeatedly to school, because of incidents of fighting, aggression and academic difficulties.

Link was, in turn, suspended, transferred to an alternative program, sent for assessments, enrolled in therapeutic courses, and eventually, arrested four times before dropping out of Grade 11, not long before his fifth arrest, for the assault on Tannis. Many people had tried to intervene and help, to little avail. He was arrested four times, but was flipped back out, four times, committing the next offence while still on probation for the one before.

The crimes showed Link's aggressive tendencies marked with a callous tone. Three of them had sexual connotations, two involving much younger children. Link's extreme immaturity and lack of social skills, combined with inappropriate "acting out" seemed to have made it impossible for him to make friends of his own age, which he desperately wanted and needed. Some of the experts who saw him said he gravitated towards much younger children because he felt more comfortable with them, while his age-related peers rejected him. The other angle is that he didn't make friends in his peer group because he was attracted to younger children.

Taken together, his three sex-related offences, his increasingly violent attitude towards females, and his earlier history of talk and notes threatening rape seemed to amount to a worsening of tendencies. Dr. T. felt these were simply displays of aggression in reaction to his being rejected (omitting the fact that a 16-year-old with "normal" sexual feelings and control would not be putting 7- and 8-year-old girls in a position to reject his advances); and he found no evidence of a sexual disorder or pedophilia. I disagreed, saying that there was a clear element of sexual deviance, although what the exact composition of that deviance was could not be determined without in-depth examination with Link's cooperation. No one had achieved that, Link having erected a solid wall of denial. In my report, I repeated that offenders who engage in brutal sexual violence are the most difficult to treat, given the deep-seated psychological disturbance that could produce such behaviour. This meant a sinister prognosis in terms of the possibility of Link re-offending in the same way, particularly without successful treatment. But given my lack of access to Link, my opinion wouldn't be worth a hill of beans in court, because it couldn't be proven beyond a reasonable doubt.

I agreed that Link had shown a marked improvement in behaviour since his last offence, and that given his relatively young age, the possibility of substantial change for the better could not be ruled out, nor could the chance that maturity could have brought him some degree of internal control. However, even exemplary conduct on a day-to-day basis doesn't mean that the person cannot continue to harbour power-

ful violent urges, as we have seen in the phenomenon, played out bold-
ly in the media, of sexually violent serial offenders who superficially
appeared to be model citizens until bodies started turning up. Link's
improvement had also occurred under the cloud of extremely serious
charges and the fear of a heavy sentence to adult prison hanging over
him. Dr. T. also expressed the need for treatment that would help determine how much the improvement had been influenced by the situation,
and whether or not it was of a transitory nature.

Our slow-moving court system had given Link a four-year "time
out", in youth wilderness camps and, later, part-time in a new community. He behaved well in the controlled and restricted circumstances of
his release, and of course wanted to present himself in the best possible
light before he was sentenced. He even came to his sentencing hearing
and said he was sorry about "what happened" (not about what he had
done), for the first time since his telephone call to Kimmy the day after
the attack.

Difficult as it is to estimate the likelihood of an individual re-offending, I was required to do so, so I chose three different methodologies, each
of which took a different approach, in the expectation that together they
would provide a balanced and comprehensive estimation of the risk.

Hare's Psychopathy Checklist is a reliable, valid and well-researched
instrument for the assessment of psychopathic traits. Psychopaths are
people whose personalities and behaviour demonstrate tendencies to
selfishness and taking personal advantage at the expense of others, for
whom they show little caring or attachment. The clinical concept of a
psychopath is related to the concept of antisocial personality, but
describes individuals who generally have more consistent and serious
problems. (Roughly speaking, the most disturbed one-third of persons
with antisocial personality diagnosis will be classifiable as psychopaths.)
Research studies have shown that individuals who score high on this psychopathy scale are more likely to re-offend, including violent re-offending, and that they also tend to continue violent re-offending later in life
than non-psychopaths. Other studies have shown that psychopaths are
less likely to cooperate or to derive benefit from treatment than non-psychopaths, including at least one study that showed that psychopaths
become worse with treatment.

The checklist rates a large range of psychological and behavioural
traits, including impulsivity, irresponsibility, failure to accept responsibility for one's own actions, juvenile delinquency, and criminal versatil-

ity. A few other factors were not applicable, and therefore not rated, because of Link's youth and situation.

Link's score was moderately high, even allowing for the typical scoring variability, which considers individual judgment and subjectivity on the part of the person doing the rating. In a random sampling of one hundred male prison inmates, only fourteen would have a higher rating — be more psychopathic — than Link.

Dr. T. dismissed his own undisclosed rating for Link, saying the score was not significant. He did allude to secondary psychopathic personality disorder, now regarded as a neurotic disorder, wherein the individual's aggressive, antisocial behaviour is a defensive reaction to protect the person's emotional vulnerability and low self-esteem. I had a hard time accepting the obvious extrapolation — that he bludgeoned a child to death (or what he thought was to death) with a rock because she hurt his feelings by not wanting to have sex with him.

Another method of evaluation I used, the Violence Prediction Scheme (VPS), came about because various researchers worked to develop actuarial schemes that took into account large-scale, systematic follow-up studies of high-risk male offenders. Link's result on this scale suggested a 76 percent risk of violent re-offending within seven years, and 82 percent within ten years.

My third measurement tool, the HCR-20, is a recently developed instrument designed to provide an estimation of violent re-offence risk. The variables are related to those in the VPS, based on a long list of personal, psychological and social factors, some of which could not be evaluated because of the uncertainty of Link's sentence, and therefore his future circumstances. However, the majority of factors that were assessed pointed to a high risk of re-offence. Dr. T. did not employ either the HCR-20 or VPS rating systems.

My opinion, presented to the court, was that Link represented a high risk of re-offending violently. It was difficult to recommend any means of reducing that risk, other than participation in a full, major sexual/violent offender treatment program. Given his continued denial and other attitude problems, I was not optimistic that his participation and treatment would be successful.

Whether or not he was a dangerous offender was up to the court. The judge pointed out that he had been given two expert reports, mine and Dr. T.'s, with differing opinions. Because he was unable to say he preferred one report over the other, he said they both must stand, and therefore he could not conclude that the Crown had established beyond a reasonable doubt the likelihood of Link's future criminal activity or of his continuing the type of violent behaviour of which he had been convicted. The dangerous offender application was rejected.

In sentencing, the judge quoted other cases of violence against defenceless children, and said that he must, as in a similar case, consider the protection of the public to be the foremost objective, as opposed to individual deterrence and rehabilitation, which might have been foremost, considering Link's age.

On both charges, Link faced up to life imprisonment. He was given nine years on both counts — eleven years reduced to nine to take into account some of the time he had already spent in custody — and both sentences to be served concurrently. In addition, he was prohibited from possessing a number of weapons — but not knives or rocks — for ten years after his release. With continued exemplary behaviour, and with or without any form of treatment (he could choose to participate or not), he could be out again within three years. While it would be a blow to my perception of my assessment abilities, for the safety of the public, I hope to be proven wrong about this young man.

V

SENTENCE ADMINISTRATION

Nothing emboldens sin so much as mercy.

— Shakespeare, *Timon of Athens*

CHAPTER NINETEEN
THE ULTIMATE

You'd recognize the type — from the media, or from knowing one — an athlete at his peak, the dot.com millionaire boarding his executive jet, the salesman closing a six-figure commission. Their eyes shine, they they are self-confident, and they know the power they wield. They are portraits of success. In 1997, at the request of the Crown, I met such a man: Clifford Olson.

The second day I saw Clifford Olson, he put his arm around me, buddy-style — "How ya doing, Doc?" — and sent the assistant prison warden scuttling off like a waiter: "What kind of hospitality is this for the good doctor? Haven't they got you coffee yet? How do you take it? Cream? Sugar?" He could have been the owner of an upscale restaurant greeting one of his best customers.

Olson had been in prison fifteen years, convicted of the separate murders of eleven children, eight girls and three boys.

Fifteen years ago, he had danced with the police who were trying to convict him, getting them to yield a $100,000 trust for his family in return for telling them where he hid the children's bodies — "cash for corpses," he called it. (He loves to point out that the original deal was $10,000 for each of ten bodies, so the eleventh was a "freebie," an act of public-spirited generosity on his part.)

Later, he toyed with the FBI, as well as the RCMP, offering to locate more "victim dump sites," in his words.

He had danced with the administrators of his life sentence, Corrections Services Canada, in every possible way, forging documents over officials' names, threatening to take hostages, pleading for admission to treatment programs then declining participation, filing grievances, launching legal suits, constantly churning out some new kind of paperwork demanding a response, and faking illness until they transported him to hospital, where a handcuff key was found tucked up his rectum.

And now he was dancing with us all — the media, his victims' families, the legal and corrections systems, even a few psychiatrists — while he invoked the Criminal Code's Section 745, the "faint-hope clause," and forced a judicial review of his case, to decide whether or not he could apply early for parole.

He had received eleven concurrent life sentences with twenty-five years to be served before he could apply for parole. However, the faint-hope clause gave him the right, after fifteen years, to apply to the court to have the parole eligibility deadline reduced; theoretically, it could be brought down to fifteen years, allowing him to apply for parole immediately. The provision was introduced in 1976, when the death penalty was replaced by the twenty-five-year minimum for first-degree murder. In addition to giving offenders a second chance in life, its intent was to provide lifers with an incentive to behave, and so make prisons safer for guards and other inmates. In 1996, the faint-hope clause was amended to disqualify serial killers, but the amendment was not made retroactive, so Olson retained the right to apply.

However, even if the court were to advance Olson's parole eligibility date as a result of this hearing, the National Parole Board could still refuse to grant parole when he applied. No one expected the judicial review to change anything, not even Olson himself. It was simply his latest strategic move in a relentless self-promotion campaign to keep him front and centre as Canada's most notorious murderer.

"I am the ultimate serial killer," he boasts.

At the time I met him, Clifford Olson saw himself as a major success, a man at the top of his field, perhaps at the high point of his life. He needs no invitation to describe his accomplishments with relish, to brag about the deeds for which he hasn't been caught, to tell you how good he is at what he does. Never mind that he is talking about a large number of gruesome murders and a career in crime and conning. It's no different, because it makes no difference to him. "I don't," he understates, "have any respect for life."

To me, and to my colleagues who have been involved in his case, Olson does represent some sort of peak. He is the quintessential psychopath, the outsider, the person who has no understanding of, or regard for, the feelings of any of his fellow human beings. He is entirely focused on getting what he wants, and what he wants is sex, killing, fame and successful trickery.

Psychopaths, the upper end of individuals with antisocial personality disorder, do not fall into the legal category of a major mental disorder, which renders its sufferers unable to understand or appreciate the nature of their acts or capable of forming the intention to do them. Psychopath offenders are capable of forming intent, know exactly what they are doing and what the consequences will be, and know that it is illegal. They just don't give a damn.

Although psychopaths comprise only about one percent of our population, they probably commit nearly half the serious crimes, and account for up to one-quarter of our prison populations. A psychopath's selfishness, predatory nature, lack of conscience, and lack of any but the most shallow emotional connection to others provide a logical fit with a life of crime.

If there are 300,000 psychopaths in Canada, and only about 8,000 of them are incarcerated (of about 32,000 total prisoners), a scary fact emerges: there are many of them out among us, psychopaths to varying degrees, leading everything from apparently normal to enormously damaging lives. They charm and manipulate their way into high-rolling careers. They do well where ambition, determination and risk-taking count, but sincere personal interaction doesn't. They are the ones who remove life savings from the elderly; they are the family members who seduce, abuse, then discard spouses or children; they are the friends who come to visit, run up hundreds of dollars in long-distance calls, disappear without mentioning it and certainly never pay; they are the hackers who send out computer viruses; they are the sons and daughters who steal their mother's crutches. In their wake, they leave anything from shock and hurt feelings to psychological or financial devastation. While many of them have learned to express regret, they don't feel it.

I have mentioned the Psychopathy Checklist, an internationally recognized instrument for detecting and gauging psychopathic traits. Developed by British Columbia psychologist Robert Hare, the PCL-R provides mental-health professionals with an in-depth means of assessing psychological and behavioural traits. Out of a maximum score of 40, 30 is considered the cut-off for formal designation as a psychopath. Clifford Olson scored 38, the highest score I have ever given, and placing him in the 99.7 percentile among male prison inmates. The psychiatrist and the forensic psychologist who both assessed Olson in 1982, before his murder trial, and again in 1997, independently, also rated him at 38, each stating that there was virtually no difference over-all between their two assessments of him, despite the fifteen-year gap. The psychiatrist added that, in some ways, he was perhaps more dangerous in 1997. Over the years, and for a number of reasons, other psychiatrists and psychologists assessed Olson. The diagnoses were essentially the same: narcissistic and antisocial personality disorders to a psychopathic extreme, as well as proclivities for heterosexual and homosexual pedophilia and sexual sadism.

Perhaps the best way to portray the challenge Olson represents to the legal system and to Corrections Services Canada, is to present him roughly as I saw him while I was going through the PCL-R rating process, drawing from his voluminous criminal and incarceration history, the assessments of others, his own writing, and my interviews with him. You may suspect I am using hyperbole, even in this abbreviated form, but I'm not.

The first characteristic on the checklist is "glibness/superficial charm" — the legendary charm of the psychopath, I've heard it called. The individual presents himself well; can be an amusing, convincing conversationalist; is likable, friendly, at ease and cooperative, but really gives out little information. He may start to answer a question, but talk about something else, leaving the impression he had answered. He can appear informed on a topic, and may employ technical terms or jargon, but his actual knowledge is superficial. The PCL-R instructions warn that these characteristics may be deft and plausible: "It will be difficult to tell who controls an interview."

I interviewed Olson under the most structured circumstances possible. First, there had been three or four letters between us: my writing to request an interview (which he could refuse), his responding in the affirmative, then sending instructions on how to write him directly, and a few procedural questions. It seemed to be all set up, a positive tone prevailing, when suddenly Olson wrote to the assistant warden, his lawyer and some other people, refusing the interview on the grounds that I would be working for the Crown. This forced a hearing, in which Olson went before a judge and the judge explained that this was not a violation of his rights, I was to be impartial, and so on. (I soon learned that this was vintage Olson, forcing ten steps where two would do.) Eventually I was allowed to present myself at the Saskatchewan Federal Penitentiary at an appointed hour.

Olson was being held in a Special Handling Unit. Here, prisoners are kept isolated from one another, and can be moved about through remote-controlled heavy steel doors, so that they seldom need come in contact with staff or other inmates. This is the highest level of security in our prison system, serving to protect Olson from being harmed by other inmates, and keeping other inmates and staff protected from Olson. At the prison, I was advised to communicate with Olson through a glass partition, using telephone handsets, but I insisted that I wanted to be in the same room with him. I was given the most vigorous warnings I have ever received in this regard, but was allowed in after signing a document releasing the prison from responsibility for my safety. Clifford greeted me in a bubbly, backslapping mode, and we were ushered into a room where we sat on opposite sides of a small table, about two feet apart.

Reports invariably describe Olson as making a good first impression and his demeanour as affable, courteous and engaging. He has a very personal way of interacting with people he wants to impress or make a point with, the psychologist had reported, and although I was prepared and experienced, I still found him to be a suave character, to the point where he had an almost hypnotic effect.

Occasionally when I'm interviewing an extremely slick, bad guy, I can find myself starting to believe something obviously untrue that he is trying to con me about, and have to give my head a bit of a mental shake to remind myself of objective reality. With Olson, this was a constant struggle, and there was a real sense that I could succumb to his will and persuasiveness if I wasn't very careful. It happened once when he was claiming sorrow or affection about an event in which he had engaged in the most abhorrent sexual sadism. However, his style and mien were so compelling that I almost started to be convinced that his ridiculous words made some kind of sense.

I was writing on my notepad, with my bare left forearm resting beside it on the table. At some point, I glanced down, and only then realized that Olson was holding my left hand with one hand, and gently carressing my forearm with the other. He had commenced this so smoothly that I hadn't even noticed. When I looked at him in some surprise, he said, "Oh, am I making you uncomfortable?" and ceased his stroking. He continued talking, relaxed and at ease, while I beat back the comparison that sprang to mind between case-hardened psychiatrists and defenceless children.

Olson moved between soft intimacy, direct eye contact and wide animated gestures. He saw his role as that of the star. Another criterion of the PCL-R was obviously functioning to the max: a grandiose sense of self-worth. He clearly sees himself as superior to other people, most of whom (particularly corrections personnel) are "fuckin' retards," as soon as they are out of earshot.

He wasn't the least embarrassed by his legal situation. To the contrary: opinionated and cocky, having done some relevant reading, he talks like a "jailhouse lawyer" and was going to act in his own defence at the faint hope hearing.

"My expertise is law," he told me. From prison he filed so many suits, mostly against prison authorities, that in 1994 he was declared a "frivolous and vexatious litigant" and prohibited from bringing any more actions without leave of the court. As to the murders for which he was convicted, the "RCMP are good, but I am, too. The law had nothing on me except what I told them." This was close to true. Ironically, his desire to boast and be recognized was probably what got him convicted.

More than anything, Olson's inflated view of his abilities and self-worth is based on his image of himself as the supreme serial killer, as an expert on the subject of serial killers as a special study subject, and as a celebrity. He seized every opportunity — and created some — to get his name into the media. He showed me a file of press clippings and the results of database searches on the subject of Clifford Olson, saying, "It's wonderful!" The famous American criminal attorney Melvin Belli had come to see him, and Olson presented me, unasked, with my own copy of the photograph taken of him with Belli. Olson told me of television programs and books that have been written about him, and offered that it was okay if I, too, wanted to write a book about him. (It hadn't occurred to me.) He said that shrinks, students, reporters and police experts are all clamouring to talk to him and study him; I don't doubt there are many who envied me this opportunity.

He is sure that nobody in the world has a clue about serial murderers, except him. Olson didn't give me his own list of 145 Questions to Ask a Serial Killer, but he did offer it to the forensic psychologist who was evaluating him for the second time this year. He claims the FBI uses it. He had been accepted into a university criminology course, he said, but he could write the textbook.

When Olson got tired of answering the same mail questions, he wrote a couple of pieces himself on serial killers, photocopied them and sent them out by the score. "Profile of a Serial Killer" is written in the third person, with descriptions of himself as "a fast-talker who could be both charming and smooth-tongued ... Olson was a braggart, a liar and a thief. He was not a violent man ...." Olson boasts of having the "gift of gab" and lists several scams he pulled off. He confesses to a "long list of crimes" and a lot of jail time before the serial murders, and he faults an incompetent corrections system for not recognizing him as a potential killer, and for letting him out time and again, "only to go straight back to crime."

He gloats over the number of prison escapes he has made (seven), and can't resist telling how he once got recaptured. (Or maybe he couldn't resist being caught when publicity was assured.) The century-old B.C. penitentiary was holding a public open house, with free tours of the building, prior to being closed for good. Clifford "paid a sentimental visit to one of his old homes," and while peeking into his cell with the rest of the crowd was recognized by one of the guards and quickly arrested.

Next in his "Profile" came "the most shocking murder spree in Canadian history." He lists his murder victims by name, age, location and injuries, and omits any mention of sexual activity. He describes how he "outwitted the best brains of the famed Royal Canadian Mounted Police" for nearly nine months, then takes credit for solving the murders himself. He follows with a play-by-play of the legal action that ensued, as the victims' families attempted unsuccessfully, through several court proceedings, to have the $100,000 returned. Olson repeats his claims that he can help solve other murders. The RCMP "believe" (he says) that he knows about twenty-three "highway murders", along with two or three others that took place in B.C. and Alberta, which Olson describes and comes just short of confessing. He further claims to have knowledge of the Green River murders and the identity of that killer, and to have worked on a deal with the FBI to provide him with immunity and a new identity in a foreign country, in exchange for finding five bodies in Washington state.

He attaches a letter, written to a broadcast reporter, to be read in its entirety on national television, in which he says he pleaded guilty to the eleven children's murders rather than put the victims' families through the agony of a trial "which would be exploited by the media for sensa-tionalism." He asks for their forgiveness. He adds pointedly that God has already forgiven him.

Having provided no new clue to the understanding of a serial killer (he later claimed the profile was a satire), Olson produced "Inside the Mind of a Serial Killer."

"[Serial killers are] a mystery to criminologists and psychologists and a frustrating nightmare to all law enforcement officials." (He got the opening part right.) "These are the people that time wishes it could for-get." He refutes a few "popular misconceptions," including the idea that serial murderers seek media attention and notoriety. Then he differen-tiates, at length, between mass murderers who explode in a one-time shooting, and serial murderers, who carry out sequential murders over time and (according to Olson) are more sly, shrewd, sophisticated and better able to get away with it longer.

He does say that serial killers can never be rehabilitated and will kill again. And that some serial killers have the overwhelming desire to control people, and gaining this control when they murder is what makes them enjoy killing.

"In my own case, this experience of pleasure, of sexual raping and murder to achieve a subjective experience of sexual pleasure and murders became an addiction."

Clifford proudly presented me with signed copies of this volume, along with another containing "his" studies of eleven serial killers — factual accounts devoid of analysis, except for "there is absolutely no way to determine who is a potential serial killer."

He also gave me a 1980s volume of Personal Reflections. It contained two poems, "A Child's Gift" and "No Love Like Mother's Love," and three Bible studies on love, friendship and abortion (he's against abortion because "taking human life is always objectively evil") that appeared to be borrowed.

Two reflections on the death penalty were also included. One, from 1983, was in favour of capital punishment, because the safety of the public came first, and "in my case" it "would have had deterrent effect to stop me from taking my little brothers and sisters lives." The second, from 1985, seemed to be against it, for religious reasons that came from different parts of the Bible than those quoted in the preceding essay. Olson said that he had been told his writing was "brilliant." I think he fancied himself as a sort of gentleman scholar serial killer.

Whether Olson wrote these pieces, in whole or in part, we will never know, just as we will never know how many of the opinions he expressed he actually held. Another common characteristic of psychopaths is habitual lying. They lie easily, even when the lie is obvious. And when they're caught, they adjust their story without embarrassment. They make promises, break them, and come up with new promises they have no intention of keeping. They take pride in their ability to lie well, especially if it helps further some criminal enterprise, some clever scam, or luring someone in. And they don't care about contradiction and hypocrisy, such as a child murderer claiming to be a pro-lifer.

Olson's files and records are full of contradictions. He claimed to be married with children a few times, long before he was, but each time he also declared elsewhere he was single. He has had one, two or three children. He made up a story about his father and a multimillion-dollar fraud. He told me he had had sex three times in a couldn't-be-more-public police cell. He claims he is strictly heterosexual, but lists off conquests of both genders. His claims of remorse and his claims of involvement in dozens more murders are regarded with major skepticism. One of the problems in evaluating Olson is that he lies to make himself look worse, as well as to look better, or to get something he wants, so you can't just assume the worst is true.

In prison, he is constantly working the system, conning and manipulating at every turn. His criminal record contains a dozen fraud or forgery charges, a skill set he carried over into prison and uses with glee. He showed me copies of postage stamps he had altered — a crude typewriter change increased the stamp's value from a penny to the amount needed for a letter. He did this for five years before he was caught, he smiled. At the time, he had laughed at the trouble he had caused, saying prison officials wouldn't do anything about it because they didn't want to take him outside to go to court, "and I'm already serving a life sentence, anyway." Every time they turned around, someone in the corrections system was receiving a letter from Clifford Robert Olson, with copies to four other people, which in turn would require several responses. Even when there wasn't a problem, he'd fire off letters "just to see what the response would be."

One of his forged documents got him access to a cordless telephone and long-distance codes. Apparently Olson kept a not-so-veiled threat in front of guards, concerning a buddy on the outside that could reach guards' families and do Olson's bidding. With many still-connected drug pushers and gang members in and out of jails, guards hear this line of intimidation frequently and it is hard to ignore. After the daughter of one of the guards was sexually assaulted, Olson hinted that he had been behind it, settling some difference with the guard in question. From then on, he got away with stuff like having pornography in his cell and using phone-sex services. Eventually, the telephone was removed, prompting Olson to launch a claim that his rights were being violated, and another round of administrative mischief began.

Sometime in 1992, Kim Campbell, who would become Prime Minister of Canada, but who was then federal justice minister, allegedly became dismayed enough upon hearing that Clifford Olson had been denied purchase of a life-size sex doll, that she wrote the penitentiary physician recommending that he be allowed to "have sexual intercourses [sic] with a female prostitutes [sic] ... as long as he uses his own personal monies. Steps should be taken right away to see that he does." I don't believe they were, despite the minister's forged signature. He can be humourous. Journalist Peter Worthington described him playing disc jockey in prison ("Your favourite DJ, the King of Kingston!") and cracking that he had a "*cell*ular phone." Some type of dyslexia makes him prone to malapropisms — anal becomes "annual" intercourse — which, because he ignores corrections, come off as quips.

Clifford worked diligently to try to manipulate his way out of Kingston Penitentiary. He would apply to enter treatment programs held at other institutions, and then when the institution did not accept him, he would initiate a flurry of grievance correspondance. It was clear he didn't want treatment; it was the spirit of the chase and the possibility of moving that motivated him. He loudly proclaims that he is not a sexual offender (he had been convicted of murder; it didn't say anything about sex, he repeats), but a few times he did apply for admission to sexual offender treatment programs. These required psychological assessments, and Olson tried to set the terms and conditions of the testing himself, or refused, or terminated testing partway through. He told me of finally agreeing to participate in an assessment in which erectile response to various visual and auditory sexual stimuli is measured by means of an elastic gauge around the base of the penis. Olson gleefully said he had placed the elastic gauge around a racquet ball instead, and jerked the elastic at will, so that the test results would show he was sexually turned on by the neutral control stimuli of mountain scenery. In many ways, Olson's deepest fulfillment and satisfaction in life seems to come from puerile mischief — akin to placing a tack on the teacher's chair.

He was an on-going disruptive force in the penitentiary, an administrative nuisance, with over twenty institutional charges racked up in the ten years he was at Kingston — for assaulting, threatening or attempting to bribe officers; for fighting; for disobeying orders, and for having unauthorized items (usually pornography) in his cell. When he was with other inmates, either he was instigating trouble or they were subjecting him to verbal abuse, spitting, throwing urine or other liquids at him. And whenever he hit the news, the hostility rose. A special cell with two doors, to provide an extra barrier, was built to protect him.

In 1992, he complained of gastro-intestinal problems and was escorted to an outside hospital for examination. Unfortunately for Olson's plans, x-rays revealed a handcuff key in his rectum. Not long afterwards, he hit national television once more. A reporter went on TV to declare that she had 150 hours of recorded telephone conversation with Olson (more calls "to his lawyer"), during which he had boasted about his smuggling out the key, boasted about his escape record, said he was biding his time and could escape anytime he wanted. Then, as a corrections officer later said, "in a move unprecedented even for him, he had the unmitigated audacity to pompously and confidently predict his escape from custody in 1993." Two routine searches of his cell produced scissors, razor blades, tape, road maps and a makeshift weapon in the form of a sharpened broom handle . He was transferred to the Special Handling Unit in Saskatchewan's federal pen. Clifford told me he had only been joking about the escape, but it got him out of Kingston, so he was happy. "It was a blessing in disguise."

Olson's biggest con, of course, was the tragic manipulation of at least eleven children whom he enticed into his car with promises of a job. He often asked his victim for directions to the employment office, saying he was looking for youths to wash windows. For the purpose, he had special business cards printed (he happily defrauded the printer), indicating he was a building contractor. He would hand them his "top of the line, laminated, fluorescent or gold-embossed business card" to prove he was legitimate, then ask them if they needed some money in advance. He would give them a $100 bill, "because I always knew I would get it back." Next came an offer of beer, or sometimes champagne — with chloral hydrate pills, an earlier crude version of what the media now refer to as "date-rape-drugs."

"These pills will counteract the alcohol," he would tell them conspiratorially, "so you won't get drunk." Olson had been manipulating kids for years, teaching them to steal and sharing the merchandise, giving them candy and toys in exchange for sex, being every mother's nightmare. He just never got caught until 1981.

One of Olson's stock defensive lines has been, "What about the hundred children I let get away?" He says he had sex with many children, and only started killing because he feared the victim would tell her mother about the sex. If only a small percentage of that is true, and he counted on young children not to talk, he was an extreme risk-taker. It is another trait of psychopaths that some are prone to boredom, constantly seeking stimulation, and so they engage in risky behaviours. Olson said he committed crimes because there was nothing else to do, and the crimes escalated.

When he found himself in custody, he upped the risk level by escaping, seven times. Knowing the prison culture well by 1976, he nevertheless put himself at risk by testifying against another inmate, providing evidence that was instrumental in getting the man convicted of murder. As a result, he was attacked and stabbed by four inmates; but once more, he testified against his attackers, and they, too, were convicted. The following year, in another penitentiary, he testified on behalf of three correctional officers whom three inmates had charged with assault. The charges against the officers were dismissed. He would be known in the prison population as a rat, but now there was a chance a few of his keepers might think slightly better of him.

Four characteristics included in the psychopathy checklist form the core of Clifford Olson's dangerousness. They are his failure to accept responsibility for his actions, his lack of remorse or guilt, his lack of emotional depth, and his callousness or lack of empathy.

Before his mail privileges were restricted, he told me, he received letters from mothers of missing children asking if he knew their fate. He would write back to them, playing along, suggesting he might know something, such as where the child's body could be located. After a few exchanges, he would make some outrageous demand, such as asking the parent to send him a photo of herself copulating with the family dog. When occasionally he actually received a compliant response out of the parent's anguish and desperation, he would reply with something like, "ha ha, I fooled you." While relating this, Olson looked at me as though he expected me to appreciate his clever joke.

He has not ceased to aggravate the heartbreak he caused. He vaunts the reign of terror he created for the families in 1980-81. He roughed up a bunch of Serial Killer Collector Cards — in the style of baseball cards — with his prison mug shots; photos of each of the victims; and his story of the murders. He sent these to several members of parliament.

He has produced voluminous files, carefully indexed and cross-referenced, in which he describes the eleven murders yet again. He insists on reading one of them to me, with comments. I have also read the terrible script in which he goes step-by-step through each murder, devoid of emotion, but replete with detail. "You need to be precise about such things," he tells me.

He says he and the RCMP have recorded a dozen videotapes on the same subject plus "all the unsolved murders I know about," which he will sell for several million dollars. When I interviewed him, he showed me the Manual of Sexual Seduction Techniques he was working on. It was a pornographically detailed description of a serial killer's seduction skills as employed prior to a murder, illustrated with photos clipped from porno magazines.

I ask him how he thinks the surviving families are affected by the tapes and scripts, and by being put through this faint-hope hearing, at which some of them will give victim impact statements. He tells me he would like to say to the parents, "You're lucky you got your child's body back, out of the goodness of my heart. You should be grateful." Then he allows that he won't challenge the families' evidence in court.

"You need to be sympathetic," he points out. "I lost a son and daughter [sic] [due to his incarceration], so I know what it's like."

We talk about guilt, and regret. I have seen no signs of either, only their opposite, in his pleasurable re-living and shameless exploitation of the murders.

"No one can tell me I got no remorse," he remarks, "but I can't keep it up after fifteen years." They shouldn't be "obsessed" with his crimes, he says. The murders are like World War II, "over and done with ... You can't live in the past."

When I'm on the stand in court, Olson questions my comment that he was incapable of feeling remorse for the families.

"Can you explain to me how empathy and remorse are shown?" he asks. I told him that by forcing this hearing, a pointless exercise when he knew there was no hope he would ever be paroled, he was dragging the families through more grief and distress.

"I'm sure it's upsetting for the whole families," he answered, "but I have the right under law, and the law must be obeyed."

He writes and talks about love in a cold, juvenile fashion, perhaps mistaking sex for love, the way he seems to equate sadness with frustration. He said he loved his wife, but then professed to having married her for the money she received in a divorce settlement, then spending it all. "I took her for a ride, shall we say." During the short marriage, ended by his incarceration, he physically abused her, cheated on her in their home with a young boy, among others, and when she wasn't there one evening, he went out and murdered someone — and then ten others. He claimed affection for his family, but following the death of his second parent in 1989, communication ceased between him and his siblings, and he didn't seem to care. He is incapable of caring, and therefore incapable of remorse.

While admitting loud and clear to the crimes, and saying he "made the choice," and he "did it of his own free will," he's not going to take all the blame. It was the alcohol. Why, he demands, did he never get any help with that? He drank heavily for the first time in his life during the ten months he committed the murders, picking up an impaired driving charge. Typically, he would have a half-case of beer before a killing, he told me, "but I was always sober enough to know what I was doing."

Quite often he blames the murders on the corrections system. If they hadn't kept him locked up in segregation so much, his thoughts and fantasies wouldn't have built up to the point where action was required.

Also (and here he shows great indignation), why didn't the police catch him sooner? They could have saved four lives if they hadn't been so incompetent!

He says he first killed for a practical reason: to prevent a rape victim from telling on him. He did not want to go to jail as a sex offender.

He says he did this in 1964; other times he says his first (or second) killing was in 1972. He realizes now it was unnecessary to kill to escape detection.

Most chillingly, I sit and listen to him say, "I got addicted to killing. It was enjoyable and habit-forming," in the same tones one might use to talk about chewing gum.

He says his victims died painlessly with no suffering or torture — "Let them say what the fuck they want about that" — and no mutilation, although he thought about it because he'd seen something in a movie. And: "I couldn't have sex with someone after they're dead — that's revolting. I'm not a psychopath, like [Charles] Manson and [Jeffrey] Dahmer. I didn't run around uncontrolled."

I couldn't disagree more. Looking through the evaluations that had been made over the years, I saw almost nothing that wasn't a perfect fit with the psychopath's cold, guilt-free use of others for his own ends, and chronically antisocial and deviant lifestyle.

Before his incarceration, he had lived parasitically, almost entirely off crime, but sometimes off public assistance, his wife, or extremely infrequent jobs. He relied on his parents, living in their house even when he got married. He was promiscuous, casual, indiscriminate and coercive in his sexual behaviour, and had nothing but short-term relationships.

His crime resume before the murder charges included a juvenile record, several revocations of conditional release, including those following his escapes and a full career of convictions, for break and entry, robbery, theft, fraud, forgery, false pretences, failure to appear, armed robbery, and impaired driving. As soon as he was released or escaped from custody, he would go right back at it.

In prison, he kept right on offending, breaking rules, assaulting someone now and again, and finding new ways to cause trouble. When his access to the media and mail was curtailed, he started sending pornography, doctored to depict him being sexually serviced by the recipient, to members of parliament.

"They can't prevent me from writing to an MP, and you can't sue for what they say in Parliament," Olson said in satisfied tones, "so I make them look like fools."

There were no signs I could see that he would change. The whole parole-eligibility hearing initiative was based on Olson's continuing, unrealistic long-term plan. He contends he was involved in dozens of murders, and is convinced that he will be able to provide the information to solve these murders to the RCMP, the FBI and Interpol, in exchange for immunity and a new identity and new life in some other country.

"No jury or parole board will ever set me loose without an immunity deal ... I'll give the letter to the Crown, and they'll whine and snivel, but I'll get recommended for parole," he tells me confidently. He was "directly involved" in five Green River murders, and he claims to have plenty of evidence about the Green River killer. According to Olson, the FBI has arranged for him to move ahead, he just needs the release from Canada. He shows me a letter allegedly from a "top-of-the-line" New York lawyer, saying arrangements have been made for the Israele (so spelled) embassy to receive him when he can leave the country.

Although he has not provided any evidence related to all this in the fifteen years he has been in prison, he says it is because "there's got to be something in it for me" before he will make any disclosures, and so far no offer has been forthcoming. There has been at least one trip with the Mounties to look for evidence, but it must have been fruitless. Olson told me he had been flown across the country five times by the RCMP, to help them solve the murders. I'm guessing that's an exaggeration, and that he has just hinted enough to keep them interested. Frustrating as it must be, as he dances around, he's still someone who can never be taken lightly. It is not beyond the realm of imagination to infer that this individual could have some information on other murders.

So we go to court. The victims' families had been lobbying, outraged, for a repeal of the faint hope clause, and they and their agony have been well covered in the media. Clifford signed one of his obscene mail pieces to MPs, "The Beast of B.C. I'm coming home, and there's not a fucking thing you can do about it." (The hearing was to be held in Surrey, British Columbia.) Five months before the hearing, an Ontario MP who had been speaking out in the House of Commons against Section 745 appeared at the families' press conference, held to announce their opposition to it, brandishing the letters, with the shocked relatives standing alongside him.

It put Olson back in the news, again beside photos of his eleven smiling young victims, and he stayed there until after the hearing. A plethora of media items featured journalists analyzing whether or not they should be giving him so much press. Clifford must have relished it all. Besides, the Clifford Olson Road Show had won him a free trip to the coast.

People at the packed hearing heard once more the words of the murder trial judge pronouncing Olson's sentence in 1982: "I do not have the words to adequately describe the enormity of your crimes or to adequately describe the heartbreak and anguish you have brought to so many people. There is no punishment that a civilized country could impose that would come close to being adequate. Parliament has set out the only punishment that I can impose ... life imprisonment without eligibility for parole for twenty-five years."

I am strongly opposed to the death penalty. It lowers society to the level of the offender, and one wrongly executed person is too many. But in Clifford Olson, I encountered the only one of all the killers I have met whom I would have readily sent to the executioner. I wondered if the sentencing judge had felt the same.

"I normally would not presume to express my views to the National Parole Board," his statement continued, "We each have our separate functions and ... responsibilities. I feel compelled, however, in this case, to express my view. It is my considered opinion that you should never be granted parole during the remainder of your days." The judge concluded by asking that a transcript of his remarks be passed on to the parole board and the Attorney General, and made part of Olson's file.

Eight members of the murder victims' families delivered emotionally wrenching victim impact statements that left everyone in the courtroom, including the tough, seasoned Crown prosecutor overwhelmed. At lighter moments, a few victim family members and Olson exchanged "the finger" and other unpleasantries through the bullet-proof barrier. Some family members did say afterwards that a measure of catharsis had been achieved through the experience of seeing Olson, for the first time in person, as such a pathetic figure, firmly in the grip of the law.

I was the last Crown witness. What I said did not dispute anyone else's testimony, or what other mental-health professionals, even those who provided reports at Olson's request, had said in their reports. Everyone but Olson was on the same side.

I testified that Clifford Olson was about the most disturbed personality I had ever encountered, that I felt he was completely untreatable, and that I believed it would be reckless in the extreme to let him out in public unless he was continuously shackled and surrounded by guards.

Olson, acting on his own behalf, sat quietly, and during his cross-examination he focused on my calling him "an extreme sexual deviant." He still didn't want anyone thinking he was a sex offender.

"Your whole report reads like a pornographic movie," he commented, "sexual preferences, sexual this and sexual that." I could feel his delight in the words.

He also criticized my limited expertise in assessing serial killers, essentially making the point that he was so special that no one was worthy to assess him.

The jury denied Olson's request to apply for early parole. In true Olson style, he soon applied for leave to appeal, based on his claims that he had been denied a fair hearing because he had not been given a legal aid lawyer and not allowed access to some documents. The court denied his request. Not long after the hearing, Corrections Canada also imposed a gag order, forbidding him contact with the media.

I have no doubt that Olson will continue to be in our faces now and again. In the year 2000, news stories appeared describing his negotiations with police in two countries. A public defender in Hawaii confirmed that Olson has offered to help locate the bodies of two women who were murdered there. They think he was in the state in 1980.

He also contrived to give a half-hour telephone interview with an Irish newspaper.

"All I am doing is trying to help authorities, around the world, find the bodies of dead men and women," he told the reporter unctuously, after boasting about a killing spree in Canada, Hawaii and Ireland. "I can find the bodies in Ireland, no problem." Irish police said he hadn't provided any useful information.

I believe that Olsen is more dangerous than he was in 1981, and that's what makes him such a conundrum for both medical and corrections people.

For public safety, he should surely be incarcerated for the rest of his life. But what to do with him? His appetite for mischief has not decreased. His sexual obsession has not diminished, even with age. At our current level of medical/psychiatric/psychological knowledge, we are unable to treat him, and he does not wish to be treated.

He says he has an addiction to murder, but then he says his killing days are over; he says he is doing a noble thing in helping to solve other murders. He believes that if he *says* he feels a certain way, it is so. He's not concerned about his destructive, wasted life. He's quite pleased with who he is.

We don't know exactly what causes psychopathy, let alone how to deal with it. Part of the secret is undoubtedly locked in our genes, some combination of genetic predisposition, brain structure and body chemistry. We do know that low levels of serotonin, a chemical that acts on emotional regulation in the brain, are sometimes linked to high levels of aggression. But we likely won't ever be able to simply say "My genes made me do it."

And we need to consider the argument that upbringing and experience can greatly affect the behaviour predisposed by the genes. Although Clifford Olson, as extreme an example of a psychopathic killer as he is, may be exceptional, it's hard to see that his "nurture" side played a big role. He didn't spring from the usual harsh, chaotic childhood. His parents were reputedly ordinary people. The family was stable, the father worked steadily, three younger siblings appeared. There was no apparent abuse of substances or children, and no great anger or trauma. If anything, his parents were too benign. Clifford's only repeated negative comment about his family was that there wasn't much discipline, but that's true of huge numbers of children who don't turn into killers.

His childhood passed fairly uneventfully. Unusually for a career criminal, his first conviction didn't come until he was 16, and if we are to average out his versions of what happened and when, he didn't start to act up seriously until he was almost in his teens. He remembered refilling half-empty beer bottles with water, recapping them and selling them to his family for a dime each; Grandma thought that was pretty cute. When he was about 12, he discovered the joy of stealing. He would pick fruit off neighbours' trees and sell it back to them. He would steal the milk money people left out for his father, a milkman at the time. People seldom locked their doors in those days, Clifford learned, and he and a pal would take the bus to another part of town and go through apartment buildings, stealing. "We were the richest kids in school." But he did poorly in school, except for sports, and left after repeating Grade 7, to do what he loved. His career took off.

Between his first arrest for car theft at 16, and his last, for murder, at 41, Olson racked up eighty-seven convictions — despite being in prison for most of his adult life. He moved from crime to crime until he found killing for pleasure.

It's clear that you have to keep a murderer with a mind like Clifford Olson's away from the rest of society, and that's a huge job for his sentence administrators, given his powers of manipulation and his determination to keep things stirred up, or to escape. He can't be forced to participate meaningfully in any treatment program, essentially because it's pointless unless he wants to change. He gets such pleasure feeding off his incredible notoriety that dull, ordinary, decent morality and behaviour could never give him the same kicks.

The combination of sadistic sexual deviance and murder is virtually impossible to treat, and most psychopaths — certainly of Clifford's level — would simply come away from treatment with an improved knowledge of how to manipulate, from having learned what is wanted or expected of them. For these hardcore cases, we refer to most types of treatment as a "finishing school for psychopaths."

Because of his unremitting rebellious behaviour, Clifford Olson is confined to his cell most of the time. He leaves for an hour of solitary exercise, to work alone as a cleaner in his area, and for occasional meetings and telephone calls. He is, at once, too dangerous and too vulnerable to being attacked to spend any time with even a small group of inmates for activity programs, socializing or meals; even treatment programs would expose too many people to risk. So his personal correctional-plan objectives have remained limited.

The goals, for him, were to remain offence free (he hasn't); to attend regular interviews with the institutional psychologist, in an effort to identify treatment needs relating to emotional and personal factors (he hasn't); to refrain from having sexually explicit material in his possession (he hasn't); to reduce his notoriety with both the inmate population and the public at large (he has somewhat, only because of the media and court bans that have been imposed upon him); to remain employed (he has carried out his paid cleaning job satisfactorily), and to complete educational programs (he had obtained his high school diploma and done Bible studies at the time of his faint-hope hearing). Out of his wages, he has been able to purchase a television, electric typewriter (perhaps by now a computer — without, I hope, Internet access) and other items, and is apparently comfortable.

The faint-hope clause has not been repealed, although it now excludes serial killers. For Clifford Olson, it was just another loophole for him to use for his own deviant purposes. It cost plenty and produced nothing except a revisiting of grief for the victims' survivors.

However, before we start clamouring for its eradication, try to imagine a killer who is the polar opposite of the cocky, remorseless inmate we have just described. In our ultra rigid sentencing system, perhaps we need a few loopholes.

CHAPTER TWENTY

VIRTUAL REALITY MURDER

He was a wisp of a boy, with his pale blonde hair, pale expression and stick-thin build. He seemed to have no energy, no will of his own, not knowing which way to turn. Meek and mild-mannered, he seemed too shy to participate in life. Robert Rocar was the last person you would think capable of bashing an old woman to death with a crowbar.

Robert had drifted through an inconspicuous and ordinary childhood, but seemed to have missed the growing-up aspects. When I met him, he was 12 to 15 years old emotionally and socially, although he was actually 24. In his early school years, what he remembered most was being picked on, and being nicknamed "Robot." In high school, he kept to himself, had no friends, never dated, didn't do sports, had a mediocre academic record. In his last year, he joined the Dungeons and Dragons Club at lunchtime, tried the game, and kind of liked it, but …. He didn't know what to do after graduation.

No career beckoned. "There's not much to me," he said, "I don't have many interests. I've never been good at anything, really. Everything I do, other people can do better."

His father had once been in the armed forces, so he suggested his son sign up, and Robert went along with the idea. He lasted seven weeks before he cracked under the pressure.

"They play head games on you. You do something right and they say you did it wrong. They keep at you, trying to find out where your breaking point is. One day, I just kind of sat on the barracks floor in a corner, doing nothing. I had a nervous breakdown, I guess."

He was found in his barracks corner, and forced back outside into training. The next day, he went AWOL. He wandered around for a week, then turned himself in. After a few inconclusive days in hospital, he was discharged from the service. His squad commander told him he was a wimp and a coward and that Robert disgusted him. "Get out," were the officer's parting words.

Robert moved back home with his parents and got a minimum-wage job in a hotel laundry. After four years had rolled past, he asked for time off during the summer. It was the hotel's busiest season, so they turned him down, and he quit. He wasn't making much more money than when he started, and he was still doing the same job, so he could see there was no future there, anyway. He went on unemployment insurance, and, because he wanted to help his parents pay off their mortgage, he engaged in a number of get-rich-quick schemes — gold-panning, lottery tickets, various send-away-to-make-big-bucks plans. Nothing paid off. He kept trying; he did want to better himself.

His jobless state offered one advantage: free time. Robert acquired, for the first time in his life, both a hobby and a friend. In the hobby, he had found something he could do well — another first for him. His lack of success in everything until now had kept reinforcing his despondency. For two years, this leisure pursuit was his main activity outside work, and virtually all his social life. Unemployed, he started spending up to sixty hours a week at it.

Dungeons and Dragons, Robert's chosen pastime, is one of a number of fantasy role-playing games that became popular in the 1980s. About the time I met Robert, as many as four million played D&D in the United States alone. It was big in England and Canada, too. Participants were almost all males between 12 and 20 years of age.

D&D players choose or "build" the characters they will assume while playing the game in a medieval, mythological setting — they can be fighters, assassins, thieves, clerics, magic users, monks or bards. They choose the proportions of these traits their characters will have: strength, intelligence, wisdom, constitution, dexterity and charisma.

The player also chooses his character's race, height, weight and alignment. Alignment is like attitude — and the choices are, in degrees, between lawful and chaotic: lawful good, lawful neutral, lawful evil, chaotic good, chaotic neutral, chaotic evil. Good and evil, I was told, are simply different orientations, without one being better than the other.

Now the character gets weapons — several dozen to chose from, depending on your "job," including combat armour, medieval weapons, hammers, poisonous gases, curses and spells. Since games can move across time, nuclear missiles and space weapons can appear as well.

The goals of the game are to steal treasure, not get killed, and to gain as much power as possible by murdering your opponents. With these objectives, most players would naturally choose the "biggest, baddest" characteristics and accoutrements for their characters.

Characters each get a god or goddess to worship, sacrifice to, obey, and if necessary, die for.

A roll of the dice determines the number of "hits" a character can take before he dies. And finally, a player gets to choose his character's name.

Now the player has a complete character whom he controls. He is encouraged, like all players, to identify with — to "become" — that character.

Robert became Dark Knight, Assassin, and lived with — or through — him for seven months.

The most powerful role in the game is that of Dungeon Master,. the player/god who runs and controls the game. He can't control the characters completely but he can restrict a character's actions — and he can destroy (kill) him. The DM creates and sets up the adventure and the intricate world in which the game will be played: the sounds, and smells; the indoor, outdoor, underground scenery; the characters that will be encountered; the actions that will occur. There are pre-generated modules of worlds and adventures, but many Dungeon Masters make up their own. Games run for days, weeks — and have been known to last a year or more. The players decide what their characters will do, react to the circumstances (rolls of the dice determine some decisions), get told by the Dungeon Master what has happened, decide what to do next, and so on.

Attacks and counter-attacks are continuous, and they may include assassinations, poisonings, spying, theft, injury, disablement, self-mutilation, cannibalism, torture, curses and mental attacks. Clerics can kill with a single word. Any number of monsters (opponents) can appear, including demons and devils, and sub-human soldiers, who are less expensive than humans, but "expect to loot, pillage, rape freely at every chance, and kill (and probably eat) captives," according to the D&D manual. Characters can be cursed with an obsession to kill others, or an obsession to commit suicide. There is hack-and-slash murder, terrorism, forced insanity. And every character must commit some of this violence. The object is to survive, and you must rob and murder, at the very least, in order to survive.

An average of five characters play with a Dungeon Master, occasionally coming together to carry out some joint action. For example, premeditated murder is the exclusive precinct of assassins, and assassins must prepare a complete plan of how the deed is to be done, considering the type of character to be killed, the value or worth of the victim and the precautions that need to be taken.

It's a complicated game, requiring some cleverness and great attention, and can be completely engrossing. And the important thing is that it takes place largely in the mind, with some details written down. The fantasies are never played out in reality. You become a character and imagine the settings, the other characters, all the actions and repercussions, and what the next stage holds. When you go home, the game keeps playing in your head. For some people, the game is a distraction; for others, it becomes their reality.

In the mid-1980s, when Robert was playing, nearly a hundred North American deaths — murders and suicides — had been linked to violence-oriented fantasy war games. A 16-year old committed suicide, with dice at his feet and a note saying, "I have finally won the game." A 15-year-old shot himself to death in the woods. Nearby, a game poem was found, instructing him to hide in the woods and "forget life, forget light." A university student who had belonged to a club in which members fought mock medieval battles with hammers, axes and swords, and played D&D games that lasted several months, killed another club member with a dagger. A babysitter killed his two young charges after dressing them in Halloween costumes.

The knee-jerk reaction to such information is usually, "But what about the nearly four million who played *without* murdering or committing suicide?" And the knee-jerk rejoinder would be, "Isn't a hundred still too many?" The majority of players probably have little trouble maintaining the difference between fantasy entertainment and reality. Thousands of college students got into it, sometimes playing all night, the way a previous generation of students played bridge.

But this type of game particularly attracts a minority of loners, social misfits, and unstable and troubled souls. It gives them some kind of life, and the macho image (and self-image) they may lack.

"I like to be something other than myself," said Robert, "The game allowed me to act out my fantasies, like being able to perform magic or feats of strength — things I can't normally do." For these individuals, and for vulnerable adolescents, the fantasy world can have a significant attraction.

Role-playing, in therapy, can be a powerful tool in changing and reinforcing a person's behaviour. Why would we doubt that it could also work negatively?

American anti-violence lobby groups have documented a great number of reported incidents of rape, bomb-making, and other deviant acts — and were able to connect them to such pastimes.

The most pernicious effect of such games — and violent entertainment in other media (television, movies, video games, Gulf War newscasts) — is their contribution to the desensitization of young people.

Where extreme violence is seen a regular, desirable and rewarding occurrence, the more normalized violence becomes. And life is cheapened.

The consequences that death and injury produce in real life are never, ever shown. No grieving families. No traumatized witnesses or terrified children. No horrible pain, or disability for life. Hey, I killed him, fifty points.

Whether it's from an overload of game-playing, watching brutal movies, or simply everyday doses of television, the more violence we are exposed to, the less significant violence becomes. And the probability that any of us will engage in aggressive behaviour rises.

In the 1970s, some parents spoke out against the violence in children's television cartoons, which continue to be violent today. In the 1980s, some people spoke out against the violence of games such as Dungeons & Dragons. This type of game continues to attract players, who can now download anything they want from the Internet. Other people have been speaking out against the violence in films, against the great number of violent video games, against television cop shows, against TV newscasters' penchant for the most violent footage, against rap lyrics that incite violence, even against hockey violence.

Yet all these forms of entertainment thrive, and have become increasingly saturated with violence. Many of them are, God help us, babysitting tools. Desensitization has crept up on us and our children like a deadly fog.

Schoolyard stabbings have almost lost their news value, but bullying, because it has driven some children to death, is a hot topic.

Dungeons and Dragons did not cause Robert Rocar to commit a murder, but as something in which he was immersed, it helped desensitize him to the situation he drifted into.

He said his motive in the homicide was "partly money, partly friendship." He went along with the planning at first, because he thought of it as a joke tied to the game. He stayed with it because he was a follower: "Other people have always made decisions for me."

He made his first good friend playing the game. Sean Mulder was three years younger, an overweight, sloppy-looking youth with stringy red hair and a goatee that looked out of place on his baby face. Sean and

Robert had been buddies for about a year, playing and strategizing D&D adventures together, watching television, and sleeping over at each other's houses. It wasn't a homosexual relationship. They joked about that, but found it hard to talk about; it didn't appeal to Robert. He had never dated a girl, either. "I'm too embarrassed," he told a psychiatrist, "I've never been able to relate to women. They make me nervous and shy." He was grateful to Sean for his friendship, so when Sean came to him with a plan that he and another young man had hatched, asking Robert to join them, he agreed. It meant everything to him to be part of a group, with Sean.

The third player was Zoltan (his D&D name) and the plot was to kill Zoltan's grandparents and aunt, leaving him the sole inheritor of a wealthy estate. His maternal grandparents had raised Zoltan. His mother died of cancer when Zoltan was a baby, and a month later, his father took off with a new girlfriend and was never seen again. Zoltan had told Sean that the grandparents were mean and physically abusive, and the aunt, who still lived at home "was a bitch and had something wrong with her head." He would get revenge on his grandparents, get rid of the aunt, and get his hands on the million he figured Grandpa had stashed away after a big career as a stock promoter.

Robert entered the story when Sean asked him if he knew anything about setting a delayed explosion. Thinking it was part of a D&D strategy Sean was devising, Robert told Sean what little he had learned about explosives during his stint in the armed forces. A week later, Sean asked him if he wanted to make some money. About five thousand dollars, he thought.

"Doing what?" Sean said it was just for plugging in a device. "What do you mean?" Sean explained that the money would be for plugging in a bomb that would kill Zoltan's grandparents.

"Oh, sure, then." Robert thought Sean was kidding, so he agreed to go along. As the plan developed and strategy shifted, he learned it was serious, but he still figured it would never happen.

Robert hardly knew Zoltan — they all lived in the same Toronto suburb and had been in a few D&D games together over the years, but he and Zoltan hadn't really connected. Still, Sean wanted Robert in on it, and Robert could see that if he refused, it would do something negative to the friendship he valued so much.

Sean had made a bomb-detonating device that would blow up a propane tank, creating a powerful and massive fireball that should level the house. The plot now was that Robert would drive Zoltan over to his grandparents with the bomb, and Zoltan would install and set the bomb in their basement. On the way over, Zoltan started sounding like he was backing out, so when Robert and Sean didn't hear from him later, Robert figured Zoltan hadn't gone through with the plan, and that would be the end of it. Next morning, Zoltan told them that while he was in the basement messing with the bomb, it set off the fire alarm, and he had to get rid of the detonator quickly. Grandpa looked around, concluded a barbecue propane tank must have been leaking, and didn't call the fire department. The bomb wires all had been pulled apart, and his grandfather was glaring at him as usual, so Zoltan went off innocently to bed.

Sean and Zoltan hatched a new plot, with poison as the chosen weapon. Zoltan had acquired two bottles of sleeping pills and he would mix them into a dessert, which he would serve his family. He worked in a restaurant, so he could say he brought it home from work, and had seen too much of it to eat any more, which would explain why he wouldn't be consuming the deadly delicacy himself. After the family passed out, the boys would kill them with painless but lethal injections of air, then Zoltan would set fire to the house. The fire would get rid of the evidence, and Zoltan could add the fire insurance claim to his inheritance.

Grandpa decided he was going out for a beer instead of having dessert that night, and left. Grandma and the aunt each had sizable helpings and soon went to bed. Zoltan called Sean and said they would go to the pub, persuade the grandfather to come out on some pretext, kill him, then go back to the house and kill the other two. Robert drove them to the pub, and waited outside in the car. They didn't come out for an hour, and when the two emerged alone, they didn't really explain what had happened. At home, Grandma vomited up the dessert and the aunt slept all night and most of the next day. It was starting to sound less like D&D heroics and more like Keystone Kops.

Undeterred, they tried to conjure up some new ideas by leafing through a game manual. The following Saturday, they tossed suggestions back and forth while they went to the mall and Zoltan cashed a cheque he had forged on his grandfather's account. They headed into Toronto, still talking, but on the way decided to check into a hotel. They would drive back home, kill the family, then return to the hotel, where it would look like they had spent the night. The trio went to the bar, where Robert, who did not drink, was joshed into downing three martinis. Before and after the bar, he did two lines of cocaine. Sean and Zoltan had persuaded him the weekend before to try coke for the first time. He didn't care much for it, and didn't think it did much for him. Like almost everything he did, he tried cocaine just to please someone else. This night, mixing drink and drugs for the first time, he said he noticed that although he knew where he was, he didn't know how to get around.

By midnight, he felt sober enough to be chauffeur again, and drove to Zoltan's house. Lights were still on, so they went to an all-night coffee shop, had hot chocolates and finalized the game plan. Zoltan would lead the way into the house, he and Sean would each take a side of the grandparents' bed, and Robert would stand guard in the bedroom doorway. Robert would count to three, then the others would hit the grandparents on the head. They had a crowbar, a baseball bat, and a gas can for the fire.

On the way to the house, Sean assumed the D&D role of Beorn, a huge humanoid cat with great strength and a history as a starship security officer. They crept into the house and up to the master bedroom, but Sean pushed Robert in with the crowbar, and held up three fingers. When Sean reached the end of the countdown, Zoltan started pounding on his grandfather with the baseball bat. Robert stood frozen with the raised crowbar until Beorn hissed a command, then he brought his weapon down.

"I had made myself callous in the game sense — that death was just death," Robert told me. "At first, I succeeded."

On the third blow, Robert heard the crack of the grandmother's skull and the grandfather's screams, and "realized what I was doing." He backed out into the hall and told Beorn he couldn't do it, while Zoltan kept hitting both victims. Sean made no move towards the aunt's room. They were each supposed to do one person. Zoltan came out, went across the hall and attacked his aunt, breaking the baseball bat. He came back, grabbed the crowbar out of Robert's hands, and went after his grandparents again. He was covered in blood. He came out and handed Sean the two women's purses.

Meanwhile, Robert was on his way outside. "I can't take it anymore," he told Sean. Sean appeared at the car just as Robert started seeing flames through a bedroom window. Zoltan arrived, and they drove off with the house burning.

They ditched the purses and the bloody shirt, then Robert drove shakily back to the hotel, where he walked straight out onto the balcony. "I was going to jump. I just couldn't live with what I had done," he would say later. "But I was scared of heights, so I backed off." He took a shower, feeling unclean, and spent the night crying. In the morning, they got Zoltan new pants and a shirt, then headed back out of the city because Sean had to work that night. They stopped for breakfast, but

Robert felt too sick to eat. The other two tried to cheer him up by congratulating each other on the points they would have earned if they had been playing D&D on this one.

Back home, Robert was trying to wash the bloodstains off his car seats when a police squad car rolled up. He answered the officers' enquiries by saying that the trio had been driving around the night before and got lost, so they checked into a hotel. That was the story they had agreed upon. The officer informed him that Zoltan's grandfather and aunt had survived the attack, and that Zoltan and Sean had already confessed. Robert told them everything.

It was a complex trial, with all three young men accused of first-degree murder; all three admitting their participation but pleading not guilty; the usual finger-pointing among the defendants, and a fleet of psychiatrists and psychologists trying to interpret for the jury the mind of the group as well as the individuals.

I testified to Robert's profound immaturity, isolation from the mainstream of society, over-eagerness to please, and desperation for acceptance and some kind of accomplishment. I said that, after the homicide, he was in a state of extreme shock and disbelief and, like any young boy, ashamed of having hurt and disappointed his parents. My first reaction had been that he was so developmentally impaired that he should have been lowered to juvenile court, though of course that was a legal impossibility.

He did not, however, suffer from any major mental disorder, aside from some ongoing low-level depression. While he was on the fantasy end of the spectrum in his perception of the offence, and particularly the planning, he was not suffering from delusions or psychosis. He lacked the normal adult appreciation of what he was doing, but at a basic, concrete level he clearly did know what he was doing. It was the worst failure to appreciate the nature and consequences of an act of murder that I had seen short of the legal definition of "insanity." Only the somewhat lame defence that he wasn't properly aware of the gravity of his actions until after the first few blows could be given as favouring a second-degree over a first-degree murder verdict.

Analyses of group dynamics featured prominently in the trial. A psychologist told the court that none of the trio was capable of acting alone. He said three components were necessary to completing any human endeavour: head, heart and hands. Sean was the "head," the brains or director (or Dungeon Master) of the murder; Zoltan was the "heart" or driver of the project, because of his hatred for his grandparents and his craving for the money; and Robert was the "hands" or willing tool who implemented the plan, although at the end he performed weakly even in that role. A psychiatrist who testified agreed that if the three hadn't been together, the awful event would never have happened. He opined that the fantasy of getting a million dollars was a "complex mind game that kept them away from the reality of it all" and that the crime was part of a group process, "sort of a game-playing situation." A characteristic of group dynamics in general, he added, is that it distorts reality.

Various claims were made trying to mitigate the guilt of each of the accused, whose lawyers took different tacks. Zoltan's defence included a medical witness who testified he was mentally ill; but another doctor diagnosed him as a classic psychopath (among other things, Zoltan had professed he enjoyed hurting and humiliating people). Robert's lawyer argued that his client's D&D obsession rendered him incapable of planning a murder (not something I had claimed). Sean's lawyer brought forth no evidence, relying on his cross-examination of the Crown witnesses.

Undoubtedly because there had been planning and deliberation — inept and perhaps fantasy-tainted as it was — the jury's verdict was guilty of first-degree murder. Each of the young men was given a life sentence with no chance of parole for twenty-five years.

Group crimes often seem to be carried out by some combination of a psychopath leader, one or more meekly passive followers or "choir boys," and others somewhere in between. With different mental states, different roles, possibly different degrees of culpability, and certainly different levels of dangerousness, vulnerability and rehabilitation potential, all three killers were sent off to exactly the same punishment. A punishment that fits the crime, to be sure, but not necessarily the individual perpetrator.

Robert Rocar seemed to me to be one of the rare killers for whom the faint-hope clause has been legislated. In the absence of a powerful psychopathic leader, he could be counted on to remain meek and mild. To emphasize the point with my wife, I remarked that if he were ever released, we could safely put him up in our spare bedroom; for some strange reason, her usually generous nature wasn't inspired to endorse that particular idea.

That I would make such a comment, even in jest, gave me pause to wonder if I hadn't taken on an overly-protective role with Robert, much as I had done occasionally with my younger brothers. There is an opportunity in every case for personal bias to creep in and cloud your judgment.

At the time of his trial, I held hope that, with treatment, Robert Rocar would one day be capable of resuming his previously ordinary, law-abiding life, posing no further threat to society. Even if he is granted a faint-hope hearing and goes on to receive early parole, however, he will certainly be a different person after fifteen years in prison. I doubt he will come out as Dark Knight, Assassin.

CHAPTER TWENTY-ONE

RELEASE: SAFETY, POLITICS OR MEDICINE?

If I had met Ryder Caslon in any other situation, my first thought might have been that I'd want to be on his side in a street fight. Tall and muscular, with menacing tattoos and dark eyes that penetrated to the point of intimidation, he might have been a biker, wearing leather and metal in ordinary circumstances.

But here he was before me, crumpled up like a handkerchief, sobbing as if his heart were broken, and talking about needing to speak to his mom. He would tell me a little of his story, then start crying again. Every so often, he would look at me pleadingly and ask why this had happened. The day before, he had killed his wife because voices had convinced him she was going to sell him as a sex slave.

Interviewing Ryder was difficult. He kept jumping around, off and on topic, and he was in such anguish.

"I don't know what came over me. I don't know why I had to do this," he wept. "I love her, I love her."

He said that he and Vicky had been separated because the Ministry for Children and Families had told them they couldn't live together for three months "because of my mental problems." He had been in and out of hospital, and "I took my anger out on Vicky in front of the kids." It wasn't physical abuse, it was shouting. Ryder's voices were insistent that Vicky was cheating on him, and worse.

Usually, when the voices got too bad, he said, he got grumpy and they'd send him off to the hospital for medication. Then one evening, he and Vicky got into an argument about money, and he shoved her. Frightened, she called the police. Two officers came and talked to Ryder, and they all agreed it was a one-time incident, and not much of one at that, but the next day, a social worker showed up and soon Vicky and the kids moved to Vancouver. The social worker said Ryder hadn't been on his meds consistently enough, and they were worried he might take his anger out on the children next time. Let's see how you are in three months, they suggested.

"I had *never* hurt the children, or Vicky," he told me, "the thing was, they thought I had been emotionally abusive to her in front of the kids." Ryder moved to Vancouver as well, into a hostel. He and Vicky called each other every day, but he obeyed the edict not to see her or even to find out where she was staying. He went faithfully to a Vancouver clinic for his long-acting injection of the antipsychotic, flupenthixol, but he ceased taking his short-acting oral antipsychotic, olanzapine. He hadn't thought about why he had stopped, "It just didn't seem like it was helping, I guess, and no one was forcing me to take it or anything." Off the olanzapine, his voices became stronger.

After a month and a half, he was allowed to see his wife, but not the children. But he and Vicky were happy, thinking the family would soon be back together.

At this point in his story, Ryder started to cry again, and I put down my pen and leaned back in my chair to give him a minute to collect himself. To my horror, he suddenly reached over, grabbed the pen and thrust it forcefully three inches deep into his neck, at exactly the spot where the carotid artery is just under the skin.

I hurled myself across the table and tried to wrest his hands from the pen. I am nowhere near his size, but adrenalin and I managed to knock him off his chair, and in the process, his hands were dislodged and I was able to remove the pen from his throat. To my great relief, the pen wasn't followed by a geyser of blood. I punched the panic button and help arrived. Responding, I guess, to my shell-shocked facial expression, a paramedic kindly offered me help as his partner attended to Ryder.

"Am I going to die?" Ryder asked hopefully. Over and over, he moaned that he wanted to die, and that he should be allowed to die.

Ryder was taken to hospital by ambulance with a prison-guard escort — fortunately the stab wound was not fatal. We were able to resume our conversation the next day, he with a major bandage and me with a firm grip on my pen. He had just wanted to be with his wife in heaven, he said about the suicide attempt. "I can't take the pain of her being away from me."

By now I also knew that the day of his arrest, as he was being escorted to a police detention cell, he had somehow shoved a wooden doorstop into his mouth, and fallen face-down to the floor in a painful but unsuccessful suicide attempt. "I killed my wife," he told the police, "I want to die."

We started talking again, this time at the beginning of all Ryder's troubles.

His voices had first chimed in when he was 18, a common age for the signs and symptoms of schizophrenia to start appearing. He began "seeing things," too. He found it hard to explain. The voices ran like a sort of chorus in his mind. A kind of nagging. Because of the voices, Ryder had been in hospital three times in the first two years after he was diagnosed. He had been taking anti-psychotic drugs ever since, and had not been admitted to hospital again. Various doctors had prescribed the appropriate medications, and these calmed him as long as he remembered to take the pills or to go for his injection. The voices stayed, but medication allowed him to ignore them. The visual hallucinations still appeared, but less often and less obtrusively.

Stabilized and on medication, he was able to work as a swamper or trucker's assistant. But, over time, it became harder for him, just as it became harder to remain conscientious about the medications.

Ryder and Vicky had been together three years and had two children. Although the younger boy was still a baby, they had talked recently of having another one. The boys were wonderful, Ryder told me, the flow of tears starting, "Man, I love my kids." Later, I learned that the older child was Vicky's from an earlier relationship, but Ryder apparently cherished them equally, and in his hopes for the future, he always spoke of them both as his children.

Vicky had been the black sheep of a prominent family. Her parents were just getting over the birth of her months-old first baby, whose father had never been disclosed, when without warning, she married Ryder. They were none too pleased, and when Ryder started going off the rails, they attempted to throw up a protective hedge around their daughter. Vicky, in turn, left town instead of accepting their offer to move home when she and Ryder were separated.

About a year before I met him, Ryder's voices had picked up the pace. They were typical persecutory hallucinations, based on "getting" Ryder. The voices told him he was a geek and a dork, a nothing and a loser, and he felt hurt. Then they began to taunt him with the notion that Vicky was going to "pimp him off" — sell him for sex. ("But she wasn't gonna do that," he broke down again.) After a while, he had confronted Vicky, asking her if it were true what the voices were saying about her cheating, and her planning to pimp him off. She started to cry. It wasn't true, she told him, and hugged him tight. But he didn't believe her, because the voices sounded so real.

After he told Vicky about them, the voices turned against him even more, so he vowed not to mention them again. But how, he wondered, did the people on television find out? TV-show hosts and actors would say things about him and Vicky all the time, about what was going on in the relationship. Ryder didn't know how he knew what these people were talking about, but they would say his name sometimes, and look straight at him. People on the radio talked about him, too.

He was so confused about his voices. He'd go for a walk and think about it. Sometimes he would decide to believe the voices, sometimes not. In any case, they were making him pretty crazy, he said.

I asked Ryder where the voices came from. He didn't know, but they came from outside him. Lately he had been sure that Vicky was making up the voices, creating them for him. It wasn't her voice, though. *Vicky is out having sex with another man. She hides her lovers in the closet so you won't know.* He had looked through all the closets, but he never caught the guy. *She even has sex with other guys in front of the kids.* He wouldn't confront Vicky about what the voices said. He was too scared it might be true.

The voices made him irritable. Doctors just told him to take the medications. He had never divulged what the voices said to any of the physicians, because he thought that if he told one doctor, all doctors — in fact, everyone else — would turn against him. Last time he had told someone (Vicky), the voices had worsened.

In Vancouver, living apart from Vicky, cut off from his children, and taking no olanzapine, the voices became more powerful. Not only was he going to be pimped off, but his baby was going to be sold on the black market. *She's had lots of babies with lots of guys, then pimps the guy off and sells the baby to another family.* They said it again and again. *She's trying to hide what she's doing. She's trying to ruin your life.*

Ryder finally got to see Vicky after two months apart, but not his children. His mother took the boys for the night, and Ryder stayed at Vicky's apartment. They had dinner, watched television, made love, had breakfast, were happy. During the second overnighter, his sister looked after the children, and Ryder and Vicky started talking about the future, moving back together, having another baby.

"Jesus Christ, I just want to kill myself now," Ryder anguished. "I had to go and screw it all up."

He didn't blame his problems before the homicide on the voices. He had been feeling terrible because he wasn't allowed even a supervised visit with the boys. "And who was responsible for me being separated from the kids? Me," he admitted, "because I was violent against my wife." He paused. Then, "Why? Oh, God!"

The third visit, his mom took the children again. Ryder walked over to Vicky's place, feeling fine, although he had taken no medication for a couple of days. *She's with another guy and she's screwing his brains out right now. She doesn't care about you.* But when he got there, she was happy to see him and was affectionate all evening. They watched a movie, went out for burgers, went to bed, and made love. *She's going to pimp you off. She's going to pimp you off!* In the morning, they made love again, had coffee, watched some television. *We're going to sell your baby.*

The voices started going on about the video cameras. He knew there were cameras on him — had been for a couple of years — and pretty much the whole world was watching him.

Now Vicky and Ryder went back into the bedroom and the cameras followed. *She's going to pimp you off. The cameras are rolling. They're everywhere. The cameras are everywhere.* As the couple began to make love, the voices became extreme, and they seemed to come from all over the apartment.

Afterwards, Vicky walked into the living room and Ryder went to the kitchen. *The cameras are on you.* He grabbed a knife. He couldn't handle the voices anymore. She was causing the voices. *Watch the camera.* He would get rid of the voices. *The cameras are everywhere.* He stabbed her, shouting, "I hate you for the voices you gave me!" *The cameras are watching you.*

"Oh, no, please don't!" she pleaded.

She managed to dial 911 and gasp out that she needed an ambulance. Ryder suddenly saw her lying on the floor, and he didn't want her to die. He picked up the telephone and cried, "Please hurry, I just stabbed my wife, she's bleeding all over, she's dying ..." The operator heard horrendous sobs, then Ryder hung up. The operator called back, and heard again, "Just hurry, she's dying, man!" Ryder hadn't realized that the call for an ambulance had already been put through and the operator was just trying to keep him on the line. "I gotta go, man, just hurry up and get here." When the police arrived shortly after the ambulance, they found Ryder lying in the hall, covered in blood, wailing, "I love her, I didn't mean to hurt her. I couldn't help it."

"I just couldn't stand the voices," Ryder was moaning to me two days later. "Why did she have to give me the voices?"

"When you stabbed her, did you know it would kill her?"

"Yes. I had to kill her to stop the voices."

"Did you have any thoughts about whether it was right or wrong?"

305

"No. I knew she would go to heaven, but I wasn't thinking about that then. My only thought was to stop the voices."

"Did you think Vicky was more than an ordinary human being, if she could cause voices?"

"No, she was a regular person. She had no special powers. Except for the voices."

"What do you think is causing your voices now?"

"I don't know. Not caring enough, I guess. Not Vicky. Oh, God." More crying.

"Are you hearing voices today?"

"Yes."

"Can you tell me what they're saying?"

"I don't know, because I'm trying hard to block them out and talk to you at the same time."

"Have you had any medications today?"

"Nothing. They gave me a heavy tranquilizer when they stitched me up yesterday."

My first interview with Ryder had concluded with the pen-stabbing. The second ended because the subject fell asleep. I had to keep raising my voice until the only way I could draw a response was by yelling, so I left him to sleep off the chlorpromazine.

The case was already unfolding in the media. "Young Mother of Two Stabbing Victim" was followed by "Daughter of Ex-Diplomat, Philanthropist Murdered." Vicky's parents were shown briefly, grief-stricken and dignified, on a television clip of the funeral. A family member was quoted as saying, "Why wasn't he in a hospital? If he hadn't been able to follow her to Vancouver, this would never have happened."

The trial, however, was short. There was a crowd in the public gallery, but it was no lynch mob. They were mostly curious, and partly looking for somewhere to put the blame, but weren't focused on Ryder. When the jury declared him Not Guilty by Reason of Insanity (the term then for Not Criminally Responsible on account of Mental Disorder) grumblings in the gallery — and later in the media — were more about whether or not such dangerous people should ever be allowed back out into the community.

It was 1985, and the judge effectively gave Ryder an indeterminate sentence. She ordered him detained in strict custody in hospital on a warrant of the lieutenant governor. He could earn increasing freedoms — a relaxation of the warrant — but he could only be released "at the pleasure of the lieutenant governor," in effect, the provincial cabinet.

Whereas the National Parole Board determines the future of offenders sentenced to prison, a completely separate provincial Review Board serves the same function for persons declared not guilty because of a mental disorder. This advisory-only group would reappraise Ryder annually and make its findings known to the cabinet, which would then make the final decision each year whether to release him or keep him in hospital.

Once Ryder was admitted to the Forensic Psychiatric Institute and placed on a program of regular and certain treatment for his schizophrenia, he became and remained free of what we refer to as positive symptoms. His voices and the associated paranoid delusions left him. For the first time in seven years, he was alone in his head. No chorus of mumbling, no insistent jeering following him around like a gang of bullies.

But now, able to think realistically, he was wrought with remorse and sorrow, appalled at what he had done, and full of grieving for Vicky. In addition to dealing with his illness, he spent a lot of time with therapists who worked diligently to gain his acceptance that it was the disorder that had made him commit his offence, and that lifelong treatment with medication was necessary to prevent anything remotely similar from happening again.

Once he was stabilized, his children were allowed to visit, which increased both his anguish at what he had done and his motivation to keep working towards release. Offering a stable family environment and the advantage of youth, Ryder's sister and brother-in-law had obtained temporary custody of the boys. Vicky's parents had put up a fight at first, but then to everyone's pleased surprise, backed off, acknowledging the children's high comfort level with their auntie, their own advanced ages, and the irony of being able to see more of the children now than their daughter had allowed. They provided financial support for the family. They were not, however, interested in Ryder being released anytime soon.

Ryder's time as a patient at FPI gave him a long period of stable mental health that allowed him to be steadily productive for the first time in his adult life, and to do things he had never done before, including becoming a skilled landscape worker on the team caring for the hospital's expansive grounds with its famous collection of heritage trees. He remained non-aggressive and peaceful in hospital, and in fact was often a stabilizing influence on the wards when other patients became rambunctious or quarrelsome.

You might think that Ryder's indeterminate sentence to the psychiatric institute would have led to the best possible conclusion of his case. Ideally, he would have received appropriate treatment to deal with both his illness and the repercussions of his crime, and when no longer dangerous, released gradually back into the community with continuing mandatory drug treatment.

Yet every year at his Review Board hearings, members expressed their skepticism that Ryder's trouble-free record was a real sign of improvement, or anything more than a skilful act, and granted him only minimal liberties: occasional, fully escorted day passes into a nearby suburb for such essential and mundane purposes as dental appointments. His annual hearing always received a mention in the media, and although none of them said so on the record, Review Board members were aware of this, and of a well-respected public figure's resistance to his release. They were reluctant to have a hand in setting him free, no doubt imagining the furor that would be unleashed if it was thought Ryder had an opportunity to re-offend. These were conscientious citizens, but only one of the board members was a mental-health professional, and all were political appointees.

The worry most often expressed in such cases is, "What's to stop a mentally disordered offender from deciding to take himself off his medication again, and doing the same thing?" Based on a lack of understanding, this legitimate question has been a major deterrent to the release of many people who were capable of going home and achieving something approaching a normal life.

Ryder's clinical history was typical of many offender patients who have been successfully released. Once out of the hospital, but still under its supervision, they continue to receive long-acting medication injections administered by a psychiatric nurse. The biggest advantage of compulsory clinic-administered injections over voluntary oral medication is the certainty that the medication has been taken; there is no need to depend on a patient's not-always-reliable word. Another factor is that even though such medication is given at, say, four-week intervals, it doesn't suddenly stop acting at the end of four weeks. Its effect gradually diminishes over several weeks, so that if a patient living in the community doesn't show up for an injection appointment, there remains a reasonable period of time in which to apprehend that individual and administer the medication before his or her condition deteriorates.

Most Review Board release orders also include provisions that patients report regularly to an outpatient clinic, and that they may be involuntarily returned to a closed psychiatric hospital if their mental condition becomes unsafe while they are in the community. At the time that Ryder became casual about going for his injections and taking his pills, he was a voluntary patient and could not be apprehended or detained to take the medication. If released after being committed by the court to hospital, he would be subject to continuous monitoring and lifelong treatment, enforceable by police apprehension if necessary.

It must be said that this monitoring and medication program is only successful for patients like Ryder whose homicidal behavior was determined by an illness treatable with medication. For killers whose behaviour is primarily brought on by other factors, including personality or situation, compliance with a medication program can't guarantee continuing peaceful behavior. Unfortunately, for Ryder, the general public doesn't usually know the difference, and in his first four years he faced a Review Board aware that it was dealing with a relatively high-profile case, and reluctant to make any move that might be perceived as risking public safety in any way. Each time, they ruled that he be kept in strict hospital custody.

When Ryder went before his fifth Review Board, he had a five-year unblemished record for his time in hospital custody and was considered by his medical-care team to be in stable, good mental health. Two psychiatrists (I was one of them) had recommended his conditional release into the community. A treatment plan with strict supervision and a social services network (including accommodation in a supervised mental-health boarding home) had been designed. His family was waiting to welcome him back into their lives.

The major hurdle was that the onus was on the patient to prove to the Review Board that he was not a significant threat to the safety of the public. If the board didn't agree with this, if it had any doubt, it did not have to recommend the conditional discharge to the cabinet.

At the time of his hearings, Ryder represented no threat to anyone, but he had been living nearly five years in a highly controlled situation with continuous supervision of his drug treatment. The mental disorder that had brought him to FPI could be controlled but not cured. Given the disastrous outcome of his past belief that he didn't really need all the medications he had been prescribed, he could promise, but not prove that he would not slide into medication-avoidance mode again. And while in his current mental state under treatment, he abhorred violence, the result of a return of hallucinations or delusions could not be predicted.

To me, the most reasonable decision both for society and for Ryder, was the one the board finally made. They recommended to the provincial cabinet that he be granted a conditional discharge, on a comparatively short leash at first, assuring maintenance of the mandatory medication treatment.

A lot of good this did, though. Even though the Review Board had been able to rise above community pressure, the provincial cabinet had not. No surprise that this and every subsequent Review Board recommendation for Ryder's conditional release came back rubber-stamped

"Release Would Be Premature At This Time." No real reasons given, no appeal, no recourse to the courts.

Between his seventh and eighth review, things changed. Bill C-30 was enacted, revising the Canadian Criminal Code, and changing the authority and composition of Review Boards. Each provincial board was now chaired by a judge or retired judge, and its other members had to include a mental-health professional (usually a psychiatrist) and a person, often a social worker, to represent the community or rehabilitative perspective. The board also began hearing representations for each case from the Crown prosecutor, who represents the province's attorney general, the patient's hospital-care team, and if deemed necessary by the patient, his or her lawyer, additional mental-health experts, and "interested parties," which can include the patient's family, victims, or anyone who can contribute appropriate knowledge or opinion. The role of the provincial cabinet in the board's decisions was eliminated. The legal-medical slant of the new board reduced the potential for a political edge in cases that earn public notoriety.

Most important, this Review Board was now the ultimate decision-maker, with the full authority to make dispositions: an absolute discharge (removing the offender from the board's and the court's jurisdiction entirely), a conditional discharge (release into the community under restrictions and remaining under the board's jurisdiction), or a conditional detention in hospital. These last two kept the offender under the board's jurisdiction, and required that the individual's disposition continued to be reviewed by the board every year.

Six months before the changes were made, the Supreme Court of Canada had found that holding a person "in strict custody" without disposition violated the person's rights as defined by the Charter of Rights and Freedoms. Now the mentally disordered offender could no longer be sent off after the verdict with an indeterminate sentence without due process rights. If the court did not make a disposition, the Review Board would, and unless the offender was granted an immediate and absolute discharge (something pretty rare), it would review that disposition annually.

With these legal changes, the Review Board's next decision for Ryder finally resulted in something better than interminable frustration for all concerned. They granted him conditional release. There was no public mention of Ryder's release, which allowed him the privacy to get on with his "new" life. After a few years in the group home, he was able to move into a small apartment of his own, still with regular visits to and from support workers and a psychiatrist, and monthly injections at the local hospital.

I have said that Ryder's most troublesome symptoms of schizophrenia, his voices and paranoid delusions, had been relieved with medication. Schizophrenics, like individuals with any mental disorder, can fit anywhere in a broad spectrum of signs and symptoms. Positive symptoms (implying something has been added to the mind) — hallucinations and delusions — can be mild to severe, and voices, fixations and imagined sights can carry many different messages to different people. In addition, victims may exhibit a variety of what we call negative symptoms (implying that something has been subtracted). These can include apathy, low energy, indecision and slow thinking. Again, the symptoms and the degree to which they affect a person vary from individual to individual. Some negative symptoms may be helped with medication. Often they gradually worsen. On top of positive and negative symptoms, the person may have to cope with unavoidable medication side effects, which are often similar to common negative symptoms. As a result of all these problems, about four-fifths of all schizophrenics are not able to gain and keep regular employment.

Ryder has difficulty making up his mind, but he is a good worker as long as he knows exactly what he has to do and doesn't have to direct anyone else. He was fortunate to find a job in a subsidized, sheltered employment company — a real business created to hire mentally disabled people — that does landscape maintenance for three seasons and snow removal in winter.

As time passed, Ryder took on more of the life of an ordinary citizen. Eventually, he remarried. Perhaps fearful because schizophrenia has a genetic component, he has had no more children. He has a good relationship with his sons. The boys remained with his sister's family, and are being raised with her husband's last name to keep them out of the limelight. The family moved out of the Vancouver area, and when Ryder was discharged he also moved to the new community.

"I am one lucky dude," he says. I think his treatment and his situation are the best they could be, for himself and for public safety.

His case continues to come before the Review Board every year. Some five years after he left the psychiatric institute, the Supreme Court of Canada came down with a ruling that has had a major impact on provincial Review Boards. The Supreme Court changed the interpretation of the Criminal Code to say that the court or Review Board must prove that the NCRMD offender *is* a significant threat to the safety of the public in order to keep the person in custody. If they cannot prove he is a significant threat, that there is a real risk of serious physical or psychological harm to individuals in the community, he must be granted

311

at least a conditional discharge, still remaining on Review Board order. If the court or Review Board cannot resolve the issue, he must be granted an absolute discharge.

The onus has been switched from the offender to the Review Board to keep the offender under the board's jurisdiction, and if board members can't make up their collective mind, the offender must be set completely free. This forces the Review Board into a more inquisitorial role, forced to search out and consider evidence, which, with its largely medical and legal perspective, it is pretty capable of doing.

The board's frequent inability to come up with convincing proof of significant risk, however, means that more absolute discharges are now being granted, and that may not be a good thing. The bar has been substantially lowered for absolute discharge, and already I'm starting to see what look to me like some rather big risks being taken, sometimes resulting in medication non-compliance and re-offences, although fortunately no serious ones that I have heard about. Still, the pendulum has swung from excessively lengthy detention to premature release of some potentially dangerous people, simply because we cannot prove they are unsafe for release. I fear we may have to see some tragedies before a healthier balance is restored. In emphasizing the civil-liberty rights of patients, the point got lost that long-term and forced treatment is also the most humane thing to do for these offenders, rather than punishment through long-term incarceration in a brutal prison environment.

In Ryder's case, and those of other NCRMD offenders, the uncertainty of his future treatment compliance has maintained his status on conditional discharge. Apparently, the Review Board agrees that there is a serious risk of Ryder once more stopping his medications if it were left up to him, and that if he did, the resulting relapse would pose a significant risk of serious violence. His history of non-compliance resulting in extreme violence offers strong proof. I expect and hope that he will remain under conditional discharge for the remainder of his life, but the shifted burden of proof now makes that uncertain.

Up to a point, the evolution of the Review Board provides a positive role model for change in bringing psychiatry and the law closer together. The question of who best decides on treatment and release of mentally disordered, serious offenders now has many examples to draw upon — of successful cases that are medically oriented, and to a lesser extent legally oriented, and not at all politically oriented. I knew of offenders who had quickly returned to normal mental health with treatment, yet, until 1992, languished in hospital for literally years, their fate in the hands of government influenced by uninformed or misinformed public opinion.

One particularly striking case involved a once-psychotic (non-schizophrenic) killer who was conditionally released almost as soon as government was removed from Review Board decisions. He had been held in custody, in excellent mental health, for nearly ten years, against all medical advice, almost entirely because of the notoriety of his case. Within a short period of time following his release, he acquired a college diploma and found a good job. He has had several promotions, thrives socially, and is in all respects a solid and responsible citizen. He is one of the vast majority of mentally disordered, violent offenders who do not re-offend, thanks to the benefits of rigorously enforced, ongoing treatment.

Annual reviews and frequent monitoring by medical practitioners and social services offer another advantage. Changes can be made fairly readily to release and treatment conditions if an individual's health or circumstances require it. The flexibility and individual adaptation provided in this kind of sentence administration could be applied across our legal system with similarly effective results for the high proportion of mentally ill inmates.

THE PSYCHIATRIST'S PRESCRIPTION

By now, readers will have discerned that I have a few quibbles with our justice system, particularly in the places where law and psychiatry try to work together.

At the most basic level, there are the fundamental differences between medicine and law that result in a mismatch in the courtroom.

Philosophically, the law believes in free will and the human ability to make completely free choices and therefore be responsible for your actions (although it fudges this in certain areas such as the Not Criminally Responsible on account of Mental Disorder defence). Psychiatry and psychology believe — in theory, if not always in practice — in the opposite: complete behavioral determinism, that is, true free choice is an illusion, and a person's actions are the product of genetics, brain structure, chemistry, and prior experiences. So we medical types are essentially incapable of addressing certain legal issues, such as the notion of loss of control, which is integral to the provocation defence. It would be like an atheist casting judgement between two church doctrines.

Differences in methodologies have, over time, driven medicine and law farther and farther apart. While medicine has progressed in leaps and bounds, and changed fundamentally in many respects, legal concepts in related areas have evolved comparatively slowly. Instead of the law adopting modern medicine, medicine is forced to continue dealing with legal concepts based on outdated or "soft" science theories that do not come up to the standards of hard experimental scientific conclusions. For instance, the "soft" notions that alcohol can eliminate your ability to intend your acts and that you can carry out complex, goal-directed actions without the involvement of your mind are at the root of the legally respectable intoxication and automatism defences. With the idea legitimized as a defence, we get juries "letting off" dangerous offenders.

Another instance of square medical pegs being forced into round legal holes involves dissociation. The psychiatric concept of dissociation is similar to the legal notion of non-insane automatism, but they are often regarded as equivalent. There is nothing in the psychiatric notion of dissociation that accurately corresponds to the legal notion of an inability to be aware of and intend your acts. But the idea is imbedded in legal precedents, so we get nice guys getting away with attempted murder.

My second big frustration in the law-psychiatry match-up lies in the way evidence concerning the mental state of a killer is delivered to the judge and jury. It is often inaccurately and incompletely gathered, partially or wrongly presented, and fiendishly difficult to assess objectively.

Months, sometimes years, can pass between a homicide and the time psychiatrists and psychologists (particularly those called by the prosecution) are asked to assess the accused. While DNA, fingerprints and other "hard" evidence won't change over time, human minds do. It doesn't take long for vivid memories to fade, or for strategic responses to become ingrained after being suggested by lawyers, fellow prisoners or even the defendant's own imagination. Often the mental-health experts called by the prosecution are given incomplete information and, because of the accused person's sacrosanct right to remain silent so as not to self-incriminate, denied any contact at all with the accused. In addition, while the prosecution is obliged to give the defence all information it gets, as soon as it gets it, concerning the accused person's mental state, the defence can withhold advance information from the prosecution until the case comes to court. At that time, it can spring the information (perhaps a psychiatric assessment supporting a controversial defence) on the prosecution, whose psychiatric witness may have to scramble for a good, on-the-spot rebuttal.

Late, early, with or without personal contact, under any circumstances, it is very difficult to provide an accurate assessment of a killer's mind at the time of the homicide. It is hard for lay eye witnesses to portray the mental state of the killer, and often the killer doesn't remember what happened, or at least claims not to. Even when the accused does claim a memory of the event, it is usually unreliable, because of the stress of the incident and intentional or unintentional memory distortions. The problem of unreliable mental-state information wouldn't be so bad if we could accurately separate, by some foolproof means, lying and other memory distortions. But our ability to catch strategic liars is relatively poor.

Because we are obliged to produce assessments based on poor information and to fit fuzzy legal concepts, psychiatrists are often encouraged to undertake some very speculative psychiatric reasoning. Some of our opinions don't even meet the legal admissibility test of being based on respectable science, as we try to assist judge and jury in areas beyond their knowledge and experience.

My third concern — and it covers a lot of territory — is the overweening rigidity of our verdict and sentencing structure related to homicide. The few verdicts that exist are so crude and simplistic, with so little leeway in the sentences inextricably paired with each one, and the stakes are so high, that defence lawyers fall back on mental-state defences even in cases where it is absurd to do so. They feel it is the only way for their client to "win," so let's give it a shot. Long, costly and overly complicated trials based on proving or disproving psychiatric defences with precious little scientific merit are the result.

Because the outcome varies so dramatically, depending on whether a psychiatric defence is successful or not, these defences are used aggressively. But primitive all-or-nothing mental-state defences are all that psychiatrists and lawyers have to deal with, and they don't reflect the complex combinations and varying importance of factors — including personality, mental illness, intoxication and circumstances — that produced the killing.

With verdicts rigidly tied to sentences, the court declares that — in order to focus on the verdict — juries must be blind to the sentencing outcome. It's hopelessly unrealistic to think juries wouldn't take the possible sentences into account when bringing down their verdict in a homicide. And if the jury isn't given correct or sufficient information, it may tailor its verdict to the disposition or sentence that jury members feel is just — even though they may be making wrong assumptions about the disposition which will result from a given verdict. I'm sure insanity defences are sometimes rejected on the false assumption that the accused will be a free person after the verdict. Although the words would never be used by the judge or lawyers, "acquitted" and "not guilty" are often associated with "not criminally responsible on account of mental disorder." But a person is virtually never set immediately free following a "mental-disorder" verdict for a homicide.

Sentencing rules are as crude and inflexible as our verdicts, particularly the minimum of twenty-five years for first-degree murder and ten years for second-degree murder before parole eligibility. These rigid rules prevent lawyers from engaging in pragmatic plea-bargaining, and pretty well block judges from adapting the sentence to the circumstances. Where a lesser sentence is achieved for someone who has killed, it is often the result of a dubious psychiatric defence yielding a manslaughter verdict, rather than reflecting the true complexity of the crime and of the accused — and the accused person's level of responsibility, treatability and future dangerousness.

Systems of sentence administration for both convicted and NCRMD offenders extend the problems imposed by the verdict-sentencing structure with serious problems of their own, including over- and under-availability of the faint-hope clause and the recent liberalization of the Review Board criteria for granting absolute and conditional discharge for NCRMD patients.

The combined effect of all these difficulties is that verdicts and sentences often make relatively little sense in relation to the facts of the crime, including the mental health of the offender, and often result in too much or not enough time spent in prison or treatment. Instead of doing the best possible job of treating and rehabilitating mentally-disordered offenders based on their own unique difficulties, we release dangerous people prematurely, waste years of persons' lives (often subjecting them to unnecessary victimization), and maintain sane offenders in hospital far too long. No wonder the process and outcome of homicide cases often leave law-abiding citizens disillusioned and disgusted with our justice system.

Some of the underlying principles in the present approach to mental-state defences in homicides are sound, but the overall structure is badly flawed.

How did we arrive at this present mess? We got here by the traditional legal process of case-law tinkering that continually adjusts the fine points, but we never step back and look at the whole structure. It's like a house that has been renovated bit by bit over many years, resulting in a mish-mash of architecture, tacked-on rooms and uneven floors — all attempts to keep the structure workable. The best solution is to rebuild from scratch, incorporating the best principles from the existing structure, but combining them into a new coherent whole.

To my mind, that simplified, practical and people-oriented structure — let's call it the "New Homicide Law," which gives us the already-familiar acronym of NHL — would have the following main features.

Homicide trials would deal only with the issue of whether or not the accused killed the victim. No psychiatric evidence would be presented, and all mental-state defences would be abolished, with rare exceptions, such as seizure-related violence, where medical evidence establishes that the accused person's brain was profoundly deranged by some clear physical cause entirely outside his or her control. If it was proved that the accused was the culprit, there would be only one possible verdict — guilty of murder — although perhaps a less-stigmatizing euphemism could be found. The specialized verdicts of first-degree murder, second-degree murder and manslaughter would be eliminated.

Psychiatric evidence would occur in the sentencing phase, after conviction. Sentencing would be much more complex and flexible than it is now, based on a set of objectives, components and principles to be adapted to individual cases. Sentencing objectives would include the traditional deterrence (for the accused and as a message to like-minded citizens), denunciation (society's public condemnation of the crime, expressed as the punitive measure of incarceration), offender incapacitation (keeping them off the streets so they don't get a chance to re-offend, usually by means of incarceration or hospitalization) and, where necessary and expected to be effective, treatment and rehabilitation. Judges would be able to sentence offenders to both much shorter and much longer terms than presently allowed, as well as more open-ended terms, based on the unique features of each case. There would be no minimums or maximums. (These were effectively banished from murder sentences in the U.K. in 1997 with the law, "the court shall impose a life sentence, unless the court is of the opinion that there are exceptional circumstances relating to either the offense or to the offender which justify it not doing so." Not a bad example.)

Psychiatric/psychological testimony, not having to relate to specific mental-state defences, would exclude speculative theorizing without a solid scientific basis and would focus instead on areas where the analysis has some reliability and meaning, such as personality (including antisocial personality and psychopathy), mental illness, intellectual deficiency, substance abuse/dependence and treatment effectiveness. Experts would also measure treatment progress at intervals during the sentence administration phase. We would be using psychology's and psychiatry's strengths instead of inviting educated guessing regarding unknowable details of the person's mental state at the time of the killing.

Consultation and collaboration would be required between mental-health professionals called upon by both defence and prosecution, another strategy to keep objectivity in place and minimize the effects of personal bias. They could use the Court of Appeal model, where the panel of judges present a common opinion and ruling, but also allow individual judges to present their dissenting opinions as they apply to particular points. Alternatively, court-appointed experts could be used, the way they already are in Dangerous Offender applications and other non-homicide sentencing situations. The defence and prosecution would still have the right to engage their own experts if they couldn't stomach the court-appointed opinion.

Access to the convicted person by all parties would be provided as part of the post-verdict sentencing assessment. Refusal to be interviewed would preclude any possible leniency in sentencing under the new law.

For sentencing purposes, the court would also consider crime-related factors including circumstances, motive, brutality, nature and degree of intent, degree of behavioural control exercised, and whether the offence was emotionally reactive or cold-bloodedly predatory. Treatability, dangerousness and the chances of re-offence under various future circumstances would be considered as well. Where psychiatric or psychological opinion is relevant concerning these factors, it would be given. Victim-impact evidence from surviving family and friends would be strongly encouraged.

Sentencing under the NHL would make use of a number of building blocks. They would include psychological/psychiatric treatment, substance-abuse treatment, rehabilitative measures such as education and job training, supervision and restriction of liberties. There are various settings in which these components could be administered or delivered, including penitentiaries, psychiatric hospitals or clinics, and the community. The judge's initial sentence would specify the building blocks and settings, generically, and the minimum number of years until eligibility for community release.

Rather than trying to use a crystal ball at the outset to determine exactly what the offender would need in the long-term for his or her own benefit and the protection of the public, we would use the kind of model presently in place for Dangerous Offenders and NCRMD patients, including regular review with great adaptability in the type of measures needed for the offender, as well as their duration. The bias would be toward public safety, with the onus of proof for safe release on the offender — rather than the system having to release the inmate if the authorities can't prove him or her to be dangerous. The only aspect of any sentence that could not be reviewed or adjusted would be the denunciation and punishment (prison-term) component, as it is based on unalterable historical facts about the nature of the crime, as determined by the court at the time of sentencing, and designed to implement society's condemnation of the criminal act.

This new organization under the NHL, designed from the ground up, should result in more just and constructive outcomes, for both offenders and society, with less waste, inefficiency and plain nonsense during and after the trial. I believe the system would also save taxpayers' money. Perhaps ordinary law-abiding citizens also would re-gain respect for the law under a system that is much less likely to allow killers to "get away with murder."

I am under no illusions that executing this grand utopian solution wouldn't raise enormous problems in some areas, and ideas for reform have been studied to death in the past. Yet if they had been tried with NHL in place, almost all the cases in this book would have had more reasonable and just outcomes, arrived at more quickly.

Terry Driver (Chapter 4) would probably have received a much longer minimum to parole than twenty-five years, based on the extreme brutality of the crime, and evidence of his total lack of remorse and his enduring pleasure in taunting the police and a terrified public. The quasi-mental-state-defence would still have been allowed, because it was used by his lawyer to try to prove he was innocent of beating and killing, rather than as a mental-state explanation for a murder and attempted murder. He was ultimately declared a Dangerous Offender, approximately the same, desired result under the New Homicide Law. If he had been originally tried under the NHL, the first trial would have run similarly, but the sexual-assault convictions from the later trials would have added extra years to his murder prison term, and we would have eliminated the need for the Dangerous Offender hearing.

Deborah LePage (Chapter 5) would have received a simple verdict of murder for the death of her two children, with similar psychiatric/psychological evidence presented at sentencing, but taken into account as a matter of degree. The final outcome would have been the same, given consensual psychiatric opinions, as we eventually arrived at, but there would have been no battle over the simple yes-or-no insanity defence verdict, no second trial, and no stretch of nearly five years with Deborah effectively in legal and treatment limbo. Similarly, our homicidal driver, Selena Collins (Chapter 6) would have received a murder verdict rather than "manslaughter," but instead of being simply freed after a short prison term, she would probably have received mandatory psychiatric treatment while serving her prison sentence, with psychiatric supervision and regular reviews of her mental health while on a very lengthy parole. Psychiatric evidence would be presented at sentencing, when it would be consensual and, again, much more useful than when presented as part of a yes-or-no battle over an insanity defence.

Drug dealer Anson Reese (Chapter 8), with his high-flying cocaine visions, would likely have received a hybrid penal, substance-abuse and psychiatric-treatment sentence under the NHL, because he exhibited limited evidence of mental illness, although it fell far short of being enough for an insanity defence.

Raymond Albertson (Chapter 9) would have been automatically convicted of murder, and received a long prison term, with his release on parole dependent on excellent substance-abuse treatment and abstinence results in and out of prison, with frequent random blood and urine testing. Dennis Young (Chapter 10), the jonesing housebreaker who stabbed a cocaine dealer to death, and Mike Mallory (Chapter 15), who murdered a gay would-be lover, would likely receive similar sentences.

Paul Wolf (Chapter 11), who killed a disabled man in a bungled, drunken burglary attempt, would, I think, have received the same conditions for release, but his previous, sincere drive to turn his young life around would have resulted in a shorter prison sentence, and some hope for a decent future.

"Clark" Kent (Chapter 12) would have been convicted of the attempted murder of his next-door nemesis, but might have received a light sentence based on the sympathy-arousing circumstances of his offence. His release would depend on good anger-management treatment results

Torval Mander (Chapter 13), the driver who accidentally killed a pedestrian because of a seizure, would have been given a total acquittal at trial, as he was. However, if the psychiatric evidence had not been deemed clear enough — a possibility had there been a trial by jury instead of by judge alone, given the skepticism with which the evidence was greeted by the public — he might have been convicted of murder, and still likely released promptly into the community, but with almost exclusively medical-supervision conditions.

Abby Dixon (Chapter 14), who killed her sister-in-law in an extreme case of caregiver burnout, would have been convicted of murder under the NHL, but received a very short prison term and been released with mandatory continuing psychiatric treatment in her community. Similarly, game-player Robert Rocar (Chapter 20) would have received a murder conviction with a significantly shorter prison term than he was given (although probably longer than Abby's), with the additional requirement of mandatory psychiatric treatment in the community upon parole. Miranda Clay (Chapter 17), of the shaken baby case, would have been handed a murder conviction, a moderate incarceration term, and continuing psychiatric treatment on parole. Vonda

Rice (Chapter 16), whose husband loved dogs, and Rod Polbert (same chapter), the cross-bow killer, would have been given much shorter prison sentences, with their developmental difficulties, histories and other personal characteristics being taken into account.

On the other hand, Link Montgomery (Chapter 18) would probably have received a longer prison term, based on the brutality of his crime of the sexual assault and near-murder of a nine-year-old, with his release dependent on very good and proven treatment results.

And under the New Homicide Law, Clifford Olson (Chapter 19) would have been permanently incarcerated with no possibility of parole ever. Period. Full stop.

CPSIA information can be obtained at www.ICGtesting.com
Printed in the USA
LVOW05s0428300115

424926LV00009B/342/P